The Bonn Republic

West German Democracy, 1945–1990

A. J. NICHOLLS

Longman
London and New York

JN
3971
.A58
N53
1997

Addison Wesley Longman Limited
Edinburgh Gate,
Harlow, Essex CM20 2JE,
United Kingdom
and Associated Companies throughout the world

*Published in the United States of America
by Addison Wesley Longman Inc., New York*

First published 1997

ISBN 0 582 49230 0 PPR
ISBN 0 582 49231 9 CSD

British Library Cataloguing in Publication Data

A catalogue record for this book is available from the British Library

Library of Congress Cataloging-in-Publication Data

Nicholls, Anthony James, 1934–
The Bonn Republic : West German democracy, 1945–1990 / A. J.
Nicholls.
p.   cm. — (The postwar world)
Includes bibliographical references and index.
ISBN 0-582-49231-9. — ISBN 0-582-49230-0 (pbk.)
1. Germany (West)—Politics and government. 2. Germany (West)—
Economic conditions. 3. Democracy—Germany (West) I. Title.
II. Series.
JN3971.A58N53   1997
943.087—dc20   96–38922
                                         CIP

Set by 35 in 10/12pt Baskerville
Produced by Longman Singapore Publishers (Pte) Ltd.
Printed in Singapore

Contents

List of Figures

Editorial Foreword

The aim of this series is to describe and analyse the history of the world since 1945. History, like time, does not stand still. What seemed to many of us only recently to be 'current affairs' or the stuff of political speculation, has now become material for historians. The editors feel that it is time for a series of books which will offer the public judicious and scholarly, but at the same time readable, accounts of the way in which our present-day world has been shaped since the Second World War. The period which began in 1945 has witnessed political events and socio-economic developments of enormous significance for the human race, as important as anything that happened before Hitler's death or the bombing of Hiroshima. Ideologies have waxed and waned, industrial economies have boomed and bust, empires of various types have collapsed, new nations have emerged and sometimes themselves fallen into decline. While we can be thankful that no major armed conflict occurred between the so-called superpowers, there have been many other wars, and terrorism emerged as an international plague. Although the position of ethnic minorities improved in some countries, it worsened dramatically in others. As communist tyrannies relaxed their grip on many areas of the world, so half-forgotten national conflicts re-emerged. Nearly everywhere the status of women became an issue which politicians were unable to avoid. The same was true of the global environment, apparent threats to which have been a recurrent source of international concern. These are only some of the developments we hope will be illuminated by this series as it unfolds.

The books in the series will not follow any set pattern; they will vary in length according to the needs of the subject. Some will deal with regions, or even single nations, and others with themes. Not all of them will begin in 1945, and the terminal date may vary; as with the length, the time-span chosen will be appropriate to the question under discussion. All the books, however, will be written by expert historians drawing on the latest research, as well as their own expertise and judgement. The series should be particularly welcome to students, but it is designed also for the general reader with an interest in contemporary history. We hope that the books will stimulate scholarly discussion and encourage specialists to look beyond their own particular interests to engage in wider controversies.

History, and especially the history of the recent past, is neither 'bunk' nor an intellectual form of stamp-collecting, but an indispensable part of an educated person's approach to life. If it is not written by historians it will be written by others of a less discriminating and more polemical disposition. The editors are confident that this series will help to ensure the victory of the historical approach, with consequential benefits for its readers.

A. J. Nichols
Martin S. Alexander

Acknowledgements

I should like to express my appreciation to the German Historical Institute in London and to St Antony's College, Oxford, for their admirable library services. I am extremely grateful to Andrew MacLennan of Addison Wesley Longman for his unfailing encouragement and patience. My most heartfelt thanks are extended to Jennifer Law and Sarah Sheldon for all their help in preparing the typescript of this book.

AJN
August 1996

The publishers would like to thank the following for permission to reproduce tabular material: Cambridge University Press for Figure 1 on p. 65, and Verlag W. Kohlhammer for Figures 2 and 3 on pages 96 and 97 respectively.

Glossary

The following German words are used commonly in the text:

Der Alte	'The old man'– Adenauer
Fraktion	Parliamentary delegation or parliamentary party
Land, plural *Länder*	The individual federal states of Germany, e.g. Bavaria, Lower Saxony, Bremen, etc.
Ostpolitik	Eastern Policy – West German relations with the Soviet Union Eastern Europe and the GDR.

List of Abbreviations

APO	Extra-Parliamentary Opposition
BBU	Federal Association of Citizens' Initiatives to Protect the Environment
BdL	Bank of the German *Länder* (1957 Bundesbank)
BDA	Federation of German Employers' Associations
BDI	Federal Association of German Industry
BHE	League of those driven from their homes and those deprived of their rights (Refugees' Party)
CAP	Common Agricultural Policy (of EEC)
CDU	Christian Democratic Union
CDUD	Christian Democratic Union of Germany (GDR)
CSU	Christian Social Union
DGB	Federation of German Trade Unions
DKP	German Communist Party
DM, D-Mark	Deutschmark – (west) German mark
DP	German Party
DDR	Deutsche Demokratische Republik (see GDR)
ECSC	European Coal and Steel Community
EDC	European Defence Community
EEC	European Economic Community
EMS	European Monetary System
EPU	European Payments Union
EP	European Parliament
ERP	European Recovery Programme
EURATOM	European Atomic Energy Community
FAZ	*Frankfurter Allgemeine Zeitung*
FDP	Free Democratic Party
FRG	Federal Republic of Germany
FUB	Free University of Berlin

GATT	General Agreement on Trade and Tariffs
GDR	German Democratic Republic (also known as the DDR)
IAR	International Authority for the Ruhr
IMF	International Monetary Fund
KPD	Communist Party of Germany
NATO	North Atlantic Treaty Organisation
NPD	National Democratic Party of Germany
NSDAP	National Socialist German Workers' Party
OEEC	Organization for European Economic Co-operation
OPEC	Organization of Petroleum Exporting Countries
SA	Sturmabteilung (nazi storm troopers)
SALT	Strategic Arms Limitation Treaty
SDI	Strategic Defense Initiative
SED	Socialist Unity Party of Germany
SPD	Social Democratic Party of Germany
SS	Schutzstaffeln (Himmler's security forces)

The Federal Republic of Germany, September 1990

Source: *Statistisches Jahrbuch 1990 für die Bundesrepublik Deutschland* (Stuttgart, 1990).

Prologue: The Impact of Defeat

On 20 July 1944 some representatives of the old ruling classes of Germany attempted to salvage their honour and their status in society by overthrowing Hitler. Their failure went some way towards achieving the first of these objectives. It ensured that the second was never achieved at all.

Although the resistance movement which organized the abortive coup against Hitler contained representatives of many different elements in German society – soldiers, diplomats, officials, former social democrats and even Roman Catholic priests – its tone was set by the protestant elites that had dominated Prussian Germany in the Wilhelmine Empire before 1918. In particular, the Junkers, the landowners of Germany's grain-producing area east of the Elbe, who had resisted the democratization of Germany most tenaciously in the period of the Weimar Republic, now wished to depose the upstart radicals in brown uniforms who had usurped their position and besmirched German honour by their atrocities during the war. A mixture of moral outrage and desperate self-interest characterized the conservative resistance in Germany. Its failure to kill Hitler was to have profound consequences for the future of the German people.[1]

The leaders of the resistance, General Beck and Carl Goerdeler, did not want to restore a parliamentary system of government to Germany. Neither the military nor the administrative elite had any emotional attachment to democracy, and most of them, including Beck and Goerdeler themselves, had welcomed the downfall of the Weimar Republic. However, although they shared Hitler's desire to break the 'chains of Versailles' and make Germany dominant in central Europe, they were not, on the whole, believers in nazi racist social Darwinism and they tended to regard the nazis themselves with fastidious distaste. Their aim was to assuage Germany's moral guilt by killing Hitler, to save Germany's 'Reich', or realm, from

1. Cf. F.L. Carsten, *A History of the Prussian Junkers* (London, 1989), pp. 183–9.

1

dismemberment, and to create a conservative, corporate state based
on private property and conservative political values.

It is most unlikely that the resisters would have succeeded in
doing these things even if they had been able to oust the nazis. The
Allied powers – Britain, the Soviet Union and the United States –
had already made up their minds to force the unconditional surrender of Germany and to occupy it completely. Furthermore, inter-
Allied discussions held during the war – the most important of which
was the meeting in Tehran at the end of November 1943 – had
agreed that Poland should receive compensation from Germany for
the damage inflicted on her by Hitler's aggression.[2] This compensation would take the form of German provinces east of the River Oder.
In fact the aim was to reconcile the reluctant Poles to the loss of
eastern territories to the Soviet Union, territories originally gained by
Stalin as the result of his infamous pact with Hitler in August 1939.
Hence the heartland of the Prussian Junkers – East Prussia, Upper
and Lower Silesia and Pomerania – would be lost to Germany.

Although the rapacity of Stalin and the needs of the Poles – who
had, of course, been the first victims of the Second World War –
may account for the establishment of the Oder–Neisse frontier, it
should not be thought that German unity was preserved by the
western powers in the face of Soviet malevolence. Neither President Roosevelt nor Prime Minister Churchill had any desire to be
'soft' on the Germans, which was hardly surprising, given the desperate struggle for survival which the British had been waging since
the fall of France in June 1940, and the enormous cost which the
war had imposed on a temperamentally isolationist United States.

Had the coup against Hitler succeeded, it is out of the question
that the western powers would have made the favourable peace
with Goerdeler and his colleagues for which they hoped. Unconditional surrender would have been enforced, the agreed occupation
zones allocated to the victors, and Goerdeler's government would
have been saddled with the odium of having encompassed German
defeat. The 'stab-in-the-back' alibi, so beloved of German nationalists,
would at once have been turned against the men who had murdered
the Führer at a time when he and the nazis were girding themselves
to withstand and repel the final onslaught.[3] Beck and Goerdeler

2. At the Yalta Conference of 4–11 February 1945, the Allies agreed to dismember
Germany, but quietly dropped the proposal in the months that followed. See J.W.
Wheeler-Bennett and A.J. Nicholls, *The Semblance of Peace. The Political Settlement after
the Second World War* (London, 1972), chs. 8 and 11.

3. Indeed, recent research has suggested that in the summer of 1944 the nazi

would have become the scapegoats for the failure of national socialism in the same way that Ebert and Scheidemann had been blamed
for the failures of Ludendorff and Hindenburg at the end of the
First World War.

As it was, Hitler suppressed the conspirators with the utmost sav-
agery, revealing the true nature of his regime by holding a grotesque
show trial and ordering the barbaric execution of the defendants by
hanging with piano wire. Stringent measures were taken to eradicate
the influence of the old conservative groups in the officer corps. The
war against the United Nations was pursued with fanatical vigour
until the end. Although in propaganda terms it was often presented
as a war to defend Europe against bolshevism, the nazi struggle in
the west was as determined as the resistance in the east. It is sometimes forgotten that Hitler's last great offensive in December 1944
was not launched against Stalin's troops pouring into eastern Germany, but against the Americans in the Ardennes. At the same time
the Allied bombing campaign continued to devastate Germany's
cities, and above all her transport networks and power supplies.

When the war ended in May 1945 Hitler himself had already committed suicide and his Reich was in ruins. Only the most fanatical
nazi (and by this time their numbers were dwindling fast) could still
cleave to the view that Hitler's own policy had not been responsible
for war and defeat. Equally discredited was the military machine
which had supported the nazis so loyally since the Röhm purge of
June 1934. The defeat of nazism was the defeat of German militarism.

It was also a defeat for Prussia. Logically, this might seem somewhat surprising, since Hitler was an Austrian by birth and his movement had begun in Munich, the capital of South German Bavaria.
Some of the regime's more revolting atrocities, such as the barbarous
campaign against Tito's partisans in the Balkans, or the organization of Jewish deportations by the SS, were partly carried out by
Austrians. Yet Austria emerged from the war with the status of a
liberated country, albeit one which was occupied by the Allied powers
and deprived of its independence until 1955.

The reason for this was, of course, political. It suited both western
and Soviet Allies to accept that Austria had been a victim of aggression, so that her status as a country independent of Germany should
not be called in question. Nevertheless, there was also a genuine

leadership sincerely believed it still had a good chance of winning the war. See
Gerhard L. Weinberg, 'German plans for victory, 1944–45', in *Central European
History*, Vol. 26, No. 2 (1993), 215–28.

belief, exemplified by the views of Winston Churchill, that Prussia was in itself a menacing factor which was responsible for the outbreak of two world wars. This was justified by the fact that, under the terms of German unification finalized in 1871, Prussia had made up roughly half of Germany's territorial area and possessed more than half of its population. For the Wilhelmine Empire the importance of the Prussian monarchy and the Prussian government was such that one might more properly refer to the 'Prussian-German' Empire.

Under the Weimar Republic, from 1919 to 1933, the powers of the Prussian government were reduced *vis-à-vis* those of the Reich administration, but the autonomy of the Prussian state remained, and the lopsided character of Germany's federal structure was so awkward that plans for so-called 'Reich reform' were constantly discussed. In all of them the position of Prussia was a major problem. This was not just a matter of size, economic power and cultural domination, although all these were important.

Just as potent was the historical tradition associated with Prussia. It was thought of as an authoritarian state dominated socially and politically by its military establishment, of which Kaiser Wilhelm II, particularly, was a devoted admirer. The military victories that had united Germany in the 1860s and 1870s had been Prussian victories. The officer corps which set the tone, not just for the German army but for much of German social life, was the Prussian officer corps. When, on 21 March 1933, Hitler and Hindenburg had clasped hands together in a public ceremony of reconciliation and fealty at the Prussian monarchy's garrison church in Potsdam, Hitler was consciously – and successfully – identifying himself with the dominant Prussian spirit in Germany.

Prussia itelf had extended across most of north Germany, from Königsberg in the east to Aachen and Cologne in the west. But its most emotively loyal Prussian lands were those in the east of the country – above all Brandenburg, and East and West Prussia and Pomerania. In most of these regions there were Polish minorities, and West Prussia had already been lost to the Reich in 1919. In the electoral map of Wilhelmine and Weimar Germany these eastern provinces had been the least accessible to democratic ideas. It was not surprising, therefore, that the destruction of Prussia loomed large on the agenda of Germany's victors. This was, indeed, one war aim which was to be attained. On 25 February 1947, Prussia was formally abolished by Allied decree.

That might have been the prelude to a major dismemberment of

Germany, and indeed, at the so-called Crimean Conference held at Yalta in February 1945, Churchill, Roosevelt and Stalin had agreed on such dismemberment, referring the detailed planning to a committee. But by the end of the war, this concept had been dropped. Neither the British Foreign Office nor the US State Department approved of it, and the Soviet government seems to have decided that its interests would be best served by keeping Germany united. This may have been because it hoped to be able to dominate Germany politically, controlling, as it did, the Reich capital of Berlin, but it is more likely that the prospect of obtaining $10 billion worth of reparations from Germany – an amount rashly promised by Roosevelt at Yalta – caused Stalin to revise his views about dividing the country. This did not, however, affect the provinces east of the Oder–Neisse frontier. They were handed over with precipitate haste to the Poles, who commenced the expulsion of German inhabitants from those territories, including some which had been almost entirely German in ethnic composition, such as Lower Silesia. Similar expulsions were carried out by the Czechs once they had recovered control of the largely German-speaking area known before the war as the Sudetenland.

In May 1945 Germany presented a scene of severe devastation. This was particularly true of larger cities, such as Berlin, Cologne and Hamburg, which had been wrecked by carpet bombing. Elsewhere, aerial attacks on communications, power stations, oil refineries and specific types of industry, such as aircraft manufacturing or synthetic rubber, had also been very damaging. In some places, such as Berlin itself, heavy ground fighting had occurred, adding to the destruction.

After the unconditional surrender of the German *Wehrmacht*, first at Rheims on 7 May 1945, and then two days later at a formal ceremony in Berlin, the Allied authorities established their own rule throughout Germany. A rump nazi regime at Flensburg in Schleswig-Holstein, presided over by Hitler's designated successor, Admiral Dönitz, was deposed and arrested on 23 May 1945, but not before its functionaries had carried out death sentences on a number of anti-nazi Germans accused of mutiny or desertion.

With its disappearance, the administration of Germany was legally as well as practically in the hands of the Allies. Already in February 1944, the Russians and the Anglo-Saxon powers had agreed on zones of occupation and worked out their boundaries. A year later at Yalta, on British insistence, the western occupiers made room for a French zone of occupation, to be carved out of the Anglo-American zones. This was to encompass the left bank of the Rhine south of Bonn, most of the Black Forest, including the city of Freiburg, and part of the Swabian Alps. The British occupied the north-west of Germany including the industrial complex of the Ruhr/Rhine area, and the Americans established themselves in Hesse, Württemberg, Bavaria and part of Baden. All the eastern area of Germany not occupied by the Poles was administered by the Russians except for Berlin, which was to be jointly occupied by the four powers.

Two other anomalies existed; one was to prove unimportant, but the other was a serious cause of difficulty. The latter was the occupation by the French of the Saar Basin, an important coal-mining region which had been a bone of contention between France and Germany between the wars, and which had only been returned to Germany after a plebiscite in 1935. It was soon clear that the French intended to amputate this region permanently from Germany, despite the almost entirely German nature of its population. The less important, but more immediately tiresome, provision was that Roosevelt had insisted on establishing an American enclave in the British zone to give American troops the possibility of withdrawing through north Germany if they felt the need to do so. The port of Bremen was to be under their control and routes to it from the American zone were carefully designated. Somewhat less attention was devoted to securing access routes to Berlin, despite the fact that it lay 150 kilometres behind the border of the Soviet zone.

For the most part, Germany's future remained uncertain. It was hoped that the next Allied conference, which was held at Potsdam from 16 July to 2 August 1945, would go some way to clarify the position. Potsdam was a seat of the Hohenzollern family, conveniently situated in the vicinity of Berlin, but in the Soviet zone of occupation. The conference met in the Cecilienhof, a bogus manor house – complete with fake Tudor chimneys – erected for Crown Prince Wilhelm, the bombastic son of the last Kaiser of Germany. It has a vaguely oppressive and unreal atmosphere which perhaps suited the character of the conference.

The last great meeting of the leaders of the 'Big Three' allies, Potsdam was bedevilled by wrangling over the administration of Poland, where the prospects of a genuinely representative government were fast disappearing. The fact that the American delegation was led by a new president, Harry S. Truman, and that the British government unexpectedly changed halfway through the proceedings, causing Attlee and Bevin to replace Churchill and Eden at the head of the British delegation, did not help the harmonious resolution of differences.

Nevertheless, so far as Germany was concerned, the Potsdam agreement was not so disastrous as might have been feared. Germany was to be administered as a unity and not broken up. This, of course, begged the question of the eastern territories occupied by the Poles or, in the case of Königsberg and part of the province of East Prussia, the Russians. So far as the latter area was concerned, the conference agreed in principle that ultimately it should be transferred to the Soviet Union. The Polish-occupied areas, on the other hand, would remain under Polish administration until the western frontier of Poland should be determined by a peace treaty. In the meantime, they should not be regarded as part of the Soviet zone of Germany – an important proviso, since it meant that food supplies from this predominantly agricultural region would not be made available to feed the Germans.

It was clear that these areas would not be returned to Germany, but formally it could be argued that, until a peace treaty finalized the frontiers, Germany still consisted of the country as it had been in December 1937 – before the nazi occupation of Austria and the Czech Sudetenland in 1938. This was to remain the west German interpretation of the legal position until the treaties which settled the unification of Germany in 1990. The Soviet government was not unhappy with this arrangement, since it left the Poles in a slightly uncertain position and made them dependent on Soviet support if they were to ensure the permanent occupation of areas east of the Oder–Neisse line. For the Poles, and not just the Polish communists, this westward expansion was essential to compensate for the territories in the east which they had lost to the Soviet Union. As their representatives pointed out when they were invited to address the Potsdam conference, the new arrangements still left Poland 20 per cent smaller than in the summer of 1919, whereas Germany herself would be only about 18 per cent smaller. In view of the aggression committed by Germany against Poland, this did not seem unreasonable, at least to the victor powers.[4]

One other Allied decision which was to have an important impact on postwar Germany was the understanding, briefly discussed at Yalta and confirmed at Potsdam, that German populations in areas either restored to or annexed by Germany's eastern neighbours could be expelled from their homes and moved west. The object of

4. Wheeler-Bennett and Nicholls, *The Semblance of Peace*, p. 335. For the Potsdam declaration relating to Germany, Königsberg and the Oder–Neisse territories, see ibid., pp. 632–42.

this exercise was to prevent the emergence of a German minority 'problem' which had proved so damaging for the Czechs and the Poles before the war.

After 1918 liberal-minded peacemakers had tried to stick to the principle of self-determination wherever possible, relying on treaty rights and, in some cases, League of Nations supervision to protect minorities. In practice this did not work. In most eastern and southern European countries, with the exception of Czechoslovakia, minorities were badly treated, and at least in the case of the German minorities, they often became agents of subversion. During the war itself Hitler and his lieutenants had not hesitated to dispossess and deport large numbers of Poles, in order to accommodate the supposed need for 'living space' (*Lebensraum*) for the Germans. The whole aim of the Second World War had been the colonization of European Russia, 'colonization' being envisaged as settlement, with the native populations being treated like Red Indians in North America. There was therefore little inclination on the Allied side to flinch from measures to remove the Germans from countries which would henceforward be independent of Germany and which would be concerned above all to prevent a recurrence of German aggression.

The only difference – and it was an important one – between the Anglo-American Allies and the Soviet Union over this matter was that the former were insistent that transfers of population should be carried out humanely, a consideration of little concern to Stalin, who had subjected his own population to brutal campaigns of deportation, starvation and murder since the late 1920s.[5]

The issue was complicated by the fact that, as the Red Army approached the eastern areas of Germany, many Germans left their homes of their own accord. The behaviour of the Soviet troops, and particularly of non-front-line formations charged with security duties, was often atrocious, rape and pillage being commonplace. Although this was perhaps understandable given the appalling behaviour of the *Wehrmacht* in the Soviet Union, it was not excusable. However, the impact of such behaviour was greatly exacerbated by a nazi

5. See Article XII of the Protocol of the Potsdam Conference: 'Orderly transfer of German Populations', in Wheeler-Bennett and Nicholls, *The Semblance of Peace*, pp. 644–5. On German and Allied policies towards expulsion of populations, see W. Benz, 'Der Generalplan Ost: Zur Germanisierungspolitik des NS-Regimes in den besetzten Ostgebieten 1939–1945', and K.-D. Henke, 'Der Weg nach Potsdam – Die Alliierten und die Vertreibung', in W. Benz (ed.), *Die Vertreibung der Deutschen aus dem Osten. Ursachen, Ereignisse, Folgen* (Frankfurt, 1985), pp. 39–69.

propaganda campaign aimed at convincing Germans that Soviet occupation would be a fate worse than death. It was small wonder that hundreds of thousands left their homes in the eastern provinces of the country, as well as in the Czech Sudenten region, even before new Slav regimes started to throw them out. Many of these people wanted to go to the Western-occupied zones of Germany to avoid Soviet control. In other cases, the Poles and Czechs expelled their unwanted Germans with rail transports targeted at the western zones, and these expulsions were often carried out in a brutal manner. The result was that the British zone, in particular, was forced to take in huge numbers of refugees and try to cope with their needs in a reasonably humane fashion.

In addition to those fleeing or expelled from the east, it should be remembered that Germany at the end of the Second World War had numerous other people displaced from their normal homes. By far the largest number were the forced labourers and concentration camp victims who had been drafted into German factories and mines to sustain Hitler's war effort. There were approximately two million of these in the British zone alone. In addition, many German families had been evacuated from major cities like Berlin to avoid exposure to Allied bombing.

This point has been laboured somewhat because it was to affect the Federal Republic in a number of ways after its foundation in 1949. First of all, the influx of nearly nine and a half million Germans from other parts of the country into western Germany between 1944 and 1950 meant that traditional regional loyalties were bound to become blurred.[6] This was particularly important in relation to confessional differences. The divide between Roman Catholics and protestants had been of major importance in German politics and society since the Reformation. It had affected political voting behaviour in the Wilhelmine Empire and the Third Reich, and was to continue to do so in the early years of the Federal Republic. The movement of population during and after the Second World War ran across traditional confessional boundaries. Roman Catholic Sudenten Germans, for example, tended to find themselves in protestant Franconia, whereas protestant refugees from the eastern districts of Prussia were transported to Roman Catholic parishes in Württemberg or Bavaria. The result was that many areas which had

6. G. Schulz, in *Wiederaufbau in Deutschland. Die Wohnungsbaupolitik in der Westzonen und der Bundesrepublik von 1945 bis 1957* (Düsseldorf, 1994), pp. 35–6, gives figures of 7.88 million expellees and 1.56 million 'migrants' who had arrived in the western zones by September 1950.

been of homogenous confessional character became mixed in religious affiliation. In 1939 Bavaria, for instance, had contained 1,424 parishes which were either wholly Roman Catholic or wholly protestant, but by 1946 this number had fallen to just nine.[7]

The refugees can also be seen as the harbinger of a new physical mobility in West Germany's population which was, if anything, to intensify during the 1950s. The waves of refugees coming out of East Germany through Berlin until the building of the Wall in 1961, to say nothing of guest workers from Italy, Yugoslavia, Spain and finally Turkey, were to have a powerful impact on the previously inward-looking and rather parochial society of the old German Reich. They were one, though certainly not the only, component in an atmosphere of restless energy which encouraged people to move from one part of the country to another, thus loosening the ties which Germans had traditionally felt to their home communities.

The concept of 'Heimat' had been an important aspect of German nationalism. It had been exploited in the nineteenth century by rulers whose legitimacy was none too obvious, but who were eager to bind their subjects together with feelings of emotional loyalty to the homeland. It helped to raise national consciousness whilst associating the nation with a conservative commitment to that 'home' which was the '. . . nursery of civic virtues and order'.[8] Nationalist theorists helped to create a myth of linkage between the Germans and their environment – a concept of organic growth which applied to communities as well as vegetation. In German primary schools from the Weimar Republic onwards, *Heimatkunde* was a major pedagogical tool, designed to combine instruction in environmental matters with the inculcation of respect for a way of life which was supposedly peculiarly German and associated with the rivers, woods, meadows and mountains of the Fatherland. Even as Germany industrialized, the myth that *Heimat* was a farming community was still propagated. The catastrophic end of the Third Reich did not immediately destroy this myth, but the population movements created by Hitler's war certainly helped to weaken it.

---

7. F.J. Bauer, 'Aufnahme und Eingliederung der Flüchtlinge und Vertriebenen. Das Beispiel Bayern 1945–1950', in Benz, *Vertreibung der Deutschen*, p. 160. This did not mean that the overall balance of Catholics and protestants in Bavaria was altered very much; it was confessional *distribution* that changed.

8. Cf. Celia Applegate, *A Nation of Provincials. The German Idea of Heimat* (University of California Press, Berkeley, CA, 1990), pp. 8–16.

CHAPTER ONE

The Legacy of the Occupation, 1945–1949

Since this book is concerned with the Federal Republic itself, it will not attempt to present a history of the Allied occupation of Germany from 1945 to 1949. The division of Germany between the four Allied occupiers and the dismemberment of the Eastern Prussian provinces were, however, not the only important results of that occupation which affected the character of the new West German state. The economic system and political culture of the Bonn Republic were also conditioned by what happened between Unconditional Surrender on 8 May 1945 and the first Bundestag elections in August 1949.

One point which should be remembered is that when the Third Reich was defeated nobody was sure how long the occupation of Germany would last. President Roosevelt, who had died in April 1945, evidently hoped to get US troops out of Germany after about two years. On the other hand, the British Field Marshal Montgomery and General Joseph T. McNarney, the American military governor until early in 1947, believed that the occupation would last at least ten years,[1] and this seems to have been the assumption upon which the British authorities in Germany operated for some time after they established their zonal administration. If it was going to be a long time before the Germans regained their independence, the occupying powers would be able to contemplate far-reaching programmes of political and even social reform.

Theoretically, according to the decisions arrived at in Potsdam, Germany was to be administered as a unity by a Four-Power Control Council in Berlin, a city in which each of the occupying powers was allocated a sector and to which their service personnel had right of

1. Michael Balfour and John Mair, *Four-Power Control in Germany and Austria 1945–1946* (Oxford, 1956), p. 183.

access. In practice the four-power system never worked properly and the powers administered their own zones without much reference to their colleagues. Most obstructive initially were the French, who resented having been presented with a *fait accompli* by the Potsdam conference, to which they had not been invited. They objected to the concept of administering the country as a unity, and refused to contemplate the national German administration agencies which were envisaged in the Potsdam agreements. However, French obstructionism soon became less important than other, more menacing, problems.

Reparations – a brake on reconstruction

The Yalta/Potsdam accords had been based on the concept that the western powers, and particularly the British, controlled the industrial heartland of Germany from which a considerable proportion of the reparations due to Russia – roughly estimated at $10 billion – would be drawn. Such reparations would be taken in kind, thus avoiding the problems of financial transfer which had bedevilled the reparations arrangements after the First World War. Most particularly, 25 per cent of industrial capital equipment in the western zones which was deemed to be unnecessary for the German peace economy should be handed over to the Russians, 10 per cent for no payment and 15 per cent in return for food and raw materials from the Soviet zone. Otherwise, reparations should be taken from the zones of the occupiers receiving them. For their part, the Russians, controlling the more agricultural eastern part of the country, would apparently be expected to provide surplus food for the more populous and industrial British zone. This was a major reason why the Allies agreed to keep the country together: the West would get the food and the Soviet Union the reparations. Both these assumptions were false. As we have already seen, most of the eastern breadbasket of Germany – including provinces such as Lower Silesia – was lost to the Poles, who were uprooting their German inhabitants and replacing them with Polish migrants from areas ceded to the USSR. What was left of the eastern zone was quite heavily industrialized and needed its agricultural resources to feed itself. On the other hand, German industrial areas, particularly in the Westphalian–Ruhr Basin complex occupied by the British, had been devastated by Allied bombing during the war. This had been particularly damaging for housing, communications and power supplies.

When the western Allies entered Germany, their main concern, as reflected in the American Chiefs of Staff occupation directive, JCS 1067, was to denazify, demilitarize and decentralize Germany and to deconcentrate German industry. Indeed, there was an implication that industrial production should be held back – an echo of the notorious Morgenthau Plan for the pastoralization of Germany which had been briefly accepted by Churchill and Roosevelt in September 1944, only to be dropped within weeks when wiser counsels prevailed.[2] Soon, however, it became clear that the main problem was going to be to get the West German economy – and particularly that in the British zone – back into production to such an extent that the Germans would neither starve on the one hand nor be a burden to the Allies on the other. The British estimated that their zone was going to cost them £80 million (well over a £1 billion in 1990's values) in the first year.[3] From 1945 to 1947 the British found themselves having to spend much of their precious supply of dollars, borrowed under what they saw as harsh terms from the USA, on feeding their zone with food purchased from the Americans. This meant that the British were eager to obtain permission to allow steel production in their zone to rise to levels which neither the Americans nor the Soviet authorities were willing to contemplate.

Although it is still difficult to be sure what Stalin's objectives were in Germany in 1945 – he may well not have been sure himself – it is evident that he wanted to secure as much industrial plant as possible from the western zones, calling in the reparations promise unwisely handed to him by Roosevelt at Yalta, whilst giving the West nothing in return from the Soviet zone, which was effectively sealed off from western influence. In the period between the end of hostilities and the spring of 1946, the Americans were eager to come to an agreement with the Soviet Union over four-power occupation, an agreement which would have severely limited the prospects for a west German recovery. In this enterprise they were blocked as much by the French – who wanted no all-German administration – as by the Russians.

For their part, the British were concerned from the summer of 1944 with the problem of the balance of power in Europe and the

2. For a description of the JCS 1067 from one who had to implement it, see Lucius D. Clay, *Decision in Germany* (New York, 1950), pp. 16–19. See also J.W. Wheeler-Bennett and A.J. Nicholls, *The Semblance of Peace. The Political Settlement after the Second World War* (London, 1972), pp. 174–87.

3. Anne Deighton, *The Impossible Peace. Britain, the Division of Germany, and the Origins of the Cold War* (Oxford, 1990), p. 30.

threat of Soviet domination. Amongst the military authorities, in particular, the obvious solution seemed to be to divide Germany, with the western powers keeping the major part of it as part of a block against the Soviet Union.[4] This would protect Britain simultaneously against German and Russian aggression in the future. Such views conflicted with opinions represented in the British Foreign Office, and amongst some politicians, that nothing should be done to upset an established alliance with the Soviet Union. It was, in any case, quite out of the question to switch loyalties from the Russians to the Germans so soon after a bitter war; neither public opinion nor the majority of those involved in British political leadership would have accepted such a move. Nevertheless, the British were determined to prevent Soviet influence seeping into their zone and worked from the beginning towards the creation of a defensive block which could protect western Europe and which would include the United States.[5]

The result of these developments was increasing tension between the Soviet Union and her western Allies. The dismantling of plant for transfer to the Russians created great indignation amongst the Germans and probably was of little value to the Soviet economy. In the end, the Russians took their reparations requirements overwhelmingly from their own zone. In 1985 Theo Sommer, the Editor-in-Chief of the respected west German weekly, *Die Zeit*, remarked that: 'The West Germans were lucky. It was the East Germans who paid the full price of Hitler's war.'[6]

This was not entirely the end of the story so far as reparations for the western zones were concerned; arrangements had to be made about German international debts, and compensation for Jewish victims of national socialism was paid in the form of aid to Israel.[7] But by comparison with the situation in the Weimar Republic, the new west German state would be remarkably free of financial burdens connected with the war. One nagging source of resentment was eliminated. Only the luckless citizens of the German Democratic Republic

---

4. In September 1944 the British Chiefs of Staff pointed out that if the USSR were to develop hostile intentions towards Britain, 'we should require all the help we could get from any source open to us, including Germany'. This implied the division of Germany, because, as they argued a few months later, the east of Germany was going to be controlled by the Russians anyhow, and to check the spread of Soviet influence into the western parts of the country they advocated setting up two separate western German states each controlled by a western democratic state. See Deighton, *The Impossible Peace*, p. 19.

5. Cf. ibid., chs. 1–3.

6. Quoted in Alec Cairncross, *The Price of War: British Policy on German Reparations 1941–1949* (Oxford, 1986), p. v. For details of the east German payments see ibid., pp. 194–218.

7. See below, Chapter 5.

were in no position to throw off the burden of Soviet reparations, since they effectively remained an occupied country.

Denazification

If the occupation forces fell out over reparations and industrial policy, their other concerns, demilitarization and denazification, also presented them with awkward problems. The former seemed at first to be relatively straightforward, since the German armed forces were totally defeated and disbanded. It was only when the Cold War became very threatening, at the end of the 1940s, that the rearmament of Germany on both sides of the iron curtain became a matter of controversy.

Denazification was altogether more difficult. For Anglo-Saxon governments it was connected with the issue of war crimes. When it became known in the West that the nazis were following policies of extermination and atrocity with respect to their occupied territories, Winston Churchill had drawn up a famous public statement making it clear that those who had 'imbrued their hands with innocent blood' could expect retribution. There was also determination in Britain to punish Germans guilty of killing British prisoners of war. But the way in which such retribution was to be administered was left vague until nearly the end of the war. The British originally thought of drawing up a list of leading nazis and having them shot, but by the summer of 1944 their Allies had rejected this arbitrary course, and on American advice it was agreed to hold full-dress trials of the nazi war leaders and those who had been involved in major crimes against humanity during the war.[8]

The trials of the major nazis who had been captured alive, including Göring, Hess, Ribbentrop, Rosenberg and Streicher, took place in Nuremberg and lasted from 20 November 1945 until 1 October 1946, when ten of the defendants were sentenced to death. Only nine of them were actually hanged, because the tenth, Hermann

---

8. Cf. Airey Neave, *Nuremberg: A Personal Record of the Trial of the Major Nazi War Criminals in 1945–6* (London, 1978), p. 322. Neave's book, which is a personal memoir, also contains a powerful defence of the Nuremberg trials, contesting the still fashionable view that they were invalidated because the victors were trying the vanquished. It has never been explained what would have been a satisfactory alternative. Allowing the nazis to go unpunished was, and remains, entirely unacceptable: ibid., pp. 330 et seq. Neave was a Conservative MP and a loyal supporter of Margaret Thatcher. He regarded nazism as 'a continuing threat to the world', a prophetic comment written in 1978, at a time when the racist right seemed to have been eclipsed. The following year Neave himself was murdered by the IRA.

Göring, cheated the executioner by taking poison in his cell. Three of the 21 defendants present at Nuremberg were actually acquitted, a fact which is not always mentioned by the critics of the trial. Interestingly enough, this was a verdict which did not find favour with the embittered German citizenry of Nuremberg, and special police measures had to be taken to protect the safety of those who had been found not guilty.[9]

Many other trials were held, both inside and outside Germany, of those accused of specific crimes. In the three western zones a total of 5,035 people were accused of war crimes or crimes against humanity; 806 defendants were condemned to death, of whom 486 were executed. Yet very many nazis who had been guilty of atrocious behaviour escaped unpunished, some of them leaving for exile in countries such as Argentina, and others remaining under cover in Germany, often protected by neighbours and friends. Despite considerable popular hostility to nazis, it was not surprising that Germans were reluctant to deliver their compatriots up to the occupying forces. Nevertheless, the ease with which many quite prominent figures in nazi local government, paramilitary formations, or concentration camp administration managed to return undetected to their native communities suggests that in many parts of the country, particularly the provincial areas where nazism had been strongly supported in the early 1930s, the sympathies of many people remained with the Third Reich. For this reason alone, the Nuremberg trials were beneficial. No matter how much they might be attacked as 'victors' justice', they presented to the public – and to historians – a record of the Third Reich which it was difficult to overlook.[10]

There was still the question of the more general 'denazification' of the German population. This was a vexatious problem, because many millions of Germans had been involved in some way in nazi organizations – the party itself, its paramilitary formation, the brownshirted SA, youth movements, women's organizations, and professional associations. Estimates presented by the Allies claimed that as many as twelve million Germans had participated in one way or the other – about one-fifth of the population.[11] Furthermore, although this was perhaps not so well appreciated at the time, many senior

9. Ibid., p. 311. The three men concerned were Hans Fritzsche, Franz von Papen and Hjalmar Schacht.

10. T. Eschenburg, *Jahre der Besatzung 1945–1949*, p. 60. This is Vol. I of K.D. Bracher, T. Eschenburg, J.C. Fest and E. Jäckel (eds), *Geschichte der Bundesrepublik Deutschland* (Stuttgart, 1983).

11. Balfour and Mair, *Four-Power Control*, pp. 170–1.

administrators and professional people who were not necessarily NSDAP members might have had much more to do with the evil aspects of national socialism – such as the extermination of gypsies and 'asocial' elements, or medical experiments on concentration camp victims – than the average nazi concierge (*Blockwart*) who spied on the inhabitants of his tenement building.

Matters were made more difficult by the fact that in the Soviet zone a quite different form of denazification – based on 'Marxist-Leninist' principles – was being implemented. This was simpler, though no more just, than that carried out by the western powers. It was based on the belief – which may well have been sincerely held by those implementing it – that national socialism had been an extreme form of capitalist exploitation and that 'fascists' could be defeated by rooting out the 'bourgeoisie' from positions of professional importance and destroying its economic power. This did not prevent the Soviet authorities using 'bourgeois' or even nazi collaborators if they felt they could rely on their obedience.[12]

In their zone the British quickly found themselves relying on former nazis for administrative and technical services in rebuilding the area's shattered economy. When complaints about this from politicians at home or anti-nazi Germans caused such people to be suspended from their posts or even arrested, the authorities tended to get the worst of both worlds, being accused both of softness on the nazis and inefficiency in administration.

In the American zone, also, the authorities faced public criticism, especially in the United States, that they were not doing enough to rid Germany of nazis, despite a commitment to uproot national socialism. In fact, both the Americans and the British dismissed and arrested large numbers of nazis during the first months of the occupation. By September 1945 66,500 people had been interned in the American zone and by the end of that year 70,000 nazi suspects were under arrest in the British zone. Literally hundreds of thousands were removed from office or had work applications refused. Had this relatively pragmatic method of dealing with former nazis been continued, it might well have been successful. As it was, the American military governor, General Lucius D. Clay, felt under pressure to produce a really comprehensive denazification scheme which could be applied to the whole of Germany. He launched an ambitious programme in his zone, using that favourite tool of American political science, the questionnaire. Germans over eighteen had

12. Ibid., p. 176.

to fill out a form containing 133 questions about their personal biography and describing their participation in any nazi organization. False answers would be punished if discovered. Respondents were then put into the following categories: major offenders, offenders, lesser offenders, followers and persons exonerated. Offenders and followers could be punished and could also be excluded from both public service and posts of any responsibility in the economy. This led to three million charges and 930,000 sentences.

Denazification tribunals were set up, manned by Germans of supposedly respectable character – including communists – to pass judgement on former nazis and pronounce on their suitability for future employment. At one point, there were 545 tribunals in the American zone, with staffs totalling 22,000. Needless to say, this procedure aroused resentments, and service on the tribunals became unpopular. The whole procedure took a long time and was bound to involve injustices in individual cases. In particular, there was the problem that even those accused of being 'followers' (the German term *Mitläufer* or 'fellow traveller' is more appropriate) were suspended from their posts, creating tremendous difficulties in administration and education. There was thus an incentive to deal with the minor cases first in order to get them out of the way and help rehabilitate those who were only found guilty of lesser involvement. It began to seem as if the small fry were being persecuted, whereas the bigger fish seemed to be unpunished. The implementation of the law created a feeling of solidarity amongst Germans – nazis and non-nazis – particularly against the Anglo-American occupiers.

The Americans had insisted that their brand of far-reaching denazification should be followed in other zones, and on 12 October 1946 a quadripartite directive was issued which made the categorizations given above mandatory for the whole of Germany. Only the British reluctantly followed the Americans' lead, and by 1 January 1949, when denazification was finally stopped, over two million persons in the British zone had been examined under similar, though rather less rigorous, procedures.

For their part, the Russians carried on without much reference to the legislation, as did the French, who acted in a far more pragmatic manner, thus enabling many competent administrators, including the future Social Democratic leader and minister, Carlo Schmid, to help in the work of zonal rehabilitation.[13]

13. For the French zone, see Eschenburg, *Jahre der Besatzung*, pp. 118–19; for the statistics in the US and British zones, see Balfour and Mair, *Four-Power Control*, p. 177. The Directive of 12 October 1946 is published in part in Beate Ruhm von Oppen (ed.), *Documents on Germany Under Occupation 1945–1954* (Oxford, 1955), pp. 168–79.

Denazification was one of the most heavily criticized aspects of Anglo-American occupation policy. Its delayed impact – in its final form it only got under way in the autumn of 1946 – its scale and its perceived unfairness discredited it among the public in the victor countries and the inhabitants of the western zones alike. Nevertheless, it had some advantages. The pressure of denazification forced nazi enthusiasts to keep a low profile at a time when the embryonic institutions of a West German state – including political parties, *Land* administrations, the press and radio, and the education system – were being established. If they wanted to keep their jobs, or at least stay out of jail, xenophobic German nationalists and racist social Darwinists had to pay lip service to the ideals of pluralistic democracy as represented by the western occupiers. In this respect the Federal Republic was to have a great advantage over its Weimar predecessor.

'Re-education'

Denazification was not, of course, just a matter of arresting and punishing former nazis, and ejecting them from state employment. The Allies wanted to create a new political culture in Germany to replace that of the Third Reich. One way of doing this which presented itself to the Allies was the notion of re-education. It was felt in Britain and the USA that the militaristic and aggressive nature of German politics was partly explicable in terms of German family life and German schooling. In fact, German families were as varied in their behaviour as those in any other part of the developed world, but the notion that secondary and university education played a significant role in disseminating authoritarian, nationalist and racist views amongst young people has, if anything, been reinforced by subsequent scholarly enquiries.[14]

There were two possible ways of changing German education: the first was by altering the structure of the German system and the second was by trying to inculcate that system with what were seen as liberal – or perhaps Western – values. On the whole, the Americans

---

14. Fritz Ringer points to the complexity of views on the right in German universities in the Weimar period, and emphasizes that there was much that was admirable in the 'mandarin' tradition. But the prevailing climate of opinion in academic circles was anti-democratic and illiberal, even if it was not crudely national socialist. F. Ringer, *The Decline of the German Mandarins. The German Academic Community, 1890–1933* (Cambridge, Mass., 1969), pp. 435–49. For the importance of pseudo-scientific research and the indoctrination of young people with racist notions in the Third Reich, see M. Burleigh and H. Wippermann, *The Racial State, Germany 1933–1945* (Cambridge, 1991), Parts I and III.

tried to do the first, the British the second, and the French essayed a rather uneasy mixture of the two. It is arguable that none succeeded, but a case could be made for the British having aimed lower and at least partially hit their target.

The Americans saw the German system of secondary education as encouraging hierarchical and authoritarian attitudes. It divided children between those, mainly of the working or lower-middle class, who would leave school at fourteen or sixteen, and the children of the better-off, who were prepared for a university education. The former spent four years in elementary school (*Volksschule*), and might then either continue there for another four years, or go on to a *Mittel* or *Realschule* until they took up a job or an apprenticeship in their mid-teens. The latter often also began in the *Volksschule*, but were prepared for the élitist *Gymnasium*, or grammar school, graduation from which guaranteed entrance to university. The restricted nature of this route can be judged from the fact that in 1932 there were 131,000 university students out of a total population of 65 million. Parents of children in secondary education had to pay school fees, and even if these by no means covered the cost of the schools to the state, they were burdensome to poorer parents, as was the cost of textbooks and other educational materials.[15] This was particularly true in the case of study in a *Gymnasium*, which lasted until the child's nineteenth year. The system of comprehensive and free public high schools in the USA seemed much more democratic and would also lead to a broader pattern of university education. The Americans saw re-education as a prerequisite for the revival of self-government in Germany and therefore hoped to be able to change the structure of schooling in their zone.

For the British, on the other hand, Germany had traditionally been an educational model to which would-be reformers had vainly aspired. Britain had herself only belatedly achieved a nation-wide system of public secondary education with the 1944 Education Act. The *Gymnasium* could be regarded as the model for the British state-maintained grammar school, to which entrance could only be gained by a highly competitive examination at the age of 11+. The one aspect of the German school system which British experts could find defective was the absence of prestigious private schools. It was hardly likely, however, that middle-class German parents, who were used to their children receiving secondary education of high

15. Alonzo G. Grace, 'Education', in Edward H. Litchfield and Associates, *Governing Postwar Germany* (Ithaca, NY, 1953), p. 446.

academic quality subsidized by the state, would find expensive private education very attractive.

Needless to say, the British did not admit to themselves during the war that their education system was inferior to that of the Germans. There was a good deal of talk of relative lack of character training in German schools, although this was a point which had to be handled gingerly, since the nazis had set up special schools for just that purpose. Nevertheless, until 1945 the orthodox British view was that re-education was something which would have to come from the Germans themselves, and could not be imposed from outside. In May 1943 R.A. Butler, at that time President of the Board of Education (Education Minister) in the British government, told the House of Commons: 'we would be wise to realise that the re-education of a people comes better from inside that people themselves ... We may hope to start such a leaven within the country that a real self-education and re-education arises'.[16] The British Foreign Office did not encourage those who suggested that new curricula or textbooks should be prepared for the Germans after the war.[17]

The general British tendency was to hope to encourage native traditions of a liberal education dating back to Wilhelm von Humboldt, a point made by Robert Birley, the headmaster of Charterhouse, in a letter to *The Times* on 8 May 1945. Birley later became educational adviser to the British military governor in Germany. He and the Education Branch of the British occupation administration avoided using the word 're-education'. In August 1948 the deputy director of the Education Branch, Herbert Walker, wrote pointedly to the Foreign Office: 'We detest the word "re-education" as much as the Germans. This is an Education Branch, not a "Re-education" Branch, and the word has never been used in our directives.'[18]

The advent of a Labour government in Britain in the summer of 1945 meant that there was rather more enthusiasm for educational reform in Whitehall. There were also some ingenious attempts to wean German prisoners of war in Britain away from national socialism. The British and the Americans were quite effective in tackling the serious problem presented by textbooks in German schools. It

---

16. Cited in Michael Balfour, 'In Retrospect: Britain's Policy of Re-Education', in Nicholas Pronay and Keith Wilson (eds), *The Political Re-education of Germany and Her Allies* (London, 1985), p. 141.

17. See Lothar Kettenacker, 'The Planning of "Re-education" during the Second World War', in Pronay and Wilson (eds), *Political Re-education*, p. 66.

18. Cited by Kurt Jürgensen, 'The Concept and Practice of "Re-Education" in Germany 1945–50', in Pronay and Wilson (eds), *Political Re-education*, p. 84.

was traditional in German education that state authorities designated the books to be used in classrooms, and these had included
a considerable amount of nationalist, militarist and racist material,
even before the nazis started to impose their own form of perverted
'science' on such subjects as history, geography and biology. The
teaching of *Heimatkunde*, which inculcated love of the homeland,
began at an early age in schools and was continued in course books
which stressed pride in national achievements. That such attitudes
were unlikely to alter simply as the result of nazi defeat in the war
was demonstrated by the types of textbooks presented for Allied
approval by authors after 1945. A proposed Greek grammar contained the statement that 'There can be no doubt that the old Indo-
Germanic ruling class was completely Nordic'. A primer for religious
instruction was proposing to tell its readers that it was from German
tribes, 'converted of their own free will . . . and under the leadership
of the German Nation . . . welded together by Christian faith . . . that
the community of Western civilisation was formed'.[19] The western
Allies refused to sanction textbooks which glorified the nazis or
encouraged extreme nationalism; political, racial or religious discrimination; militarism; or cruelty and morbidity.

The teaching of history was a particular problem. In December
1946 a History Working Party was set up in Braunschweig (Bruns-
wick) in the British zone, and under the guidance of Professor Georg
Eckert it began to produce a series of booklets on recent history.
From this initiative emerged an institute devoted to international
co-operation in the production of history textbooks and a journal,
the *Internationales Jahrbuch für Geschichtsunterricht* (*International Year-
book for History Teaching*), which flourished throughout the history
of the Federal Republic and which helped create an atmosphere
of mutual respect amongst history teachers in different European
countries.[20]

Attempts to alter fundamentally the structure of German education were far less successful. In the British zone some efforts were
made by social democratic *Land* governments to reform the system
by introducing comprehensive education, but they aroused intense
hostility from those who feared a loss of status if the *Gymnasium* was

19. Cited in Kathleen Southwell Davis, 'The Problem of Textbooks', in Arthur
Hearnden (ed.), *The British in Germany: Educational Reconstruction after 1945* (Lon-
don, 1978), pp. 116–17. See also Arthur Hearnden, 'The Education Branch of the
Military Government of Germany and the Schools', in Pronay and Wilson (eds),
Political Re-education, pp. 97–106.

20. Davis, 'The Problem of Textbooks', pp. 124–5.

abolished, and were unsupported by the British authorities.[21] The Americans, for their part, tried to insist on changes in their zone; they pressed for the abolition of school fees, and for the introduction of a six-year period of elementary schooling followed by comprehensive high school education. But the *Land* governments in their zone showed little enthusiasm for such experiments, and they were especially unattractive to the CDU/CSU. Christian Democrats were more concerned about establishing the right to create separate confessional schools in the public sector, an obsession which hampered educational development in *Länder* such as Bavaria, but which did at least arouse parental interest in educational matters.[22]

By 1948 the Americans had given up attempting to press their structural reforms on the Germans, and tried instead to influence by encouragement. They did succeed in getting the *Länder* in their zone to abolish school fees and provide free textbooks, an example which was generally followed, though with reluctance by CDU-dominated *Land* governments, in other western zones.[23]

In the field of university education, very little was changed in the German system. This was in many ways a pity. Before 1933 German universities had been famous as centres of research. They had not, however, attempted to provide rounded programmes of teaching for large numbers of students. As a result of nazi persecution, many of the best scholars had left Germany, either voluntarily or as the result of racist and political purges. The postwar era might have been an opportunity to change the university system to make it more flexible by increasing the number of junior teaching staff and reducing the absolute authority of professors. Neither the British nor the French were in a position to do that, the French because their universities were as top-heavy as the German ones, the British because public university education was relatively unimportant in English life, the older universities still being regarded as social as much as educational institutions. The best model to follow would have been that of the USA, with its combination of undergraduate colleges and graduate schools.

21. Hearnden, 'The Education Branch of the Military Government', p. 104. Hearnden fairly points out that the British were concerned about the rushed and secretive nature of the proposals in Schleswig-Holstein and Hamburg in 1948 and 1949 respectively. However, it seems unlikely that a man like Birley would have looked kindly on comprehensive education. See his own description of British policy in 'British Policy in Retrospect', in Hearnden (ed.), *The British in Germany*, pp. 47–63.

22. Eschenburg, *Jahre der Besatzung*, pp. 252–4.

23. For these developments in the US zone, see Grace, 'Education', p. 459. The school system in the Soviet zone was made considerably more egalitarian, but fell under the ideological control of the communist regime there.

However, in the desperately difficult economic situation of the occupation period, such a reform was bound to have a low priority, and the vested interests entrenched in German universities were able to assert themselves against reformers and denazifiers alike. The university system, which had been one of the major breeding grounds of national socialism, was left virtually untouched – an instructive indication of how powerful the forces of continuity in German society were, despite talk of the 'Hour Zero' in 1945.

The senior civil service

Since the end of the eighteenth century, universities in Germany had been funded by the state for a state purpose – the training of senior civil servants. This category of occupation – which was more broadly defined than in most Anglo-Saxon countries – included secondary school teachers and university professors as well as judges. But most important were the senior administrative officials in the *Länder* and the Reich. Persons in the senior civil service qualified for what was described as the 'well-established rights of German officialdom', which meant that they could not be dismissed or made redundant except for proven malpractice, and that their salaries and pensions, as well as the pensions of their dependent relatives, would be guaranteed by the state. In the Weimar Republic these rights had been written into the Constitution.

In order to qualify for this status most officials needed a university education which, as we have seen, meant in practice that they would come from the wealthier sections of society. Furthermore the administrative officials, who wielded great influence under the Wilhelmine Empire and the Weimar Republic, were expected to be qualified in law – a training which required both university education and a period of unpaid apprenticeship before official appointment.

Critics of the German civil service felt that it was too subservient to the rulers of the state, and did not concern itself enough with its duties to the mass of the population. It was also argued outside Germany that the so-called *Juristenmonopol*, the monopoly of lawyers, had created a narrowly legalistic attitude to administrative problems, quite apart from the way in which it excluded many able people from the highest ranks of the civil service. Promotion from the lower ranks of officialdom was virtually impossible. The nazis had tried to open things up slightly by including trained economists amongst acceptable candidates for senior posts, but this had altered the make-up of the official cadres very little.

In the years 1945–48 there seemed a great opportunity to carry out root-and-branch reform of the German administrative civil service, many of whose members were in any case suspended on suspicion of national socialist sympathies. The Americans wanted to end the lawyers' monopoly, and abolish the distinction between *Beamten* and salaried employees. Recruitment should be more flexible and openly competitive. On the other hand officials should be prevented from presenting themselves for election to parliament, as many had done under the Empire or the Weimar Republic. They should be politically neutral and appointed by independent personnel offices in each *Land.*

These reform schemes foundered on German opposition. The issue did not arouse much public concern, but the vested interests involved had powerful political friends. The Christian Democrats and liberals sympathized with the senior officials and did not want change. The Social Democrats were attracted by the abolition of caste differences between different grades of official, but they, like the other parties, were determined not to accept restrictions on officials' political rights. This was, of course, a double-edged matter: if the officials were allowed to be politically active, the parties could hope to attract them and create for themselves a source of patronage.[24]

German prevarication over this issue eventually caused so much irritation to the Anglo-Saxon occupiers that they demanded a reform be presented to them by 1 October 1948. When this was put off into February 1949 the military governors lost patience and announced that they were imposing an Allied law on the Anglo-American zone (Bizone) with effect from 15 March 1949. This aroused great indignation amongst the German politicians, and although it remained formally in effect, it was never implemented. Once the Federal Republic was established it was clear that the West Germans would regulate the official question themselves, and in 1953 the Bundestag passed a federal civil service law which was mainly based on that promulgated by the nazis in 1937.[25] Meanwhile the Basic Law, the constitution of the Federal Republic, also recognized the well-established rights of officials, so that no change in their status could occur without a two-thirds majority in the federal parliament.

---

24. For a good description of the situation of the German senior civil service between the wars, see Jane Kaplan, *Government without Administration. State and Civil Service in Weimar and Nazi Germany* (Oxford, 1988), especially ch. 1. For the American reform plans, see Eschenburg, *Jahre der Besatzung*, pp. 255–62.

25. Eschenburg, *Jahre der Besatzung*, p. 418. It should be pointed out that the nazi law itself was based on drafts drawn up in the Weimar Republic. These in turn reflected traditional official attitudes which dated back to the late eighteenth century.

The result was not as catastrophic as some Western critics might have feared. The old authoritarianism of officialdom was tempered in the Federal Republic by the much greater power of parliament and the political parties, and by the existence of an inquisitive press. Nevertheless, the cost of officialdom in the Federal Republic was high, and the inflexibility of the system – like that of the universities – was to prove economically damaging in the last decades of the Bonn Republic.

Judges and doctors

There were one or two areas of German officialdom, however, in which the evasion of reform proved more serious. These were the judiciary, which was a branch of the public service with a career structure of its own, and the medical profession, many of the most important of whose members were state functionaries, either as university professors or public health officials. Both these groups had been heavily compromised during the Third Reich, with high levels of NSDAP membership.[26] So far as judges were concerned, many had been suspended after the war, but the need for them was so great that most had to be re-employed, even during the period of military rule. Soon nazi judges were widespread in West Germany. In Lower Saxony, for example, the summer of 1948 saw 51 per cent of judges and state prosecutors holding the same posts they had filled during the Third Reich, and 71 per cent of them had been members of the NSDAP. In May 1949 the Bavarian Justice Ministry employed 5,000 staff, of whom 67 per cent were former nazis. As for the really evil measures carried out by the nazi judiciary during the Second World War, hardly anything was done to bring their perpetrators to book. Not one judge who had served in Hitler's notorious 'People's Court' was condemned for his activities. When the Ulbricht regime in East Germany released information to embarrass western judges, they dismissed it as 'communist propaganda'.[27]

It was therefore a fact of life that for the first two decades of the Federal Republic quite a lot of those involved in administering the

26. On doctors, see M. Kater, *Doctors under Hitler* (North Carolina, 1989); on judges, see L. Gruchmann, *Justiz im Dritten Reich, 1933–1940. Anpassung und Unterwerfung in der Ära Gürtner* (1988), and I. Müller, *Furchtbare Juristen* (1987).

27. R.J. Evans, *Rituals of Retribution. Capital Punishment in Germany, 1600–1987* (Oxford, 1996), pp. 744–58, and Dick de Mildt, *In the Name of the People: Perpetrators of Genocide in the Reflection of their Post-war Prosecution in West Germany. The 'Euthenasia' and 'Aktion Reinhardt' Trial Cases* (The Hague, 1996), p. 322.

law had either enthusiastically supported or at least collaborated with the nazi regime. In day-to-day legal affairs this might not matter much, but it was not conducive to the investigation and punishment of nazi crimes or the provision of compensation for the victims of nazi oppression. When it came to dealing with the perpetrators of peculiarly abhorrent crimes of mass murder, especially those involving professional, middle-class defendants, the courts seemed to excel themselves at finding ingenious excuses for acquittal or lenient sentences. One disturbing area in which this phenomenon was noteworthy related to the mass killing of patients in German mental hospitals in the early years of the Second World War. The so-called T4 programme, in which supposedly incurable patients were selected for deportation to killing centres where they were gassed, aroused public indignation and the gassing was suspended in the summer of 1941, but not before 70,000 patients had been murdered. Thereafter numerous patients – including many children – were quietly poisoned or starved to death in psychiatric institutions.

Whilst Germany was under Allied occupation rule quite a number of those involved in these crimes were arraigned, and the supreme court in the British zone (OGHBZ) insisted that lower courts take the issue seriously. But once the Federal Republic established its own higher Court, the *Bundesgerichtshof*, the situation changed. Various excuses were accepted for complicity in nazi 'euthanasia', even though the victims had for the most part been Germans. Those involved in the action were praised for their professional integrity and honourable lifestyles, and their testimony was believed even when there were obvious inconsistencies in their evidence. The Federal Court accepted the argument that evil acts could not be criminal if the perpetrators had not realized that they were doing wrong, and enlisted the aid of great minds in history – Seneca and Plato, for example – to question the view that 'the extermination of life-unworthy life was to be absolutely and a priori considered immoral and conflicting with a higher legal order'.[28] It was not for a long time that the judicial atmosphere in west Germany changed to one more critical of such viewpoints, and for this reason the medical profession remained almost untouched by the aftermath of the Third Reich. Both in its organization and its personnel, it maintained continuity with an older, more authoritarian Germany.

28. De Mildt, *In the Name of the People*, p. 137. For information concerning the attitudes of the German courts on this issue, see ibid., pp. 316–18 and passim. For details of the nazi euthanasia programme, see M. Burleigh, *Death and Deliverance. 'Euthenasia' in Germany 1900–1945* (Cambridge, 1994), esp. chs. 3–5.

The press and radio

Another institution which was obviously going to be of great importance to any new democratic German state was the press. The fate of
the press and radio in Germany during the Third Reich had been
symptomatic of that country's decline from a civilized society to a
totalitarian state. Before 1933 Germany had possessed a rich press
culture, with thousands of newspapers and magazines representing
the broadest possible spectrum of views. The provincial press had
been particularly strong; Berlin newspapers did not enjoy the same
dominance as London papers in Britain. However, the fact that there
were few papers with large circulations also meant that the economic
position of the press was often fragile. In the Weimar Republic many
apparently 'non-political' papers fell under the control of right-wing
business interests, and their capacity to resist the collapse of parliamentary democracy was thereby limited.[29] Under the Third Reich
opposition newspapers were closed down and their plant taken over
by the nazis. Many 'bourgeois' newspaper publishers were bullied
into selling their firms to the nazi publishing empire, and even those
who remained in business had to obey the dictates of the Reich
Propaganda Minister, Josef Goebbels.

At the end of the war the western Allies closed down all German
press activity and issued official bulletins of their own. For some time
the German press was 'blacked out' until it was realized that the Russians were licensing newspapers in their zone and that these were
conducting pro-Soviet propaganda. By November 1945 the American
zone could boast only eighteen licensed German newspapers; there
were none in the British zone at all. It was not until January 1946
that the British issued their first licence – to a newspaper in Bruns-
wick. By the end of that year, however, 44 newspapers had been
licensed in the British zone.[30]

Licences were distributed carefully in an attempt to create a
balance between different party political viewpoints, although the
parties themselves were not the licensees. By 1947 the licensing of

29. In 1932 only 1.4 per cent of German newspapers had a circulation of over
50,000 copies: Kurt Koszyk, 'The Press in the British Zone of Germany', in Pronay
and Wilson, *Political Re-education*, p. 127. For the decline of the liberal press in the
Weimar period, see Modris Eksteins, *The Limits of Reason: The German Democratic
Press and the Collapse of Weimar Democracy* (Oxford, 1975).

30. These included two weeklies and the semi-official *Die Welt*. In general, the
term 'newspapers' used in this chapter includes weeklies such as *Die Zeit* and news
magazines such as *Der Spiegel*. For details of British policy towards the press, see
Koszyk, 'The Press in the British Zone', pp. 107–38.

newspapers became the task of the *Land* governments under Allied supervision. The Anglo-Saxon occupiers were eager to stress objectivity in reporting and a clear distinction between news and views as desiderata in a democratic press. Perhaps most important was the fact that they allowed a new and intellectually more independent generation of journalists to start up newspapers without being hamstrung by proprietors who were themselves either nationalistic by temperament or under the influence of business interests with little concern for democracy.

The old newspaper publishers were not allowed to re-emerge as proprietors, but in many cases they retained control over their printing presses, and the new licensees, who were often inadequately capitalized, had to pay for their use. In the early days of the new 'licensed press' this did not matter because the main problem was not so much lack of money as shortage of newsprint, which was strictly rationed by the Allied authorities. After the currency reform in June 1948, however, financial difficulties became more serious, because printing costs had risen sharply in real terms.

The old newspaper publishers were mobilizing to re-enter the market once occupation restrictions were lifted, and there were fears – especially in London – that anti-democratic and even pro-nazi papers would start to flood the market once the Federal Republic had been established. In fact this did not happen. Certainly many of the old newspaper publishers re-entered the field. At the end of 1949 there were nearly 150 licensed newspapers and periodicals in the western zones. Within three months these were challenged by 437 newspapers run by the pre-war proprietors, some of them under their old names. Among them was the *Frankfurter Allgemeine Zeitung*, the successor to the distinguished *Frankfurter Zeitung* of the pre-war era. Yet the impact of this change was not as immediately disastrous as the British feared. Although the numbers of the 'new' papers were large, their circulations tended to be small, and they were often restricted to regional or local sales. The papers licensed by the Allied authorities, on the other hand, had already established relatively large circulations – 80 per cent of them sold more than 50,000 copies each. Many of the magazines and newspapers licensed in the occupation period, such as *Die Zeit, Der Spiegel* and the *Süddeutscher Zeitung*, retained their prominent position. So did some of the early group of Allied licensees. One example was Axel Springer, the proprietor of the *Hamburger Abendblatt*, who, in 1953, was to take over *Die Welt*, and whose mass circulation tabloid, *Bild Zeitung*, was to become one of the genuinely national papers of the Federal Republic.

In general, the pressure of occupation policy and the fear of communism combined to produce a West German press of higher quality and greater variety than that in most of the victor countries themselves. For the first decades of the Federal Republic, at least, it was a happy mixture of the best traditions in both pre-1933 German journalism and the well-meaning prescriptions of Anglo-Saxon occupiers, whose own press culture rarely matched up to their expressed ideals.[31]

Radio broadcasting was under direct military control in the occupation period, having been completely centralized by Goebbels in the Third Reich. The western occupiers wanted to establish a German broadcasting system which would be independent of state and party political influence. However, the Anglo-Saxon Allies represented two different philosophies of broadcasting: the Americans were used to private, commercially funded radio, the British to the independent but non-profit-making British Broadcasting Corporation (BBC), which had gained prestige throughout Europe for the quality of its broadcasting during the war. The BBC model was also nearer to the pre-1933 German system which, though more subject to state control than the BBC, had been funded by fees collected through the German Post Office.

To start with, each of the western zones developed its own broadcasting system. In October 1946 the British set up the North West German Radio (NWDR) in Hamburg, which was to function as the radio system for Germans in the British zone. It was headed by Hugh Carleton Greene, who had been director of the German Department of the BBC in the war. He recruited a staff of anti-nazi Germans, some of whom had been identified in POW camps in Britain.[32]

In 1947 Greene negotiated a set of statutes for the NWDR with the various German bodies which claimed that they should have an influence over broadcasting. His aim was to set up an independent governing body modelled on the BBC. This did not prove entirely possible, because the *Land* governments and parliaments (*Landtage*),

---

31. It was commonly claimed, for example, that American and British newspapers carefully separated 'news' from 'views', a notion that would have amused readers of the *Daily Express* and other popular British newpapers in that period. For details on the licensing of newspapers in the British zone, see Koszyk, 'The Press in the British Zone', pp. 118–29. For a detailed description of the development of the German press under occupation, see Kurt Koszyk, *Pressepolitik für Deutsche, 1945–1949; Geschichte der deutschen Presse* Part IV (Berlin, 1986).

32. See the description of broadcasting in the occupation period given by Eschenburg in *Jahre der Besatzung*, p. 138.

which were already becoming too important for the Allies to ignore, wanted to control the radio. However, something of the British system was incorporated into the NWDR; instead of being controlled directly by the states, as the *Länder* would have liked, it was to be run by a board which would include the four *Land* premiers, four educationalists, and representatives of the churches, employers' associations and, later on, the trade unions. The political complexion of the board was to be regulated by the Austro-German principle of *Proporz*, that is to say that it should be balanced roughly according to the political complexion of the area served by the broadcasting station. A somewhat similar system was arrived at by the Americans in their negotiations with the four *Länder* in their zone, since privately funded broadcasting hardly seemed an option in Germany given its straitened economic circumstances. In the US zone each *Land* had its own radio service regulated by *Land* legislation, but the Americans were able to insist on Radio Councils in each *Land* which should represent a broad spectrum of interests and not just those of the state or political parties.

The upshot of these wrangles over radio (TV was not yet a problem, but its organization would be fundamentally the same as that for sound broadcasting) was that there was established an administrative structure which contained elements of both the British and the pre-Hitler German system. As with the British and German systems, it was funded by fees from the public rather than by advertising, and it was non-profit-making. Unlike the previous German and the British systems, it was genuinely decentralized, broadcasting being organized on a regional basis. Legislation about radio was a matter for the *Länder*, not the Federation. On the other hand, the radio stations were protected from government direction by Article 5 of the Basic Law of the Federal Republic which expressly forbade censorship. Where the Germans diverged from the intentions of both the British and the Americans was in the extent to which party politics entered into the appointment to radio boards and even into the selection of senior staff. The result was a predictable amount of political wrangling and tension within the broadcasting bodies, especially the NWDR. Nevertheless, that aspect of the matter may not have been quite so damaging as the Allies and some later historians have perceived it to have been.[33] At least it meant that the political

---

33. Theodor Eschenburg evidently regards it as a weakness in the German system. Cf. idem, *Jahre der Besatzung*, pp. 138–43.

influence was openly admitted, and that appointments would be made according to some sort of proportionally weighted method, which could be defended in public.

In the Federal Republic broadcasting remained a public service, and radio stations were required by their statutes to reflect a broad range of ideological, scientific and artistic perspectives. News broadcasts had to be general, independent and objective. Broadcasting remained decentralized, and the *Länder* successfully defended their influence over it. TV channels were organized in much the same way as radio, with governing bodies drawn from a wide variety of political, social and cultural groups.[34] The general quality of broadcasting was high, and the public was exposed to a variety of views as well as reasonably objective news reporting. It was not until the final years of the West German state that the threat of commercialization began to creep in with the appearance of cable and satellite TV, but when Germany was unified in October 1990 it still possessed one of the most respectable broadcasting services in the world. The fruitful tension between occupiers and German politicians, 1945–55, had played an important part in this development.

If one compares the starting conditions of the Weimar Republic in 1919 and the Federal Republic 30 years later, one can see that, on the face of it, the latter had far greater difficulties to overcome: the division of Germany, the loss of territories in the east, the devastation which had laid waste to so many of Germany's large towns, the burden of refugees from the east, to say nothing of the large numbers of bereaved and mutilated war victims – in all these ways west Germany seemed worse off than its Weimar counterpart. But these appearances were at least partly deceptive. The very depth of misery created by defeat had discredited militarism amongst large sections of the population. There could be no 'stab-in-the-back' explanation

34. The board of the 'Second German Television', for example, which served the whole federation, had 66 members, including representatives of the federal government, the *Länder* governments, the protestant and Roman Catholic Churches, the Central Council of Jews, the trade union federation, the employers' federation, German agriculture, the association of skilled trades, representatives of newspaper publishers and of journalists' organizations, of charities, municipal government associations, sports associations, refugees, youth, and the free professions as well as specialists in education, arts and science, family issues and women's work. See Detlev Karsten, 'Interest Groups and the Media', Document 11, in Carl-Christoph Schweitzer, Detlev Karsten, Robert Spencer, R. Taylor Cole, Donald Kommers and Anthony Nicholls, *Politics and Government in the Federal Republic of Germany 1944–1994: Basic Documents* (2nd revised edition, Providence, R.I., 1995), p. 396.

for the German catastrophe. Whereas in 1918–19, apparently revolutionary disturbances had frightened Germany's property-owning classes and associated democracy with bolshevism, the miseries of the postwar era could be blamed either on Hitler or on the occupying Allied authorities, but hardly on newly established German political parties. As for the fear of bolshevism, that was now attached – with much more justification – to the menace posed by the Red Army in East Germany and the pro-Soviet regime there. Democracy, and in particular that variant supported by the Americans, seemed to be the only real guarantor of German security against communist penetration. The influence of the Allied occupation on the institutions of the Federal Republic had not been as far-reaching as many idealistic reformers – particularly in Washington – had hoped. But it had created the environment and set the agenda in a fashion which prevented that authoritarian, nationalist intellectual atmosphere, which had proved so damaging to the Weimar Republic, from reappearing in West Germany.

It is to the embryonic democratic political system created in postwar Germany that we must now turn.

CHAPTER TWO

The Embryonic Party System

Federalism

If many features of West German society had been shaped during the occupation period, it cannot be emphasized too strongly that Allied decisions relating to the structure of the state were also crucial to its future stability. The federal principle was most important here. Like many successful aspects of postwar Germany, federalism was a combination of native historical experience and imported Anglo-Saxon concepts. In this case the British had little to offer. They did not themselves possess a federal structure, although dominions like Canada and Australia were organized along federal lines. French traditions were even less sympathetic to federalism. But both the British and the French were happy to accept a weakened central German authority, and the Americans were strongly in favour of a decentralized federal system.

For their part, the Germans had a long history of regional loyalties which predated unification. Many Christian Democrats, and some liberals, regretted the form unification had taken, 1866–71, based as it was on the domination of Germany by the authoritarian state of Prussia. One acute observer of the German scene in 1945, the liberal economist Wilhelm Röpke, claimed that the true Germany was western Germany, the land of thriving small industrial towns, self-sufficient farmers and free-thinking intellectuals, and that the subservience of those areas to East German Prussianism had been a tragedy from which Germany had never recovered. Similar ideas were propagated by Christian democratic publicists in the Rhineland.[1]

1. For Röpke's views, see Wilhelm Röpke, *Die deutsche Frage* (Erlenbach-Zurich, 1945), pp. 10 and 224 and for Christian democratic notions of German federalism, see Hans-Peter Schwarz, *Vom Reich zur Bundesrepublik. Deutschland im Widerstreit der*

As mentioned earlier, one Allied war aim had been the abolition of Prussia, and that was achieved by Four-Power decree on 27 February 1947. It remained to determine what sort of structure would replace the old, Prussian-dominated German Reich. In the American zone, the situation rapidly became clear. The south Germans had preserved a number of autonomous states, or *Länder*, the largest of which was Bavaria, a country which had always jealously guarded its particular identity until the Third Reich smothered it. Bavaria emerged from the war as the largest German state which still possessed its historic frontiers, and most political parties there were keen to stress Bavarian autonomy – if not virtual independence. The Americans did not encourage separatism, but they were happy to accept the notion of Bavaria as an administrative unit, and on 28 May 1945 appointed Fritz Schäffer, a Roman Catholic politician and former Bavarian state official, as prime minister.

Other German states, such as Württemberg and Baden, were disrupted by the boundary of the French zone, but by September 1945 they had been reorganized, so that fragments of Hesse and the old Prussian province of Hesse-Nassau were fused into new *Länder* of Württemberg-Baden and Greater Hesse. A fourth American-administered *Land* was created in the northern enclave of Bremen a year and a half later. In the British zone, where Prussia had been predominant, a number of new *Länder* were created, Lower Saxony, Schleswig-Holstein and Hamburg. Most significant of all was the decision to create a large new *Land* which would cover much of the industrial region of the lower Rhine and the Ruhr. This state, which became the most populous in the Federal Republic, was North Rhine-Westphalia, with its capital in Düsseldorf. Its creation was a cause of controversy, the British wanting an effective administrative unit to cover the Ruhr area, especially in view of French and Soviet efforts to detach that region from Germany altogether. German politicians in the region were eager to have a counterweight to Bavaria in the south, but the Social Democratic leader, Kurt Schumacher, disliked the project because he thought the creation of powerful *Länder* might jeopardize the restoration of a unified German state. However, in July 1946 the British decided to establish the new *Land*, and appointed its first prime minister in August.

In the French zone three *Länder* were set up: Württemberg-Hohenzollern, Baden and the Rhineland-Palatinate. The first two were parts of historic *Länder* the rest of which was in the American zone, and the third was made up of a province which had belonged to Bavaria and a section of the middle Rhine as far north as Coblenz. To the south-west of this state lay the Saar valley, a coal-mining region which the French had coveted since the Napoleonic wars. It was administratively separated from the French zone and French propaganda urged them to persuade its inhabitants to accept association with France.[2]

Although each of the western powers initially administered its zone in a different way from the others, and although political leaders in the *Land* governments were at first arbitrarily selected, once the *Länder* were set up they became the focus of German political activity. Their premiers, such as Karl Arnold (CDU) in North Rhine-Westphalia, Hans Ehard (CSU) in Bavaria, Hinrich Wilhelm Kopf (SPD) in Lower Saxony and Reinhold Maier (FDP) in Württemberg-Baden[*] were significant figures in the occupation period, supported as they soon were by elected *Land* parliaments and a German ministerial apparatus. It was very important for the future of the Federal Republic that these states predated the establishment of the federation. Each of them had its own administrative and political capital. With Berlin's authority eclipsed by the menacing presence of the Red Army, the concentration of talent and power in one place which had characterized Germany under previous regimes since unification in 1871 could not take place. When Bonn was finally chosen as federal capital, the danger of arrogant centralization was ruled out for 40 years.

The parties of the left: Communists and Social Democrats

If the Germans were going to be given administrative responsibility through the *Länder* and other Allied-controlled bodies, they would, sooner or later, have to be given the right to set up their own political organizations.

2. For the establishment of *Länder*, see Robert Spencer, 'The Origins of the Federal Republic of Germany, 1944–1949', in Carl-Christoph Schweitzer *et al.* (eds), *Politics and Government in the Federal Republic of Germany, 1944–1994. Basic Documents* (2nd edn, Providence, R.I., 1995), pp. 2–3, and T. Eschenburg, *Jahre der Besatzung 1945–1949*, pp. 77–102 (Vol. 1 of K.D. Bracher, T. Eschenburg, J.C. Fest and E. Jäckel (eds), *Geschichte der Bundesrepublik Deutschland* (Stuttgart, 1983)).

* This was later to become Baden-Württemberg once the Federal Republic was established and the French zone no longer existed.

Whereas the Russians had been quick to license what they described as 'anti-fascist' parties in their zone, the western powers moved rather ponderously when it came to allowing the Germans political rights. It was not until September 1945 that political parties were allowed to organize in the western zones, and even then they were kept under strict supervision and limitations were put on their activities.

Two of these, the Social Democratic Party of Germany (SPD) and the Communist Party of Germany (KPD), had emerged from exile and repression, having played an important, though in the latter case destructive, part in the history of the Weimar Republic. In the final stages of the Third Reich some communists and social democrats had joined other anti-nazi individuals in so-called anti-fascist (antifa) groups to try to resist the nazis and take over the civil administration at a local level. They reflected a view, which had always been present amongst rank-and-file members of the two parties, that working-class unity would be the key to establishing democratic socialism in the country. In fact, however, their numbers and influence were very small. They cannot even be compared in importance to the dissident groups which heralded the collapse of the German Democratic Republic nearly 45 years later.[3]

The attitude of experienced functionaries in both parties – exemplified by the returning exiles, such as the Communist leader Walter Ulbricht or the Social Democrat Erich Ollenhauer – was one of mutual suspicion created by years of bitter rivalry. In addition to historical mistrust dating back to the 1920s, there was the fact that during the war the Communists in exile had accepted Allied plans for dismembering Germany as set out at the Yalta conference, and were even willing to see Germany burdened with some form of collective guilt to justify reparations to the Soviet Union. For Social Democrats, quite apart from their rejection of Stalinist tyranny as a model for Germany's future, there seemed no reason why they should apologize for the Third Reich. They had, after all, been persecuted by the nazis at a time when the British government had been appeasing Hitler. It was up to the Germans themselves to deal with nazi criminals, and this would require a change in the social structure of the country. But the mass of the people had no need to adopt an attitude of penitence.

3. For the anti-fascist movements, see M. Fulbrook, *The Divided Nation. A History of Germany, 1918–1990* (Oxford, 1992), pp. 135–6. For the 1989 GDR revolution, see D. Grosser (ed.), *German Unification: the Unexpected Challenge* (Oxford, 1992), chapters by Hannelore Horn and Uwe Thaysen.

The SPD regarded itself as the natural heir to power in Germany, as the only major democratic party in Weimar which had never bowed the knee to nazi tyranny – in March 1933 its Reichstag members had voted against the Enabling Act which allowed Hitler to establish his dictatorship. In 1945 social democrats looked for a new beginning in which they would create a strong democracy, free from the weaknesses of Weimar. They sought to do this by reducing the power of landowners and capitalists and creating a planned but democratically controlled economy.

The most determined and eloquent expression of these views came from Kurt Schumacher, a former SPD Reichstag member who, having already lost an arm serving in the First World War, then had his health completely undermined by incarceration in Dachau concentration camp. Freed towards the end of the war as a person incapable of further political activity, he used his home base in Hanover to establish a centre of authority over the party in West Germany. This was an important development, because leaders of the party in Berlin were eager to claim that the headquarters of political activity should be in the capital of the Reich, and among them there were some, like Otto Grotewohl, who wished to contemplate a merger with the KPD. Schumacher publically rejected any such idea in May 1945, when he pointed out that the KPD was firmly bound to the Russian state and the furtherance of its foreign policy interests.

Initially these initiatives for a merged working-class party had come from the leaders of the SPD in Berlin as well as from some independent left-wingers, and were an expression of distaste for Western capitalism. They certainly did not imply subservience to the Soviet Union, and perhaps for this reason were rejected by Ulbricht in June 1945.[4] Soon, however, the obvious preponderance of SPD support over that of the KPD inclined Ulbricht and the Soviet authorities towards a merger which would enable the Communists to manipulate an apparently united socialist party. There followed a campaign of intimidation and propaganda aimed at bullying the Social Democrats into accepting union with the Communists. On 21 April 1946 the Socialist Unity Party (SED) was set up. The official leaders were the veteran Wilhelm Pieck, a founder member of the KPD, and Grotewohl himself for the SPD, but the real power lay with Ulbricht, who had access to the Soviet authorities.[5] Soon, loyal Social Democrats were being purged and arrested, and many who had endured nazi concentration camps found themselves in Soviet ones. Those

4. Eschenburg, *Jahre der Besatzung*, p. 125.
5. Ibid., p. 128.

Social Democratic leaders in Berlin, like Gustav Dahrendorf, who had genuinely believed in the possibility of a united working-class movement which would create democratic socialism, were faced with a tragic dilemma. They could either bow to Soviet pressure and see their party turned into a tool of Soviet communism or leave the eastern zone altogether. Dahrendorf and his family were helped to escape to Hamburg by the British authorities. Grotewohl remained a hapless creature of the Soviet occupiers, and duly received the reward for which his vanity craved when he was made prime minister of the German Democratic Republic on its foundation in 1949. But real power lay with Ulbricht and the Soviet authorities.

The foundation of the SED laid the foundations for a communist dictatorship in East Germany. It also, as Schumacher realized, marked an important stage in the division of Germany. Thanks to Schumacher himself and to the SPD members in the western sectors of Berlin who refused to accept SED authority, the party outside areas of Germany under Soviet control remained independent and became firmly anti-communist. This was an early and essential prerequisite for the healthy development of political life in a new West German state.

Political liberalism: the Free Democrats

Of course, the socialists and communists did not have a monopoly of political activity in the postwar era. German liberalism had a long tradition stretching back at least to the abortive revolution of 1848. It was, however, severely damaged by its association with intolerant nationalism. It had also been disunited since the time of Bismarck, when issues such as free trade versus protection, or individual rights and constitutional propriety versus power politics, had caused serious divisions in liberal ranks. During the Weimar period liberalism had been fragmented amongst at least three parties, and by the early 1930s it was in total eclipse, many of its former adherents having deserted to the nazis.

After 1945 liberalism, which had always been strongest amongst Germany's protestant middle class, re-emerged, and although its supporters were not able to create a mass 'people's party', they did manage to avoid the damaging divisions which had plagued them in the Weimar period. The liberals had always been quite strong in the protestant parts of south-west Germany, where they were supported by provincial bourgeoisie and independent farmers. In north Germany the movement was more nationalist in character, and attracted

rather too many ex-nazis. The liberals stressed the need for the protection of private property and individual rights, although at first they
were not at all wedded to free market capitalism, and accepted the
need for planning. In the early stages protestant resistance to Roman
Catholic pretensions – especially in fields such as education – was
an important motivation for the founders of liberal parties. These
had different names in different regions, sometimes calling themselves Liberal-Democrats, but the title accepted in west Germany in
December 1948 was that of the Free Democratic Party. Their leaders
included Reinhold Maier, the prime minister of Württemberg-Baden,
and Theodor Heuss, a respected journalist in Heidelberg who had
formerly been a Democratic (left-liberal) deputy in the Reichstag
during the Weimar Republic. He was to become the first president
of the Federal Republic in 1949.

The parties of the right: the German Party and the Christian Democrats

More overtly nationalist parties could not reappear in the occupation period. One rather odd exception to this was a separatist movement in Hanover which – since the 1860s – had been supporting
the lost cause of Hanoverian independence from Prussia. After the
occupation of their region by the British, its supporters hoped that
the memory of the Hanoverian connection would work in their
favour. When the *Land* of Lower Saxony was established, they seemed
to have gained their objectives and changed their name to German
Party (*Deutsche Partei* or DP). They stood for opposition to any form
of socialism or land reform, demanded an end to denazification and
made a big point of defending the interests of former members of
the *Wehrmacht*. A north German regional party which never extended
its influence very far, it was to play a significant role in the early
history of the Federal Republic. Its most prominent figure, though
not its leader, was Hans-Christoph Seebohm, whose role in the Third
Reich was later to provide propaganda material for the east Germans
in their attacks on Adenauer's government.[6]

More important than the creation of a united, but relatively small,
liberal party, and certainly much more important than the DP, was
the realignment of powerful political forces in Germany under the
banner of Christian Democracy. Neither in the Wilhelmine Empire

6. Ibid., pp. 205–6.

nor in the Weimar Republic had there been a major conservative party which could appeal to the broad range of social and confessional groupings in Germany. The Christian population was divided between the Roman Catholic Centre Party (from which a Bavarian variant, the Bavarian People's Party, split off in November 1918) and a number of protestant conservative or liberal parties appealing to various interest groups and social strata. It was this situation that had enabled the NSDAP to mop up so much support from a fragmented German middle class, and particularly from the protestant areas of provincial Germany.[7]

In 1945 the position of the non-Marxist German intelligentsia was not enviable. Many had collaborated with, or even participated in, the nazi movement. This also applied to many practising Christians. Both the protestant and the Roman Catholic churches had welcomed the Third Reich, and only as time passed had some elements in them – the confessing church in the case of the protestants, and brave individuals, like Bishop Galen of Münster, among the Roman Catholic clergy – essayed opposition to godless national socialism. This had not prevented the churches being persecuted by the nazis. It was obvious that, had Hitler won the war, the Roman Catholic Church, in particular, would have been destroyed. Shared experience of repression had caused some Christians to reconsider confessional rivalries, although there was no suggestion of doctrinal compromise between the two major churches. Among non-Marxists who engaged in various forms of resistance against Hitler, including those who supported the abortive coup of 20 July 1944, there had been priests and pastors, as well as sincere Christian laymen from both confessions, but particularly from the Protestant Church. Therefore at the end of the war Christianity offered the most attractive spiritual home for many people after the fall of the nazi regime. It was not tainted with either nazi or Marxist ideology and it alone seemed to offer a tradition from the past which had not been discredited by the events of the twentieth century.

It was also not without importance that the churches themselves played an important role in providing succour for refugees and homeless people in the immediate postwar years. They tended to be

---

7. It is not the task of this book to describe nazi inroads into the German electorate at the end of the Weimar Republic. The reader is referred to Thomas Childers, *The Nazi Voter: the Social Foundations of Fascism in Germany* (Chapel Hill, NC, and London, 1983), and idem (ed.), *The Formation of the Nazi Constituency* (London, 1986). For the disintegration of the liberal parties, see Larry E. Jones, *German Liberalism and the Disintegration of the Weimar Party System* (Chapel Hill and London, 1991).

used by the Allied and German officials as agencies for the relief of suffering. Claims of a religious revival in this period are difficult to substantiate – the main characteristic of Germans noted at this time was apathy – but in establishing a popular party of the right the Christian connection was very useful, and if the confessional division could be overcome, many regional barriers to a national movement of a socially conservative character would also be removed.

Hence it was very important that, as political activity revived in occupied Germany, the old Centre Party made little headway, and a new political force of Christian Democracy emerged in all four zones of occupation.[8] It is still a little difficult to understand the burgeoning of inter-confessional Christian Democratic groups after the war. The shared experience of repression by and in some cases of resistance to nazi oppression certainly had something to do with it. As the Roman Catholic writer and co-founder of the Christian Democrats in Cologne, Leo Schwering, wrote, the new inter-confessional political movement was a symptom of the fact that representatives of both confessions were coming together with a newly awakened awareness of 'Christian Western thought, Christian culture and Christian morals in German-speaking territories . . . the destruction of which had led to the most painful German catastrophe'.[9] There was also a widespread view, expressed in the programmes of early Christian Democratic groups, that a new start was needed, and not just a return to the Weimar Republic.

Also helpful, however, was the policy of the Allied occupiers, who tended to seek political support from different groups of Germans regarded as anti-nazi. 'Christians' were one such category. When the Allied forces entered Germany they set up advisory committees of Germans at local level on the basis of 25 per cent communists, 25 per cent socialists, 25 per cent Roman Catholics and 25 per cent protestants.[10] In such circumstances the continuation of confessional jealousies seemed inappropriate.

In the summer and autumn of 1945 Christian Democratic parties

8. For a brief but moving description of an intelligent adolescent's development from national socialism to conservative Christianity and then pro-American liberalism in the 1940s and 1950s, see Waldemar Besson, 'Wie ich mich geändert habe', in *Vierteljahrshefte für Zeitgeschichte*, Vol. 19, No. 4 (October 1971), 398–403. For the failure of the Centre Party to re-establish itself as a serious force in west German politics, see N.D. Cary, *The Path to Christian Democracy. German Catholics and the Party System from Windhorst to Adenauer* (Cambridge, Mass., 1996), chs. 10–12.

9. Cited in Winfried Becker, *CDU und CSU 1945–1950: Vorläufer, Grundung und regionale Entwicklung bis zum Entstehen der CDU-Bundespartei* (Mainz, 1987), p. 27.

10. Cf. Eschenburg, *Jahre der Besatzung*, pp. 120–1.

were established in various parts of Germany, most notably Berlin, Frankfurt am Main and Cologne. They presented varying programmes: among principles espoused were the denunciation of militarism and racism, the rejection of both uncontrolled individualism and materialism on the one hand, and of collectivism which damaged human values on the other. So far as social and economic policy was concerned, the state was certainly not just to be a night watchman. It should concern itself with the social welfare and the planning of the economy. Various proposals were put forward for publicly owned industry, and the Berlin Christian Democrats, doubtless with an eye on their Soviet occupiers, proposed the nationalization of natural resources (*Bodenschatz*). The element of Christian Socialism in the movement should not be overlooked, even though it proved ephemeral. It reflected the widespread belief that capitalism had been discredited by the inter-war depression and the participation of big business in the Third Reich.

In Berlin, where Andreas Hermes and Walther Schreiber tried to establish a nation-wide party, and were actually responsible for the adoption throughout most of Germany of the title Christian Democratic Union (CDU), demands for public ownership were combined with commitment to small business and private property, and it was evident that Christian Socialism was seen as a defensive measure against its more menacing Soviet alternative. After Hermes and Schreiber had been deposed by the Soviet authorities, their successor, the former Roman Catholic trade union leader, Jakob Kaiser, stressed the need for a socialist economy and tried to present the concept of a united, independent Christian socialist Germany functioning as a bridge between the capitalist west and the communist east. This was an idealistic vision, for which Kaiser and others struggled manfully, but it had no chance of success. It was not attractive to the western powers, and socialist parties were not enthusiastic about what they saw as clerical rivals. Above all, however, it ran counter to the intentions of the Soviet occupation authorities. They had been willing to encourage the east German CDUD, as it was called, to establish its authority throughout the Reich, but that had proved impossible. Otherwise they simply wanted the CDUD to be as subservient to Ulbricht's Socialist Unity Party as were the other so-called block parties which had been legalized in the Soviet zone in the early summer of 1945. By December 1947 Kaiser's opposition to SED manipulation had become so tiresome to the Soviet authorities that they effectively neutralized his influence. In 1948 he fled to the West.

In fact, the Christian Democrats in the western zones, like their counterparts in the SPD, had never accepted the authority of the Berlin party. It was one of the features of Christian Democracy that it remained relatively loosely organized by comparison with the SPD under Schumacher's leadership. This was not just a matter of chance. The CDU in the west, and even more its Bavarian sister party the Christian Social Union (CSU), tended to favour decentralization as a matter of principle. In one of the earliest CDU programmes it was stressed that the state should be subordinate to the values of society and justice, relating this to the theories of the separation of powers and of federalism.[11]

Christian Democracy was indeed strongly supported in the *Land* which was most sensitive about its right to autonomy, the self-styled 'Free State' of Bavaria. The Christian party in Bavaria kept itself completely separate in its organization from those elsewhere, and adopted the title of Christian Social Union (CSU). It tended to be more conservative politically and socially than the CDU, and stressed the particular interest of Bavaria in a decentralized system of government with the maximum possible rights for the individual states. For much of the occupation period the prime minister of Bavaria was the CSU leader, Hans Ehard, who dedicated himself to the establishment of a German federation in which Bavaria retained the maximum freedom. Nevertheless, the CSU was not a separatist party. Its close links with the CDU prevented the sort of split which had occurred between the Centre Party and the Bavarian People's Party in the Weimar period.

Party leadership: the case of Konrad Adenauer

The most important leader of German Christian Democracy to emerge at this time was Konrad Adenauer. His career illustrates the importance of chance in history, but also the possibilities of achievement for a man of determination, dedication and relentless industry. Adenauer was born in 1876. He was thus two years older than Gustav Stresemann, the distinguished Chancellor and Foreign Minister of the Weimar Republic, who died in October 1929. The

11. For comments on the Rheinhessen CDU programme, see Becker, *CDU und CSU*, pp. 34–5. On 18 December 1945 a CDU meeting at Bad Godesberg resolved that the collapse of the Hitlerite centralism and the defeat of those forces which had kept the nazi regime going had paved the way for a new federal organization of the country. This would protect freedom against excesses of power. Ibid., p. 359.

Weimar Republic was ill-starred in the matter of death: apart from Stresemann's untimely end, the first president of the Republic, the Social Democrat Friedrich Ebert, died in office at the age of 54, whereas his aged and ultimately disastrous successor, Field Marshal von Hindenburg, lasted until he was 86, by which time he had handed over power to Hitler.

For the Federal Republic the fates were kinder, although it must be pointed out that politicians, like sportsmen, make their own luck. Konrad Adenauer, a lawyer and member of the Roman Catholic Centre Party, was appointed mayor of Cologne in October 1917. He retained this position throughout the Weimar period, shrewdly avoiding office in any Republican administration in Berlin. He built up Cologne to be one of the model cities which so impressed British visitors to Germany at that time, with a new university, a new bridge over the Rhine, fine civic buildings and public amenities, and a green belt to give the town a decent environment. His grandiose projects were not at all popular with Reich governments or with the Reichsbank, and there were critical comments on his own remuneration. One rumour had it that his salary was 'somewhere between that of the Reich Chancellor and the Lord God, but nearer the latter's'.[12] Great German cities were accused of damaging the economy by high levels of municipal spending, but the deflationary policies of their critics were to prove even more disastrous, and the collapse of Weimar democracy was the result.

Once Hitler came to power, Adenauer's days as mayor were numbered. He was ejected from office by the nazis, having refused to fly the swastika flag over civic buildings when Hitler came to Cologne for an election rally. He was falsely accused of treasonable dealings with the French in the early 1920s, and his salary and pension rights were cut off. It was not until 1935 that he was able to obtain a pension, and then he lived quietly in a villa in Rhöndorf, overlooking the Rhine not far from Bonn. In the wake of the anti-Hitler plot in July 1944 he was arrested and held in prison by the nazis for two months. In March 1945 he was appointed mayor of Cologne again by the Americans when they liberated the city. After Hitler's death and German surrender, the city became part of the British zone, and Adenauer proved rather too wilful a German administrator for the taste of the British officer in charge of the Northern Rhine province, Brigadier Barraclough, who would also not have been attracted

---

12. Harold James, *The German Slump: Politics and Economics 1924–1936* (Oxford, 1986), p. 21.

by Adenauer's Roman Catholicism. In October Adenauer was peremptorily dismissed by Barraclough for 'incompetence', and forced to leave Cologne, ostensibly because he was reluctant to cut down trees in Cologne's green belt for firewood in line with Barraclough's instructions.

The situation was made worse by the fact that Adenauer's wife, whose health had been undermined by wartime privation and nazi persecution, was hospitalized in the city, and Adenauer would be unable to see her. She never fully recovered and died in 1948. Fortunately, the British officers in charge of the city's military administration, Alan Prior and Colin Lawson, were furious over Barraclough's high-handed action, and discreetly allowed Adenauer to visit the hospital. Potentially even more disastrous for Adenauer's career was a ban on political activity in the British zone. An astute British political officer, Noel Annan, made it his business to get this restriction overridden, and Adenauer was able to resume political life everywhere except in the city of Cologne itself.[13]

Some space has been devoted to Adenauer's background because his personality played a vital part in shaping the Federal Republic, and his legacy remained powerful until after the achievement of German unification in 1990. Before describing his activities as a party leader, one or two other points about him should be noted. He was, of course, a Rhinelander and a Roman Catholic. Under Weimar he had been interested in establishing a new west German state in the Rhineland which would be independent of Prussia, though not – as the nazis falsely alleged – separate from the Reich itself. The aim of a federally organized Germany fitted in very well with his political predilections, especially since it would mean that protestant-dominated Prussia would disappear. Once he had become chancellor, Adenauer's critics, including the outspoken proprietor of the *Spiegel* news magazine, Rudolf Augstein, accused him of having little interest in the reunification of Germany since a western federal state suited him very nicely. He was supposedly a parochial Rhinelander who had no desire to regain the peoples of the Soviet zone because they were predominantly protestant and would therefore be less likely to vote for the CDU.

13. For Adenauer's career up to 1945, see H-P. Schwarz, *Adenauer. Der Aufstieg 1876–1952* (3rd edn, Stuttgart, 1991), pp. 131–478. The circumstances of his dismissal by the British are described on pp. 467 et seq. Adenauer's wife died on 3 March 1948. Schwarz's biography has been translated by Louise Willmot as *Konrad Adenauer. A German Politician and Statesman in a period of War, Revolution and Reconstruction* Vol. 1 *From the German Empire to the Federal Republic, 1876–1952* (Providence, R.I., 1995).

These accusations were unfair, but not entirely devoid of substance. Against them it has been pointed out that Cologne under the Wilhelmine Empire had been enthusiastic to demonstrate its loyalty to the Reich, and Adenauer's father was a Prussian civil servant. Nor was Adenauer himself just a parish pump politician. During the Weimar Republic he was president of the Prussian *Staatsrat*, the upper chamber of the Prussian parliament. This function took him to Berlin at regular intervals, even though he does not seem to have been attracted by what he saw there. In many ways Adenauer was a man of the pre-Weimar era, and his preconceptions were those of an intelligent and civilized – if not particularly sophisticated – young man who grew to maturity at the turn of the century. Nevertheless, there remains something in the critical caricature. Adenauer was not a member of the Wilhelmine 'establishment'. His provincial environment and his confession saw to that. He was aware that, under the Prussian-German system, somebody of his background could not have risen to great heights in society. Nor did he have any emotional commitment to the old Prussian lands lost to the Russians and the Poles. For him the reunification issue did not burn as largely as it did for Schumacher, and he was able to put it towards the rear of his list of political priorities.

Adenauer's dismissal by the British was his chance for a new career, and he sometimes ironically thanked the British for it. In fact, however, the outlook must have seemed very bleak for a man of nearly 70 whose wife was dying. Adenauer was unlikely to regard the British with much affection, especially since Cologne itself had been devastated by the attentions of Air Marshal Harris during the war. Nevertheless, he did have an opportunity to devote himself to party work at a time when other former politicians untainted by national socialism were in demand as administrators, and when the concept of party politics was still widely unpopular.

He threw himself into the establishment of the new Christian Democratic Party, and cleverly turned his apparent handicap – his age – to his advantage. On the one hand, his seniority gave him status in a political situation in which few established political leaders existed, and on the other, his evident superannuation lulled younger rivals into a false sense of security. At first he put his efforts into building up the CDU organization in the British zone and, at one crucial meeting of CDU politicians in Herford in January 1946, he coolly took the chair on grounds of seniority. He did not relinquish it.

Adenauer also turned his attention to the party's programme. He seized on the essential elements in Christian Democracy's appeal and winnowed out the dangerous illusions harboured by some of his new colleagues. The first casualty of this process was Christian Socialism. Adenauer saw that the CDU could not successfully be conservative and revolutionary at the same time. His career as mayor of Cologne had demonstrated that he had no dogmatic hostility to public services, but he instinctively preferred private enterprise to state bureaucracy. He was also shrewd enough to realize that socialism was not popular with the bulk of the German people. He once remarked that for every voter attracted by socialism, two others were scared away. He therefore avoided too clear a commitment to socialist objectives, even though the CDU apparently accepted planning and the nationalization of some major industries in its Ahlen programme of February 1947. Yet Adenauer also avoided the suggestion that the CDU would be a supporter of *laissez-faire* liberalism backed by big business. He was happy to encourage Christian trade unionists and idealistic believers in social welfare to support his party so long as they were ready to accept the principle of private property. The more radical aspects of the Christian Socialist programme were effectively, though not always formally, abandoned.

Adenauer was also eager to overcome the narrowly confessional attitude which had characterized the old Roman Catholic Centre Party. His ideal was an inter-confessional Christian party of a socially conservative character. It was in this sense that he built up the CDU in the British zone.

In 1948 Adenauer was still only a zonal politician, and the German equivalent of *Who's Who* did not list him. His chance to impress his personality on the Christian Democratic movement as a whole came in September 1948, with the establishment by the western occupiers of a Parliamentary Council to draw up what would be in effect a constitution for all three western zones. Again, trading on his age and experience, Adenauer was elected president of this body. Even Social Democrats were happy to have Adenauer – referred to by one of them as an 'awkward old niggler' – kicked upstairs into this post, since it was imagined that it was largely decorative and that the real work of the Council would be done by its main sub-committee, chaired by a Social Democratic minister from the French zone, Carlo Schmid.[14]

This turned out to be a serious mistake. The West Germans were

14. R. Morsey, 'Der politische Aufstieg Konrad Adenauers 1945–1949', in R. Morsey and K. Repgen (eds), *Adenauerstudien* Vol. I (Mainz, 1971), p. 32, cited in Anthony Nicholls, 'Adenauer', in Lord Longford and Sir John Wheeler-Bennett (eds), *The History Makers* (London, 1973), pp. 184–5.

still under the authority of the Allied powers, and any future German constitution would have to be approved by them. The person responsible for communicating with the Allied military governors was the president of the Parliamentary Council – i.e. Adenauer. He therefore gained public recognition as the spokesman of the Germans *vis-à-vis* their occupiers, and his polite but firm negotiating technique won the respect, if not always the approval, of the occupation authorities. Furthermore, his status as president of the Council helped him to impose his authority on the regionally fragmented CDU. Whilst the Social Democrats wrangled over the small print of the Basic Law, Adenauer spent a good deal of time preparing his party for the elections which would be held throughout west Germany once the new constitution was promulgated. It was to prove a shrewd investment of effort.

The political developments in West Germany which led up to the founding of the Federal Republic cannot, however, be understood without giving some scrutiny to the economic situation in the immediate postwar period. Most Germans had little time for party politics after 1945. They were too busy with problems of survival.

CHAPTER THREE

Economic Crisis, 1947–1948

Political squabbles in the Anglo-American Bizone

After Germany's defeat, the need to prevent mass starvation was the prime concern for most of the Allied occupation personnel in the western zones. The Americans were unhappy that the hermetically sealed nature of the four occupation zones was making rational administration impossible, and they feared that they were going to be the paymasters for the ensuing chaos. On 11 July 1946, the US Secretary of State, James Byrnes, suggested to a conference of Allied foreign ministers meeting in Paris that the German occupation zones should be merged into an economic unity, without prejudice to any future political arrangements. In the same month the American military governor offered the possibility of union with the American zone to his Allied colleagues on the Four-Power Control Council. Only the British took up this suggestion.

The burden of provisioning and administering their zone was becoming too great for the British, whose own economy was enfeebled after the war. Their very limited dollar resources were being depleted by the need to buy food to prevent the Germans in their zone from starving.

The creation of a joint Anglo-American zone would also be in line with the British aim of keeping the Americans in western Europe. A more conciliatory attitude towards the west Germans on the part of the Americans was signalled by Byrnes on 6 September 1946 when he delivered a speech in Stuttgart which has since been regarded as an important stage in the development of the Cold War. Negotiations between the British and the Americans became intensive in the same month, and in December 1946 the two governments agreed to the joint administration of their zones. 'Bizone', as it was called, was formally established on 1 January 1947.

Bizone was effectively the core of the west German state as it emerged in 1949. In many ways it was a well-balanced society, with heavy industry and industrial raw materials – especially coal – in the north, many processing industries in the central region and agricultural production well balanced between both areas. It contained just over 60 per cent of the population of all four occupation zones and just under 59 per cent of the agriculturally usable land.[1]

Nevertheless, it took a considerable time for the institutions of the two zones to be happily co-ordinated. The Americans had favoured a federal model from the beginning, whereas the British had operated with centralized administrations, their *Länder* having initially a rather less important role than in the American zone. It was decided to set up combined bizonal administrations for Agriculture and Food, Economics, Finance, Posts and Telegraphs, and Transport. To avoid giving the impression that a west German state was being created, these were not to be concentrated in one place, but would be distributed between the two zones, and each would be established in a different location. The results were not happy so far as efficient bizonal operations were concerned.

This did not mean that there were no political developments within the Bizone. The most important related to economic policy. The Economics Administration was first established at Minden, where the British had their zonal offices to oversee economic affairs. It was initially headed by Rudolf Mueller, a politically independent but liberally minded economics minister from Hesse, in the American zone. However, as the result of the creation of new *Länder* in the British zone and coalition shifts in their south German counterparts, the Social Democrats took over most of the economics ministries in the *Länder* and in January 1947 they ejected Mueller, replacing him with a hard-line socialist, Viktor Agartz. This act, which aroused some disquiet amongst the occupying powers, was believed to have been ordered by Schumacher's SPD headquarters in Hanover. It was evident that the SPD wanted to control economic policy in Bizone and orientate it towards socialist controls and planning. This apparently trivial incident was to have important consequences for the political constellation which appeared in the Federal Republic.

The CDU and FDP were furious and went into *Landtag* (state parliament) elections held in the British zone in April 1947 attacking

1. Cf. Wolfgang Benz, 'Vorform des "Weststaates": die Bizone 1946–1949', in *Geschichte der Bundesrepublik Deutschland* Vol. I: T. Eschenburg, *Jahre der Besatzung 1945–1949* (Stuttgart, 1983), p. 376. This is, of course, a very rough description; there were industrial centres like Nuremberg or Augsburg in Bavaria, but generally speaking there was more industry in central and northern Germany than in the south.

'the establishment of a centrally planned economy like that of the Soviet Union'. It has been seen as the first political confrontation between the CDU and the SPD at bizonal level.[2] It set a pattern which was to repeat itself in 1948 and 1949.

The bizonal administrative arrangements sketched out above soon proved unsatisfactory. It was clear that better co-ordination was needed, and in April 1947 it was agreed to put all the bizonal administrations at one central location. Frankfurt was an obvious choice, both because it was well placed for communication with all other parts of the Bizone, but also because it had been the home of the German *Bund* or confederation in the nineteenth century, and had hosted the brief but historically important attempt made in 1848 to create a German nation on the basis of liberal idealism rather than force of arms.

This latter point was more attractive to the Germans than to their occupiers. When, on 25 June 1947, black, red and gold flags were hoisted over public buildings, the Allied authorities promptly insisted that they be removed. The cause of this demonstration was the first meeting of the Economic Council (*Wirtschaftsrat*), an indirectly elected representative body which, until the election of the first Bundestag in August 1949, would be the nearest approach to a parliament which could speak for the whole of the Anglo-American zone.[3] The *Wirtschaftsrat* was supposed to be dealing only with economic affairs and officially the Allies did not regard it as a political body. But it could enact legislation on matters falling under the competence of the different administrations, and in practice it was dominated by the political parties. The CDU and the CSU set up a linked but not united parliamentary delegation. Between them they had twenty seats, as did Schumacher's SPD. However, the CDU/CSU were sure of the support of the DP, and the four liberals tended to agree with them on economic questions. The SPD had no real allies, although three Communists could be counted on to oppose the market economy.

When the question of electing the various directors of the administrations came up – on 23/24 July 1947 – it became clear that the CDU/CSU were not willing to accept the SPD demands that the Economics Director should be of their party. The upshot of an impassioned debate was that all the administrations were to be directed by non-socialist candidates acceptable to the CDU/CSU and their

2. Ibid., p. 382.
3. See ibid., pp. 388–9.

allies, the SPD having refused to vote for any candidates. This meant that the Social Democrats had accepted that they would form the opposition in the bizonal 'parliament' – a situation from which they doubtless hoped to profit during the hard times that lay ahead. On the other hand, the fact that non-socialists dominated the administrations meant that their policies would be orientated more towards decentralization and market economics than towards centralization and planning.

These early proceedings in the *Wirtschaftsrat* were not received well in public. It was believed that Adenauer and Schumacher were behind the combative attitude of both party groups, although neither party leader was a member of the *Wirtschaftsrat*. Adenauer's victory seemed likely to give the new regime in Frankfurt an excessively right-wing flavour, and the parties were accused of playing politics in an irresponsibly divisive fashion.[4] But, by facing up to the need to choose between two fundamentally different types of economic policy, the party leaders had actually done west Germany a service.

One issue which loomed large in the discussions in the *Wirtschaftsrat* was the problem of surviving the next winter. The winter of 1946/7 had been probably the worst this century, and had exacerbated an already desperate situation so far as food supplies were concerned. This had been one of the major concerns of the Allied occupiers, and had encouraged them to intensify their bizonal co-operation.

A failing economy: West Germany, 1946–47

In many respects the achievements of the Allied occupiers in the years 1945–48 were remarkable – particularly in the British zone, where carpet-bombing of cities had been extensive, where there were large numbers of refugees and where communications were particularly badly damaged. By the end of 1947, despite the serious setback caused by the severe winter, most railway bridges and canals had been repaired, and power stations were in production. The physical infrastructure, though battered and war-torn, had been restored. But precisely at the end of 1947 the situation in the western zones looked particularly grim. Food rations were very meagre, causing riots in parts of Bavaria in January 1948. Production was stagnating, despite a reasonably rapid rate of recovery after the war finished. At the same time, the threat of communism seemed to

4. Ibid., pp. 394–5.

be growing. The Communist Party (KPD) had more voters in the Ruhr area than had been the case in the early 1930s.[5] In the Soviet zone, as we have seen, apparent readiness by the Russians to allow the formation of 'anti-fascist' political parties soon proved to be a manoeuvre behind which communist control could be established. At the same time, the Soviet threat to countries like Finland, Norway, Turkey and Czechoslovakia was evidently growing, and in February 1948 Czechoslovakia actually succumbed to a Soviet-orchestrated communist coup.

It is sometimes suggested that west German recovery was progressing satisfactorily in 1947 and that no special measures were needed to help the recovery either of the German economy, or that of mainland western Europe. This is quite wrong. The situation in western Europe after 1945 was in some ways similar to that after 1918, when an initial postwar boom had been followed by stagnation, inflation and impoverishment for many central European countries. Capital was desperately scarce, and governments were dependent on loans or other aid from the United States. By 1947 these sources of funds were beginning to dry up, and the US Congress was in no mood to keep on making hand-outs of American taxpayers' money to Europeans, especially those like the British, who seemed to be using the money to fund socialist experiments. Had the situation which existed in Germany been allowed to continue, the whole of western Europe would have experienced an economic and political crisis. This was partly because before the war Germany had been an important supplier of manufactured and semi-finished goods to neighbouring countries and a major market for their products. Unless Germany recovered, Europe could not recover.

The main factors inhibiting recovery can be divided into internal and external restraints. The external restraints were those imposed by the occupying powers on German trade and to a lesser degree on her industry. All bizonal trade was strictly controlled by the joint Export/Import Agency, and imports would only be allowed if they were paid for in dollars. This provision was insisted upon by the Anglo-American occupiers to protect their zones against claims from formerly occupied continental countries which had built up large trade surpluses with Germany under the Third Reich and which, not unnaturally, wanted to be able to buy German imports with the otherwise worthless Reichsmark credits they had accrued during the war. The dollar rule meant, however, that the possibility of expanding

5. The KPD claimed 300,000 members in West Germany at this time. Details are given in Patrick Major, *The Death of the KPD: Communism and anti-Communism in West Germany, 1945–56* (forthcoming in 1997, OUP).

Bizone's exports was very limited, and that, in turn, caused western European countries to depend very heavily on American supplies at a time when dollars were difficult to earn.

On the other hand, the domestic situation of the German economy was anything but satisfactory. Here again, a number of myths have to be discarded. The West German economy had not recovered strongly after the war. Production in west Germany was only at about 50 per cent of the pre-war levels at the end of 1947. This was not due to shortages of labour or materials but to the thoroughly inefficient way in which the factors of production were organized in the postwar era. Partly this was inevitable: many of the homeless refugees and expellees had had to be billeted in the countryside because there was no room in bombed-out cities. Numerous younger German males were still in prisoner-of-war camps.

Planning and controls stifle enterprise

Mainly, however, the dislocation and low productivity was caused by a suffocating system of rationing and controls, the so-called *Zwangswirtschaft*, inherited from the Third Reich. Hitler's economic policy had begun with an apparent acceptance of capitalism, working according to the laws of supply and demand. It soon developed into a command economy in which the entrepreneur retained his property – so long as he was 'aryan' – but was forced to produce for the state if he wished to stay in business. Market forces and competition were seen as 'liberalistic' concepts incompatible with national socialism. With the inauguration of Göring's Four-Year Plan in 1936, public spending shot up but prices were strictly controlled. This gave the illusion that Hitler's regime had created full employment, economic growth and stable prices. The fact that the nazis ruled by terror had helped the apparent success of this policy. Hitler claimed that his answer to inflation was an SA man, and shopkeepers who tried to increase prices were liable to be beaten up or taken to a concentration camp. In fact, of course, inflationary pressures were building up relentlessly in the economy. Consumer goods became scarce and of poor quality. A large excess of purchasing power was created, and a condition of suppressed inflation (*zurückgestaute Inflation*) developed. In 1944 the future economics minister in Bonn, Ludwig Erhard, had reckoned the public debt to be about four billion Reichsmarks.[6]

After the war the Allies felt they had little alternative but to carry

---

6. Ludwig Erhard, *Kriegsfinanzierung und Schuldenkonsolidierung. Faksimiledruck der Denkschrift 1943/44* (Frankfurt/Main, 1977), pp. 104b–104c.

on with the nazi system of rationing, price controls and the allocation of raw materials to factories by administrative action. However,
they were not so frightening as the SS and Gestapo had been, and
the Germans were in any case less willing to obey restrictions imposed
upon them by foreigners. It was also important that the standard of
living of most Germans had declined radically from about the end of
1943. For most of the war the Third Reich had plundered occupied
Europe and German living standards had remained reasonably high.
With defeat, things changed drastically. Shortages of food, clothing
and fuel added to the miseries of homelessness. The black market
flourished and money became virtually worthless, even though the
prices of goods still appeared relatively low.

Many workers attended their jobs in order to draw wages which
could pay for such items as fares, school fees and the small amount
of food which could be obtained on ration cards. Otherwise the
cleverer ones absented themselves to engage in barter dealings,
black market transactions, or even such wearisome tasks as scaveng-
ing for coal or the cultivation of tobacco in window boxes. Needless
to say, productivity remained low, and absenteeism was chronic.

As for employers, they had little incentive to increase productivity. The production of goods for sale was not so important as the
husbanding of stocks of material and labour against the day when a
real profit might be made from them. So there was substantial overmanning in most west German factories. Although entrepreneurs
constantly complained about shortages, investigations of factory in-
ventories showed that many of them had stockpiles of material larger
than those they had possessed in 1936.[7] Most debilitating was the
need to engage in complicated barter transactions in order to obtain
spare parts or other production items. Classically trained economists
regarded barter, or *Kompensationsgeschaft*, as more damaging for the
economy than the black market, since at least the latter had some
relation to supply and demand. One German economist wrote in
1948: 'As the result of price-controlled inflation [*preisgestoppte Inflation*], our economy has degenerated from that of a modern industrial nation enjoying the benefits of the division of labour, and has
reverted to the stage of a primitive mediaeval barter system.'[8]

7. See Christoph Buchheim, 'Die Währungsreform 1948 in Deutschland', in
Vierteljahrshefte für Zeitgeschichte, Vol. 36, No. 2 (April 1988), 197.

8. C. Fischer, *Entwurf eines Gesetzes zur Neuordnung des Geldwesens (Homburger Plan)*
(Heidelberg, 1949), p. 61. See also Wendy Carlin, 'Economic Reconstruction of
West Germany, 1945–1955: The Displacement of "Vegetative Control", in Ian Turner
(ed.), *Reconstruction in Post-War Germany. British Occupation Policy and the Western Zones,
1945–1955* (Oxford, 1990), pp. 47–53.

The result was what has been described as the 'vegetative' condition of German industry, in which businesses stagnated and investment remained negative – i.e. plant was wearing out faster than it was being replaced.

Something had to be done to rectify this situation, but it was by no means clear what measures could, or would, be taken. On the one hand, the worthlessness of the currency would have to be overcome; an economy running on barter, cigarettes and other forms of black market payments could not expect to regain its health. Somehow the excess of worthless paper money in circulation had to be severely curtailed. This was a matter which could only be solved by the occupying powers, since they controlled the presses on which notes were printed. So long as the attempt was being made to continue a four-power occupation policy, measures for a fundamental reform of the currency were difficult to contemplate. Plans had been drawn up by American experts for a reformed currency to replace the Reichsmark as early as 1946, a scheme which would involve savagely reducing the money supply by writing off the face value of much of the existing German money, including bank deposits and other personal savings. However, the Americans could never trust the Russians not to increase the money supply in their zone if a new currency were introduced throughout Germany, and the Soviet authorities would not allow any reform over which they did not have equal rights of control with the Americans. So monetary reform would require there to be a clear breach between the western zones – assuming that the French would collaborate with the Anglo-Americans – and the Soviet zone.

This was not just a matter of controlling the money supply. The divergences between the western zones and the Soviet zone were growing steadily larger as the SED tightened its grip on east Germany. It was obvious that a capitalist, market-orientated system was being replaced by a socialist command economy, although the implementation of that policy was to take more than a decade to complete. Clearly a new monetary system would function very differently according to the type of economic policy being implemented in Germany. In the east the choice was clear. In the west things were more complicated.

The period after the Second World War was marked by economic interventionism, not only in Soviet-controlled countries, but in many western ones as well. The memory of the disastrous slump of the early 1930s was still fresh in the public mind. *Laissez-faire* capitalism seemed to have been finally discredited by the experiences of the depression, and the rise of national socialism had been associated with the failings of the capitalist system. Even the Americans were not immune from such views. Roosevelt's USA was, after all, the country of the New Deal, and some of the American experts who came to Germany were enthusiastic 'New Dealers'. So far as the British were concerned, orthodox Conservative economic policy had been tarnished by its association with appeasement, and during the war a national coalition had vigorously organized the economy, paying more attention to the mobilization of labour than to the sensibilities of the previously all-powerful Treasury.[9] Rationing and controls over all aspects of economic life became the order of the day, and in 1945 they were extended by the Labour government into the peacetime economy. Even outside the ranks of the Labour Party, belief in a form of Keynesian demand management designed to stimulate growth and ensure full employment meant that the old orthodoxies of classical free market economics were no longer regarded as valid.

In France, as in other continental countries, the Left had been strengthened by the war, and the Communist Party seemed a force to be reckoned with. But from the Vichy period onwards, interventionist policies in the field of industrial development and social welfare were accepted by Left and Right as the way forward. These factors, combined with a not unnatural desire to retain control over the German economy as long as possible, meant that the policies of the western powers were by no means helpful towards a liberalization of the German economic system. Both the British and the Americans did set their faces against attempts by the Social Democrats to take major industrial enterprises in *Länder* they controlled into public ownership, but they justified their refusal by arguing that such matters would have to be decided upon by a properly constituted German government – a reasonable enough argument considering the fundamental character of the policy decisions involved.

There was therefore very considerable danger that, even if the decision was taken to break with the Soviet Union in Germany and to introduce a new currency – the banknotes for which had already been printed and secretly brought to Germany by the Americans in 'operation Bird Dog' before the end of 1947[10] – the discredited and

9. Ernest Bevin at the Ministry of Labour and John Anderson, Lord President of the Council, were more powerful figures in the War Cabinet in London than the Chancellor of the Exchequer, Sir Kingsley Wood. This situation changed somewhat when Wood died in September 1943 and Anderson took over the Treasury. Cf. J.W. Wheeler-Bennett, *John Anderson, Viscount Waverley* (London, 1962), pp. 291–315.

10. Lucius D. Clay, *Decision in Germany* (New York, 1950), pp. 211–12. Clay claims that at that time he was worried that the Soviet authorities might introduce their own currency in Leipzig.

collapsing control system would remain in place, and the new currency would start to go the way of the old.

The orthodox view amongst Allied officials, German administrators and many German politicians, particularly those of social democratic or Christian democratic persuasion, was that some form of planning allocation of materials for industry, price-fixing, controls over commercial activity and rationing of personal consumption would remain necessary for many years to come. These restraints were thought to be unavoidable at a time of scarcity. It was feared that the liberation of the economy to release market forces would put unbearable burdens on the mass of the population and create civil unrest.

When, in November 1947, Ludwig Erhard, who was at that time heading a German enquiry into the possibility of currency reform, asked one of the leading American experts, Edward A. Tenenbaum, whether it would not be best to restore the free price mechanism as soon as possible, he was told that 'sometime' it might be restored but it was not going to be easy. There was no great pressure from the Americans to jettison controls in the winter of 1947/8. Leading officials in the German economics administration were also happier with controls than with the free price mechanism.[11]

The social market economy

There were, however, still adherents of classical economic theory in Germany who believed that only by restoring the free market could the economy be brought back into efficient operation. These included Walter Eucken, professor of economics at Freiburg, who had devoted his academic life to encouraging competitive markets, Franz Böhm, a severe critic of the cartelization of German industry which had been such a feature of Weimar Germany and had been institutionalized under the nazis in the Third Reich, and Wilhelm Röpke, formerly a professor of economics at Marburg who had been dismissed by the nazis for his fearless expression of liberal views and had gone into exile, first in Turkey and then in Geneva, whence he had launched fierce attacks on all forms of collectivism, be they communist or fascist. It is important to note that these economists, and others of like mind, did not advocate a simple return to nineteenth-century *laissez-faire* capitalism. They accepted that this had led to

11. A.J. Nicholls, *Freedom With Responsibility. The Social Market Economy in Germany, 1918–1963* (Oxford, 1994), p. 206 et seq.

market distortions and social injustice; especially the form of proletarianization connected with mass enterprises and urban deprivation. Two main principles differentiated them from the dogmatic supporters of *laissez-faire* such as Ludwig von Mises or Friedrich von Hayek, even though the latter's anti-collectivist tract *The Road to Serfdom* was well received. The first was an acceptance that the economy had to be firmly regulated by the state to prevent over-mighty economic forces denying competitors access to the market. In particular, cartels and monopolies should be prohibited. The cycle of boom and slump should not simply be tolerated if – as in the early 1930s – it was evident that self-correcting mechanisms would be insufficient to prevent extensive social – and even political – damage. But measures to stimulate economic activity should always be in conformity with market trends (*Marktgerecht*) and they should also be self-liquidating – permanent subsidies should be avoided.

The second modification of *laissez-faire* ideology was a willingness to see public action taken to alleviate poverty where individuals could not be expected to survive in the market through illness or infirmity. There should therefore be a social net to catch the casualties of the capitalist system, which might involve a modest level of redistributive taxation, although the neo-liberals, as the supporters of this position came to be known, preferred contributory systems of insurance to heavy burdens on the exchequer.

Neo-liberalism was a brave attempt to wed the free price mechanism and market competition to a socially responsible policy which would promote the welfare of the under-privileged, protect the environment and avoid the horrors of nineteenth-century industrialization. One of its most active adherents after the war was Alfred Müller-Armack, a professor of economics at Münster who later moved to the University of Cologne. It was he who invented the expression 'social market economy' to describe the programme of the market-orientated 'middle way' between collectivist socialism and *laissez-faire*. Even more important was the fact that neo-liberal views were taken up by an economist in Bavaria, Ludwig Erhard, who had been active in market research before the war, and had already been drawing up plans for the transition to peacetime economy in 1944. Erhard was appointed economics minister in Bavaria by the Americans in 1945, and although he was ousted as the result of party political intrigues the following year, he remained an active supporter of currency reform and market liberation.

In March 1948 Erhard was appointed to be the new director of the economics administration in Bizone, following the dismissal of his CSU predecessor for critical remarks about Allied policy. Erhard was independent of any political party, although his candidature was furthered by the FDP. His election was the result of a deal between the Christian Democrats and the liberals on the Economic Council, and was by no means a foregone conclusion. It was, however, one of the most important personnel decisions of the occupation period. Erhard was able to draw support from the economic experts advising his administration, many of whom were of neo-liberal persuasion, to determine that, once currency reform was achieved, the hated *Zwangswirtschaft* should be dismantled as quickly as possible. Had a different director been elected, this fundamental decision could easily have been fudged or postponed.

The importance of Marshall aid

Of course, Erhard had some advantages not vouchsafed to his predecessors. The Marshall aid programme, announced in the summer of 1947, included west Germany as a potential recipient of funding. Indeed, one view of the Marshall scheme is that it was introduced as a means of helping rehabilitate west Germany without upsetting her former enemies too much, thereby enabling the Americans to shed the heavy financial burden of occupation within measurable time. Undoubtedly the aid programme was welcome to the Anglo-Saxon Allies in Germany, but the genesis of Marshall aid was the result of a complex mixture of economic and political motives. The important point was that, by June 1948, American funding was about to be made available for West Germany, thus providing the external credits which market economists had seen as being necessary if the stifling control system was to be replaced. Food supplies were also becoming a little easier; rations could be increased in the summer of 1948.

With the aid of hindsight, some historians have been tempted to belittle the impact of Marshall aid on the German – and therefore European – postwar recovery. It is suggested that the aid was slow to arrive and was only marginal in its effects. The latter point is, of course, true: Marshall aid accounted for only a small percentage of West Germany's GDP. But in crucial areas such as food and raw material supplies – cotton for the textile industry, for example – Marshall funds paid the bills. Even more important was the confidence created by the American commitment to the West German economy, and the knowledge that the West Germans were being treated on the same footing as other Europeans.

Revisionist historians have recently taken the anti-Marshall case a step further and claimed that the Germans paid much more to the western Allies in reparations, occupation support costs and artificially low prices for coal deliveries than they received in aid. This is a somewhat pointless discussion, because it was hardly to be expected that Germany would be a prime target for western financial assistance after the war, or that West Germany could expect to be guarded by the western powers against a Soviet threat without paying for it. The figures for costs and benefits in this period are also unclear; the price for German coal was not as unrealistic as was claimed, and the Germans tended to ignore the foreign currency spent in west Germany by Allied occupation forces. What was important was the sense of security and hope given to the West Germans by American policy, hope which could be exploited by Erhard.[12]

West Germany's central bank

The Allies had also taken an important preliminary step towards reforming the West German economy in March 1948 with the establishment of a central bank in Frankfurt, the *Bank deutscher Länder* (*BdL*). This was to be renamed the Bundesbank in 1957. The bank was to be independent of the central government and of other political bodies, a characteristic insisted upon by the occupiers.[13]

This central bank was to prove one of the most successful and important institutions of the Federal Republic. Its predecessor, the Reichsbank, had enjoyed a chequered career; it had encouraged inflationary note-printing in the early years of the Weimar Republic and had presided over the first destruction of the German currency. Under the Third Reich its president, Hjalmar Schacht, had invented

12. See Christoph Buchheim, *Die Wiedereingliederung Westdeutschlands in die Weltwirtschaft 1945–1958* (Munich, 1990), p. 94, where he points out that, after September 1947, German coal prices were comparable with British, Swedish and Polish prices. For the overall cost/benefit analysis of the occupation, see ibid., pp. 77–99. For views on the Marshall Plan in general, see John Gimbel, *The Origins of the Marshall Plan* (Stanford, CA, 1976), and Michael J. Hogan, *The Marshall Plan. America, Britain and the Reconstruction of Western Europe, 1947–1952* (Cambridge, 1987). For sceptical views about the seriousness of the crisis in 1947, and about the critical nature of the Marshall Plan, see Alan S. Milward, *The Reconstruction of Western Europe, 1945–1951* (London, 1984), pp. 231–53, and W. Abelshauser,'The Re-entry of West Germany into the International Economy and Early European Integration', in C. Wurm (ed.), *Western Europe and Germany. The Beginnings of European Integration, 1945–1960* (Oxford, 1995), esp. pp. 37–44.

13. Hans Giersch, Karl-Heinz Paqué and Holger Schmieding, *The Fading Miracle. Four Decades of Market Economy in Germany* (Cambridge, 1992), p. 37.

camouflaged methods of credit creation, thus allowing Hitler to indulge in reckless public spending on arms production. The bank established by the Allies was both democratic, in that its directorate was elected by the central banks of the various West German *Länder*, and independent – or at least, more independent of government interference than was the case with most central banks. Its primary duty, imposed by its statutes, was the protection of the value of the German currency. From the summer of 1948 onwards, encouraged by Erhard, the presidents of the bank opposed political attempts to loosen its control over West Germany's money supply. Public and private credit were reined in by interest rate measures and by other forms of restraint, such as increased reserve ratios demanded from private banks. When the West German state came to its end in October 1990, the Bundesbank was perceived by Germans and foreigners alike as one of the most successful institutions of the Federal Republic.

Allied currency reform

On Sunday, 20 June 1948, the Allies carried out the long-awaited currency reform. The old currency was abolished as legal tender and replaced by the new Deutsche Mark (DM). Individuals each received 40 of the new marks at a rate of 1:1 with the old. Two months later they were able to claim 20 more DM in cash. All bank deposits and private cash balances exceeding these allowances were to be scaled down so that only one DM would be received for every ten marks of the old currency. Even then only half of the balances could be exchanged immediately at that rate, and when the rest came to be exchanged in September 1948, fears of inflation led the authorities to cut this amount still further so that effectively bank balances over 600 Reichsmarks were repaid at 10:0.65 instead of 10:1.

Most private debt was devalued by a ratio of 10:1, so creditors did marginally better than bank depositors. Firms were granted an allowance of DM60 per employee, and public authorities had the equivalent of one month's revenue in the new currency. The old Reich debt was wiped out and banks received low-interest 'equalization claims' amounting to about 4 per cent of the Reich debt in May 1945.[14] Hence there had been a drastic reduction of the money supply and a restructuring of private and public debt, largely at the expense of

14. Giersch *et al.*, *Fading Miracle*, p. 37.

those who had little property or other real wealth such as stocks and shares in industry.

The Allies put in place safeguards to prevent the new money going the same way as the old; the *BdL* became the sole provider of legal tender in West Germany, and budget deficits by public bodies were forbidden. This was a major and drastic step – the second time in the twentieth century that the Germans had seen their worthless money replaced by new currency. It has been suggested that only under a foreign occupation could such a controversial and – in many quarters – unpopular step have been taken. Certainly in July 1990 the federal government bullied a reluctant Bundesbank into announcing a very much more generous level of exchange for largely worthless East German marks when monetary unification was achieved. The result was to appease consumers initially but to hasten the ruin of East German enterprises. The political circumstances were, however, quite different from those in 1948, and a more relevant year for comparison might be 1924, when a German government carried through an equally drastic currency reform by itself – though once again, under pressure from powerful former enemies.

Erhard's liberalization

However, it is not clear how far these measures would have proved lastingly effective without the complementary action taken by Erhard as Economics Director of the Bizone. On the Sunday of the currency reform, Erhard announced to the German people over the radio that controls on most industrial products and some foodstuffs were abolished, thus allowing the prices to be fixed by market forces. The following day there occurred the famous 'shop-window miracle' when consumers in the Bizone found themselves faced with consumer goods which had long since been virtually unobtainable. Prices were undoubtedly high, but the controlled prices had often been rendered meaningless by scarcity. It had been estimated in 1946, for example, that a woman in the Rhineland could expect to wait 350 years for a winter coat and 29 years for a pair of stockings. The real comparison was with black market prices under the old system, and these rapidly began to come down.

This had an electrifying effect on productivity. Absenteeism dropped sharply and production shot up as workers had an incentive to earn money and firms to deliver goods to the market (see Figure 1). Even more important in the long run was the rise in industrial investment. During the period 1945–48 such investment had been negative, that is to say industrial plant was deteriorating faster than

FIGURE 1 *Productivity, wages and prices after the currency reform of June 1948 (% change)*

	30.6.1948– 31.12.1948	31.12.1948– 31.12.1949	31.12.1949– 30.6.1950
Labour productivity[a]	17.7	26.0	8.8
Nominal wages[b]	15.0	8.4	2.1
Consumer prices[c]	14.3	−6.3	−5.7
Producer prices[d]	3.5	−5.7	−2.0
Real wages[e]	0.6	15.6	8.3

[a] Index of output per man-hour in industry (1936 = 100).
[b] Index of gross hourly earnings per worker in industry.
[c] Consumer price index for representative household (four persons; 1950 = 100).
[d] Index of producer prices in industry (1950 = 100); only available from 31.7.1948 on; figure in table is estimated, based on backward extrapolation to 30.6.1948.
[e] Nominal wage index as defined in note b divided by consumer price index as defined in note c.

Source: H. Giersch, K.-H. Paqué and H. Schmieding, *The Fading Miracle: Four Decades of Market Economy in Germany* (Cambridge, 1992), p. 51.

it was being replaced. Capital stock had fallen by 7.3 per cent since the end of the war. After currency reform this picture was transformed. Capital stock grew at an annual rate of 5.6 per cent in the second six months of 1948, and industrial output grew at a rate of 137 per cent.[15]

Lest it be thought that this was simply the result of Marshall aid and the currency reform, it should be pointed out that Erhard's writ did not run in the French zone of occupation, where the new currency had also been introduced. General Koenig, the French military governor, refused to relax controls, and so his zone represented what Wilhelm Röpke described as a laboratory experiment of currency reform without liberalization. The results were not happy. Production did not increase nearly as fast as in Bizone, and the pressure exerted by its example forced the French authorities to relax controls themselves or face the effective disintegration of their system.[16]

Despite the enthusiasm over the appearance of consumer goods which had previously been virtually unobtainable, the liberalization had its darker side, and its critics were vociferous. For poorer, larger

15. Ibid., pp. 39–40. For textile supplies under the controlled system, see A. Drexler, *Planwirtschaft in Westdeutschland 1945–1948. Eine Fallstudie über die Textilbewirtschaftung in der britischen und Bizone* (Wiesbaden, 1985), p. 113.
16. Nicholls, *Freedom with Responsibility*, p. 218.

families the increased prices for such items as bus and train fares, school fees and rationed food – prices which were still controlled but which were now reckoned in DM at a rate of 1:1 to the old currency – were a very serious burden. Furthermore, market pressures began to bear down on the workplace. Increased productivity was a matter of necessity as much as choice, and firms began to shed labour as overmanning suddenly became intolerable for their balance sheets. Public authorities also were forced to make severe cuts in spending.

The SPD and the trade unions angrily denounced Erhard's policies as pandering to the rich and leaving those without a 'life-jacket' of property or real wealth to sink in the cold waters of the unprotected market economy. Erhard was also accused of allowing the economy to run in precisely the wrong direction, because his market liberation encouraged consumer goods production, whilst he did nothing to implement costly schemes drawn up by the Allied authorities for state investment in heavy industry or the transport infrastructure.[17]

In fact, however, Erhard's policies were not quite so radical as they appeared at first sight. By comparison with developed economies in the 1990s, West Germany was still very severely controlled in 1948. Erhard's economic advisers had prescribed the retention of rationing for basic foodstuffs, as well as controlled prices for rent and fuel. Although West Germany became far freer of controls than a country like Britain, whose government was insisting with puritanical zeal on a campaign of austerity, enough control was retained to prevent mass starvation, and rations were actually increased in the summer of 1948, so that for the first time in three years workers had enough to eat. Partly for this reason, but mainly because the dynamic upturn in the economy was too emphatic to be overlooked, trade union protests, and a one-day general strike in November 1948, proved a failure. The consumer-led boom roared on, but inflation was held down by restrictive monetary policies deployed by the *BdL*, and by the fact that there was a great deal of slack in the economy which had been disguised by the inefficiencies of the *Zwangswirtschaft*.

Inherent strengths of the German economy

One point which should be stressed about the West German economy in the postwar period is that, despite the appalling devastation created

17. Ibid., p. 220 and pp. 231–3.

by bombing, devastation exacerbated by Allied policies of dismantling which went on until 1949, the fundamental resources available to German industry were still very impressive. Under the Third Reich there had been huge investment in machine-tool plants and other industrial enterprises supporting military expansion, by no means all of which were directly connected with armaments. During the war this expansion had continued until 1943, and although the Allied bombing campaign had been effective in slowing down production, it had destroyed more houses and communications than machine tools. Therefore German industry had a potential for expansion once the burdens of a wartime command economy and the postwar *Zwangswirtschaft* had been removed. The most obvious example of this was the case of the Volkswagen plant, a nazi public enterprise in Wolfsburg in Lower Saxony which was supposed to produce the much-heralded 'people's car', but which before 1945 had in fact served only the NSDAP and the *Wehrmacht*. In the free market environment of Erhard's regime it became a major export earner for west Germany, the symbol of the 'economic miracle' in the 1950s.

Nor were machine tools West Germany's only advantage. If one compares the situation in Eastern Europe in the early 1990s – including the former GDR – with that of Bizone in 1948, it becomes apparent that Erhard could rely on a powerful infrastructure for a market economy. Banks, insurance companies, wholesalers and retailers had all survived the Third Reich, even if they had operated under a blanket of government-directed cartelization. In the case of Soviet-dominated economies 40 years later this was not true.

Lastly, there is the point that labour in West Germany was unusually flexible and willing to accept sacrifices. The hardships of the postwar period had meant that the prospect of work for wages which could buy something overshadowed the resentment at poor living standards and obvious inequalities of wealth which became very glaring in the early years of Erhard's 'miracle'. Even then, people were less likely to dislike opulent businessmen in an open market than they were to detest black marketeers who exploited the failings of the old control system.

Women and reconstruction

The loosening of controls made life much easier in particular for women, who in many ways had been the heroines of the immediate postwar reconstruction period. It was they who had had to cope with shortages, inadequate rations, and the destruction of their homes, whilst at the same time clearing rubble in devastated cities and often acting as bread-winners for families whose fathers were dead, missing, mutilated or in prisoner-of-war camps. For them, the new consumer freedom was a blessed relief, and it is no coincidence that the housewife's basket featured in CDU propaganda in early Bundestag elections.

Erhard and the CDU

Erhard's success predated the Federal Republic, but it had a great impact on its political character. As has been mentioned, the Social Democrats angrily rejected the 'social market economy'. They claimed it was a sham, and that the word 'social' was just a cosmetic device behind which discredited – and even pro-nazi – capitalist forces were restoring their position. They demanded responsible planning and a juster method of distribution. This proved to be a serious tactical mistake, for it saddled the SPD, however unfairly, with the burden of the discredited control system. Indeed, it was difficult to see what halfway house could be found between Erhard's free market and the old *Zwangswirtschaft*. Schemes for markets divided between a controlled and an uncontrolled sector promoted by social democratic economists seemed unconvincing and would almost certainly have proved unworkable. Either there was a free market mechanism or there was not. As one supporter of Erhard's course remarked, a wildlife park was no substitute for the real jungle. By making Erhard a central target for attack, the SPD alienated those who felt liberated by the new economic developments.

Adenauer moved fast to capitalize on this situation. Although Erhard had not been a CDU nominee and had no contacts with the party, he depended on Christian Democratic support for his measures in the Economic Council. Adenauer invited him to address CDU party gatherings and in February 1948 he convinced a meeting of CDU functionaries in the British zone that Erhard's social market economy should replace the existing, rather vague, Christian Democratic economic policy, and that it should be a major plank in the forthcoming elections for a West German parliament. This duly occurred when the CDU issued the 'Düsseldorf principles' in July 1949. They stressed the superiority of the free market over collectivism, whilst rejecting *laissez-faire* and stressing a Christian commitment to social welfare.

By this time measures had been taken to establish a West German state closely bound up with the western powers which were creating a united front against Soviet communism. The summer of 1948 had witnessed events which created a new and unwonted feeling of solidarity between the Germans and their former enemies.

The Berlin blockade, 1948–49

Partly as the result of the western currency reform, the Soviet authorities began to exert serious pressure on Berlin. The German capital, which lay 150 kilometres behind the frontier of the Soviet zone, was supposedly under quadripartite administration, although each occupying power had effective control of its own sector of the city. The German administration of Berlin was, however, a unified *Magistrat* which was elected by all the city's adult inhabitants. Since 1946, the largest party in this body had been the SPD, with the CDU also coming ahead of the communist-dominated SED. The Russians were unhappy about this, and did their best to obstruct Social Democratic leadership of the German administration; in particular they refused to recognize the mayor (*Oberbürgermeister*) elected in 1947, Ernst Reuter, and his place had to be taken by an acting mayor, the Social Democrat Louise Schröder. The political parties in the western sectors of Berlin began distancing themselves from the Soviet-dominated parties in the east of the city and in the Soviet zone itself. In this they were discreetly assisted by the western occupiers. By March 1948 it had become clear that the western powers were going to create a German state of some sort out of their zones, and in March the Soviet Marshal Sokolovski walked out of the Allied Control Council. It never met again. In some ways this could be regarded as the date on which Germany was divided.

In the months which followed, land traffic to Berlin from the west was subject to delays imposed by the Soviet authorities. The critical situation of Berlin came to a head in June 1948 as a result of the currency reform. At first the western powers had hesitated to introduce the new DM into their sectors of Berlin, but when the Russians responded by carrying out a currency reform of their own and insisting that the new East German marks should be used throughout the city, West Berlin political leaders, and especially Reuter himself, refused to accept such a move. When the Russians rejected requests from the western commanders that the quantity of east marks in Berlin should be under their control, the western powers introduced the new western DM into the western sectors of Berlin. Soviet displeasure soon manifested itself. By 4 August 1948 land traffic from the west was completely blocked.

The western powers – with Ernest Bevin, the British Foreign Secretary, showing particular determination – resisted Soviet pressure, but did not risk a war by an armoured thrust into East Germany. Instead they took the unexpected course of supplying West Berlin by air, a colossal undertaking given that there were 920,000 west Berliners and that aircraft payloads were still relatively small. But by flying round the clock from eight airfields in West Germany, the western Allies were able to lift enough food and other vital materials into Berlin to keep the city going. However, the victory over the blockade would not have been possible without the fortitude of the Berliners. Their resolution attracted a great deal of publicity in the west, and this helped to create a much better atmosphere between the victors and the vanquished. By February 1949 8,000 tons of supplies were being flown into West Berlin daily – nearly twice the amount regarded as a minimum for survival. On 12 May 1949 the blockade was lifted.[18]

The tension and excitement of the Berlin airlift provided the backdrop for the transformation of the western occupation zones into a West German state, even if this would not mean the restoration of German sovereignty, something to which the French, in particular, were very much opposed. The nature of the constitutional arrangements with which the Federal Republic began its life in September 1949 will be discussed in the next chapter. But by the autumn of 1948 it was clear that a West German parliament would be in place before too long, and that West German elections could be expected.

The first Bundestag elections, 14 August 1949

In those elections the importance of domestic issues – and in particular the state of the economy – was self-evident. As described above, when Erhard's social market economy survived its early difficulties and showed itself to be working, its political value did not escape the attention of Konrad Adenauer.

Adenauer's own views on the economy were not entirely clear. He regarded Erhard as a useful ally against the Social Democrats, but in other respects judged him to be an 'idealist' – which was a definite

18. Eschenburg, *Jahre der Besatzung*, pp. 447–58.

insult in his vocabulary. Adenauer sympathized with consumer freedom, respect for the rights of property and encouragement for small businesses, but he was by no means wedded to free competition if this would upset the interests of big business, upon whose support the CDU, like other non-socialist parties, depended for their funding. Nevertheless, for the time being, Erhard and Adenauer were on the same track. Erhard was, indeed, a very important electoral asset to the CDU, and the Free Democrats, who had been responsible for his election as Economics Director, were bitterly disappointed when he agreed to fight the election on the CDU list in Baden-Württemberg. His role in the economy had made Erhard better known in the western zones than any other politician except Schumacher – not excluding Adenauer himself.[19]

The Social Democrats, however, did not only lose electoral ground because of their economic policy. Schumacher had played a nationalist card in his negotiations with the Allies, and although West Germans were patriotic, many of them had an uneasy feeling that without Western protection they might find themselves exposed to Soviet domination. Above all, the CDU seemed likely to enjoy American approval; Adenauer was indeed more attractive to Washington than his prickly socialist opponent. Lastly, Schumacher made no secret of his anti-clerical inclinations, and in particular his hostility to the Roman Catholic Church. A reference to the papacy as the 'fourth occupying power' was unlikely to limit the partisanship of Roman Catholic clergy for the CDU/CSU.

Thus it was that in the first Bundestag election on 14 August 1949, the SPD, which had claimed the right to govern Germany in the postwar era, emerged with less votes and seats than the combined totals of the CDU/CSU constellation. Even so, it had been a close-run thing: the SPD had 131 seats and 29.2 per cent of the vote; the Christians had 139 seats and 31 per cent of the vote. Even though the smaller parties were mainly on the right of the political spectrum, it would have been difficult to exclude the SPD from power if it had emerged as the largest party.

As it was, Adenauer firmly opted for a 'small' coalition of CDU/CSU, Free Democrats and DP – the same coalition that had been supporting Erhard's social market economy in the Economic Council. He resisted calls from *Land* premiers, including the CDU prime minister of North Rhine-Westphalia, Karl Arnold, for a great coalition with the Social Democrats along the lines of the Republican coalition which had launched the Weimar Republic. Such a solution seemed sensible to administrators, but was rightly rejected by the party politicians. Had there been a fudged coalition with the SPD, Erhard could not have continued as economics minister and the electors would have seen the policy they voted for jobbed away by politicians.

For his part, Schumacher believed that Erhard's economic policy would soon lead to such mass emiseration that the electorate would see the error of its ways. He could also hope to gain from disillusionment over the division of Germany, and a spell in opposition seemed to have advantages for the SPD. It seems reasonable to speculate that the lessons of Weimar were in the minds of many politicians at this point; Schumacher doubtless remembered the odium incurred by the SPD in having to take hard decisions during the formative years of the Weimar system. As it was, the Federal Republic was established on the basis of a Christian–liberal alliance. Theodor Heuss of the FDP was backed by the CDU/CSU for the post of federal president. He in turn nominated Adenauer as the first federal chancellor and on 17 September 1949 this was put to the vote in the Bundestag. Adenauer won on the first ballot by one vote – which was, as he was later fond of asserting, his own. In fact the matter was not really in very much doubt, since his chances would have improved in subsequent ballots had they been necessary. The vote did, however, underline the apparently fragile nature of the new government. A septuagenarian heading a motley coalition with a narrow majority did not seem too likely to make a lasting impression on German politics. In fact, he was to dominate them for the next fourteen years.

CHAPTER FOUR

The Bonn Republic is Founded

Bonn and Weimar

When Adenauer took up office as federal chancellor in September 1949 he had a number of advantages over his predecessors in the Weimar Republic. On the face of it, this was rather surprising, since West Germany represented only a truncated German state which had been born of total defeat. Its cities still bore the scars of extensive bombardment during the war, even if many of the ruined houses had been cleared away and their rubble deposited in urban slag heaps, or *Trummerhaufen*, which loomed on the periphery of many urban centres. Nine and a half million Germans from eastern areas had sought refuge in west Germany, one and a half million of them having moved from the Soviet zone since 1945.[1] To feed these millions, West Germany had proportionately far less agricultural land than was available to the German Reich in the inter-war period.

In terms of status, also, the situation was apparently disastrous. When the Constituent National Assembly which founded the first German republic met in Weimar in February 1919, only a part of Germany – the Rhineland – was occupied by the troops of the Entente powers. In September 1949 the Bundestag convened in a country which was still entirely occupied by the former victors, whose military governors, or High Commissioners as they were now described, still possessed the rights of control and could exercise their veto powers over the actions of the West German government. Although in 1919 Germany had lost provinces in both east and west, it was still fundamentally a united country. In 1949 it was divided

1. Wolfgang Benz, 'Vorform des "Weststaats": die Bizone 1946–1949', in *Geschichte der Bundesrepublik Deutschland* Vol. I: T. Eschenburg, *Jahre der Besatzung 1945–1949* (Stuttgart, 1983), p. 385.

in a fashion which many feared would be permanent, especially since the Soviet authorities had responded to the creation of a west German state by establishing the German Democratic Republic (GDR), under the subservient rule of Ulbricht's Socialist Unity Party. The Red Army, with its enormous superiority in conventional forces over those of the West, loomed menacingly on the line of the Elbe, and the threat of Stalinist communism seemed all too real to those living under its shadow.

Yet Adenauer was still more fortunate than his former colleagues in the Weimar Republic. The obvious point has to be stressed that most of the harsh decisions necessary for German recovery had already been taken under Allied occupation by the time the Federal Republic was founded. Nobody could blame its leaders for the defeat in 1945. Hitler's obstinacy, the Allied policy of Unconditional Surrender and the failure of the bomb plot in July 1944 had ruled out a 'stab-in-the-back' myth. There were no 'November traitors' to act as scapegoats for nationalist displeasure. The difficult problem of negotiating peace did not arise in the case of the Bonn Republic either. There was no peace. All the time the Cold War between East and West was intensifying there could be no compromise over Germany and no final settlement.

Economically, the tribulations associated with a turn-over from war to peace had been experienced under the direct rule of the Allied powers. The British, in particular, were very unpopular by the end of the 1940s as the result of the austerity in their overcrowded and underfed zone. Whereas the first democratic German governments had been forced to struggle with food and coal shortages, demobilization, and runaway inflation culminating in the destruction of the currency in 1923, the Bonn Republic had these traumas behind it. As we have already seen, the Allies had taken the drastic measures necessary to reform the currency, and Ludwig Erhard had followed these up with the restoration of the free price mechanism and the free market. The economic recovery which was to be such a remarkable feature of West German life in the 1950s was already under way when the Federal Republic started. Food rationing was eliminated by the end of 1949, a fact noted with envy by Germany's British occupiers, who were not able to destroy their ration books until 1954.

Bonn's constitution: the Basic Law

A further problem which Adenauer did not have to solve was that of Germany's constitution. As was mentioned above, the political and legal structure of the Federal Republic had been worked out by a special body, the Parliamentary Council (*Parlamentarischer Rat*), of which Adenauer had been elected president.[2] This convened in Bonn from 1 September 1948 until the end of April 1949. Bonn was chosen largely because it was felt that such a meeting ought to be held in the British zone, since other bodies such as the Economics Council had been established in the American zone. Bonn was also convenient from the point of view of rail communications and had been relatively undamaged in the war. There was no intention to make it into the capital of West Germany, an honour which most people supposed would go to Frankfurt.[3]

The arrangements worked out by the Parliamentary Council were not to be described as a constitution; a demand by the Allied powers in July 1948 that the West Germans should take it upon themselves to create such a constitution, and that this should be ratified by a referendum, was unacceptable on the grounds that it would apparently rule out a reunification of Germany, and would give a propaganda weapon to Ulbricht's SED. The discussion of this matter once again illustrated the importance of Germany's great cities and their mayors. It was the acting mayor of Berlin, Louise Schröder, who urged her West German colleagues not to create any permanent constitutional arrangements until Berlin had been organically integrated into the west. It was the mayor of Hamburg, Max Brauer, who invented the term 'Basic Law' to describe the provisional statute which should regulate a West German state until the German people as a whole could decide on their future.[4]

The basis of the new West German state was an occupation statute, which secured the rights of the western Allies in the country and gave them power to intervene in German politics or even to veto legislation if they felt it threatened their interests, and the new Basic Law, which set out the rights and duties of west German citizens, established a federal legislature, and delimited the competence of the West German *Länder* and the new federal institutions.

When it met in September 1948, the Parliamentary Council had before it an extensive discussion document about the new constitution and a draft of the Basic Law. This had been drawn up by representatives of the eleven *Länder* governments at a meeting in August on the picturesque island palace of Herrenchiemsee in Bavaria. The

2. See above, Chapter 2, pp. 48–9.
3. See below, pp. 78–80.
4. Theodor Eschenburg und Wolfgang Benz, 'Der Weg zum Grundgesetz', in Eschenburg, *Jahre der Besatzung*, p. 464.

Bavarian government had thus been able to exercise considerable
influence over the proposals, which stressed the need for a federal
rather than a unitary state.

The Parliamentary Council itself, however, represented the political parties rather than the *Land* administrations. Its 65 members
were selected by the parties from their delegations in the various
Land parliaments in proportion to the results they had achieved in
the most recent elections and according to the size of the population
in their *Land*. This meant that the CDU/CSU and SPD each had
27 seats, the liberals came next with five seats and the Communists,
the DP and the Centre Party received two seats each.

Both Adenauer and Schumacher made it clear they did not wish
to be bound by the Herrenchiemsee drafts, but the CDU was generally far less opposed to their general tenor than the Social Democrats.
The SPD had always believed in strong national government, regarding local particularism as reactionary. The Christian Democrats were
more suspicious of central power, and in this their inclinations
chimed in with those of the Allies, who had their own reasons for
avoiding a strong German executive. Last but not least, the Bavarians
led by their eloquent and determined prime minister Ehard, wanted
as little federal power over their country as possible. They took the
lead in trying to influence the Parliamentary Council's decisions in
a manner favourable to the *Länder*. They were helped by the fact
that the Bavarian Christian party, the CSU, although allied with
Adenauer's CDU, retained its autonomy and was even willing to
negotiate separately with the SPD in order to obtain its objectives.[5]

The nature of west Germany's federal structure

The core of the problem facing the legislators was the federal character of the future West German state. The north Germans tended to
want to accept an American-style Senate, in which the *Länder* would
be represented by directly elected members, as in Washington. This
would have meant that the *Land* governments themselves would have
no say over federal legislation, and would face a federal legislature
with a powerful mandate in both its houses. The American system
gave the individual states more independence *vis-à-vis* the Federation

5. For Bavarian policy at this time, see K.-U. Gelberg, *Hans Ehard. Die föderalistische
Politik des bayerischen Ministerpräsidenten, 1946–1954* (Düsseldorf, 1992), Ch. VIII, esp.
pp. 199–201.

by ensuring a complete separation of financial resources and administrative functions between Washington and the state capitals. For the centralizers in the SPD, that would be unwelcome, especially because they hoped to carry through socialization measures throughout west Germany when elected.[6]

The SPD and the CSU therefore agreed to a second chamber which would be weaker than the US Senate in its constitutional functions but which would represent the governments of the *Länder* rather than their populations. In this respect, the west Germans were harking back to their own traditions of federalism, which had been designed to protect the particular interests of the various German states when the country was united between 1866 and 1871. The title of the second chamber, the Bundesrat, was to be the same as that used in Bismarck's time, although its function was to be somewhat different.

The west German parliament therefore consisted of the Bundestag, elected on a democratic basis by all west German adults, and the Bundesrat, a body of 41 members chosen by the *Land* governments and varying in numbers from three to five according to the size of the *Land* concerned. The fact that the members were simply to be agents of their governments was highlighted by a rule that each *Land* delegation could only vote as a bloc. The Bundesrat could conclusively veto Bundestag legislation which affected the vital rights of the *Länder* – for example, by altering the federal constitution, creating new federal agencies or affecting taxes which went to the *Länder* or to municipalities. It could veto other legislation, but its objections could then be overruled by the Bundestag if a majority so wished.[7]

The institution of the Bundesrat meant that federal governments in Bonn would need to placate their counterparts in the *Länder* if legislation was to pass smoothly. Clearly life would be difficult for a federal coalition which differed from the political constellation in a majority of the *Länder*. The influence the *Land* governments could exercise over the federal system also tended to increase the importance of *Land* politicians within the system. One of the features of the Bonn Republic was to be the function of *Land* parliaments and administrations as springboards to power in federal politics. After

6. Cf. Eschenburg, *Jahre der Besatzung*, pp. 494–6.
7. See R. Taylor Cole, 'Federalism: Bund and Länder', in Carl-Christoph Schweitzer *et al.* (eds), *Politics and Government in the Federal Republic of Germany, 1944–1994. Basic Documents* (2nd edn, Providence, R.I., 1995), pp. 324–70, and Eschenburg, *Jahre der Besatzung*, pp. 495–6.

Adenauer only one Chancellor – Ludwig Erhard – did not play an important role in *Land* politics before taking up ministerial office in Bonn.

The extent to which the *Länder* were able to retain their influence over the new Republic was certainly affected by the fact that they pre-existed it, and their success owed much to the determined lobbying of individual *Land* governments, particularly that of Bavaria. Ironically, the politicians in Munich were unhappy with the concessions they had obtained in Bonn, and Bavaria was the one German *Land* to refuse to ratify the Basic Law. Nevertheless, the Bavarian *Landtag* agreed to accept a majority decision if the other *Länder* voted for the Law, which effectively meant that it was saying yes to the Federal Republic. Bavaria's sturdy particularism was to stand it in good stead during the years which followed, so that it became one of the most prosperous parts of western Germany.

Bonn as federal capital

One other factor which strengthened the *Länder* against the rapacity of powerful central government was the choice of Bonn as capital. This was by no means foreseen in the autumn of 1948. Bonn was a quiet Rhineland city, best known for its university and for its attractions to retired civil servants or army officers. It did enjoy good communications, being on the main north–south rail axis. But the real reasons for its choice as federal capital were political. The British occupation authorities were happy to see the capital of west Germany in their zone, and although they did not press the issue, they were co-operative over such matters as the use of Wahn military airport for civilian purposes once the capital was established. When the question of the capital was raised in the Parliamentary Council in autumn 1948, a number of German cities started competing for this honour. The favourite seemed to be Frankfurt, already the seat of the Economic Council and a city with a proud history – home to the German *Bund* or confederation in the nineteenth century, and the city in which the first attempt at German unification had taken place in 1848. Most Social Democrats wanted Frankfurt, a large town which would command respect for the federal government. But the SPD in Berlin, whose voices carried particular weight at this time even though they were not given votes in the Parliamentary Council, were against Frankfurt precisely because it was impressive, and it might therefore appear to be a permanent solution, whereas

Bonn could only be provisional. Frankfurt was also not popular with the Bavarians, and the CSU agreed to support Bonn. The powerful government of North Rhine-Westphalia wanted the capital within its frontiers, and thus supported Bonn also.

Above all, the president of the Parliamentary Council, Konrad Adenauer, was determined to opt for Bonn. Personally that choice would suit him well, since his home in Rhöndorf was conveniently placed for it. Politically Bonn represented the provincial, middle-class Roman Catholic Rhineland, from which Adenauer drew his support. He put all his influence behind Bonn, and on 10 May 1949 the city was chosen by a narrow majority on the Parliamentary Council. This was not the end of the matter, because Frankfurt fought a strong rearguard action. Matters were not helped by the fact that Bonn was occupied by Belgian troops, and it took some careful diplomacy by the British military governor, Brian Robertson, to remove them. The Americans, also, would evidently have preferred Frankfurt, but this was probably one of its main handicaps, since many German politicians did not want to feel the overpowering presence of the American occupation authorities, with their headquarters in the IG Farben building in Frankfurt.

Nevertheless, it is probable that, if the Social Democrats under Schumacher had won the first Bundestag elections, the seat of government would have been moved to Frankfurt.[8] As it was, a Bundestag committee which visited Frankfurt in October 1949 was not happy with the ostentatious American presence there and recommended that Bonn be established as provisional capital. This was confirmed by the Bundestag on 1 November on condition that as soon as free elections could be held throughout Germany the capital should move to Berlin at once.[9] The provisional nature of this capital was always stressed in public pronouncements, even by the municipal leaders of Bonn itself, who had worked hard to gain its selection. Needless to say, their views on this matter changed abruptly in 1990, when the prospect of a return to Berlin became more than a pipe dream.

The choice of such a modest capital for the Federal Republic also made it more natural that many of the most important institutions of the federation should be situated in other parts of the country.

8. For the complexities of the struggle over the capital city, see R. Pommerin, *Von Berlin nach Bonn. Die Allierten, die Deutschen und die Hauptstadtsfrage nach 1945* (Cologne, 1989), pp. 145–6.

9. Ibid., pp. 180–93. The committee noted the large numbers of 'Ami-Mädel' (prostitutes) on the streets.

The central bank had already been established in Frankfurt and stayed there, underlining that city's role as the country's financial centre. The Constitutional Court and the Federal Supreme Court were established in Karlsruhe. The federal archives were situated in Coblenz and Freiburg. Overmighty centralism was combatted by geography as well as constitutional theory.

The federal president

Another fundamental issue which had to be tackled was that of the federal presidency. A head of state seemed necessary, but the members of the Parliamentary Council – all of whom wished to avoid the errors of the Weimar Republic, and some of whom had even been members of the Weimar Constituent Assembly – were aware that a popularly elected president could be a rival to the Bundestag and might prove a threat to parliamentary democracy. So it was decided that the president should fulfil mainly ceremonial functions and should be indirectly elected by members of parliament. A body called the *Bundesversammlung,* or Federal Assembly, would be summoned by the speaker of the Bundestag. It would consist of all elected Bundestag members and an equal number of members of the various *Land* parliaments or *Landtage.* The latter would be elected by each *Landtag* on the basis of proportional representation, so that the half of the *Bundesversammlung* members drawn from the *Länder* would reflect the political complexion of the various *Land* parliaments, and not just those of a majority within them. The federal president would be elected for five years – thus avoiding clashes with the Bundestag which had a four-year electoral cycle. Presidents could be re-elected once only. Although they seemed to be largely ceremonial in character, they did in fact exercise an important influence, and could expect to be kept informed of political affairs. During the early years of the Republic it was important that the president was a protestant liberal (FDP) leader, Theodor Heuss, whose reputation as a man of letters assured him public respect. He could offset the suspicion that West Germany was dominated by a clerical and largely Roman Catholic regime. He was also tactful in his dealings with Adenauer, and never attempted to impose his own political ideas on the government. Adenauer's situation was hence much more comfortable than that of Weimar politicians like Gustav Stresemann or Hermann Müller who, from 1925, had had to deal with the popularly elected President Hindenburg, a former field marshal in the Imperial army who enjoyed the support of the Reichswehr and the administrative bureaucracy.

The powers of the chancellor

Adenauer also benefited from the decision of the Parliamentary Council to strengthen the position of the federal chancellor within the parliamentary system. It was agreed that party squabbles under the Weimar system had weakened parliamentary government and lowered its prestige in the country. So it was made more difficult to depose a chancellor once he had been appointed. At the beginning of each four-year legislative period, the federal chancellor was to be elected by the Bundestag on the proposal of the federal president. Once elected he was responsible to the Bundestag, but could not be forced to resign unless the Bundestag majority designated his sucessor in a so-called 'constructive vote of no-confidence'. Throughout the entire history of the West German state this device was only used once with success – when Helmut Kohl replaced Helmut Schmidt as chancellor on 1 October 1982.

The pre-eminent position of the chancellor became a noted feature of government in the Federal Republic, and was even given the journalistic label 'Chancellor Democracy'. In Adenauer's long period of office it was assumed that he exercised an authoritarian control over his cabinet and that his influence also extended over the parliamentary delegations of the CDU and CSU. Certainly Bundestag elections became as much personal conflicts between chancellor candidates as competitions between parties, and in this respect west German politics became more like those of the USA than of the Weimar Republic. Nevertheless, the power of the chancellor should not be exaggerated. The authority of the office depended to a considerable degree on the personality and skill of its holder, as was demonstrated when the apparently popular Ludwig Erhard was unable to survive as chancellor in 1966, despite having only recently won an election victory for his coalition government. Adenauer himself was highly successful in election campaigns, and in 1957 he became the only chancellor in the history of the West German state to obtain an overall majority of the popular vote. Yet the formation of Adenauer's cabinets was always a lengthy and wearisome business, which involved concessions to smaller parties like the FDP or the DP, concern for confessional balance between Roman Catholics and protestants and, last but not least, regional considerations – above all, the need to appease the sensibilities of the Bavarian CSU. Adenauer had to show all his toughness and guile to retain control of his unruly and ill-organized political supporters.

The electoral system

Other lessons the Parliamentary Council learned from the failure of Weimar were not always so helpful to Adenauer, though initially they may have worked in his favour. The electoral system was adjusted to avoid the supposedly damaging effects of pure proportional representation during the 1920s. The Bundestag was to be elected by a split voting system: each elector had two votes – one for a personal candidate in his own constituency and one for a *Land* party list. The directly elected candidates were chosen by simple majority, the list candidates according to proportional representation, taking into account the number of votes cast for political parties in the country as a whole. Directly elected candidates would be subtracted from a party's entitlement to election from the list, so that in reality the second vote distribution really defined the distribution of seats in the Bundestag. The only exception to this would be if a party gained more directly elected Bundestag members than the number to which it was entitled from the distribution of second votes. Then it would be allowed to keep all its directly elected members, and the number of seats in the Bundestag would be temporarily increased to take account of such a result.

Lastly, the electoral system was defined in the 1950s so that only parties which gained 5 per cent of the total of second votes cast or three directly elected members could be represented in the Bundestag at all. This so-called '5 per cent hurdle' – which also applied to *Landtag* elections – was to prove important in keeping fringe parties out of parliament, and was a constant threat to more established smaller parties like the FDP and DP. It was a contributory factor, though not necessarily a decisive one, in the reduction of parties in the Bundestag in the 1950s. When he took office in 1949, Adenauer's coalition consisted of three parties – or even four if the CSU was considered a separate organization from his own CDU. In the opposition were not only the Social Democrats, but also the Communists, who had proved so disruptive in the Weimar Republic, and smaller refugee or regional groups. Yet by 1957 most of the smaller parties – including the Communists – had disappeared and the Federal Republic was effectively represented by a three-party system of Christian Democrats, Social Democrats and the liberal FDP.

The defence of democracy and protection of human rights

The danger of radical, anti-democratic parties threatening the new Republic was diminished still further by a constitutional provision which enabled the government and the courts to ban political organizations which, by the aims or by the actions of their adherents, threatened the democratic political system. It was used against the crypto-nazi Socialist Reich Party in 1952, and against the German Communist Party in 1956. This provision had its limitations. Radical parties could formally disguise their intentions, and a genuinely popular radical movement would be difficult to suppress by legal action. Nevertheless, in the early days of the Republic the safeguard helped to intimidate anti-democratic elements, and to reinforce the view amongst the German nationalist right that collaboration with the new regime would be better than obstruction. Such attitudes were, of course, even more strongly affected by the Cold War, which presented the immediate threat of communism. It was evident that only by collaborating with western democracies could German security be maintained and so, for the time being at least, racism and social Darwinism were confined to the lunatic fringes of German politics.

Just as important for the political health of the new Republic was the stress laid in the Basic Law upon the individual rights of citizens. The Parliamentary Council adopted only the 'classical' human rights, ignoring more rarefied demands such as the need for opportunities for career advancement or the suppression of anti-social profiteering.[10]

Article 3 of the Basic Law specifies that all human beings are equal and that men and women have equal rights. Equality of the sexes had also featured in the Weimar constitution, but it had not been followed up by legislative changes ensuring that women enjoyed social as well as political equality. Most members of the Parliamentary Council thought they were just restoring a fairly harmless Weimar constitutional provision ensuring women the right to vote and participate in politics. However, one SPD delegate, the redoubtable feminist Elizabeth Selbert, aroused public support for a wider interpretation, which would require women's legal position *vis-à-vis* men to be revised and improved. The sentiment that women had

10. Eschenburg, *Jahre der Besatzung*, pp. 502–3. The rights mentioned were in the Bavarian and Weimar constitutions respectively.

helped Germany to recover in the worst days of the postwar period was evidently a potent force behind this move, which would otherwise have found little sympathy in a predominantly middle-aged and male assembly.[11]

The Basic Law also guaranteed freedom of religious worship and incorporated sections of the Weimar Constitution which had given the churches special rights, even though there was no state church. Most important was the right to levy taxes on their members. Church taxes in the Federal Republic were levied in the same fashion as income tax, and were a not inconsiderable burden. Of course, citizens could avoid them by refusing to join a church, but this was embarrassing, not only because it would deny individuals access to such rituals as marriages and funerals, but also because nearly all forms to be filled out in West Germany contained a box marked 'religion'. There was a strong suspicion that employers and others in authority would look with displeasure on openly godless people. This was particularly true in the tenser periods of the Cold War, when atheistic communism seemed to be threatening the western way of life. So membership of both protestant and Roman Catholic churches remained high, even if participation in church life dropped off towards the end of the Bonn Republic's history.

Most important were the sections of the Basic Law which established the individual's rights to political freedom, to privacy and to protection against arbitrary actions of the state. These could not be altered, even by a two-thirds majority in Bundestag and Bundesrat – which was otherwise needed for reforms of the Basic Law. Such concern for individual rights reflected the bitter lessons of the interwar period, in which such rights had been suspended by presidential decree, at first to protect the republic, but then to establish the nazi dictatorship.

The Constitutional Court

Underpinning both the liberal nature of the Basic Law and the rights of the federal states *vis-à-vis* the central government was the institution of the *Bundesverfassungsgericht*, the Federal Constitutional Court. The judges in the court were elected in equal numbers by the Bundestag and the Bundesrat. The court could test the compatibility of federal or state laws with the prescriptions of the Basic Law, and

11. E. Kolinsky, *Women in Contemporary Germany. Life, Work and Politics* (2nd edn, Oxford, 1993), pp. 41–5. For the legal reforms affecting women, see below, Chapter 5.

could act to protect the rights of individuals if they felt them to be compromised by unconstitutional government action. The court, which was established at Karlsruhe, became a very important feature of West German political life, and its judgments did not always please the governing authorities. The concept of Germany as a *Rechtstaat*, a state based on a rule of law which restrained the highest as well as the lowest, had always been a German liberal ideal. It was only in the Federal Republic that this ideal was properly realized.[12]

There was, of course, a negative side to this concern with legality. Firstly, it tended to reduce political issues to points of law, thus clogging up the political process and in some cases threatening to jeopardize popular but controversial innovations – such as the policy of *détente* with the eastern bloc and the GDR in the early 1970s, which was challenged, albeit unsuccessfully, in the Federal Constitutional Court.[13] There was also the fact that so many of those involved in politics and administration were themselves lawyers by training or even by profession. The majority of the members of the Parliamentary Council, which drew up the Basic Law, were themselves legally trained officials.[14] It was therefore to be expected that German politics would be characterized by a certain legalistic pedantry. Indeed, it is perhaps surprising that, despite the possibilities of obstruction offered by the decentralized, federal nature of west German politics, buttressed as it was by the federal courts, the system functioned so smoothly. Undoubtedly one reason for this was the domination of Christian Democracy in the early years of the Federal Republic, and the perception by the administrative élites that, with Hitler defeated and Stalin at the gates, the Bonn government under Adenauer was as good as anything they were likely to get.

Winning over the middle classes

One of the main tasks of the new Republic established in west Germany in 1949 was to reconcile the so-called *Bildungsbürgertum* – literally the educated middle class – to parliamentary democracy.

12. For a description of the Constitutional Court's function and a translation of the relevant parts of the Basic Law, see Donald P. Kommers, 'The Judiciary' and 'Basic Rights and Constitutional Review', in Schweitzer *et al.* (eds), *Politics and Government in the FRG*, pp. 272–324. It is worth noting that judges in the Constitutional Court were elected for a period of twelve years only and in any case had to retire at the age of 68.
13. See below, Chapter 9.
14. Eschenburg, *Jahre der Besatzung*, p. 504.

This had not occurred in the Wilhelmine Empire or in the Weimar Republic. The *Bildungsbürgertum* was made up of middle-class men who had usually been educated at universities – including specialized technical universities – or who, at the very least, had graduated from the prestigious *Gymnasien* which prepared pupils for university entrance. They included senior government officials, university professors and secondary school teachers, as well as members of the free professions such as law and medicine. They were mainly protestant, especially in Prussia, where Roman Catholics – not to mention Jews – were regarded as outsiders.

Although there were, of course, many individual exceptions, one can say that, by 1914, two attitudes characterized this section of the population: fear of 'the masses' and commitment to an almost mystical form of German nationalism. Since the masses could not be trusted, only strong and authoritarian leadership could ensure victory for German cultural values, which such people generally assumed to be superior to any others. The experience of the First World War strengthened this attitude: in 1917 many academics and professional people joined the government-sponsored *Vaterlandspartei* working for total victory and, when the revolution of 1918 overthrew the Wilhelmine Empire, they were quick to blame the masses for having 'stabbed Germany in the back'.

A good example of the opinions of a relatively moderate, conservative academic in this category can be found in a letter of 19 February 1919 from the young historian Siegfried Kaehler to his former university supervisor, Friedrich Meinecke. Meinecke, the most distinguished historian of his generation, was one of those German intellectuals who had supported a compromise peace during the war, and who was willing to accept a democratic parliamentary republic if it could create a decent future for Germany. Kaehler was horrified by such a prospect. In his letter he complained that the German people had betrayed their past and delivered themselves up to slavery, especially spiritual slavery: 'You cherish the belief in the creative will of our people', he wrote; 'when in our long, doleful history has our "people" built anything unless it was subjected to iron leadership? . . . I would say that the fundamental feature of the German character is not [strength of] will but reluctance [*Widerwillen*] towards the most immediate and most necessary [tasks] . . .' He went on to make clear that he rejected the Republic because he thought that the masses did not seek social peace but wanted 'naked class domination'. Therefore an attempt by him as a middle-class citizen

(*Bürgerlicher*) to adapt himself to the socialists in a democratic republic would be bound to fail.[15]

There were many who thought as he did and who maintained their opposition to the Weimar Republic throughout its short lifetime. Although he was not a nazi, he retained his contempt for the Weimar Republic even after Hitler's takeover. Despite their experiences under the Third Reich, conservative, protestant intellectuals of his type remained fundamentally opposed to democracy, and were not immune to social and confessional prejudice. At the end of the war Kaehler urged resistance to 'Jewish-democratic defamation' of Germany. In February 1946, by then a full professor of history at the relatively undamaged University of Göttingen, he wrote to the leading figure in the conservative historical school, Gerhard Ritter of Freiburg, complaining about the overcrowding of his university, which would lead to a hopeless 'academic proletariat' being created.

He then went on to agree with a comment by Ritter to the effect that former attempts to restrict the number of Jews in German universities could be defended without accepting anti-semitism of the nazi type. Kaehler recalled with distaste that, in autumn 1932, five out of seventeen chairs in his faculty had been occupied by 'pure Jews' (*Volljuden*) and one by a 'half or quarter aryan'. So a full third of the chairs were in Jewish occupation at an old university which, according to its statutes, should only have admitted protestants. Kaehler approvingly remembered one distinguished Jewish archaeologist at Marburg who urged the Prussian authorities not to appoint a Jew as his successor because the faculty would not put up with it. His comment on this was: 'Not all Jews were as clever as he, had they been so the unpleasant events of 1933 would not have occurred . . .'[16]

The purpose of citing this correspondence is not to denigrate a distinguished scholar, but to illustrate the fact that the cultural inheritance of large parts of the German intelligentsia was alien to pluralistic parliamentary democracy. It was symptomatic that Kaehler was a protestant academic at strongly protestant universities. The legacy of protestant Prussian-German nationalism was not going to

15. Kaehler wanted a monarchist restoration or at least a strong, undemocratic state. Interestingly, he combined an apparently fanatical nationalism with contempt for the German people. W. Bussmann and G. Grünthal (eds), *Siegfried A. Kaehler. Briefe 1900–1963* (Boppard am Rhein, 1993), Doc. 24, pp. 154–8.

16. Bussmann and Grünthal (eds), *Kaehler. Briefe*: for the reaction to nazi takeover, Docs. 56–60, pp. 221–31; for the letter to Ritter on 25 February 1946, Doc. 103, pp. 334–6.

disappear overnight, despite talk of a 'zero hour' (*Stunde Null*) after Hitler's death.

There were indications of this problem at the birth of the Federal Republic. The president of the protestant church in Hesse and Nassau was Pastor Niemöller, a nationalist clergyman who had become a staunch opponent of Hitler and was incarcerated in a concentration camp from 1938 to 1945. He enjoyed considerable prestige inside and outside Germany, and his criticism of the new regime was especially embarrassing for the CDU. In December 1949 he claimed that the Federal Republic was a child 'conceived in the Vatican and born in America'. He argued that it was German protestantism that had lost the war; eastern Germany had been colonized by Catholic Poles, central Germany was under Russian control and West Germany had become a Roman Catholic state. He seemed to suggest that, if the choice was to be between German unity under communism and a long-term division of the country, the former option should be chosen.[17] This kind of talk was disturbing for Adenauer because the CDU had only won 25 per cent of protestant votes cast in the 1949 Bundestag elections, and the imbalance between Roman Catholics and protestants in the CDU ranks was also noteworthy. He had to take care that his newly established Christian people's party appealed to the conservative protestants as well as to Roman Catholics.

A difficult beginning, 1949–53

Having mentioned the advantages possessed by the Bonn Republic when Adenauer took up office in September 1949, we should not, however, overlook the extent to which in the early years of its existence it seemed anything but secure. A provisional regime born out of international crisis, with huge economic and social problems, its political structures did not look nearly so impressive to start with as they would do after 40 years of successful operation. Nor did public opinion polls suggest that there was deep-rooted enthusiasm for pluralistic democracy among the west German population.

As for Chancellor Adenauer, he was 73 years old. In August 1949 he had told potential ministers that his doctor had assured him he could carry on for as long as two years. This hardly guaranteed the prospect of stable leadership – or of cabinet loyalty. That Adenauer's

17. Hans-Peter Schwarz, *Die Ära Adenauer: Grunderjahre der Republik, 1949–1957* (Stuttgart, 1981), p. 123. Niemöller proposed that Germany be occupied by neutral powers – a suggestion unlikely to have much practical effect.

regime actually lasted for fourteen years was due to his own grit and determination as much as to fortuitous circumstances. Had he faltered in the early stages of his administration, the success story of the Federal Republic might have ended much earlier – and in disaster.

The first of Adenauer's wise choices was his preference for the small coalition of anti-socialist parties. The political constellation in the Bundestag, although it looked insecure, made it relatively easy for Adenauer to get his way. He had already established a rapport with the western Allies whilst carrying out his duties as president of the Parliamentary Council, and this in itself gave him a certain prestige which could be used to intimidate those who might be tempted to rebel. He could impress the doubters amongst the coalition parties by his apparent expertise and inside knowledge. At the same time, the intemperate opposition of the Social Democrats, and in particular of their leader Kurt Schumacher, tended to drive the non-socialist parties into the arms of Adenauer even if they were often uneasy about policies which seemed to be deepening the division of Germany rather than overcoming it.

Schumacher's offensive against the government, 1949–50

Kurt Schumacher, the SPD leader, believed that the reunification of Germany should be his party's first and essential objective. He opposed the policies of the western powers: the continued dismantling of large industrial undertakings in the British zone, the French action in separating the Saar from the rest of Germany, the Americans' supposed preference for capitalism, which Schumacher blamed for his failure to establish social democracy in the Federal Republic and, of course, the Russian depredations which had cut off the eastern territories of Germany and given them to Poland or even the USSR. This meant that Schumacher, who was certainly more sympathetic to the West than to the Soviet Union, presented himself in public as an obstructive and nationalistic opponent of western integration.

One of the awkward issues with which Adenauer had to deal was the future of the important industrial complex in the Ruhr basin. The official Allied policy was to internationalize the Ruhr and have it controlled in such a way as to avoid a resurgence of German national power buttressed by heavy industry. The French were particularly insistent on that. An International Authority for the Ruhr (IAR) was to be set up, and Adenauer was eager that the Germans should take up their representation on it. In this way he hoped to be able to negotiate an end to the Allied dismantling policy and obtain the return of heavy industry to German ownership. But to Schumacher any collaboration in the IAR was a form of treason. When this matter was debated in the Bundestag on 24/25 November 1949, Adenauer rather mischievously suggested that the SPD would prefer to see Allied dismantling carried through to the bitter end than to send a representative to the IAR, a comment which provoked the furious response from Schumacher that Adenauer was acting as 'the Chancellor of the Allies'.[18]

This became a famous moment in the early parliamentary history of the Federal Republic. Schumacher was banned from the debating chamber for several days. In other respects too it helped Adenauer by making him seem even more indispensable so far as the western powers were concerned, and by alienating his opponent from possible allies in parliament. Schumacher, however, was confident that his time would come, and that a strong Social Democratic Party would take over the reins of power once the social market economy had demonstrated its fundamentally unjust character. Then the German people would be able to insist on reunification. How this latter objective was to be achieved was never convincingly explained either by Schumacher or by his party; it remained a will-o'-the-wisp which undermined the SPD's credibility throughout the 1950s.

In a sense, the situation seemed the reverse of that in the early years of Weimar: then the SPD had been saddled with responsibility for 'fulfilment' of Allied demands, now the CDU would have to take on that burden. In the summer of 1952, when the unification issue was very much on the agenda and when German public opinion showed strong resistance to rearmament, Schumacher might hope that his awkward stance would benefit the SPD. However, the redoubtable but prickly Social Democratic leader had reckoned without the forces of nature. On 20 August 1952 Schumacher, who had already suffered a serious stroke the previous December, died suddenly. He was nineteen years younger than Adenauer.

His death certainly spared him the humiliation of an unexpected and resounding electoral defeat in the Bundestag elections of 1953, when the SPD obtained less than 30 per cent of the vote and Adenauer's Christian supporters won an overall majority of

---

18. Ibid., p. 65. See also Lewis D. Edinger, *Kurt Schumacher. A Study in Personality and Political Behaviour* (Berkeley, LA, and London, 1965), chs. 7 and 8.

parliamentary seats in Bonn. With his looming presence removed, reformers in the SPD could try to modify their party's inflexible resistance towards both the free market and Western integration. But his successors were grey men trained in the administrative apparatus of the Socialist Party; it was not until the end of the decade that new policies and new leaders made a real impact on the electorate. In the field of foreign policy, indeed, his death had an unfortunate consequence for the SPD. Schumacher had been determined to extract immediate concessions from the Allies for German contributions to Western defence, and he refused to take steps which might prejudice reunification. But he would certainly not have been willing to make concessions in the other direction either – towards the Soviet Union or Ulbricht's regime in Pankow.[19] His successors were not quite so clear about that, and continued his opposition to European integration and Western defence whilst making it appear that they might be willing to trade reunification for concessions to the Soviet Union which could undermine Western security. The CDU/CSU were quick to pounce on such unpopular notions, and foreign policy became a weakness rather than a strength for the opposition.

Schumacher is, however, rightly revered as one of the founding fathers of the Federal Republic, even if his contribution was not so substantial as that of men like Adenauer or Erhard. His unflinching commitment to freedom and moral rectitude, and his association of social democracy with the cause of national reunification, created respect for his party and for democracy in west Germany, even if it did not arouse affection.

Above all, his stern rejection of Soviet communism meant that the Federal Republic was not threatened from within by enemies on the left, as the Weimar Republic had been. The communists themselves were completely discredited by their obvious subservience to Ulbricht's SED – a subservience amply documented by east German archive materials once the GDR collapsed in 1990. They had only managed to gain 5.7 per cent of the votes for the new Bundestag in 1949, and in the subsequent elections of 1953 they fell out of the federal parliament altogether, failing to reach the 5 per cent hurdle which had been erected by the electoral law. When, in 1956, the Communist Party was declared illegal by decision of the Constitutional Court, it was already a spent force. Nevertheless, the court's decision helped to demonstrate that the new Republic

19. Pankow was a suburb of East Berlin in which the GDR government established its administration. For a contemporary discussion of Schumacher's policy, see Fritz René Allemann, *Bonn ist nicht Weimar* (Berlin/Cologne, 1956), pp. 139–41.

was not inclined to allow the enemies of democracy to abuse its free political system in order to destroy it, as had happened between 1919 and 1933.[20]

The Soviet threat to German integrity

In the early 1950s, however, it was evident that the most serious threat to German freedom came from outside the borders of the Federal Republic. The power of the Soviet bloc had been consolidated in the late 1940s, despite measures taken by the western Allies to defend themselves. Most important was the establishment of NATO in April 1949, an alliance of great importance for west Germany, but one from which she was naturally excluded as an occupied enemy country. The establishment of the Federal Republic itself was mirrored in the east by the creation of the German Democratic Republic (GDR), a communist dictatorship effectively run by Walter Ulbricht. His regime adopted an aggressive tone towards the West in general and Bonn in particular. The GDR began to recruit a paramilitary police force, the *kasernierte Volkspolizei*, which looked remarkably like an army and which, it was feared, might be used to attack vulnerable points in West Germany – especially West Berlin – without involving Soviet forces.

In June 1950 the international outlook darkened even further with the outbreak of the Korean War, a clear test of western resolve which seemed to present an immediate threat of global conflict. The prompt and firm response of President Truman, Clement Attlee and the French administration ultimately overcame the crisis, but not before it had caused a bloody regional war and a world shortage of raw materials. Both aspects of the situation, the economic turbulence and the threat to security, seemed especially damaging to the Federal Republic.

20. The KPD was not, of course, the first party to be suppressed under Article 21 of the Law. That distinction belonged to the crypto-nazi Socialist Reich Party, which was banned by order of the Constitutional Court in October 1952. This party had made serious gains in *Landtag* elections in Lower Saxony in May 1951, and seemed to be growing in popularity – to the dismay of the government, not least with an eye to its image abroad. When the indictment was presented against the SRP the government decided it would have to launch a similar case against the KPD, but it proceeded much more slowly with that, fearing possible problems in negotiations over all-German elections. So the KPD ban was not decided until 1956. Cf. Schwarz, *Ära Adenauer, 1949–1957*, pp. 130–5, and D. Kommers, 'Basic Rights and Constitutional Review', in Schweitzer *et al.* (eds), *Politics and Government in the FRG*, pp. 297–310.

CHAPTER FIVE

The 1950s: Economic Success and Social Consolidation

Crisis times for Erhard

So far as the economy was concerned, Ludwig Erhard found that his 'honeymoon period' as director of the west German economy was coming to an end by the time he was appointed federal Economics Minister in Adenauer's government in September 1949.

Euphoria over relaxed controls and more lavish supplies of consumer goods was giving way to resentment at living standards which were still generally meagre, levels of unemployment which seemed worryingly high and glaring imbalances of wealth associated with a period of industrial growth and economic opportunity. Erhard himself believed that the way to overcome these problems was to press ahead with deregulation and decontrol, thereby freeing both the dynamic forces of the market and returning ownership of German industry – especially heavy industry in the Ruhr area – to German hands. In this way the free market policy also served German national interests, since several key industries, such as coal and steel, were still effectively controlled by the Allies, who were committed to breaking them up into small units.

Erhard's other objective was the restoration of West Germany's freedom to trade with her neighbours. This was essential both for German and continental European well-being since, without German industrial production, Germany's neighbours could not be expected to experience a lasting economic recovery. Erhard therefore did everything he could to encourage the relaxation of Allied controls over German trade. In this he was encouraged by the Americans, who wanted to see multilateral trade patterns restored, but opposed by more cautious institutions such as the British Treasury, for whom liberalized commerce might pose a threat to the status of sterling as a reserve currency.

In the early months of the new federal government Erhard was under pressure to create jobs by increased public expenditure. Supported by the central bank, he refused to do any such thing and the economy quickly turned in a different direction. As private investment, stimulated by export-led demand and tax concessions, took off, demand for imports grew, and Germany's balance of payments went into deficit. The Korean War exacerbated the crisis, which at one stage threatened to blow Erhard's policy off course altogether. Fortunately, however, a new mechanism to ease trade between countries in receipt of Marshall aid, the European Payments Union (EPU), had been established under American patronage. It was formalized by treaty only on 19 September 1950, but its provisions covered transactions starting in July 1950. The EPU enabled member countries to trade with each other using limited credit made available within the organization, thus obviating the need to pay in gold or dollars. Embarrassingly enough, the Federal Republic quickly ran up a large deficit, and was the object of foreign criticism as a result. It looked as though drastic measures of restriction were going to have to be imposed on West German trade, but two independent experts appointed by the EPU, Per Jacobsson and Alec Cairncross, recommended that the Germans should be granted a special credit of $120 million to tide them over until the following April.[1]

Even so, the Korean crisis initially posed a serious threat to Erhard's policies. As shortages of coal and other raw materials grew worse, the bluff optimism of the federal Economics Minister seemed inappropriate. Public opinion polls began to register dissatisfaction with his performance, and demands for controls on prices and imports became more strident. Most dangerous of all was pressure from an unexpected quarter – the United States government. Since the Korean War was putting a great burden on the American taxpayer – not to mention the conscripted US soldiers who were being sent to the front – the Americans saw no reason why other western countries – especially a former enemy country – should not exercise self-discipline too. On 6 March 1951 McCloy, the US High Commissioner in Germany, wrote to Adenauer demanding the rationing of raw materials in the Federal Republic, a demand which seemed to imply the end of Erhard's free market policies. Erhard had to admit to

---

1. Hans Giersch, Karl-Heinz Paqué and Holger Schmieding, *The Fading Miracle. Four Decades of Market Economy in Germany* (Cambridge, 1992), pp. 101–2.

the Bundestag that the German people would have to accept sacrifices as the result of the Korean War and that 'some freedom will have to be replaced by planned and sensible regulation'. This admission brought forth howls of derision from the Social Democratic opposition, whose spokesman in the Bundestag declaimed: 'Professor Erhard, what you have brought to this podium today is the mummified corpse of your market economy. When you look at yourself in the mirror, I should like to ask if you can actually recognize yourself.'[2]

Nevertheless, Erhard kept his nerve, and Adenauer supported him. An emollient reply was sent to McCloy, but Erhard was not forced to alter fundamentally the main thrust of his policies. The allocation of scarce raw materials was entrusted to industrial associations and there was also a levy on consumer industries for the benefit of capital investment in heavy industry.

West Germany's boom begins

These apparently *dirigiste* measures did not, however, mean a return to a general regime of controls and rationing. Instead, the market forces upon which Erhard had pinned his faith began to operate in Germany's favour. The opportunities presented by the world-wide demand for machine tools and high-quality manufactured goods meant that German exports started to boom, reversing the trade deficit and pushing West Germany into surplus. The policy of tight money pursued by the central bank with Erhard's support meant that German prices remained competitive, and manufacturers had every incentive to seek out export markets instead of relying on artificially stimulated home demand. At the same time investment in domestic industry grew unusually fast, creating growth and reducing unemployment. This was the next phase of the German 'economic miracle', and in some ways the most remarkable. Annual gross domestic product rose by 8.2 per cent in the years 1950–1960, an achievement exceeded in this period only by Japan (see Figures 2 and 3).[3] A combination of low inflation, encouragement for domestic investment and a well-trained, motivated labour force enabled West Germany to catch up rapidly on her initially more affluent neighbours.

2. Erik Nölting before the Bundestag, 14 March 1951, cited in A.J. Nicholls, *Freedom With Responsibility. The Social Market Economy in Germany, 1918–1963* (Oxford, 1994), p. 284.

3. Giersch *et al.*, *Fading Miracle*, pp. 4–5. The growth rates for the United Kingdom over the same period were 2.8 per cent, and for the USA 3.3 per cent.

FIGURE 2   *Economic development of the Federal Republic, 1951–63*

	Growth rate[a]	Price rises[b]	Unemployment[c]	Trade surplus[d]
1951	10.5	7.9	9.1	1.9
1952	8.9	2.0	8.5	2.5
1953	8.2	−1.7	7.6	3.8
1954	7.4	0.1	7.1	3.4
1955	12.0	1.6	5.2	2.4
1956	7.2	2.5	4.2	3.4
1957	5.7	2.3	3.5	4.1
1958	3.7	2.0	3.6	3.9
1959	7.3	1.1	2.5	3.4
1960	9.0	1.4	1.3	2.6
1961	4.4	2.3	0.9	2.2
1962	4.7	2.9	0.7	1.2
1963	2.8	3.0	0.9	1.5

[a] Percentage growth in GNP at 1980 prices.
[b] Annual adjustment of the price index for living costs of a four-person family in the wage-earning category.
[c] Percentage of those unemployed out of the total of employed and unemployed workers.
[d] Exports minus imports expressed as a percentage of GNP at current prices.

Source: D. Grosser, T. Lange, A. Müller-Armack and B. Neuss, *Soziale Marktwirtschaft: Geschichte, Konzept, Leistung* (2nd edn; Stuttgart, 1990), p. 229.

It should, of course, be noted that West Germany had some advantages which would not be likely to recur. Firstly, there was still no German army, so that the share of GDP devoted to defence – even accounting for the cost of support for Allied troops in the Federal Republic – was lower than in many comparable countries. From 1952 the German Finance Minister, Fritz Schäffer, did have to take into account the probability that a new German army, the *Bundeswehr*, would have to be funded in the future, and he therefore budgeted for a surplus of income over expenditure. Since the *Bundeswehr* was actually slow in being established, the money built up into a kind of war chest, nicknamed the *Juliusturm*.* This initially helped in the overall dampening of public spending, although in 1957 Schäffer's colleagues rebelled and raided the *Juliusturm* for popular expenditure in election year. By this time, however, the economic recovery was well established, and tax revenues often exceeded budget forecasts.

* The *Juliusturm* had been a tower in Berlin in which, after the defeat of France in 1871, the French indemnity had been stored.

FIGURE 3   *Percentage growth of GDP in industrialized countries, 1951–65*

	1951–55	1956–60	1961–65
Belgium	4.5[a]	2.6	5.0
FRG	9.5	6.5	5.0
Denmark	2.0	4.4	5.3
France	4.1	5.0	5.8
Britain	3.9[b]	2.6	3.1
Italy	5.5[c]	5.5	5.2
Netherlands	5.1	4.0	4.8
Austria	6.6	5.5	4.3
Sweden	3.4	4.3	5.2
Switzerland	5.0	4.3	5.3
Spain	5.2[d]	3.5	8.5
USA	4.1	2.3	4.6
Japan	7.2[b]	8.6	10.2
AVERAGE	5.1	4.5	5.6

[a] 1954/5
[b] 1953/4
[c] 1952/5
[d] 1955

Source: D. Grosser, T. Lange, A. Müller-Armack and B. Neuss, *Soziale Marktwirtschaft: Geschichte, Konzept, Leistung* (2nd edn; Stuttgart, 1990), p. 232.

Other factors in the German economy besides sound money and free markets should not be overlooked. Firstly, although Erhard himself was genuinely determined to make the West German currency convertible as quickly as possible – he was nicknamed 'Mr. Convertibility' by the Americans – for most of the 1950s foreign exchange controls remained in force throughout western Europe, including the Federal Republic. This fact was combined with tax incentives for domestic investment and an economic culture in which foreign investment had never been as attractive to investors as had been the case in countries like the United Kingdom. So there was no danger of a flight of capital from West Germany during this period, or indeed later. By the time foreign exchange regulations had been completely relaxed, the DM was so strong that West Germany attracted money rather than exporting it.

Secondly, in the 1950s the West Germans benefited from the fact that their restrictive, deflationary policies were being pursued against a background of economic growth elsewhere in the western world. The combination of military expansion and post-Keynesian commitments to deficit spending and full employment meant that there was no danger of a world slump which could have crippled the West German export drive. It could be claimed that the Bonn Republic owed its prosperity to the misguided profligacy of others, but if all governments had followed the policies preferred by Bonn, the resulting recession might have damaged the political as well as the economic stability of the new West German state. As it was, the speed and effectiveness of the industrial recovery did much to restore German self-confidence and engendered respect in other western countries.

West Germany's 'economic miracle' has been the object of much interest on the part of economists and politicians outside Germany. Erhard himself denied that the term 'miracle' should be applied to it, since it was simply the result of correct economic theory, sensibly applied. However this may be, certain myths about West Germany's economic development should not be allowed to obscure the facts about the early years of the Federal Republic. The decision to rely on market forces and competition to stimulate growth was a very sound one. But it should not be thought, as is the current wisdom in Britain in the 1990s, that this must involve a return to unregulated *laissez-faire*, vigorous repression of trade union activity and the readiness to tolerate mass poverty as a means of creating 'healthy' imbalances of wealth. Neither Erhard nor Adenauer was particularly fond of trade unions, but both appreciated the value of industrial peace, and neither believed in salvation through mass suffering. One cliché Erhard never uttered was, 'if it ain't hurting, it ain't working'. On the contrary, he believed in incentives for consumers and producers alike.

Trade unions and co-determination

So far as the industrial trade unions were concerned, these had been allowed to reappear after 1945, not least because the Allies realized that their leaders and members had been generally more opposed to national socialism than many other sections of society. In the British zone the trade unions were also seen as helpful in resisting communist attempts to dominate works councils in heavy industry. The British had agreed to trade union proposals for co-determination in large-scale mining and steel production companies in their zone. This arrangement gave employees as much representation on the supervisory boards of such companies as the shareholders. The trade unions regarded this as a vital development in industrial democracy and were determined to retain it.

With the establishment of a West German state, the trade unions organized themselves on a federal basis. In October 1949 they set up an umbrella organization for the whole of West Germany, the German Trade Union Federation (DGB), headed by a moderate and experienced leader, Hans Böckler. Attempts to recreate a Roman Catholic trade union movement proved unsuccessful, and the DGB came to represent most unionized workers in the Federal Republic.

The new federal government was under pressure from the FDP and employers' representatives to abolish the type of co-determination established in the mining and steel industries; the DGB, on the other hand, wanted it extended to other industries. Within the cabinet there were differences between the trade union wing of the CDU, represented by Anton Storch, the Minister of Labour, and those who sympathized with the employers, like Erhard. In January 1951 the DGB threatened a strike in the Ruhr if co-determination was not confirmed and extended by the federal government. Adenauer, although he was no friend of the trade unions, cannily avoided a confrontation over this issue. He invited Böckler, whom he had known during the Weimar period and who was actually a year older than himself, to his official residence in the Palais Schaumburg in Bonn. There, on 11 January 1951, the two elderly men agreed on a compromise. Co-determination should be confirmed in industrial undertakings which had more than 1,000 employees and which were engaged in production of iron and steel and/or in the mining of coal or iron ore.

The strike was called off, and Adenauer stuck to his side of the bargain, despite opposition from the FDP and DP. The Co-determination Law was passed in April 1951 with the votes of the Christian Democrats and the Social Democrats. The following year, in July 1952, a Works' Constitution Law was passed which established the rights of workers in other large firms to have a voice in their conditions of work and to be informed on management decisions by participation in works' councils. There were also to be employee representatives on the supervisory boards, but they would be in a clear minority and would not be able to interfere in the commercial operations of companies. This was very far from 'workers' control', but it was an attempt to make working life more humane and was consistent with the principles of the social market economy. In the 1990s the possible introduction of works' councils into British industry as the result of European laws caused outrage amongst right-wing advocates of *laissez-faire*, and was one reason why the British government refused to accept the Social Chapter at Maastricht.

It is nowadays fashionable to play down the significance of co-determination as a factor in West Germany's economic success,[4] but during the first 30 years of the Federal Republic's existence the relatively harmonious labour relations enjoyed by West German industry were the envy of many European neighbours. This was not simply due to the feebleness of German trade unions, or the supine nature of their membership. In the 1950s there were signs of militancy amongst the rank and file, and the government was cautious when it came to confronting labour troubles, such as a three-week engineering strike in Bavaria in the summer of 1954.[5] Neither Adenauer nor Erhard, despite their commitment to free market capitalism, made a name for themselves as union-bashers; on the contrary, the government liked to project an image of harmony between capital and labour, and this seems to have had a positive impact on both industrial relations and the West German electorate.

Taxation and social welfare

Nor is it right to regard the Federal Republic as a society with low taxes and low social spending by comparison with other European countries. In 1913 the burden of taxes and social security payments in Germany was just over 10 per cent of GNP; in 1938 it had reached 28.4 per cent, but in 1951 it was up to over 32 per cent.

The demands on the budget were formidable. Some 36 per cent of it was taken up by Allied occupation costs in 1949–50. But this did not mean that social spending was jettisoned. In the early 1950s West Germany spent proportionately more on social welfare than other countries – in part a measure of the appalling legacy of the world war.[6]

It is true that Erhard and Schäffer both preferred to lower direct taxes on personal income. These had been excessively high under Allied occupation – a factor of marginal importance before currency

---

4. Cf. Giersch *et al.*, *Fading Miracle*, pp. 86–7, which gives a clear description of co-determination, but seems to regard it as a liability which fortunately did not damage German industry.

5. H.K. Rupp, *Politische Geschichte der Bundesrepublik Deutschland* (Stuttgart, 1978), p. 89; Hans-Peter Schwarz, *Die Ära Adenauer: Grunderjahre der Republik, 1949–1957* (Stuttgart, 1981), p. 235. The problems were made easier for the federal government in 1954 because the official bodies dealing with labour unrest at that time were the *Land* of Bavaria and some municipal authorities.

6. H.G. Hockerts, *Sozialpolitische Entscheidungen im Nachkriegsdeutschland* (Stuttgart, 1980).

reform, since the old Reichsmark had been worth very little anyhow. There was also the point that a relatively high proportion of income tax had to be devoted to funding the municipalities and the rest was divided between the federal government and the *Länder*, whereas a larger share of excise duties and turnover taxes went to the federation. The result was a strong inclination to increase indirect taxes and cut higher levels of income tax. This helped to reduce mass purchasing power in the home market, thus encouraging industrial investment in export growth. But the government did not ignore social policy in order to encourage upper-class wealth creation.

In the early years of the Federal Republic a number of measures were taken to meet the needs of those most seriously damaged by the outcome of the war. There was already a legacy of pensions to be paid to wounded ex-servicemen, war widows and victims of the bombing.

Housing

Then there was the housing shortage. In West Germany over 2,300,000 dwellings, or about a fifth of the homes available, had been destroyed or made uninhabitable during the war. Many more dwellings had been damaged. In addition, there was the pressure on housing created by the influx of refugees and expellees from the east, who in September 1950 numbered nine and a half million and made up 16 per cent of the West German population. Since few new houses or flats had been built since the outbreak of the war, there was also a demand from newly created households. The authorities reckoned that nearly five million dwellings would have to be built to get things back to something like normalcy, and there were gloomy predictions that three decades would be needed to remedy the deficit.[7]

It was obvious that this problem could not be overcome by relying solely on the invisible hand of the market, and no political party

7. Even then, there is some doubt about 'normalcy', since the situation in the Third Reich had not been ideal so far as poorer levels of housing were concerned. For a discussion of the whole problem, see G. Schulz, *Wiederaufbau in Deutschland. Die Wohnungsbaupolitik in der Westzonen und der Bundesrepublik von 1945 bis 1957* (Düsseldorf, 1994), pp. 33–40. Figures on the estimated need vary. R.C. Führer mentions that in 1950 the housing shortage was reckoned to be 4.4 million dwellings; see his 'Managing Scarcity: The German Housing Shortage and the Controlled Economy, 1914–1990', in *German History. The Journal of the German History Society*, Vol. 13, No. 3 (Oxford, 1995), 326–54, esp. 341.

dared to suggest such a solution. Rent controls were retained. For the first time in German history a special Ministry of Housing was established (*Wohnungsbau*, literally 'dwellings construction', since most of the dwellings would be flats). Fortunately the housing shortage was recognized as a national, rather than a class, issue by all the major parties, even if there were differences of opinion about how to tackle it. The SPD favoured subsidies and controls, the Free Democrats wanted to liberate market forces to help private landlords and the CDU/CSU were keen to encourage home ownership for as many families as possible. The interaction of these views in the democratic process, exemplified by long debates in the Bundestag, produced remarkably positive and rapid results. Responding to a Social Democratic scheme presented in October 1949, the government produced its own draft legislation within a very short space of time, and the proposals were then modified in lengthy discussions, so that by 23 March 1950 they could pass the Bundestag committee stage by general agreement. On 13 April the Federal Dwellings Construction Law (*Wohnungsbaugesetz*), which Adenauer himself described as the most important piece of legislation so far put before parliament, was accepted by the Bundesrat. The speed with which the new democratic system, despite its pluralism and its consultative procedures, was able to cope with this issue, demonstrated that the Federal Republic could be every bit as effective as its predecessors, and considerably more humane.

The new law, which was supposedly only to operate for one year, but which was extended regularly thereafter, was designed to further the building of 'social dwellings' (*sozialer Wohnungsbau*) affordable by poorer tenants – usually under the auspices of the *Länder* and the municipalities. The means used to achieve this were to be public loans with low interest or none at all, floated and guaranteed by the *Länder*; guarantees for other housing loans; and very generous tax advantages for those investing in new building. A big effort was made to release land for building, and housing controls were to be relaxed. Housing was to be divided into three segments. Firstly, there were publicly supported building projects for flats of limited size with strictly controlled rents available only to poorer tenants taken off lists provided by housing offices. Secondly, there was tax-benefited housing, which could be for larger dwellings at higher, though still restricted, rents, and without limitation on the type of tenants who occupied them. Lastly, there could be privately financed construction which would be unrestricted in either size or rent. The government also pledged itself to encourage insurance companies and banks to invest in housing, and to extend tax concessions on housing to the mass of the population.[8]

More than half the funds channelled into housing in the 1950s were public, either in the form of public building schemes, guaranteed low-interest loans to private firms or tax exemptions.[9] In 1952 the west Germans built about 430,000 dwellings. Five years later, in 1957, 591,000 dwellings were constructed, a record in German history. During the period 1950–57 over four million homes were built, of which 57 per cent were 'social' in character. From 1955 to 1957 the Federal Republic built 99 dwellings for every 10,000 of its inhabitants, whereas in Britain the figure was only 57 per 10,000 and in France 35. The improvement in living standards resulting from such construction was demonstrated by the fall in the number of people living as lodgers or sub-tenants. In 1948 these had made up 13 per cent of households; by 1960 they had fallen to 5 per cent.[10]

The conquest of the housing crisis in Germany was a major triumph for the Bonn Republic. It seemed to demonstrate that a sensible compromise, involving public sector regulation and funding and private enterprise investment, fared better than either *laissez-faire* or socialist planning. Claims that an entirely private enterprise system could have produced a better result cannot be disproved, but they lack credibility.[11] By the 1960s housing ceased to be an area of hardship and became a mark of West German affluence. The nature of the house-building programme meant that rents remained relatively low, and as a proportion of household income they were substantially less than in earlier periods. From 1959 to 1967 rent made up on average only a little over 10 per cent of family budgets, whereas the figure had been well over 15 per cent before 1914 and not much less under the Third Reich. It was not until the last decade of the Bonn Republic that housing costs were to rise to something approaching their pre-war proportion of household outgoings. Of course, poorer

---

8. Schulz, *Wiederaufbau in Deutschland*, pp. 210–52.

9. Giersch *et al.*, *Fading Miracle*, p. 84.

10. Schulz, *Wiederaufbau in Deutschland*, pp. 336–7.

11. The suggestion that a system of free rents and private enterprise housing could have 'done the same job, maybe with fewer negative by-products' is made in Giersch *et al.*, *Fading Miracle*, p. 84. It does not seem to be confirmed by the experiences of the United Kingdom and other *laissez-faire* economies in the 1980s. For other details about social housing, see Schulz, *Wiederaufbau in Deutschland*, pp. 335–7, and Hans-Peter Schwarz, *Geschichte der Bundesrepublik Deutschland. Die Ära Adenauer: Epochenwechsel, 1957–1963* (Stuttgart, 1983), p. 164.

households tended to pay a larger proportion of their income in rent than was the case with wealthier ones.[12]

By the early 1960s the housing market could return to something like normal. Housing offices, which had allocated tenants to social housing, were closed. Under a plan introduced in May 1960 by Housing Minister Paul Lücke of the CDU, rent control was abolished by stages and in different localities until it was scheduled to disappear by the end of 1965. Rents rose gradually, and to offset the hardship for the really poor families, *Wohngeld*, or rent allowances, were introduced for those incapable of paying the market rent.[13] This was the implementation of the theories of the social market economy. By the time the CDU left government in 1969, more west Germans were living in decent accommodation than at any time in their history.

Women and the family

Another aspect of Christian democracy which cannot be overlooked is its commitment to strengthening the family. This meant improving the status of women, although not always by means of which the German feminist movement, which had an impressive history reaching back before the First World War, would have approved. After the currency reform of 1948 and the triumph of Erhard's social market economy at the polls the following year, women's position in West Germany had been subject to contradictory pressures. On the one hand, chances for employment were reduced and many women found themselves having to make way for men as the job market shrank. Women civil servants could be dismissed if it was demonstrable that their husbands had an adequate income. Outweighing this, however, was the improvement in the quality of life created by better supplies of food and consumer goods. Sinister diseases associated with privation, such as typhus and TB, were overcome.[14] Most

12. D. Saalfeld, 'Mieten und Wohnungsabgaben in Deutschland 1880–1980', in G. Schulz (ed.), *Wohnungspolitik im Sozialstaat. Deutsche und Europäische Lösungen, 1918–1960* (Düsseldorf, 1993), p. 202. In 1988 the poorest citizens of the Federal Republic, with earnings of less than 800 D-Marks per month, spent 40 per cent of their income on rent, whereas for those in the wealthiest category, only 11.1 per cent of their incomes went on rent. See Führer, 'Managing Scarcity', p. 354.

13. Führer, 'Managing Scarcity', p. 348.

14. K.-J. Ruhl, *Frauen in der Nachkriegszeit 1945–1963* (Munich, 1988), p. 107. The dismissal of female civil servants to make way for men was based on the Nazi Officials' Law of 1937; ibid., pp. 74–7.

omen seem to have been happy to retire into the normalcy of
amily life, even if conditions were still difficult, and even though
ie excess of women over men meant that many were forced to live
ndependently of male partners.

The Adenauer government established a Family Ministry under
ranz-Josef Wuermeling of the CDU, a ministry strongly influenced
y pressure groups associated with the Roman Catholic and protest-
nt churches. The main aims of the ministry were to overcome the
ousing shortage and encourage home ownership, to provide finan-
ial support for families through tax relief and family allowances, to
rotect morals and to encourage large families. As we have seen, the
overnment was to be highly successful in overcoming the housing
roblem. So far as family allowances were concerned, the Christian
emocrats wanted to help larger families, but not as pensioners of
ie state, since 'our children are not children of the state but chil-
ren of the family'.

This was a conscious differentiation of the Bonn Republic's view
f the family from that of racist nazis on the one hand and Ulbricht's
ommunists on the other. In November 1954 the CDU/CSU pushed
irough a family allowance system which paid allowances indirectly
irough a 'family equalization payments office' which they hoped
ould be run by private organizations so that the money would not
ppear to come directly from the federal budget. Only families with
t least three children would benefit, children after the second be-
ig paid for at DM25 per month. This figure was increased in sub-
equent years, and in 1961 an official Child Allowance Office was
stablished to deal with the payments. So, under Christian Democratic
uspices, an important element of the welfare state was established
i west Germany.[15]

Even more important were changes in German civil law which be-
efited women. This was the result of the stipulations in the Basic
aw noted in the previous chapter.[16] Under the old Civil Law Code
hich had been drawn up towards the end of the nineteenth cen-
iry, men were given authority within the family. A wife was required
y law to look after her family and could not take up employment
ithout her husband's permission. Property and wealth accumulated
uring the marriage belonged to the husband. On the other hand,
 the husband could not keep himself in the manner to which he
as accustomed, the wife had a duty to go out to work to help him,

15. Ibid., pp. 110, 135–6.
16. See above, Chapter 4.

despite having to run the household as well. Divorce was based on
the concept of guilt. If the wife left home she lost everything, including rights over her children.

In July 1957 a measure of reform was introduced which meant
that wealth or property acquired during marriage were to be jointly
owned by husband and wife. The latter was also able to go out to
work if this was compatible with her household responsibilities – in
other words, she was not dependent on her husband's permission.
Nevertheless, the aim of the law remained to protect an ideal of marriage in which a housewife remained at home to look after husband
and children. In 1959 an important decision of the federal Constitutional Court ruled that it was unconstitutional to grant fathers
sole custody of children, and that decisions about child welfare had
to be taken jointly by both parents.[17] All this seemed compatible
with the Christian Democratic ideal of a protected family, in which
women's rights would be strong enough to ensure the happy up-
bringing of children.

But at the same time, in the 1950s another aspect of west German womanhood came to the fore – the so-called 'woman miracle'
(*Frauenwunder*). This was a favourite topic with popular illustrated
magazines, even including such political heavyweights as the *Spiegel*.
The American *Time* magazine also noted with approval the change
in German females from the frumpy, overweight Brunhilda type to
the chic and attractive Americanized women who featured increasingly in the fashion and society pages. During the occupation period
church authorities and male-dominated educational establishments
had tried to resist this Americanizing trend, and women were up-
braided for yielding too easily – and too literally – to the embrace
of Anglo-Saxon occupiers.[18] By the middle of the 1950s, however, this
particular battle had been lost: women took pride in their appearance as well as in their homes, and the model they chose to imitate
was an American one, transmitted to them by Hollywood films and
Madison Avenue advertising. In this, women were no different from
their menfolk, relatively few of whom were able to visit the USA
but most of whom believed living standards there to be far higher

17. Eva Kolinsky, *Women in Contemporary Germany. Life, Work and Politics* (2nd edn
Oxford, 1993), pp. 48–9.
18. M. Höhn, 'Frau im Haus und Girl im *Spiegel*. Discourse on Women in the
Interregnum Period, 1945–49, and the Question of German Identity', in *Central
European History*, Vol. 26, No. 1 (1993), 57–90. One – unjust – sneer by German men
at their womenfolk was: 'it took the Allies six years to defeat the German men, but
German women fought for less than five minutes': ibid., p. 59. Ultimately the women
gained a greater victory than any their menfolk had achieved.

than in Germany.[19] Despite disapproving noises from conservative clergy and left-wing intelligentsia, the mass of the population began to enjoy the new prosperity of the consumer society. It provided them with a personal form of expression free from bureaucratic interference or hierarchical intimidation.

Agriculture

The desire on the part of Christian Democratic politicians to protect the family extended even more strongly to the position of family farmers in agriculture. There had always been something slightly mystical in the way in which German conservative circles regarded the family farm, symbolizing as it did a way of life rather than just an economic activity.[20] Even the FDP shrank from insisting on the application of liberal economic principles to agriculture, and Erhard's Ministry of Economics had no authority over it. The farmers' lobby, or 'Green Front', was highly organized in west Germany. The fact that the East Elbian estate owners, who had exerted a dispropor-tionate influence over agricultural policy in the Weimar period, had now been dispossessed and uprooted by the Soviet authorities or the Poles, meant that the interests of relatively small or medium producers were paramount. Farmers were particularly important electorally in some *Länder*, such as Bavaria or Baden-Württemberg, and they were influential as pressure groups within the CDU, CSU and FDP. The Federal Republic therefore carried on a system of agri-cultural protection and subvention which was not dissimilar to that operated by the Third Reich. Although rationing for consumers was ended quickly, imports were strictly controlled, and protection for the agricultural sector was built into the system.[21]

One reason for this was a concern for social peace in the coun-tryside. Another was a general horror of food shortages inherited from the immediate postwar period, a sentiment which inclined politicians to prefer paying well over the world market price for food if self-sufficiency, or something like it, could be sustained. Even

19. See information on public opinion surveys given by A. Sywottek, 'The Amer-icanization of Everyday Life? Early Trends in Consumer and Leisure-Time Behaviour', in M. Ermath (ed.), *America and the Shaping of German Society, 1945–1955* (Oxford, 1993), p. 152.

20. H. Kötter, 'Die Landwirtschaft', in W. Conze and M.R. Lepsius (eds), *Sozial-geschichte der Bundesrepublik Deutschland. Beiträge zum Kontinuitätsproblem* (2nd edn, Stuttgart, 1985), p. 116.

21. Kötter, 'Landwirtschaft', p. 123.

industrialists, who might have been expected to demand lower food prices, were happy with protection if it afforded them access to European Community markets.[22] There was also the widespread view that the rural section of the community was not keeping pace with the prosperity of the industrial sector, and that this should be counteracted by government action. Already the Federal Republic employed a smaller proportion of its people on the land than had been the case for Germany before the war – one in five as against one in four – and with growing opportunities in urban areas the numbers were bound to shrink further. In the election campaign of 1953 all major parties urged support for agriculture, and in September 1955 a bill was introduced into the Bundestag committing the government to present an annual 'Green Plan' of measures to support the farmers, measures which would include tax concessions, assistance with investment and social welfare benefits for the rural population.[23]

These measures, which were later subsumed into the Common Agricultural Policy of the EEC, certainly enabled west German farmers to enjoy one of the most prosperous periods in their history. They continued to meet two-thirds of domestic food needs (three-quarters if animal fodder is included) until well into the 1980s. They enjoyed artificially inflated prices and were encouraged to modernize their production methods. Many smaller producers used their farms as a base from which to engage in other forms of economic activity, so that they were no longer vulnerable to fluctuations in the food market. Despite government help, the numbers directly involved in agriculture continued to fall; by the last decade of the Bonn Republic only about 5 per cent of the working population was employed in agriculture. But the measures taken by government, measures which aroused remarkably little domestic controversy, smoothed the transition, so that – despite occasional rumblings – the farming lobby did not represent the alienated sector which had troubled the Weimar Republic in the late 1920s.[24]

Equalization of burdens

There were other pressing social problems which could not be overlooked. Measures had to be taken to meet the needs of those

22. G. Hendriks, *Germany and European Integration. The Common Agricultural Policy. an Area of Conflict* (New York, 1991), pp. 75–81.

23. Ibid., p. 37.

24. Cf. Kötter, 'Landwirtschaft', pp. 115–39.

who had suffered special hardship as the result of the war and its aftermath. The millions of German refugees who could not return to their former homelands behind the iron curtain organized themselves into effective political groups. In particular, the nationalistically inclined *Bund der Heimatvertriebenen und Entrechteten* (BHE) fought elections in the *Länder* with considerable success. There was also a strong refugee element in the CDU which threatened to break away and join forces with the BHE if nothing was done to meet the needs of refugees. The issue was complicated by a general commitment, made by political parties at the time of the currency reform in 1948, to achieve a more equal distribution of the burdens of hardship arising from the war and postwar inflation.

The result was the *Lastenausgleich* (equalization of burdens) law which was passed by the Bundestag in May 1952. This mainly benefited refugees and took the form, not of any serious redistribution of wealth or property, but of a relatively mild tax on wealth, the proceeds from which would be distributed to those most damaged by the war. Small claims could be paid in full, but larger losses would only be met up to a maximum of 2 per cent. The process of claiming the money was lengthy and bureaucratic. Nevertheless, by the end of 1971 about 82.8 billion marks had been paid out, 67 per cent of which had gone to refugees and 20 per cent to war wounded. The *Lastenausgleich* bitterly disappointed the Social Democrats, who were demanding more radical measures to overcome the injustices created by the currency reform. But the government's measures were practical, and demonstrated to the refugees that the new Republic could take action on their behalf. They helped to reconcile many of them to Adenauer's government.[25]

The problem of former nazis

Others who needed to be reconciled to the new democracy were the large numbers of middle- and upper middle-class Germans who had supported Hitler's Third Reich. As we have seen, Allied attempts to denazify Germany had not been very successful. Many former members of the NSDAP and its associated organizations were well-educated and articulate people who could be relied upon to cause trouble if they were not integrated into the new pluralistic

25. For a rather critical view of the *Lastenausgleich*, see Rupp, *Politische Geschichte*, pp. 124–5. For total cost, see Schwarz, *Ära Adenauer, 1949–1957*, pp. 166–9.

parliamentary system. On the other hand, relatively few of such people were fanatical nazis and, if offered a sufficient share of the loaves and the fishes in the Federal Republic, might be expected to bed down without too much trouble in a socially conservative, economically successful, West German state.

Adenauer's government allowed them to do this. In May 1951 the Bundestag passed a law reinstating 150,000 officials and public employees who had lost their positions as a result of denazification. Public administrations at federal, *Land* and municipal level were forced to set aside 20 per cent of their salary budgets to pay for such people. On the other hand, officials and employees who had been cleared of nazi associations received no such protection and were less likely to be appointed. Ministries and other public bodies had to meet quotas of such former nazi appointees before they could take on anybody else. When in March 1951 the west Germans were allowed once again to set up their own Foreign Office, almost two-thirds of the staff were former members of the NSDAP.[26]

Adenauer himself was notably unfussy about the involvement of his associates with Hitler's movement so long as they had not been obviously prominent nazis and so long as they were loyal to him. In 1953 he appointed as his personal state secretary and troubleshooter in the federal chancellery, Hans Globke, an official who had drawn up a commentary on the notorious Nuremberg race laws which enshrined discrimination against the Jews in 1935. Globke remained a faithful henchman of Adenauer throughout his career as chancellor.

This apparent myopia towards the recent past was, of course, aided by the Cold War, which seemed to present an immediate totalitarian threat of a very different kind. Former nazis were only too happy to commit themselves to a campaign against communism. If parliamentary democracy was the only state form on offer which could protect them against 'bolshevism', most of them were willing to work with it. In a number of areas, such as the state intelligence services, ex-nazis became influential.

Had Schumacher's SPD been in office in 1950, the continued exclusion of former collaborators in the Third Reich might have been continued, with the result that a disaffected minority of articulate and often well-to-do citizens would have been irrevocably opposed to the new regime. By adopting a more tolerant attitude, Adenauer's government defused this potential opposition and encouraged those concerned to support the coalition parties.

26. Rupp, *Politische Geschichte*, p. 118.

Public attitudes to the nazi past

However, it has to be said that the influence of such persons on public life in Germany in the 1950s was far from healthy. It encouraged an attitude inclined to forget the recent past or indeed to blame Germany's enemies for contemporary problems. Had they not, after all, been the allies of Stalin? Such views came to the fore in strident demands that gaoled war criminals should be released and that the *Wehrmacht* should be publicly recognized as honourable, free from responsibility for atrocities committed during the war. The Free Democrats and the Deutsche Partei, but also sections of the CSU and even the CDU, were vocal in this campaign.

In schools and universities, those who had collaborated with the Third Reich were either reinstated or had not been removed in the first place. This was particularly true of such faculties as law and medicine. Most of the judiciary and much of the higher civil service remained as it had been during the Third Reich. If awkward questions were asked about this at all, the usual claim was that professors or judges had not been serious members of the NSDAP and that they had gone along with the regime to prevent worse happening if they resigned. Even the version of recent history which was presented to young Germans by their teachers was curiously apologetic. National socialism was presented as an aberration to be blamed on unGerman 'mass politics' and the hypnotic personality of Adolf Hitler. There were striking exceptions to this complacent doctrine, such as the veteran historian Friedrich Meinecke who, in his courageous and illuminating book *Die deutsche Katastrophe* (*The German Catastrophe*, 1946), insisted that the Germans should look to the history of their own spiritual and national development when explaining Hitler's rise to power. But the general tendency was either to ignore the Third Reich or to bracket it with Stalin's Russia as a form of totalitarianism. Public opinion polls suggested that there was still a substantial minority willing to vote for somebody like Hitler; in 1952 32 per cent of those asked described him as an admirable leader who had made a few mistakes.[27] Even as late as 1961 more west Germans were negative than positive in their judgements about the resistance to Hitler in the Second World War.

There were, however, intellectual forces at work which would soon

---

27. Ibid., p. 91, citing K.D. Bracher, *Die deutsche Diktatur. Entstehung, Struktur, Folgen des Nationalsozialismus* (Cologne, 1969), p. 519.

challenge this complacency. Most important was the attraction of the United States, where many young German academics received an introduction to western scholarly methods – including those developed by refugees from Hitler's Germany. The establishment of research institutes, such as the Institute of Contemporary History in Munich or the Centre for the Study of Nazism in Hamburg, meant that serious, objective investigations into the Third Reich and its origins began to be undertaken. But the results of this research did not have much impact until the end of the decade.

The Federal Republic and the Jews

One matter which remained a looming shadow over the reputation and self-esteem of the new Germany was the fate of the Jews during the Second World War. It took a very considerable time for the true horror of nazi policies towards the Jews to penetrate into the public mind, not least because many of those involved were determined to forget about it. Anti-semitism of a low-key variety remained common amongst the West German population. Before 1949 the Allies had insisted that individual Jews could make claims for restitution against the German *Land* governments, but this only applied to German Jews resident in the country at the time of persecution. The much wider issue of compensation for the millions of Jews whose families had been destroyed and who had been uprooted from their homes throughout Europe was not addressed. As early as 1941 the Jewish World Congress had raised the possibility that Germany should pay an indemnity to the Jews, but this had not even been accepted by the Allies, let alone the Germans themselves.

Early in 1951, when it was clear that the Federal Republic was likely to regain sovereignty more rapidly than had at first been thought, the Israeli government wrote to the four victor powers demanding that Germany be made to pay one and a half billion dollars as a debt to Israel for accommodating Jewish refugees who had escaped from occupied Europe. This elicited no reply from the Soviet Union and only sympathetic noises from western governments.

Adenauer himself took the courageous step of expressing west German contrition by negotiating a settlement with Israel according to which the Federal Republic would pay compensation to the Israelis and to international Jewish organizations for the crimes committed by Hitler's regime against European Jewry. On 27 September 1951 he told the Bundestag that the whole German nation was not responsible for the crimes against the Jews committed by the national socialists, but that he was ready to accept a German responsibility for restitution. Such a proposal was popular neither in Germany nor in Israel, and the negotiations had to be conducted in great secrecy. There were many powerful reasons for not tackling the issue at all; Adenauer's government was not under serious pressure from the western Allies to compensate Israel, which had not existed at the time of the Third Reich. There was also the problem that Bonn was negotiating with the Allied powers for a final settlement of Germany's outstanding war debts, and to offer large sums to Israel might damage Germany's claims for lenient treatment from her other debtors. However, after secret meetings with the President of the Jewish Claims Conference, Nahum Goldmann, Adenauer insisted, in the face of considerable domestic resistance, that the settlement with Israel be finalized. The Federal Republic should pay three billion marks to Israel over eight to twelve years, plus 450 million marks for distribution to Jewish organizations. All payments were to be in goods rather than money.

Although bankers like Hermann Abs and the Finance Minister, Schäffer, claimed that this was beyond their country's capacities, Ludwig Erhard pointed out that the expanding German economy would be able to provide the manufactured goods required, and that their export might even help German industry. His optimism was justified. The fact that the Israeli merchant fleet was equipped with German vessels, for example, did not do any harm to west German shipbuilders. Despite these beneficial spin-offs, the extent to which the Federal Republic honoured a debt to the Jews which had been incurred by another and very different regime deserves respect. Apart from the deliveries to Israel, compensation paid by West Germany to individual Jewish victims had reached the colossal sum of 80 billion marks by 1980.[28] The behaviour of other countries was less honourable. It was perhaps only to be expected that Ulbricht's GDR, controlled as it was by a rapacious Soviet Union, would refuse to pay anything, but the response of Austria, so many of whose citizens had participated with enthusiasm in the campaign against the Jews, was also niggardly and belated.

Adenauer evidently sincerely believed that there was a moral obligation involved, although doubtless he also appreciated that a gesture to the Jews would improve West Germany's image abroad.

28. Günther Gillessen, *Adenauer and Israel* (The Konrad Adenauer Memorial Lecture, Oxford, 1986), p. 17.

But it was noteworthy that parliamentary support for the measure came more wholeheartedly from the Social Democratic opposition than from the coalition parties. When the matter was put to the Bundestag on 18 March 1953 less than half of the 239 members in favour of the settlement came from the government side, whereas about 90 government supporters abstained or voted against the measure. Amongst those abstaining was Franz-Josef Strauss.[29]

Adenauer's electoral success, 1953

As the first Bundestag drew to its end, in the summer of 1953, it was clear that Adenauer's coalition had weathered its most serious storms. The economy was not only booming, it was beginning to satisfy consumer demand in a fashion not witnessed in Germany since the late 1920s. The Federal Republic had ceased to be just an object of foreign control and had started to play a role in foreign affairs, as we shall see below. Furthermore, the Korean crisis, and the increasingly repressive nature of the regime in the German Democratic Republic, meant that the public was more and more inclined to seek safety under the wings of the American-led Western Alliance. Adenauer's party, and not the opposition, stood to gain by that. In particular, the CDU began to be associated with stability in conservative protestant circles, which perceived Adenauer's more strident nationalist critics to be endangering the security of bourgeois Germany. It was the moment when the Prussian *Bildungsbürgertum* lost its innocence; when faced with a choice between idealism and material interest, it chose the latter. The choice was a wise one.

The death of Stalin on 5 March 1953 might have been expected to encourage a more flexible approach to the Soviet Union, but the popular uprising which took place in east Berlin and other industrial centres in the GDR on 17 June 1953, and its brutal repression by Soviet tanks, reinforced the popular view that communism was a deadly threat to West Germany's existence. In the Bundestag elections which followed in September 1953, Adenauer relentlessly hammered home the dangers of voting for a Marxist party. Despite the staunch anti-communism of the SPD, he did everything to suggest that to vote for the opposition would be to open the way for communist subversion. 'All Marxist roads lead to Moscow!' was the theme of one election poster. Adenauer also claimed without much

29. Schwarz, *Ära Adenauer, 1949–1953*, p. 186.

foundation that SPD functionaries were receiving funds from east Berlin. The combination of anti-Soviet feelings and the recognition that economic life was improving rallied the electorate behind the CDU/CSU. Adenauer's party became the first in German history to win an overall majority of the seats in a parliamentary election, although it had received only just over 45 per cent of the votes cast. In percentage terms the SPD and the FDP fell back slightly, but the real losers were the smaller parties of the left and right or those representing regional interests; for them the newly introduced 5 per cent hurdle proved fatal. Whereas in the 1949 Bundestag 80 out of 402 seats had been won by smaller parties, in the second Bundestag elected in 1953 only 45 were gained by such parties and eighteen of those, three for the Centre and fifteen for the DP, were the result of combined lists with the CDU, a circumstance which made them virtual dependencies of Adenauer's party. The Communists, the Bavarian and Schleswig-Holstein parties dropped out altogether. Only the BHE refugee party just managed to scrape in under its own steam with 5.9 per cent. West Germany had achieved a stable, conservative government which evidently could command the acceptance, if not the affection, of most of its electorate – the turnout for the elections had been nearly 86 per cent. For Adenauer himself it was a personal triumph and illustrated the fact that by 1953 popular confidence in his leadership had consolidated itself. Before that year as many – and sometimes more – West Germans had been dissatisfied with his policies as had supported them. Thereafter until the end of the decade public opinion polls showed a healthy surplus of supporters over opponents.

Despite his greatly strengthened position, Adenauer continued the small coalition with the Free Democrats and the DP, and shrewdly extended his cabinet to include a leader of the BHE, the controversial ex-nazi, Theodor Oberländer, who became Minister for Refugees. This gave Adenauer the two-thirds majority he would need to enable him to establish a West German army, and the necessary amendment to the Basic Law was passed by the Bundestag in February 1954. In the same year attempts at four-power negotiations to end the Cold War failed and the provisional west German state looked even more permanent. Adenauer's tough-minded and consistent foreign policy, to be described in the next chapter, was beginning to bear fruit. For the public at large, however, the joy at seeing West Germany unexpectedly winning the 1954 World Cup football competition in Switzerland probably outweighed many other aspects of West Germany's consolidation, including her balance of payments surplus in

the European Payments Union and the prospect of entering NATO
as an equal partner with her former victors. On 5 May 1955 the
High Commissioners of France, the United Kingdom and the United
States signed a proclamation declaring that the Federal Republic
was no longer an occupied state. It was not the end of the world
war for Germany, but it was the beginning of a new phase in her
postwar development.

CHAPTER SIX

West Germany Achieves Sovereignty

Adenauer and the Allies

Despite all the vexing domestic problems that the Bonn Republic had to face – the need to establish loyal institutions and to rebuild its economy, the huge numbers of refugees from the east and the problem of former nazis – the real issue which faced Adenauer when he took up office as chancellor was a diplomatic one. How could he restore German sovereignty without making sacrifices which might return to haunt Germany in the future? In some ways Adenauer was aided by the limitations imposed upon the Federal Republic by the Occupation Statute, which the Allies had insisted the west Germans should accept before regaining any independence. This meant that German foreign policy would have to be conducted in agreement with the occupying western powers, whose governors were now described as High Commissioners. The military men, Clay, Koenig and Robertson, were replaced by civilian officials such as John Jay McCloy, André François-Poncet and Sir Ivone Kirkpatrick, but in foreign affairs the west Germans remained subordinate to their erstwhile conquerors. At first there was no foreign minister and only an embryonic Foreign Ministry.

This situation was, in fact, tailor-made for Adenauer because it meant that he alone controlled the Federal Republic's foreign policy. He once remarked that the only minister he could trust in his cabinet was the Minister for Foreign Affairs – who was, of course, himself.

Konrad Adenauer's foreign policy was systematically devoted to establishing the sovereignty of West Germany and her acceptance as an equal partner in the Western Alliance. During the Weimar Republic Germany had been generally isolated in foreign affairs, despite a period of synthetic bonhomie associated with the Locarno Treaties of 1925 and Germany's entry into the League of Nations the following year. Weimar foreign policy had been characterized by a series of oscillations between a sensible, but unpopular and necessarily half-hearted, attempt to conciliate the western powers, favoured by Gustav Stresemann, and an understandable but misguided attempt to enlist the Soviet Union on Germany's side. This was exemplified in the Rapallo Treaty of 1922 and subsequent trade treaties with the Russians, not to mention clandestine co-operation with the Red Army.

There would have been a natural temptation in Germany after 1945 to play off the Soviet Union against the western powers in order to attain German unification or at least some form of independence from both sides. During the 1950s, support for this type of *Schaukelpolitik* (see-saw or swing politics) was sometimes implied in the criticisms levelled at Adenauer's foreign policy by critics among the Social Democrats or the more nationalistic liberals in the FDP.

It was one of Adenauer's great achievements that he established the reputation for absolute reliability and unswerving commitment to the West. This was partly due to his own distaste for Russia, which he saw as a threat to Germany both as the home of bolshevism and as a restless Slavonic giant, whose perpetual expansion had already threatened western Europe before 1914.[1] Therefore Adenauer followed a consistent western policy, supporting NATO, accepting the need for a German military contribution to western defence, and doing all he could to further moves towards western European integration.

This did not mean, of course, that he acted from some sort of selfless supranational European idealism. In the field of defence, for example, Adenauer was quite clear that West Germany needed to be rearmed. Partly this was due to a genuine fear of the Soviet Union and a pessimistic belief that sooner or later war would be inevitable. He was also very concerned about the mischief which Ulbricht might initiate with his paramilitary *Volkspolizei*, a fear which became widespread in the summer of 1950, when the Korean War broke out. Western Europe was generally regarded as defenceless, and the French High Commissioner even suggested that the federal government should prepare itself for exile in Canada. Adenauer declared

1. Hans-Peter Schwarz, 'Adenauer and Russia', in *Adenauer at Oxford: The Konrad Adenauer Memorial Lectures*, St Antony's College, Oxford, and the Konrad Adenauer Stiftung (Oxford, 1983), pp. 26–7.

he would stay at his desk and await the Russians' arrival, but the fear of Soviet attack, either then or at the latest in 1952, remained very strong.[2]

The outbreak of the Korean War was certainly a fillip for the cause of German rearmament, but Adenauer had been committed to this in his mind for several years. He regarded it as essential for a sovereign state to possess the means of self-defence, a *Wehrmacht*. He wanted West Germany to be on terms of equality, at least with her European neighbours, and that meant creating a German army. Later on he even hoped to gain access to the charmed circle of powers controlling nuclear armaments, a goal which – perhaps fortunately – escaped him. Yet this did not mean that he was simply a ravanchist reactionary hoping to recreate Germany's former military glory. Adenauer had no high opinion of military leaders, having noted their subservience to Hitler in the Third Reich. He was determined that any new German army should be under civilian control.

For the time being all his objectives, except that of nuclear armament, chimed in with those of the Anglo-Saxon powers, and particularly the USA. The Americans wanted a German contribution to the defence of the West; they were themselves trying to further western European integration to strengthen the Western Alliance and help relieve Washington of financial burdens. They were also suspicious of any German attempts to initiate independent relations with the Soviet Union. Since Adenauer retained control over foreign policy by acting as his own foreign minister, there was no danger of ambivalent signals coming from Bonn. The Federal Republic was given permission in March 1951 to reopen its own Foreign Ministry, but it was not until 1955 that a separate Foreign Minister, Heinrich von Brentano, was appointed and even then he was kept firmly under Adenauer's thumb. Foreign policy remained the prerogative of *der Alte*, at least so far as high politics were concerned, until he left office in 1963.

Adenauer had already gained the high regard of the Truman administration when he had represented the Parliamentary Council to the Allied military governors in 1948–49. His parliamentary triumphs over the raucous and apparently anti-American Kurt Schumacher also counted in his favour. After the election of Dwight D. Eisenhower as president in the autumn of 1952, Adenauer's identification with American policy became even stronger. He was a great favourite of

2. Hans-Peter Schwarz, *Adenauer. Der Aufstieg 1876–1952* (3rd edn, Stuttgart, 1991), pp. 747 and passim.

the Republican Secretary of State, John Foster Dulles, and, in so far as Adenauer had a sentimental attachment to any politician, he seems to have regarded Dulles with genuine personal warmth. For the next few years Bonn was seen from Washington as the ideal ally, socially conservative, economically liberal and staunchly anti-communist. Adenauer did not necessarily trust the Americans, but he was impressed by their power and determined to retain their support in Europe.

In addition, however, Adenauer struck out in a new direction for German foreign policy, namely a systematic attempt to improve relations with France, and to further the cause of European integration. It should be remembered that the Basic Law of the Federal Republic, with which Adenauer was particularly associated as the former president of the Parliamentary Council, committed the German people in its preamble to membership of a united Europe, and under Article 24 the Federal Republic was empowered to transfer sovereignty to supranational institutions. It was this *Westpolitik* which was to prove such a successful feature of Bonn diplomacy. In Adenauer, the Rhinelander who had experienced the disaster of passive resistance to the French occupation of the Ruhr in 1923, the Federal Republic had a leader who could pursue it with consistency and determination. It was not an easy option, given the understandable fears of the French, who had so recently been defeated and occupied by the Germans.

There was also a particular bone of contention which dogged Franco-German relations in the early years of the Federal Republic: the question of the Saar basin. This region, which contained important coal resources, had been treated by the French as separate from the rest of their zone of occupation, and it was clearly their intention to detach it from Germany permanently. Since the population was German in speech and loyalty, this was a serious breach of the principle of self-determination. It was unacceptable to most German political parties, and although Adenauer himself seems to have regarded it as a tiresome problem in Franco-German relations, even he could not ignore the domestic consequences of too many concessions to the French on this matter. Apart from anything else, the creation of a permanent French Protectorate in the Saar would undermine Germany's case for the re-examination of Polish occupation of German areas east of the Oder–Neisse frontier, since it would pre-empt the peace treaty without which Germany's frontiers were not supposed to be permanently altered.[3] It was one of Adenauer's

3. Ibid., pp. 690–9.

greatest achievements that he managed to create a new relationship with Paris, despite all the historical enmity between the two peoples and despite the constant irritant of the Saar issue.

Well before he became Chancellor, Adenauer had opened up contacts with the French and with other European politicians inclined towards some form of European integration. In May 1948 he attended the Congress of the European Movement at The Hague where Edouard Herriot, the former French premier, and Winston Churchill were present. Thereafter Adenauer and other Christian Democrats continued to have confidential meetings with French politicians in Geneva during 1948–49. In October 1948 Adenauer had a long, private discussion with Robert Schuman, the French Foreign Minister, who also happened to have been brought up as a German citizen, since he had been born in Lorraine in 1886. Adenauer urged economic integration as the best method of overcoming France's understandable fears about renewed German aggression. He argued that the people in West Germany were less prone to Marxism and nationalism than those in other parts of the country; this might be caused by the different confessional development in that part of Germany – a reference to the Roman Catholic religion which dominated in France as well as the Rhineland. For his part Schuman made comforting noises about the Saar basin and admitted some mistakes in French occupation policy. More important, the two men seem to have established a basis of cautious trust.[4]

By the time the Federal Republic was founded it was clear that the CDU was the main exponent of European integration in Germany. The SPD and the FDP were both luke-warm or even hostile. Schumacher was certainly not attracted by any sort of alignment which might compromise German unity; he had not even attended the European gathering in The Hague in May 1948. Generally speaking, the push for integration came amongst the Christian Democratic, Roman Catholic countries of continental Europe. The Council of Europe, a forum for western European debate which had aroused hopes amongst the federalists when it first met in August 1949, was divided between the British and the Scandinavians on the one hand, who wanted only inter-governmental co-operation, and the six west European countries – Benelux, France, Germany and Italy – whose leaders wanted supranational integration, on the other. When it became obvious that the British and the Scandinavians would not support serious integration, the other six countries were inclined to move forward on their own.

4. Ibid., pp. 561–3.

Nevertheless, in the first year of the Federal Republic's existence, Adenauer and his colleagues did not seem to be particularly well disposed to the French. He and François-Poncet, the French High Commissioner, were locked in a series of rows over the control of heavy industry in the Ruhr and the vexed issue of the Saar. To observers with memories of the inter-war period, like US High Commissioner McCloy, things seemed to be developing in as unhelpful a manner as they had in the early 1920s. Adenauer was determined to improve West Germany's inferior status and the French were equally determined to hold the Germans down, an enterprise viewed sympathetically by the Anglo-Saxon occupiers, even though they did not always approve of French methods.

Nor did some embarrassing manifestations of nationalism in the new Federal parliament reassure the western Allies. The constant demands for an end to the punishment of war criminals, or the statement by a DP deputy in the Bundestag doubting that the mass murder of the Jews had ever taken place, seemed to suggest that German nationalism would be as dangerous as ever were it allowed to revive.[5] For his part, Adenauer was a genuine patriot and wished to eliminate foreign control from his country. But even had he been willing to submit meekly to the Allies, the nationalist posturing of the SPD and some of his own coalition partners would have forced him to adopt a more intransigent tone than he might have wished. The Americans therefore had to pin their rather meagre hopes on the French. If they could offer a solution to the issue of Ruhr heavy industry, the pro-western elements in the German government might be able to hold the initiative in Bonn.

The Schuman Plan

The first major step came with the Schuman Plan in May 1950. The aim of the scheme was to create a European coal and steel pool, with market rules administered by a supranational European authority. It is important to remember that the basis of this plan was Franco-German collaboration, and that it met the national needs of both the French and the Germans. Schuman had already informed Adenauer of his intentions in a confidential letter before he announced his Plan, and he would have known that Adenauer would welcome the

---

5. See, for example, Thomas Alan Schwartz, *America's Germany. John J. McCloy and the Federal Republic of Germany* (Cambridge, Mass., 1991), pp. 87, 298.

principles underlying it. The Plan specifically mentioned pooling Franco-German iron and steel resources, and Schuman made it clear that it could go ahead even if only France and west Germany participated in it. For the French, the Plan removed the nightmare of West German economic domination once the occupation era had passed; for the Germans, it meant a step towards equality of status and almost certainly the end of the hated International Authority for the Ruhr. But for both parties it was seen as a move towards genuine political integration.

For this reason British participation was not very keenly sought, since London was evidently unenthusiastic about such a policy. The British government duly rejected the Plan, and the six countries carried it forward, with the support of the USA. The American High Commissioner, John McCloy, knew and admired Jean Monnet, the French businessman who was the real architect of the Schuman Plan, and thoroughly approved of his initiative. The European Coal and Steel Community was established by treaty on 18 April 1951.

This was a very significant development in European and west German history. The Schuman Plan was based on Franco-German co-operation, and it was aimed, not just at limited industrial collaboration, but at the 'establishment of common bases for economic development as the first step in the federation of Europe'.[6] Adenauer was initially suspicious of the French, but Monnet convinced him of their good intentions and persuaded him to appoint as chief German negotiator, not a self-interested Ruhr industrialist, but a distinguished professor of international law, Walter Hallstein. Adenauer now came out wholeheartedly in support of the Plan; the opposition only grudgingly accepted it.[7] This meant that if it succeeded the Christian Democrats would reap the political benefits.

The European Defence Community and German rearmament

The next European initiative related to defence. As we have seen, the continued, and apparently very real, threat from the Soviet Union and its East German satellite had created a common view between

---

6. D.W. Urwin, *The Community of Europe: A History of European Integration since 1945* (London, 1991), p. 46.

7. Schumacher indeed privately disliked the Plan, both because it would seal the division of Germany and because it would create a 'Europe of the Managers' rather than a socialist Europe. Schwartz, *America's Germany*, p. 111.

Adenauer and the Anglo-Saxon Allies that Germany should be rearmed and should make a substantial contribution to western defence. When, in September 1950, the three western Allies met in New York to discuss their future military policy, the American and British military authorities were pressing for a German army of fifteen to twenty active divisions, and the British General Staff even went so far as to envisage a tactical German air force.[8] The Anglo-Americans were ready to accept West German membership of NATO so long as German forces were integrated in the Alliance and not under independent national command.

But these plans were easier to adumbrate than to implement. They faced very serious political obstacles. The first was the aversion to German rearmament on the part of the French, who flatly rejected the Anglo-American schemes. The French political establishment was not yet ready to swallow a German army. The second was sensitivity amongst the public in Germany to any suggestion of rearmament. Adenauer, who had been discreetly preparing for rearmament since before he became Chancellor, was aware of this and had therefore kept even his cabinet colleagues in the dark about military developments. When, at the end of August 1950, he drew up a memorandum for High Commissioner McCloy which he could use to present the West German case to the Allies at their deliberations in New York, he immediately ran into trouble with his Minister of the Interior, the former mayor of Essen, Gustav Heinemann, who threatened to resign over Adenauer's promise to provide German divisions for an international west European army – a promise for which Adenauer had no cabinet authority. The fact that Adenauer did not even show his colleagues copies of the memorandum illustrates how sensitive the issue was.[9]

Attempts to get Kurt Schumacher to agree to a bipartisan defence policy had failed; growing popular unrest over the issue made it difficult for the SPD to saddle itself with responsibility for a measure which seemed likely to be bitterly unpopular. Schumacher took the line that, since the western Allies were occupying Germany, it was up to them to defend it. He pledged that the SPD, the party of German patriots, would 'fight against attempts to integrate any part of Germany with other nations in advance of German unification'.[10]

Nor was it only politicians on the left who attacked the concept of

    8. Schwarz, *Adenauer. Der Aufstieg,* p. 751.

    9. Ibid., pp. 764–8.

    10. Lewis J. Edinger, *Kurt Schumacher. A Study in Personality and Political Behaviour* (Berkeley, LA, 1965), p. 172.

West German rearmament; a section of the protestant clergy headed by the influential Pastor Niemöller denounced it as against the will of God, and nationalist elements in the FDP and DP argued that only if the Allied powers released war criminals and gave West Germany an independent *Wehrmacht* could the Germans be expected to participate in western defence.

The only way round these dangerous obstacles seemed to be to approach the matter as a European issue. Adenauer had made a number of statements implying that any west German defence contribution would have to be part of a supranational force, and early in August 1950 the Assembly of the Council of Europe had passed a resolution, warmly supported by Winston Churchill, demanding that a European army be established as soon as possible, with full West German participation. The British government had vetoed this in the Council of Ministers, but the French persisted. They realized that pressure to rearm the Germans would soon be irresistible, and saw the precedent set by the Schuman Plan as a way of restraining the Germans whilst harnessing their power.

Adenauer and the British preferred a more rapid creation of a West German army of about 150,000 men. This could block the threat of aggression from Ulbricht's regime in the GDR, which was making belligerent noises after the outbreak of the Korean War, and which was building up its own armed forces.[11] However, McCloy and Truman were less keen on German rearmament. The former remarked: 'Germany always had two bosses; one the General Staff and the other the Rhine industrialists ... We still have the latter only a little chastened. Let us not take on the other for a while.'[12]

So in September 1950 the Americans had pressed for a package which would include the creation of a German army, but with more American troops in Europe and all continental European forces under one, American, commander. The French government was shocked into action and produced a scheme for an integrated, supranational European army. This proposal, called the Pleven Plan after the French Premier who presented it to the French parliament on 24 October 1950, envisaged a European defence community (EDC) headed by a European Defence Minister responsible to a

---

11. The notion that the East Germans would fulfil the role of the North Koreans in the scheme of Soviet aggression did not seem too fanciful. Ulbricht claimed that the East Germans did not need to build a new seaport of their own, since they would soon control Hamburg and Lübeck. Schwartz, *America's Germany*, pp. 125–6, 135–5.

12. Ibid., p. 123.

supranational control body. It was specifically envisaged as a further step towards political integration. However, from the German point of view it had serious disadvantages: the Federal Republic would be in an inferior position to other countries since its army would be entirely controlled by the supranational leadership, whereas the other European countries could keep some of their forces for purely national purposes.

Although Adenauer welcomed the EDC Plan, he and his military advisers pressed hard to modify it so that West German forces should be on an equal footing with those of other member states. He stipulated that when the scheme came into operation West Germany's status as an occupied country should cease, and the Federal Republic should obtain full sovereignty. It might indeed seem that Adenauer's motive in accepting the creation of German armed forces and in supporting European integration was simply to escape from the controls of the occupation regime. This would be untrue. As we have seen, he was committed to both military defence against the Soviet threat and to the concept of west European integration well before the concrete possibility of trading these policies off against west German independence was on the agenda. What is true is that he was determined not to allow the establishment of a German contribution to NATO and a west European economic community without ensuring that the West Germans would enjoy full equality of status within these frameworks.

Adenauer between East and West

Although Adenauer certainly was a genuine supporter of German rapprochement with France and of European integration, he was always aware that the key to German security lay with the Americans. His first priority was to keep on good terms with Washington and to prevent any inclination among the Americans to withdraw from Europe. His greatest fear was that they might come to some sort of arrangement with the Soviet Union which would undermine German security.

This was Adenauer's greatest nightmare, the return of the 'Potsdam' solution to the problems of Europe at the expense of Germany's vital interests.[13] It would weaken western Europe and encourage the Americans to go home, as they had done after the First World War.

13. Schwarz, *Adenauer. Der Aufstieg*, p. 833.

It would leave Germany vulnerable either to communist subversion or to a renewed outburst of misplaced nationalism.

For the eighteen months after Pleven had announced his plan for a European army, Adenauer struggled to ensure that the EDC treaty should be signed, and that it should be accompanied by recognition on the part of West Germany's occupiers that the Federal Republic was a sovereign state and an equal among the western Allies. Those allies should be required to protect West Germany's security as well as their own. To this end there should be a German armed force, though not an independent German national army, and a vastly strengthened Allied military presence to deter a Soviet attack, thus preventing West Germany becoming the battlefield in a war between East and West. More than 50 western divisions would be required, at least six of them German.

These objectives did not seem at all easy to realize in the autumn of 1951. It was clear that the SPD would oppose both the rearmament of Germany and any commitments to the western Allies which seemed likely to rule out German reunification in the near future. Their doubts were shared by many Free Democrats, who were part of Adenauer's governing coalition, and influential members of his own party, including the Minister for German Questions, Jakob Kaiser, and the leader of the CDU parliamentary delegation, Heinrich von Brentano. The latter occupied a key position so far as Adenauer's support in the Bundestag was concerned, and matters were not made easier by the fact that Brentano himself was eager to take over the post of Foreign Minister in the federal cabinet.

The Soviet response to the prospect of NATO and the European Defence Community was also a cause of anxiety. On 3 November 1950 the Soviet government sent a note to the western Allies urging a conference of foreign ministers to draw up a peace treaty with a demilitarized Germany from which all occupying troops should then be withdrawn. There should be a constituent German assembly made up of representatives from the Federal Republic and the GDR which should prepare the way for a provisional German government. Although Adenauer firmly rejected such offers as being designed to leave Germany a helpless victim of future Soviet aggrandizement, it was clear that amongst sections of the West German intelligentsia the option of trading neutralization for unification was not unattractive, especially if it meant avoiding the necessity of rearmament.

As for the western powers, only the determination of the Americans to block Russian policy, and the crudeness of Soviet methods, prevented Paris and London from entering on the slippery slope of four-power negotiations. Public opinion in Britain and France still disliked the idea of West German rearmament, and the appearance of a neo-nazi political movement, the Socialist Reich Party (SRP), which made electoral gains in Lower Saxony in May 1951, had not served to improve the Federal Republic's image abroad. In particular, the French government had to be concerned about anti-German feeling, given that its own support in the Chamber of Deputies was narrow, and that the Gaullists and Communists were both opposed to concessions towards Bonn.

Repeated offers of unification came from the GDR and Moscow during the period in which Adenauer was trying to press ahead with the Western Treaties. In September 1951 the East German parliament urged the Bundestag to enter into negotiations, and even suggested that there might be free elections within Germany – a concession which seemed to meet one of the major objections to negotiating with the east. This put even strongly anti-communist Social Democrats, like Ernst Reuter, the mayor of Berlin, in a very awkward position.[14] But Adenauer stayed firm, and the Americans backed him up. In later years controversy raged over whether the early 1950s had seen a missed opportunity for unification, sacrificed because Adenauer's conservatism and obsession with western European integration prevented him from negotiating with the Communists. In fact, there is little doubt that Adenauer was right, and that Soviet moves were mainly designed to sow confusion in the west. As Adenauer himself pointed out, the Soviet bloc could hardly liberate the East Germans from its grip without raising dangerous hopes amongst the Czechs, Hungarians, Poles and other subject peoples of the Soviet empire in Eastern Europe. Nor did the fact that the SED-led regime in the GDR was busily sovietizing East German society and establishing a one-party tyranny east of the Elbe chime in with a readiness to envisage unification on genuinely democratic terms.

The battle for sovereignty

In August 1951 serious negotiations began over the revision of the Occupation Statute. It soon became clear that Adenauer's hope of achieving full sovereignty and equality of status with the western

14. Reuter told the American High Commissioner, John McCloy, that if there was a genuine choice between a freely united democratic Germany with neutral status and immediate integration into the West, he would find it difficult not to opt for reunification. Schwarz, *Adenauer. Der Aufstieg*, p. 881.

powers was not going to be fulfilled – the Allies wanted to maintain their right to keep troops in Germany, and even to interfere in domestic politics if these seemed to threaten them. Adenauer knew that he would have to be able to offer a major change in West Germany's status to the Bundestag if the General Treaty (later to be known as the German Treaty) were to be ratified in Bonn. Things looked particularly black because in 1951 polls showed the popularity of Adenauer's federal government to be low, and *Land* election results were anything but encouraging.

Nevertheless, with American help, Adenauer battled on. One area in which success could be registered was that of West Germany's international creditworthiness. When the western Allies had discussed the return of sovereignty to the Federal Republic in September 1950, they had made it clear that this could not occur unless the West Germans satisfied their creditors in the West on the issue of German indebtedness. This applied to debts incurred before the war – such as American loans associated with the Dawes Plan – and to credits extended to west Germany after 1945, including Marshall aid payments and loans from Britain. Although the federal Finance Minister, Schäffer, and the President of the central bank, Wilhelm Vocke, were opposed to putting burdens on the FRG's fragile budget at such an early stage in its career, private banking circles wanted to clarify West Germany's credit position, and Adenauer needed an agreement with the western powers. He left the negotiations in the hands of his trusted acquaintance, Hermann Abs, later to be director of the *Deutsche Bank*. At the debt conference convened in London in February 1952 Abs was able to whittle down the payments expected from West Germany very considerably, and eventually it was agreed that the FRG should pay annuities of DM567 million, rising to DM765 million from 1958. The Germans made it clear that if the question of reparations were to be raised in the future they would not be able to continue their debt repayments. The conference also insisted that all debtors present their claims at that point, so that the west Germans could feel secure in the future.[15]

The upshot of all this was that West Germany was free of the damaging and apparently open-ended debt burdens which had plagued the Weimar Republic. The decision to press ahead with the negotiations proved fully justified; the Federal Republic's economic expansion soon meant that the repayments proved very little problem to

15. Hans-Peter Schwarz, *Die Ära Adenauer: Grunderjahre der Republik, 1949–1957* (Stuttgart, 1981), pp. 181–4.

Bonn, and indeed, at times of embarrassing balance of payments surpluses the FRG was happy to repay the debt prematurely. Had the settlement been delayed, the creditor countries would probably have been far more rapacious than they showed themselves in 1952.

Meanwhile Adenauer pressed ahead with the scheme for a European Defence Community. From October 1951 a delegation headed by Adenauer's putative defence minister, Theodor Blank, negotiated over this case in Paris. At the same time Adenauer himself, supported by the formidable forensic skills of Walter Hallstein, who had negotiated the ECSC package, wrestled with the Allied High Commissioners over the small print of the General Treaty. Adenauer also raised the prestige of the federal government by visits to Paris, Rome and London, at the last of which, in December 1951, he tried to convince Churchill that German unification could only come after the Federal Republic had been firmly integrated into the West.[16] By February 1952, when the death of King George VI gave Adenauer another opportunity to confer with his allies in London, it was clear that the Americans and British were determined to accept Adenauer's policy, though not without driving a hard bargain over such matters as their residual rights in Germany and the costs of stationing troops there. The French, however, remained obstructive. One contemporary joke had it that the French wanted a German army which would be bigger than the Russian but smaller than the French.[17] Only American pressure – made possible by the French need for arms deliveries in respect of their war in Indo-China – prevented Paris torpedoeing the Western Treaties.

Despite another desperate attempt by Stalin on 10 March 1952 to sabotage western policy with his demand for a four-power conference on uniting Germany, Adenauer was able to hold his partners on course, and on 26 May the foreign ministers of the three western Allies met in Bonn to hammer out the final details of the General Treaty which would virtually restore sovereignty to at least the western part of Germany.

This event had been preceded by serious tensions in Bonn itself. In his usual fashion, Adenauer had kept the full details of the treaty from his cabinet and his own parliamentary party until the last possible moment. When he revealed the draft text of the General Treaty there was consternation in his own ranks, since some of his colleagues argued that West Germany should be offered full sovereignty

16. Schwarz, *Adenauer. Der Aufstieg*, p. 894.
17. Fritz René Allemann, *Bonn ist nicht Weimar* (Cologne/Berlin, 1956), p. 192.

with no limitations and no further rights for the occupying powers. Brentano claimed there would be no Bundestag majority for such a treaty. The cabinet, most of whose members were in fact aware of the general tenor of the treaty and were ready to support it, nevertheless instructed the Chancellor to renegotiate one particularly offensive clause (VII,3) of the treaty, which seemed to imply that a future united Germany would have to shoulder the same restrictions and obligations as those accepted by the Federal Republic under the General Treaty.[18]

Adenauer showed extraordinary physical and moral stamina as he chaired a series of lengthy cabinet meetings, held discussions with his parliamentary party and conducted negotiations with the three Allied High Commissioners. He knew that, far from the Germans being likely to win further concessions, the real problem would be that the Allies, and above all the French, would not accept even the draft settlement that was on the table. The French were fundamentally unhappy with the whole concept of German rearmament. They wanted to obtain guarantees against renewed German aggression from the British and the Americans, and although the latter were willing to make reassuring declarations, they could not convince those French politicians who were still obsessed by Anglo-Saxon unhelpfulness in the years between the wars.

On the weekend of 23/25 May 1952, the Allied foreign ministers, Anthony Eden for Britain, Robert Schuman for France and Dean Acheson for the United States, met with Adenauer in Bonn for what had been announced as the conclusion of negotiations. After the General Treaty was signed, the foreign ministers, including Adenauer, would fly to Paris for the signature of the EDC treaty, without which the French would not accept the revision of the Occupation Statute. Schuman, whose political star in Paris was on the wane, seemed gloomy, and it was known that the French cabinet was in session, wrangling over the treaty. At one point the French tried to insert a claim to reparations from Germany into the draft, a manoeuvre which Adenauer was only able to thwart by suggesting that he would make concessions over military dispositions within the EDC treaty.[19]

In Bonn itself the text was far from finalized, and legal hairsplitting continued. To satisfy German critics of the offending clause VII/3 a formula was suggested by Acheson, whereby the rights given by the General Treaty to the Federal Republic would be passed on

18. Schwarz, *Adenauer. Der Aufstieg*, pp. 925–43.
19. Ibid., pp. 950–1.

to a future united Germany so long as it accepted the duties in the treaty as well. Since another clause would prevent the Federal Republic entering into an agreement against the wishes of its partners, this in practice did not alter the situation.[20] Nevertheless, it was a prestige-saving piece of logic-chopping which seemed to satisfy at least those parties which supported Adenauer's coalition. It did not, of course, do anything to meet the objection that by signing the Western Treaties, as they became known, the West Germans were accepting that unification in the near future was very unlikely.

When the statesmen went to their formal dinner on the evening of 25 May, it was still not certain whether the whole negotiation was about to collapse. At any moment they could expect a veto from Paris. Had this happened, the history of the Federal Republic, and indeed of western Europe, might have taken a very different turn. Adenauer's press chief Felix von Eckardt, who was with Adenauer during this fateful weekend, wrote in his memoirs that Adenauer's whole policy was at stake in those two days:

> If the treaties had not been signed he [Adenauer] would have lost the political game because . . . a catastrophe of that sort, before the eyes of the whole world, could hardly have been overcome. Success in domestic politics was also at stake. If the treaties had collapsed, the Social Democrats would have gained a victory and would undoubtedly have won the Federal elections in the following year.[21]

It should be remembered that the Federal Republic was less than three years old at this juncture. Neither its political structure nor its international status had been consolidated. Had Adenauer's gamble failed, the old Franco-German conflicts, the old inter-Allied rivalries and the old domestic German wrangles which had riven the Weimar Republic might have surfaced again.

As it was, Sunday 25 May 1952 was a turning point which actually turned. The text of the General Treaty was hammered out, the Damocletian sword poised in Paris failed to fall. On Monday 26 May the treaty was signed in a formal ceremony in the Bundesrat. The delegations then flew to Paris, where on the following day, and with considerably less jubilation, the EDC treaty was signed.

The signature of both treaties was only the beginning of a wearisome process, because they had to be ratified by the legislatures concerned. There was not much doubt about London and Washington,

20. Schwarz, *Ära Adenauer, 1949–1957*, p. 164.
21. F. von Eckart, *Ein Unordentliches Leben. Lebenserinnerungen* (Düsseldorf, 1967), p. 189, cited in Schwarz, *Adenauer. Der Aufstieg*, p. 949.

especially because neither Britain nor the USA was going to be a member of the EDC. In Bonn the critics of the treaties were still vocal. Something of the danger Adenauer had been in on 25 May can be gauged from Kurt Schumacher's public declaration that any-one who accepted the General Treaty would cease to be a German, a menacing statement reminiscent of nationalist attacks on Repub-lican governments in the Weimar period, and one which was used as a slogan in demonstrations against the treaty.[22]

By now, however, Schumacher's time was running out and Aden-auer's successes were having an impact on public opinion. Those opposing Adenauer's foreign policy were shown by opinion polls to be losing ground, and optimism about European integration was growing. There was more scepticism about reunification, and in July 1952 a poll asking people which issue they thought more vital, reunification or security from the Russian threat, found that more than half those responding chose the Soviet threat as more import-ant, whereas only a third chose reunification.[23] Even so, the Social Democrats and their FDP allies in some *Länder* governments such as Baden-Württemberg still tried to block the treaties, and it was not until 15 May 1953 that they passed the Bundesrat.

The real stumbling block, however, lay in Paris. The treaties had only been signed by the French because critics in the government privately thought they would never be ratified. In the two years which followed, the situation worsened as the French economy was increasingly debilitated by the colonial war in Indo-China. Success-ive French governments prevaricated about ratifying the EDC treaty, but on 30 August 1954, Premier Mèndes-France presented it to the National Assembly, which voted against even discussing it.

The European Defence Community was thereby jettisoned and the future of the General Treaty (henceforth to be called the German Treaty) was also in jeopardy. Franco-German relations, still bedevilled by the Saar question, seemed to have hit a new low. But matters were not so serious as they would have been if this reverse had been suf-fered two years earlier. In the meantime the position of the French in the Western Alliance had been seriously weakened. The Federal Republic, on the other hand, had been gaining in economic and po-litical importance, and its government was far more secure, Adenauer having won a resounding triumph in the Bundestag elections of September 1953. The fact that the ailing Truman administration in

22. Schwartz, *America's Germany*, p. 277.
23. Schwarz, *Ära Adenauer, 1949–1957*, p. 166.

Washington had been replaced by a non-isolationist Republican government under Eisenhower and Dulles also strengthened the west German position.

The French needed the support of their Anglo-Saxon allies in negotiating their way out of the Indo-Chinese imbroglio after the catastrophic defeat at Dien Bien Phu in May 1954. Within an almost amazingly short time what had seemed a disaster for the Federal Republic turned into a triumph. Mèndes-France agreed to deal with the German Treaty separately and, under severe pressure from the Americans, showed himself willing to accept the end of the Occupation Statute and its replacement by the German Treaty. The British Foreign Secretary, Anthony Eden, proposed an arrangement whereby the Brussels Treaty of 1948, which had committed the British to defend a number of western European countries in case of attack, should be expanded to include the former enemy countries, Germany and Italy. An existing stipulation that this treaty was directed against renewed German aggression was to be replaced by a vague commitment 'to promote the unity and to encourage the progressive integration of Europe',[24] and the signatories were to become part of that rather shadowy organization, the Western European Union (WEU). Attempts by the French to control German arms production through the WEU were resisted, although eventually it was agreed to set up a WEU arms control office which would simply verify arms levels. More important as a means of bringing the negotiations to a conclusion was Adenauer's commitment that the Federal Republic would voluntarily abstain from the production of weapons of mass destruction, heavy warships, long-range guided missiles and strategic bombers. Nor was this the only concession Adenauer had to make. More embarrassing for him politically was the linkage made by the shrewd Mèndes-France between the German Treaty and the fate of the Saar. To obtain French ratification of west Germany's sovereignty and membership of NATO, the international status of the Saar region – which in practice meant its satellite status *vis-à-vis* France – would have to be recognized as effectively permanent. Curiously enough, this concession also turned out to be a blessing in disguise for the West Germans, as we shall see below.

At conferences in London and Paris in October 1954 the Western Treaties were finally accepted. The Occupation Statute was to be replaced by the German Treaty (*Deutschlandvertrag*) and the Federal Republic should join NATO. All her armed forces should

24. Urwin, *The Community of Europe*, p. 69.

be integrated within it. In effect the result was that there would be a federal German army, but that all its forces would be operating within the framework of the Alliance. This solution, which was far nearer what the British and the Americans had always hoped for, was also well in line with the intentions of Adenauer. Indeed, the upshot of this diplomatic marathon was far better than he could have expected in 1952.

With the disappearance of the EDC many of the obviously discriminatory aspects of rearmament had gone also. In most respects West Germany was now a partner of equal status, if not yet of equal weight or self-confidence. In the German Treaty itself the objectionable Clause VII/3 was dropped altogether, since it no longer seemed relevant. On the other hand the German Treaty contained commitments by the signatories – the three western occupiers and the Federal Republic – to work towards a comprehensive peace treaty between the whole of Germany and her former enemies in which the frontiers of united Germany would be finally decided. This enabled the West Germans to claim that the legal frontiers of Germany remained those of 1937 until a peace treaty should rule otherwise. Furthermore, the three Allied powers committed themselves to work peaceably to achieve a united Germany which should possess a free, democratic political system like that of the Federal Republic and should be integrated into the European Community. It was a commitment they hardly expected to have to honour, but it was a commitment just the same. In 1990, to everybody's surprise, the Germans were able to call in this particular debt, and the Allied powers were bound by their promise.

For the time being, however, Adenauer had succeeded in gaining for the Federal Republic its release from the status of an occupied and humiliated enemy. In practice this did not seem to have much effect. Under the German Treaty the western Allies kept their right to station troops in Germany, although these were now for the purpose of European defence, not occupation. In Berlin the four-power occupation status still remained, and the west Germans supported this to protect the western sectors against Soviet pressure. Nevertheless, Bonn had secured most of its cake whilst eating it: the western powers would remain to defend Germany, whilst the West Germans could create their own armed force of up to 500,000 men; the Soviet Union and not Germany was now marked out as the main enemy of the West, and German foreign policy could operate without restraints other than those imposed by the problems of the Cold War. When, in May 1955, the Western Treaties came into operation, the

Federal Republic emerged from the shadows of defeat and joined the Western Alliance as a respected partner. To have attained this goal in less than six years was a noteworthy achievement.

Adenauer followed this up the same year by the enunciation of the Bonn Republic's famous 'Hallstein Doctrine', named after Walter Hallstein, the senior civil servant in the Foreign Ministry who had negotiated the ECSC treaty and who was also a distinguished professor of law. According to that 'doctrine', Bonn would break off diplomatic relations with countries which recognized the German Democratic Republic, thus underlining the claim by the West German government to be the only legitimate representative of the German people. For fifteen years this policy certainly hindered the GDR's relations with non-communist countries; on the other hand it also handicapped Bonn's own attempts to get on terms with states in the 'socialist camp'.

The Saar settlement

One other development took place as a result of the Western Treaties which helped to stabilize the Federal Republic in the form it was to assume until October 1990. This was the Saar crisis. As we have seen, Adenauer had agreed to accept that the international statute for the Saar which had been proposed for it by the French should be accepted in return for French agreement to the German Treaty. This statute, which bound the Saar economically to France, would last until a definitive peace treaty settled Germany's borders – a distant prospect. The arrangement was that the statute should be presented to the people of the Saar for acceptance by plebiscite. The plebiscite would only be a 'Yes/No' vote for the statute and offered the people of the Saar no alternative. It was supported by the premier of the region, Johannes Hoffmann, and by Konrad Adenauer, who had decided that Franco-German co-operation and west German sovereignty were worth the sacrifice of the Saar.

In this matter, however, the old Chancellor was not to have his way. The SPD, and above all the Free Democrats, were determined that the people of the Saar should be given the right to return to Germany. When, during the negotiations in autumn 1954, the French had insisted on a plebiscite, it was assumed that the citizens of the region, which had been politically isolated from West Germany, would be inclined to vote for the statute. Saar parliamentary elections in November 1952 had produced a majority for the pro-French parties. However, by the spring of 1955 it was evident that opposition to the statute was growing, and the campaign hotted up. When the votes were counted on 23 October 1955, 67 per cent of those voting rejected the statute and, in subsequent elections to the Saar *Landtag*, parties supporting the statute received only 28 per cent of the vote. A strongly pro-German coalition took over, and it was clear that preventing the Saar's return to Germany would be very difficult.

Once again, the time factor was important, as was the general atmosphere to which Adenauer's pro-western policy had so greatly contributed. The French had begun to lose interest in the region since the importance of coal was no longer so great, and it had become obvious that the steel industry in the area would need expensive restructuring. The economic issue had been an important reason for turning the population back to Germany, and the French found the prospect of hanging on to a potentially expensive rust belt against the wishes of its people decidedly unappealing. Furthermore, the mid-1950s saw another stage in the move towards European integration with the consolidation of the ECSC and the proposals for a European economic community, and the French cabinet was dominated in October 1955 by 'Europeans' like Premier Guy Mollet and Foreign Minister Antoine Pinay. So the loss of the Saar no longer seemed particularly critical to the French, and after extracting some economic concessions from Bonn, they agreed that the region should join the Federal Republic.[25]

On 1 January 1957 the Saar became the eleventh federal state, or *Land*, in the FRG. Although a relatively obscure area, its story is interesting for two reasons. The first is that its return to Germany took eleven years after the Second World War, whereas it had taken nearly sixteen years after the First and had then been handed back, not to the democratic Weimar Republic, but to Hitler's Third Reich. The situation after 1919 was clear-cut because the Versailles Treaty stipulated a referendum after fifteen years, whereas after 1945 the French seemed determined to separate the area permanently from Germany, and their Anglo-Saxon allies were not inclined to obstruct them. Bonn therefore seemed more successful than Weimar in overcoming this particular problem.

There is a second aspect of the Saar question, however, which turned out to be of some significance. When it entered West Germany, it did so on the basis of Article 23 of the Basic Law which

25. On 4 June 1956 Adenauer and Mollet agreed to the incorporation of the Saar in west Germany. For an admirable description of this issue, see Schwarz, *Ära Adenauer, 1949–1957*, pp. 282–6.

simply listed the constituent *Länder* of the Federal Republic and stated that in other parts of Germany the Basic Law would operate once they had joined the FRG. Thirty-three years later it was to this simple procedure that the ruling parties in Bonn and East Berlin would turn when the time came to incorporate the GDR into the Federal Republic. Such had not, of course, been the intention of the founding fathers of the Basic Law. They had, in Article 146, specifically provided for the termination of the law at the moment when the united German people freely voted itself a constitution. The Saar also presented a precedent for 1990 in another way. Its incorporation turned out to be considerably more expensive than had been envisaged when its return to Germany was agreed. Nevertheless, the funding for it was found from the Federation and the wealthier *Länder*, and the *Saarland* settled down as a reasonably prosperous backwater in a free and sovereign west German state.

Hence, whereas repeated attempts at national resistance pursued by Weimar governments in the 1920s had simply led to humiliation and instability, Adenauer's consistently pro-western policy had the paradoxical result of restoring West German sovereignty. As the perceptive contemporary Swiss observer, Fritz René Allemann, noted, it was ironic that in 1949 Adenauer's ministry had set out into the wilderness with its compass pointing to European integration as the only route towards equality of treatment for the Germans, and yet when they emerged from that wilderness in 1955 they found themselves back upon the broad and clear road of national sovereignty they thought they had left behind forever.[26]

26. Allemann, *Bonn ist nicht Weimar*, pp. 150–4.

CHAPTER SEVEN

Adenauer's 'Chancellor Democracy' and the Beginnings of Change, 1955–1963

The mid-1950s saw Adenauer at the pinnacle of his popularity and power. A West German public opinion poll carried out in December 1955 to discover the most admired living man found that 45 per cent of those asked selected Adenauer for this distinction, whilst his nearest rival, the medical missionary Albert Schweitzer, polled only 14 per cent.[1] Adenauer was seen as combining authority, energy and a sense of duty with a commitment to democracy, a combination which many Germans had believed impossible before 1949. He personified continuity and stability.

Adenauer's electoral victory in 1953, his achievement of sovereignty for the FRG in 1955, and the booming economy, which saw production levels twice those of 1936, together with almost full employment, seemed to mark a transformation in West Germany's fortunes. There were, of course, many people still living in hardship as the result of war damage, mutilation or displacement. Large west German cities still bore the scars of bombardment, though they were being restored much more rapidly than their counterparts in the east. But already at the time of the 1953 election the consumer society was beginning to make itself apparent in the Federal Republic. Americanization, which had been regarded with horror by both the Weimar intelligentsia and Hitler's nazis, was now on the agenda, and it proved highly popular.[2]

For Adenauer, 1955 was the year of what he considered in later years to be his greatest triumph. In September he travelled to

---

1. Fritz René Allemann, *Bonn ist nicht Weimar* (Cologne/Berlin, 1956), p. 332.

2. See below, Chapter 8. For a recent discussion of this issue, see R. Pommerin (ed.), *The American Impact on Postwar Germany* (Providence, R.I., 1995), especially the chapter on 'West German Reconstruction and American Industrial Culture' by V.R. Berghahn, and that on 'Daily Life and Social Patterns' by Hermann Glaser.

Moscow, where he negotiated the return of nearly 30,000 military and civilian prisoners from camps in the Soviet Union. This achievement, which required brinkmanship of a high order, including the traditional tactic of ordering his aeroplane to be ready to take him home before the end of the conference, was in return for the establishment of normal relations with the USSR – a ticklish matter, since the Soviet side made no concessions to West German sensibilities about future unification.

Adenauer's advisers were unhappy about his giving recognition to the protectors of Ulbricht's GDR, but the Chancellor showed his mettle as a leader by brushing aside legalistic quibbles. He was strengthened by a message from President Eisenhower giving him a free hand. The agreement to open diplomatic relations with the Soviet Union was not consistent with Bonn's refusal to deal with countries recognizing the GDR – the so-called Hallstein doctrine – but it was clearly in Germany's interests that the one freely elected German government should be able to negotiate directly with the Soviet superpower. The FRG issued a unilateral declaration that it still regarded itself as the only true representative of the German people, and in practice nothing changed. Without mutual recognition between Bonn and Moscow, however, no progress could possibly be made towards a settlement of West Germany's differences with the East.

But for most of the public, the important achievement was the return of the prisoners in October 1955. Years after Adenauer's death, opinion polls showed that this was appreciated more highly than Adenauer's success in integrating western Europe or even than that of creating a stable democracy in Bonn.[3] The prisoners returned to whatever part of Germany (FRG or DDR) they came from, since the Russians applied the concession to both Bonn and Pankow. But it was Adenauer whose toughness and flexibility had created the chance for their release.

'Citizens in uniform': the Federal Republic's army

In the next few years another of Adenauer's objectives was realized: the Federal Republic obtained an army. Of course, the need for a

---

German contribution to western defence was one major reason for granting the FRG her sovereignty. Yet the actual creation of the new army, the *Bundeswehr*, did not prove easy. During the Weimar period the aim of the German government and the *Reichswehr* had been to circumvent Allied restrictions on Germany's armed forces. In the 1950s the situation was quite different, since the Anglo-Saxon Allies, at least, wanted a large German army to help solve their own strategic problems. But the planning and logistics required for such a military establishment were not simple. Surprisingly enough, finances were not the most difficult problem. As we have seen, Finance Minister Schäffer had been piling up budget surpluses since 1952, and yet the expected expenditure did not materialize. Despite a great deal of informal pre-planning, the German armed services could not be created very rapidly.

This was partly due to domestic opposition to conscription, the well-known 'ohne mich' ('without me') sentiment, and to the need to amend the Basic Law before an army could be created. The opposition made it clear that it would challenge the decision to integrate west Germany in the European Defence Community in the Federal Constitutional Court, and there was considerable confusion when the government tried to pre-empt this by persuading President Heuss to ask for an opinion on the issue from the court in June 1952. The manoeuvre backfired when it seemed that the court would take so long to make up its mind that it might compromise ratification of the EDC treaty, and so the discomfited Heuss had to withdraw his request. After the elections in September 1953 the government possessed the necessary two-thirds majority to push any necessary army laws through, but there were still many hurdles to be overcome.

The delay in establishing the army gave the Bundestag parties every opportunity to involve parliament in shaping the new force. The SPD decided to play down its root-and-branch opposition to rearmament and insist that, if armed forces were going to be created, they must be free from militaristic, anti-democratic tendencies. Younger, more pragmatic members of the party like Fritz Erler and Helmut Schmidt played an important part in Bundestag discussions of this issue. In the CDU/CSU and FDP also there were many who were determined to see any new armed force kept firmly under civilian, and preferably parliamentary, control.

The army must not threaten the democratic order, as the *Reichswehr* had done by its lack of commitment to the parliamentary system during the Weimar Republic. This problem was met by creating the concept of the 'citizen in uniform' to describe the new *Bundeswehr* soldier. Army officers were to be instructed in methods of leadership which encouraged an independent-minded attitude on the part of their troops. This so-called *innere Führung* was something of a curiosity, and seems in practice to have been ignored or minimized at platoon or battalion level. However, taken together with a serious commitment to the institutions of parliamentary democracy and with the clear subordination of the *Bundeswehr* to control by the Bundestag, these changes effectively prevented a military 'state within a state' developing in Bonn as it had in Weimar. The establishment of a military commissioner, an Ombudsman, for the *Bundeswehr* also made it more difficult for officers to abuse their positions *vis-à-vis* their inferiors or engage in subversive activities without being reported. The annual reports of the military commissioner also drew attention to weaknesses in *Bundeswehr* personnel policy which could then be followed up in parliament.

Perhaps just as important as these precautionary measures was the fact that the *Bundeswehr* was being created in quite a different atmosphere from the old *Reichswehr*, which had been a professional army of long-serving volunteers kept deliberately small by the provisions of the Versailles Treaty. Its first task had been to combat left-wing attempts at revolution, whilst itself being tarred with complicity in right-wing machinations to overthrow the Republican constitution.

The *Bundeswehr* was created as part of a western military alliance against communism. It would depend for most of its more sophisticated weaponry on the USA. Because a major contribution to western defence was required, it would have to be a conscript army. This meant that popular feeling – which was often decidedly unenthusiastic for military adventures – would make itself felt within the army. For most of its life the officers in Bonn's army had to worry more about the indifference and apathy of many of their recruits than about their enthusiasm for war.

One serious problem was the selection of officers for the *Bundeswehr*. A number of senior officers from the former *Wehrmacht*, such as Generals Gerhard von Schwerin and Hans Speidel, had prepared plans for the new army, and other former officers were clearly hoping to be involved in it. There was also a demand that all those imprisoned for war crimes should be released and that the honour of the *Wehrmacht* under the Third Reich should be recognized by the western powers. The DP and sections of the FDP were particularly strident in making such demands. It seemed that in the new Cold War atmosphere there was a real danger that the professional officers needed even by a conscript army would carry with them a legacy of anti-democratic militarism going back to the time of Bismarck, if not Frederick the Great. More to the point, a survey of former *Wehrmacht* personnel in July 1952 showed that 44 per cent of those questioned had a high opinion of Hitler, and that 21 per cent of officers thought he was the greatest statesman of the twentieth century.[4]

Had the army been rushed together in the early 1950s, as seemed likely at the time of the Korean crisis, it would have necessarily been recruited from trained personnel from the former *Wehrmacht*, many of whom were still unemployed. In that case its political complexion would have been open to criticism.[5] As it was, the immediate crisis passed over, and the creation of the *Bundeswehr* was delayed until the relevant treaties were ratified. As we have seen above, that problem was not finally resolved until 1955. The selection of senior officers could therefore be approached with more deliberation.

In 1952 Theodor Blank, the CDU politician entrusted by Adenauer with the task of preparing the ground for the new army, suggested that there should be a Personnel Advisory Committee appointed by the government to make recommendations about the appointment of senior officers from the point of view of their character and political dependability rather than just their military competence. The Bundestag took up this proposal and strengthened it, so that the committee was appointed by parliament, not the government, and was equipped with formidable veto powers. All the first round of appointments to the rank of colonel and above had to be vetted by the committee, and if a proposed candidate was not supported by two-thirds of its members he would automatically be rejected for service in the *Bundeswehr*.[6] This meant that the upper echelons of the new army were free of anti-democratic taint.

It also demonstrated the very different power position of the *Bundeswehr vis-à-vis* earlier German armies. Civilian ministers, exemplified by Konrad Adenauer himself, and the Bundestag, made it clear that the army would be the servant of the civilian leadership. The fact that the civic institutions of the FRG were already firmly established before the *Bundeswehr* made its appearance was not unimportant in this respect. The Basic Law made it illegal to plan for an offensive war, so the *Bundeswehr* would have to be committed to

4. Allemann, *Bonn ist nicht Weimar*, p. 402.
5. Schwarz, *Ära Adenauer, 1949–1957*, p. 287.
6. Allemann, *Bonn ist nicht Weimar*, p. 399.

defence. However difficult such a provision was to implement in practice, it could always put a brake on headstrong military initiatives. The Defence Ministry, headed by a party politician, was to control the army, and there was no equivalent to the former Chief of the Army Command such as had existed in the Weimar Republic. Ministerial personalities in Bonn, such as Franz Josef Strauss, Kai-Uwe von Hassel and Helmut Schmidt were far more prominent than the leading generals of the *Bundeswehr*.

So far as the officer corps was concerned, it was inevitable that those who volunteered for military service were likely to be of an authoritarian frame of mind, and that some of them might sympathize with radical nationalist groups. They were targeted by the *Soldatenzeitung*, a journal which glorified the exploits of the *Wehrmacht* in the Third Reich. The monitoring committee mentioned above could not affect the appointment of junior officers or their subsequent promotion into the higher ranks. From time to time incidents did occur which suggested that neo-nazi tendencies were manifesting themselves in particular units, and the naming of barracks after Third Reich generals was not an encouraging sign.

Nevertheless, throughout the history of the Bonn Republic the *Bundeswehr* remained an obedient tool of the civilian leadership and a co-operative member of the NATO alliance. Close links were forged with Allied armies and many senior officers had experience of working on intimate terms with their American, British and French colleagues. At its senior levels, at any rate, the *Bundeswehr* developed an entirely different culture from that of the old Prussian/German army. It reflected society much more broadly in its recruitment, its leaders were more open in their political attitudes – the SPD Chancellor Schmidt was probably respected more than most other Bonn politicians for his knowledge of military affairs – and it demonstrated a far more cosmopolitan, pragmatic approach to the task of national defence than had been the case with its predecessor before 1945.[7]

7. For a good description of the establishment of the *Bundeswehr* and the discussions about such matters as *Innere Führung*, see Schwarz, *Ära Adenauer, 1949–1957*, pp. 287–302. For a helpful description of the position of the *Bundeswehr* in the FRG, with extracts from the major relevant documents, see Carl-Christoph Schweitzer, 'Defence Policy and the Armed Forces', in C.-C. Schweitzer *et al.* (eds), *Politics and Government in the Federal Republic of Germany, 1944–1994. Basic Documents* (2nd edn, Providence, R.I., 1995), pp. 150–74. A far more critical picture of the *Bundeswehr* is given in the volume edited by Franz H.U. Borkenhagen, *Bundeswehr. Demokratie im Oliv? Streitkräfte im Wandel* (Berlin/Bonn, 1986), which includes an introduction by Graf von Baudissin and an interesting memoir by Claus Kress, 'Disziplin muss sein – Schikane auch?', in which he points out that the political education of recruits in the early 1980s was very poor, and that unemployed men joining the army were less likely to stand up for their rights than their predecessors had been: ibid., pp. 90–105.

The necessary addition to the Basic Law having been passed by the Bundestag in March 1956, a consequential conscription law was accepted in December of the same year. Conscripts – who would only be male – would serve for twelve months, a period later extended to fifteen months. Provision was made in a later law for conscientious objectors to perform civilian service, which would, however, last longer than military service. As time went on, the proportion of conscripts opting for civilian service rose, and by the 1980s serious concern was being felt about the falling numbers of young men ready to serve in the *Bundeswehr*. There was even talk of conscripting women, but the collapse of the Cold War eased that problem, at least for the time being.

The arguments surrounding the establishment of the West German army had an important political consequence. When preparations had begun for it in 1950, the politician foreseen for the post of defence minister was Theodore Blank. When the ministry was formally established in 1955 he was indeed the first incumbent. But Blank, though trusted by Adenauer, was not popular in the Bundestag, where he was felt to be too receptive to the views of traditional *Wehrmacht* officers. He was also blamed, doubtless unfairly, for difficulties which arose in 1955 when the FRG, having waited so long for permission to rearm, was faced with NATO commitments which apparently required an army of nearly half a million men. Barracks had to be built and equipment found; it was clear that it would all take much longer than Blank had envisaged. There was also the difficulty that NATO strategy was changing, with more stress being laid on technical superiority and nuclear weapons than on manpower.

Blank's position was made more difficult because he faced a ruthless rival for his position in the ambitious and energetic Bavarian CSU politician, Franz-Josef Strauss, who had come into the Bonn government after the 1953 elections. In autumn 1956 Strauss persuaded the CDU/CSU parliamentary delegation that Blank's plans for the development of the *Bundeswehr* were faulty, envisaging as they did a force of 485,000 men by the end of 1959. The build-up should be slower, with more emphasis on quality, and particularly on modern armament. Adenauer saw he could no longer protect Blank, and in October Strauss became defence minister. He was also destined to be the most controversial politician in the Bonn Republic.[8]

In the 1950s the whole issue of the German army was highly

---

8. W. Krieger, *Franz Josef Strauss. Der barocke Demokrat aus Bayern* (Göttingen, 1995), pp. 34–8; also Schwarz, *Ära Adenauer, 1949–1957*, pp. 299–302.

sensitive, both inside and outside Germany. But in the history of
the Bonn Republic itself the *Bundeswehr* as an institution played a
marginal role. By the time it was established at full strength, the
major threat from the East had apparently passed. Politically it had
little weight. From 1955 to 1990 no German soldier was killed in action against an enemy, nor was it ever necessary to deploy *Bundeswehr*
troops against domestic rioters. Nevertheless, without it West Germany could not have become a respected partner in the Western
Alliance. Service in the *Bundeswehr* was also a fact of life for literally
millions of German males from 1956 onwards. Its impact on their
political beliefs or social attitudes seems, however, to have been
remarkably small.

One less publicized aspect of West German defence policy under
Franz-Josef Strauss was its impact on relations with Israel. As we have
seen, in 1952 Strauss himself had not voted for the reparations package for Israel in the Bundestag, but by the time he became defence
minister he realized that this measure had improved Bonn's standing with her western partners. So when, towards the end of 1957,
Shimon Peres and an Israeli defence delegation secretly visited him
at his home in Rott am Inn, Strauss was happy to arrange a confidential arms deal for Israel. This involved helicopters, anti-tank
weapons and transport aircraft, some of which were purchased in
France. Strauss also helped to develop the Israeli armaments industry by purchasing from it supplies for the *Bundeswehr*. The Israelis, for
their part, supplied secret information about Soviet weaponry and
communications systems gleaned from captured Arab equipment.[9]
Although the government – and even the parliamentary opposition
– were informed about this, it was kept secret until 1964, and caused
considerable embarrassment for West Germany in its relations with
other Middle Eastern countries when it did become public.

Troubles in the coalition

Political difficulties of a different kind soon began to affect the
Bonn government, and some of them were to contain the seeds of
Adenauer's eventual downfall. The problems arose with the smaller
parties in his coalition. It was clear to both the FDP and the BHE[10]

9. Krieger, *Strauss*, pp. 43–4.
10. The BHE was formally designated GB/BHE: *Gesamtdeutsche Block/Bund der
Heimatvertriebenen und Entrechteten*, thus stressing their commitment to German
reunification and restoration of lost territories.

that if Adenauer's policy went on so successfully, their own future would be very bleak. In addition, both parties were unhappy about the growing permanence of Germany's division, and the apparent willingness of the Chancellor to abandon the Saar to the French did not reassure them. In the summer of 1955 the BHE delegation in the Bundestag split, and at the party's congress of October the same year it was decided to leave the coalition. This did not worry Adenauer particularly, especially since their most capable leader, Oberländer, preferred to stay on in his ministerial office. But soon it became clear that the FDP was also getting very restless; its parliamentary leader, Thomas Dehler, disliked Adenauer and was furious when the post of foreign minister was given to a member of the CDU, Heinrich von Brentano. He attacked the western policy of the government, including the agreement at Messina to go forward with the European Economic Community.[11]

Adenauer wished to split the FDP, and it was clear that some FDP members of his government, such as Blücher, would go along with him. But he was foolish enough to threaten a reform of the electoral system to increase the importance of directly elected seats as against the party lists, a prospect which would spell doom for smaller parties like the FDP. It was at this point, in February 1956, that the importance of the Bonn Republic's federal system became apparent, because tensions at *Land* level also affected politics in Bonn and vice versa. In Düsseldorf, the capital of the important *Land* of North Rhine-Westphalia, there had been a CDU/FDP coalition headed by the Christian Democrat Karl Arnold, who had been premier since 1947. A group of FDP 'young Turks', dissatisfied with Adenauer and his policies, overthrew Arnold and helped replace him with an SPD-led government in which the liberals (FDP) received more ministerial places. This not only deprived the CDU of power and patronage in Adenauer's own home territory, it also shifted the balance of forces in the Bundesrat against the government. Simultaneously the FDP in Bonn split, and most of its members went into opposition. Although the coalition with the CDU was to be restored after the 1961 elections, the basis of trust between Adenauer and the FDP was never repaired. The fact that the 'young Turk' rebellion in Düsseldorf had been planned in the flat of an FDP politician called Walter Scheel was not without interest. In 1969 Scheel was to be an architect of the first federal government that did not contain the CDU.

11. See below, p. 153.

For the time being, however, the political climate remained set fair for the Christian Democrats and their leader. The party had proved itself capable of attracting a wide spectrum of electors from most regions of Germany outside Bavaria, where its CSU associate was expanding its support. Socially, too, it was a genuine people's party, attracting votes from a variety of class backgrounds. Even the confessional issue, which seemed likely to prove a problem, began to dwindle as some specifically Roman Catholic policies in educational and family matters were quietly shelved. The fact that issues of this kind were treated at a *Land* level rather than in Bonn made it easier for Adenauer to gloss them over. As Adenauer himself became associated with stability and economic success, so more protestants began to support the CDU. The losers were the smaller parties of the right.

Adenauer and Erhard: frictions begin

Adenauer himself seemed extremely powerful in the mid-1950s. His federal Chancellery, presided over by the ruthlessly efficient Globke, monitored the activities of government departments to ensure ministerial loyalty to the Chancellor, and his press spokesman, Felix Eckardt, presented the Chancellor to the public in a very positive light. In the Bundestag Adenauer could rely on the unswerving support of the former general secretary of the Centre Party, Heinrich Krone, who in 1955 became leader of the joint parliamentary delegation (*Fraktion*) of the CDU/CSU in Bonn. Pressure groups also looked to the Chancellor for help, and supported him in their turn. Bankers like Robert Pferdemenges and Hermann Abs, and businessmen like the head of the German Industrialists' Association (BDI), Fritz Berg, had warm relations wih him. Adenauer often seemed to prefer the advice of 'practical' men of business to the 'academic' views of Ludwig Erhard, with his social market economy. However, this did not mean that Adenauer was able to exercise some sort of dictatorial power in Bonn. The limitations of a pluralistic democratic system applied to him as to others.

This was illustrated by the 'Gürzenich incident', which occurred in May 1956. For some time both Erhard and Schäffer had been worried that the economy might be overheating. Supported by the central bank, they wished to apply the brakes, if only in a mild fashion. Erhard was keen to discipline German industry by cutting tariffs on imports, whereas Berg was demanding more tax concessions and cheap credit. On 19 May 1956 Wilhelm Vocke, president of the *Bank deutscher Länder* (federal central bank), raised the central bank discount rate to 5.5 per cent, a measure he was entitled to take independently but which he had cleared with Erhard and Schäffer beforehand. Adenauer, however, had not been informed. A few days later, on 23 May, the octogenarian Chancellor attended the BDI's annual conference in the huge Gürzenich Conference Hall in Cologne. He listened without apparent dismay as Berg delivered a ferocious attack on the economic policy of the government and the central bank (*BdL*), complaining about Erhard's proposed cuts in import duties and new high-interest payments which were crippling German industry. Adenauer himself then rose to speak and warmly seconded Berg's views, saying that the central bank was responsible to nobody and that its policies were damaging the interests of the 'little man', a person hardly well represented at the BDI conference. The Chancellor assured his audience that he would at once call the relevant cabinet ministers – Erhard and Schäffer – to account.

At a cabinet meeting the following day he did indeed excel himself in a display of ferocious sarcasm at the expense of Erhard, in particular. Pointing out that the coalition would need money to fight the next election, he asked the hapless Economics Minister: 'Can you somehow pay for it, Herr Erhard? Have you perhaps got the money with you? Then put it here on the table and I will be shown to be wrong ... [a pause] ... So, you haven't got it ....'[12] Unpleasant though this experience may have been for Erhard, who was not at his best in the cut and thrust of cabinet debate, it did not alter the policy of either his ministry or Vocke's central bank. Despite rumours that Erhard was about to be dismissed, Adenauer knew perfectly well that the Economics Minister was too valuable an electoral asset to jettison and that he had strong support from sections of the CDU in the Bundestag. Globke was active behind the scenes in arranging a rapprochement, and on 30 May Adenauer was blandly telling the cabinet that he had probably not heard Berg correctly owing to the acoustics in the Gürzenich Conference Hall. He then left for a well-publicized visit to the USA and Erhard's tariff cuts were accepted by the cabinet with some generous exceptions for agriculture.[13]

This incident illustrates the interplay of vested interests, ministerial authority and political chicanery which characterized much decision-making in Bonn. It may not have been heroic or always

12. D. Koerfer, *Kampf ums Kanzleramt: Erhard und Adenauer* (Stuttgart, 1987), p. 121.
13. Ibid., pp. 123–4.

consistent, but it often provided effective answers to immediate problems and allowed the powerful German economy to go roaring on without too much restraint.

Erhard and cartels

In the economic sphere Erhard was working to complement his elimination of physical controls with measures against private distortions of the market. The first of these was his anti-cartel law, which he had to fight through the Bundestag in the teeth of opposition from vested interests such as Berg's BDI and supposedly pragmatic politicians, among whom Adenauer himself was often prominent. Erhard saw the abolition of cartels and price rings as an essential element in the social market economy, since otherwise west Germany would remain a corporation of producers dominated by heavy industry, with the consumer's interests being neglected. He also saw open access to the market as essential, not only for economic efficiency but also for a healthy democracy.

He was supported in parliament by a strong group of Christian Democrats, the so-called 'Erhard Brigade'. Their most effective spokesman on the cartel issue was Franz Böhm, who had been campaigning for an end to price rings since the 1930s. The core of the argument was whether cartel contracts should simply be ruled illegal, thus making them indefensible in courts of law, or whether they should be allowed in principle but controlled by the government. The latter tactic had been tried before and had simply resulted in the protection of cartels by the state. Thanks to the bitter opposition of vested interests in industry and within some public administrations, such as the post office, Böhm's vision of a cartel-free Germany could not be achieved. Nevertheless, the final version of the legislation, passed in July 1957, did accept the fundamental principle that cartels should be regarded as illegal, even though it was so riddled with exceptions to satisfy the business world that it would not be very effective. It also established the Federal Cartel Office, which was not only to combat price rings, but also to try to prevent private monopolies from so dominating markets that they could exclude competition.

This was part of a very healthy development in German economic life which can be described as 'Americanization'. It was only partly due to Erhard's policies, although his staunch defence of free trade and free competition gave it respectability. It was also influenced by the tremendous prestige gained by American industry for its production methods during and after the war, and the tendency for ambitious young German managers to want to obtain experience and training in the USA.[14] It was not unimportant that the old smoke-stack industries of coal and steel, which had so dominated the German industrial economy since the middle of the nineteenth century, were now dwindling in importance as oil imports, encouraged by Erhard, provided competition for coal and finished goods were becoming more profitable than steel production. The shift in the industrial centre of gravity in Germany from the Ruhr area southwards to the Main/Rhine confluence, parts of Baden-Württemberg and Bavaria, which had already been visible under the Third Reich, was now intensified. Economic and social rigidities were being undermined in a fashion which made the old nationalist clichés harder to justify.

Social welfare

As the economic boom thundered on, so pressure for a reform of West Germany's complicated social welfare system intensified. It was estimated in 1953 that 20 per cent of the west German population were in receipt of some form of pension or public payment, but pensioners were very badly off by comparison with the rest of the population, and the network of support for those suffering deprivation was complex, bureaucratic and inconsistent in its application. There was an opportunity in the mid-1950s to introduce a coherent set of social payments based on the principles of the social market economy. This would have involved the maximum possible use of the insurance principle, with individuals protecting their own future by contributions, and the use of state funding only to deal with the really helpless and needy, or with situations of sudden crisis. However, this opportunity was lost, largely because arguments about social policy took the form of a struggle between the Finance Ministry, which wanted to introduce stringent means-testing and cut costs, and politicians who were anxious to gain the favour of pensioners, refugees and other victims by offering them a greater share of West Germany's new prosperity.

14. On this issue, see V.R. Berghahn, *The Americanisation of West German Industry, 1945–1973* (Leamington Spa, 1986), and the same author's chapter, 'West German Reconstruction and American Industrial Culture, 1945–1960', in Pommerin, *American Impact on Postwar Germany*, pp. 65–81. For the ambivalence of some industrialists' attitudes towards Americanization, see V.R. Berghahn, 'Resisting the Pax Americana? West German Industry and the United States, 1945–55', in M. Ermath (ed.), *America and the Shaping of German Society, 1945–1955* (Oxford, 1993), pp. 85–100.

Adenauer was especially concerned not to allow the SPD to gain electoral advantage by exploiting the pensions issue. It was agreed that, since recurrent inflations – in the early 1920s and after the Second World War – had rendered contributory pension schemes worthless, each generation would have to pay for its own pensioners. Such a view meant that pensioners could be given their share of prosperity by linking the level of pensions to the general level of wages, so that pensions would keep up with the cost of living. So West German citizens received the benefit of the 'dynamic pension' which seemed to ensure them the prospect of a rising standard of living in old age. It was highly popular, but has been seen by economists as disastrous. In the 1950s and 1960s, steady growth rates made it seem that such pension burdens could easily be shouldered. But as growth began to slow down, and as the proportion of elderly people in the population increased, so the burden of the pension commitment bore more heavily on both public finances and individual workers, whose social security payments constantly rose.

Whatever the long-term dangers, the pension law gained much credit for the government when it was passed in January 1957. It came into effect the following month but took some time to implement, so that many pensioners received substantial back-payments in the summer, a circumstance which did not harm the CDU's chances in the forthcoming Bundestag elections.

These were held on 15 September 1957 and were indeed a great triumph for the old Chancellor. The Christian Democrats won 50.2 per cent of the votes cast – the first and only time that a German political party gained an overall electoral majority in a national election. They reflected support for Erhard's social market economy and Adenauer's staunch commitment to the West, a commitment which assuaged the public's fear of communism. The campaign was one of personalities, and Adenauer undoubtedly stood head and shoulders above his rivals. The bespectacled and corpulent SPD chancellor candidate, Erich Ollenhauer, was completely outclassed in this respect, as was the respectable but uncharismatic FDP leader, Reinhold Meier. Above all, the electorate voted for no change. For once things were going well for the West Germans, and they did not want to upset the apple cart. Adenauer's electoral poster promising 'no experiments' was very effective.[15]

---

15. For a collection of – not very impressive – electoral posters from the 1957 Bundestag elections, see U.W. Kitzinger, *German Electoral Politics. A Study of the 1957 Campaign* (Oxford, 1960), plates between pp. 112–13. It was not until the 1960s that party propaganda in Germany took on the slickness of American public relations techniques.

Adenauer's foreign policy: safety first

Certainly the consistency of Adenauer's foreign policy had made his opponents appear confused or irresponsible. His commitment to NATO was clear, but he also pressed on in the field of European integration, accepting the challenge of the European Economic Community (EEC) set up by the Treaty of Rome, signed in March 1957. The SPD and the liberals were unhappy about developments which seemed to foreclose German unity, and the SPD was prone to producing unlikely schemes for the effective neutralization of a united Germany. The latest of these was Wehner's *Deutschlandplan* (Plan for Germany) which was announced in spring 1959 and which envisaged a step-by-step unification and merging of the Federal Republic with the GDR. The new Reich would be neutralized and disarmed as part of a central European arms control zone encompassing the two German states, Hungary and Poland. The whole scheme was hazardous and impracticable, and was controversial within the SPD itself. Nevertheless, it reflected a common fear among left-wing parties in western Europe that nuclear armaments would lead to mutual devastation. Adenauer, on the other hand, was determined that no steps should be taken which would weaken NATO or prevent German forces being armed with nuclear weapons. His views would prevail, but at the end of the 1950s this was not at all self-evident.[16]

One serious shock was the collapse of the Fourth Republic in France in May 1958 and its replacement with the regime of Charles de Gaulle. The German Foreign Office had not prepared Adenauer for this, and he was disturbed at the thought of a more nationalist, and possibly anti-German, French government. It seemed at first as if de Gaulle might even reconsider French participation in the EEC, and although he actually accepted it, his unco-operative attitude within NATO worried Bonn.

More alarming was the behaviour of the Soviet government. On 27 November 1958 Khrushchev, who had now established himself as Soviet dictator, delivered an ultimatum to Bonn, London, Paris and Washington in which he demanded the demilitarization of West Berlin and its transformation into a 'free city'. If this were not

16. In 1959 Adenauer himself was having to consider plans which might involve recognition of the GDR and a special status for Berlin. Cf. Hans-Peter Schwarz, *Geschichte der Bundesrepublik Deutschland. Die Ära Adenauer: Epochenwechsel, 1957–1963* (Stuttgart, 1983), pp. 86–8. For the SPD's *Deutschlandplan*, see Kurt Klotzbach, *Der Weg zur Staatspartei. Programmatik, praktische Politik und Organisation der deutschen Sozialdemokratie 1945 bis 1965* (Berlin/Bonn, 1982), pp. 487–94.

done in six months he would hand over the Soviet rights in this area to the German Democratic Republic. For the next three years, the West would be faced with constant threats of unilateral Soviet action *vis-à-vis* Berlin, accompanied by sinister background music in the shape of massive Soviet nuclear tests in Siberia, and the startling development of Soviet space technology. The first man-made satellite, the *Sputnik*, had been launched into space from the USSR in 1957, and from then on a series of Soviet achievements involving satellites and space rockets unsettled the West. The shooting down of an American spy plane, the *U2*, in May 1960 apparently underlined the advance of Soviet missile development.

Adenauer presented all this as malevolent Soviet pressure which should be resisted stoutly lest it undermine western security. In this view he was supported by the American Secretary of State, John Foster Dulles, but the latter's death on 24 May 1959, together with growing uncertainty about the health of President Eisenhower, caused Adenauer great anxiety. He doubted the determination of his western partners. He was already very distrustful of the British, who seemed willing to come to an arrangement with the USSR, even if this meant recognizing the GDR and thus scuppering the prospects of Germany unity, an objective which few British statesmen regarded with enthusiasm anyhow.

But Soviet policy was not just a matter of communist pressure on the West, despite Khrushchev's bombast about overtaking the western world or even 'burying' it. There was a genuine problem for the Communists in the GDR. Ulbricht's regime was deservedly unpopular there. As we have seen, on 17 June 1953 there had already been a rising in East Berlin and other cities in the GDR. Although this was later minimized as an outburst of labour discontent against increased work norms, subsequent research has illustrated that it reflected widespread political hostility to the SED and a desire for reunification with West Germany.[17] Ulbricht's government was momentarily paralysed and the rising was suppressed by Soviet forces. Tragically, the result was to strengthen Ulbricht's position in East Germany, since he was seen by the Russians as their most reliable functionary there. The regime pressed on with socialization of the economy and, in particular, with the collectivization of agriculture.

17. For a description of the 1953 events in the GDR, see Mary Fulbrook, *The Divided Nation: Germany 1918–1990* (Oxford, 1992), pp. 226–71. For recent German scholarship: A. Mitter and S. Wolle, *Untergang auf Raten* (Munich, 1993); M. Hagen, *DDR – Juni 1953* (Stuttgart, 1992), and T. Diedrich, *Der 17. Juni 1953 in der DDR. Bewaffnete Gewalt gegen das Volk* (Berlin, 1991).

The totalitarian features of the political system became more marked, including the increasingly pervasive *Stasi* or secret police, faithfully modelled on the Soviet example.

The response of many Germans in the former GDR was to vote with their feet. That this was possible was due to the strange position of Berlin as the result of the Allied occupation arrangements. Whereas Germany west of the Oder–Neisse had been divided up into occupation zones effectively administered by the victor powers concerned, the capital supposedly remained under four-power control, although it too was divided into four sectors, each under the authority of one of the occupiers. Since 1947 the city had been effectively divided between the three western sectors, administered by a democratically elected mayor and senate, and the eastern sector, run by the SED. In theory, however, the occupation rights of the four powers still existed within the city, and members of Allied forces could claim the right to go anywhere within it. The importance of this was that in many practical ways the city remained a unity; the underground railway and inner-city trains (the *S-Bahn*) ran throughout Berlin, and there was no physical barrier between the various sectors. A substantial number of workers who lived cheaply in Soviet East Berlin commuted daily to jobs in the western sectors.

However, from the point of view of the GDR government, the situation was most unsatisfactory, because GDR citizens who got to Berlin could slip across the sector boundary, seek haven from the West Berlin authorities and fly out to a new life in the Federal Republic. Every year hundreds of thousands did just that. They included a high proportion of young, skilled people whom the East German economy could ill afford to lose. For some enthusiastic Cold Warriors in the west this process seemed to be the answer to the German problem, and even perhaps to the supremacy of the Soviet Union east of the Elbe. It was hoped that the 'disappearing satellite' in East Germany would soon cease to function and that the Soviet bloc would then be forced to make concessions.[18] This expectation proved a little naïve. From a military viewpoint West Berlin was virtually impossible to defend, surrounded as it was by powerful Soviet forces. At first, Khrushchev tried to bully the western powers into recognizing the GDR and accepting a new free city status for West Berlin which would have prevented East German refugees using it as a transit station. This would have meant that the Germans would have had to

---

18. Cf. George Bailey, 'The Disappearing Satellite', *The Reporter* (New York), 16 March 1961, pp. 20–3. This is not to imply that Bailey himself was a Cold Warrior.

accept that in future there would be two Germanies, one communist-controlled. Reunification would be ruled out. Such an agreement would have clearly breached the commitments made by the western Allies to the Germans in the German Treaty (*Deutschland-Vertrag*) of 1955, as well as solemn NATO declarations. It might have aroused anti-western resentment in the Federal Republic, and would certainly have weakened faith in NATO as a serious military alliance. Nevertheless, there was no great enthusiasm in London – or even Washington – to die for Berlin. Adenauer became very suspicious that the Anglo-Saxon Allies, and especially the British, might be going to do a deal with Khrushchev over his head.

Adenauer was not the only player on the German side when it came to the Berlin question, however. The city had benefited from the leadership of a series of courageous Social Democratic mayors – Louise Schröder, Ernst Reuter, Otto Suhr and, since October 1957, Willy Brandt.

Brandt was determined to protect the people of West Berlin from the threat of communist domination. On the other hand he himself was a democratic socialist from a genuinely working-class background. He had actively resisted Hitler's Third Reich, both inside Germany and in Norway, Spain and Sweden. His name was actually an alias he had used when travelling to a socialist conference in 1933. This sort of career aroused resentment amongst those who regarded themselves as his social superiors, especially if their own record of resistance to nazism had been less than perfect.[19] Brandt was young, cheerful, good-looking and spoke fluent English. As a former journalist he mingled easily with the press. He was well equipped to meet the demands of the new media age – especially with respect to television – which was burgeoning in the late 1950s. The Berlin crisis was to propel him into the limelight not only for Germans but for the whole of the western world.

If Adenauer was suspicious of the western Allies, Brandt had no great confidence in Bonn. He believed that Adenauer had written east Germany off – western inactivity during the June 1953 uprising

---

19. Brandt was born in 1913. His father was John Möller of Hamburg, but he was not married to Brandt's mother, whose name was Frahm. Brandt thus remained Frahm until he went into exile in Norway in 1933 at the age of nineteen, returning as a socialist agent at great risk to himself in 1936. He later returned to Norway and thence to Sweden after the nazi invasion of the former country. Nevertheless, there was nothing mysterious about his origins, despite the heavy weather made of them by his opponents, especially Adenauer and Strauss. Willy Brandt, *My Life in Politics* (London, 1992), p. 74. See also B. Marshall, *Willy Brandt* (London, 1990), pp. 5–25, 44–5.

had been an illustration of that – and he was not impressed when, at the time of Khrushchev's November 1958 ultimatum, a German Foreign Office official told him that he should be prepared to accept the 'free city' option for Berlin. Brandt stoutly resisted Soviet threats. On 1 May 1959, less than a month before the Soviet ultimatum was due to run out, he told a crowd of 600,000 Berliners: 'Look at the people of Berlin and you will know what the Germans want.' The ultimatum ran out without anything happening, but the pressure remained on Berlin. Brandt continued his public resistance, despite nervous noises from such people as Defence Minister Strauss, who told him in May 1960 that the city could not be defended.[20] The SPD itself was, of course, busily drawing up the 'German Plan' which involved at least initial recognition of the GDR and neutralization of Germany. Brandt had no part in that and disapproved of it.

He was, however, an enthusiastic supporter of moves towards a more pragmatic and liberal policy direction within the SPD. Ever since Schumacher's death in 1952 there had been attempts by reformers such as Willi Eichler and the Hamburg economist Karl Schiller to modernize the party, weaning it away from class war ideology and the command economy. After the crushing electoral defeat of 1957 Eichler's group was able to make real headway, and the result was the Godesberg Programme of November 1959. This specifically distanced German social democracy from Marxism, which was now seen as just one among a number of influences upon socialist thought, influences which included the Sermon on the Mount. The planned economy was rejected in favour of Schiller's formula, 'as much competition as possible, as much planning as necessary'. The SPD seemed to be accepting the social market economy, and Ludwig Erhard sourly accused the party of plagiarism.[21]

The Godesberg Programme aroused much favourable comment in the press, and although it did not involve changes in SPD foreign or defence policy, the atmosphere in the party created by Godesberg's success made it easier to swing over to a western orientation. Brandt played a leading role here, speaking out for principles which would place the SPD much more in line with government thinking on the East–West conflict. He argued that there was common ground between the major parties over Berlin's linkage to the Federal Republic, the commitment to the West on the part of the Germans, the

20. Brandt, *My Life in Politics*, p. 24.
21. For the German Social Democrats' conversion to market competition, see Nicholls, *Freedom with Responsibility*, ch. 16.

rejection of any form of commmunism or soviet German policy, the need to do everything to help Germans living in the GDR, and the avoidance of any actions which might split the non-communist world or endanger world peace.

In Bonn, Herbert Wehner, the SPD leader who had been most involved in drawing up the controversial 'German Plan', now saw that the common anti-Soviet front policy was more popular, and on 30 June 1960 he committed the SPD to supporting European unity, the Western Alliance and the defence of the West. Disengagement and neutralization were jettisoned. The SPD accepted that the right of self-determination expressed through free elections should be the basis for future reunification.[22] This bipartisan approach to the East was not welcomed with great enthusiasm by the government, since it would knock away a major plank in the CDU case against the Social Democratic opposition. It was also evident that the focus on Berlin and its charismatic mayor was not at all attractive to a governing party which was itself beginning to show signs of stress.

As we have seen, the first cracks in Adenauer's government had revealed themselves in February 1956, when the bulk of the FDP broke with his coalition.[23] His triumph in the 1957 elections seemed to render that issue unimportant, but soon other problems appeared. One obvious issue which could not be put off for much longer was that of Adenauer's successor. The Chancellor would be 85 by the next Bundestag elections in 1961. Many of his own followers thought he should stand down before then, and the favourite candidate of the CDU to succeed him was Ludwig Erhard, whose economic 'miracle' had done so much to benefit the party electorally. Adenauer himself had no intention of standing down, and was particularly unenthusiastic about Erhard as his successor. He regarded the professor of economics as unworldly and too weak to govern Germany. The two men also disagreed fundamentally over the European Economic Community, which Adenauer supported for political reasons, but which Erhard regarded as a protectionist cartel which would damage German trade. He campaigned in favour of a free trade area including Britain, a breach of cabinet discipline for which Adenauer did not forgive him. Tensions arising from this rivalry would dog the government until Adenauer finally did resign in 1963.

22. Klotzbach, *Staatspartei*, pp. 497–503. Wehler chose to give this assurance in the form of answers to questions publicly posed by Franz-Josef Strauss, a leading scourge of the SPD who, nevertheless, seems to have got on quite well with Wehner. In 1966 the latter was quite happy to welcome Strauss as a coalition colleague. Cf. Krieger, *Strauss*, p. 61.

23. See above, p. 147.

Tensions over the presidency, 1959

Meanwhile an awkward constitutional issue presented itself. The federal president, Theodor Heuss, was due to end his second phase in office in 1959. According to the constitution he could not be re-elected, although he was regarded as having discharged his functions with distinction. Had he been asked by the major parties to stay on, the rules could have been changed for him and he probably would have agreed to serve. However, the government allowed time to slip by, and Heuss decided to remain aloof. On 12 February 1959 the SPD announced that it would put forward Professor Carlo Schmid for the presidency. He was in many ways a strong candidate: moderate, urbane, cultured and a good linguist. Since the FDP – Heuss's party – was in opposition and the election would be carried out by the *Bundesversammlung*,[24] the CDU could not be sure that Schmid's candidature would fail. So a convincing CDU candidate had to be found.

Adenauer first thought of killing two birds with one stone by proposing Erhard for the post. But on reflection the Economics Minister saw the intention behind this and refused the nomination. Adenauer's next step, in April 1959, was more fateful. He decided to stand as president himself, apparently under the misapprehension that he would be able to exploit the constitutional position of the presidency to control foreign policy and to appoint his successor as Chancellor. He may have been influenced by the success with which de Gaulle, whom he had met the previous September, was establishing an authoritarian regime in France on the basis of presidential power. In fact, Adenauer's manoeuvre turned out to be a complete fiasco. The suggestion that he might become president immediately opened up the question of his successor as Chancellor, and it became clear that his own preference – Franz Etzl – would not have an easy run in the party caucus. Once Adenauer stood down, Erhard would probably win. It was also evident that Adenauer's generous interpretation of the president's power did not chime in with that of legal experts. Showing his usual nerve and iron will, Adenauer did another about-turn and withdrew his candidacy, claiming that the international situation required that he stay on as Chancellor. The relatively unknown Minister of Agriculture, Heinrich Lübke, was hustled in as candidate and duly elected on 1 July 1959.

In some ways the presidential fiasco illustrated Adenauer's extraordinary power over his party and his government. In others,

24. See above, pp. 80–1.

however, the incident was damaging for him. Public reaction to the confusion in CDU ranks was negative. Furthermore, the succession issue was now a matter of open discussion, and Adenauer knew he would face increased pressure from supporters of the 'crown prince', Ludwig Erhard. There was one other aspect to this affair which would have some importance in the future. Despite being Adenauer's choice, Lübke did not get on personally very well with the Chancellor, and he was even less sympathetic to Erhard. Although Lübke was not a political heavyweight, he did have experience from the Weimar period, when he had been a left-wing member of the Centre Party in the Prussian parliament (*Landtag*). He remembered the collaboration between the Social Democrats and Centre in Prussia which had been a feature of successful Prussian government, 1918–32. He therefore retained a preference for the Weimar style of coalition between the major parties, the CDU and the Social Democrats. It was to be in his period of office that the only 'great coalition' of the Bonn Republic came into being.[25]

The succession problem for the CDU was underlined on 24 August 1960, when Willy Brandt was nominated as chancellor candidate for the SPD in the Bundestag elections due the following year. For the first time since the death of Schumacher Adenauer would find himself facing a personable and popular opponent on the hustings.

TV and politics: the Constitutional Court stands firm

One way in which Adenauer tried to strengthen his party's political position after 1957 was in his attempt to introduce commercial television into the Federal Republic. The existing TV stations were the responsibility of the *Länder* and, as we have seen, had carefully balanced governing bodies designed to ensure their public responsibility. As is not unusual, Adenauer regarded such balanced reporting as biased against his government, and believed that commercial TV, established on the basis of business interests close to the CDU, would guarantee more favourable coverage. He proposed a federally organized commercial system which would give Bonn far more influence over the organization of the new channel.

This led to a revolt within his own party and an embarrassing

25. For a discussion of Lübke's election, see Arnulf Baring, *Machtwechsel. Die Ära Brandt-Scheel* (Munich, 1984), pp. 29–32. Baring points out that presidential elections in the FRG often had a 'seismic significance' because they revealed trends and attitudes beneath the surface of politics.

conflict with the Roman Catholic Church. The controversy revealed that the federal structure of the Bonn Republic was not so unimportant as some of its critics believed. Adenauer was blocked not only by the opposition parties and by ecclesiastical outrage, but by the 'state princes' (*Landesfürsten*) from his own party in the various *Land* capitals. The *Länder* were determined to retain control of TV, and the churches were rightly concerned about the impact commercialization would have upon the moral tone of TV programmes. Adenauer pressed ahead with his scheme, but its opponents in SPD-controlled *Länder* demanded that it be tested in the Federal Constitutional Court, and on 28 February the latter ruled against the Bonn government. The Second German TV channel (ZDF) was placed under the control of the *Länder* with much the same balance of interests represented in its governance as had been established for the existing channels. Its headquarters was established in Mainz, the capital of the Rhineland-Palatinate, whose CDU premier, Peter Altmeier, had been one of Adenauer's fiercest opponents in the whole TV struggle.[26] Although some finance came from commercial advertising, the pressure of market forces on the programmes was minimal.

In this way the FRG escaped, for almost the first 35 years of its existence, the relentless commercial pressure towards down-market programming and lopsided news coverage which was to characterize TV culture in most Anglo-Saxon countries. It was only in the 1980s that cable and satellite TV infiltrated the German system and began to undermine the ethos of public service electronic media which had already been established in the pre-history of the Bonn Republic.

By 1961 thoughts were turning to the forthcoming Bundestag elections due on 17 September. Despite the improved position of the SPD, which had attracted favourable media coverage as the result of its Godesberg Programme, the tense international situation could yet be beneficial to Adenauer, since 'no experiments' still seemed a useful slogan in face of the Soviet threat.

The Berlin Wall

However, in August 1961 the Berlin crisis boiled over. Threatening noises from Pankow and Moscow, together with increased pressure on farmers and horticulturalists facing collectivization, led to a surge

26. Cf. Hans-Peter Schwarz, *Geschichte der Bundesrepublik Deutschland. Die Ära Adenauer: Epochenwechsel, 1957–1963* (Stuttgart, 1983), pp. 165–9; R. Taylor Cole, 'Federalism, Bund and Länder', in Schweitzer *et al.* (eds), *Politics and Government in the FRG*, pp. 148–50.

in refugees pouring into West Berlin. During the first six months of 1961 120,000 had fled into the western sectors, and this accelerated sharply in July, when 30,000 GDR citizens went to the West.[27] This time the Soviet/East German response was carefully planned. Huge quantities of concrete building blocks and barbed wire were brought into strategic positions around East Berlin. The people's police and factory militias controlled by the SED were mobilized, and in the small hours of Sunday 13 August, the East German authorities, discreetly supported by their Soviet masters, started to divide East Berlin from West Berlin and to build the notorious Berlin Wall. This monstrous structure, one of only two man-made objects visible to astronauts on the moon, was to incarcerate the citizens of the GDR until their country's liberation began on 9 November 1989.

The personal tragedy of the Wall cannot be overstated. Many families were divided, and had no prospect of seeing their relatives again. Furthermore, the sealing up of East Berlin meant that the population of the GDR lost their hope of a better life in the west. Escape now became a very dangerous business, and a number of East Germans were killed attempting it.

The building of the Wall also created a backlash in the west. The bombast of some western observers had led to the belief that Allied troops would defend *East* Berlin against Soviet pressure. When they did nothing of the kind, disillusionment was considerable. One distinguished journalist, Sebastian Haffner, published an article which began with the following dialogue:

> Khrushchev (suddenly): 'Give me Berlin!'
> The Western Allies: 'No, no. Never.'
> Khrushchev: 'All right then, give me Germany.'
> The Allies (perplexed, humming and hawing a little): 'Mhm, mhm . . . all right.'[28]

Reports were rife that the Soviet step was only the first phase of pressure on West Berlin, and that all confidence among West Berliners was being undermined. West Berlin removal firms were reported to be booked up for months ahead, with families moving to West Germany. The western Allies, and especially the British, were blamed for their lack of resolve. It was suggested that West German opinion would rebel against the ineffective support from NATO

27. Figures given in Brandt, *My Life in Politics*, p. 46. The rush was partly stimulated by the spectacular failure of a summit meeting between Khrushchev and Kennedy at Vienna on 3 and 4 June 1994.
28. S. Haffner, 'Germany, Russia and the West', in *Encounter* (October 1961), 62–7.

allies. In the article cited above, Haffner argued that the Germans had only accepted the Paris treaties of 1954 because the West had promised to support German unification, even if it had to be deferred for a time. In choosing western partnership, as against unification on Soviet terms, the Germans had done the West 'an immense favour', thereby saving NATO. If the western powers' answer was to be an 'eagerly contrived anti-German Munich', they could not expect the continuance of an alliance which from the German national viewpoint would be 'meaningless and suicidal'.[29] In fact, of course, the West Germans had joined NATO to protect their own way of life from Soviet pressure. They showed no more enthusiasm to rescue the East Germans by force than did their Allied partners. But Haffner was right to point to the crisis as one of confidence within the Western Alliance.

Certainly western responses to the events in Berlin were initially unimpressive. Brandt, who was about to embark on his federal election campaign, found himself isolated in the old Reich capital. Nearly a day passed before the first Allied military patrols appeared on the sector boundary. Forty hours elapsed before a formal protest was sent to the Soviet Commandant in Berlin and it was 72 hours before this protest actually reached Moscow.[30] There was no enthusiasm in London or Washington, let alone Paris, to risk a world war for the citizens of the GDR. It did not escape the notice of policy-makers in western capitals that by sealing off their population the East Germans were solving their problem without attacking western territory. Already in May 1961 the NATO Council of Ministers in Oslo had announced that it would defend the freedom of *West* Berlin and its people, a formulation which must have reassured Pankow and Moscow.[31] The Kennedy administration in Washington had for some time been seeking an alternative to 'massive retaliation' using nuclear weapons as the only strategy with which to respond to Soviet pressure. The Berlin crisis hastened the adoption – at least in practice – of 'flexible response'.[32]

However, it should not be thought that caution was confined to West Germany's allies. Brandt got even less support from the Bonn government. On 13 August his only message from the federal capital was a phone call from Foreign Minister von Brentano urging

29. Ibid., pp. 64–6.
30. Brandt, *My Life in Politics*, pp. 2–3.
31. R. Pommerin, 'Die Berlin-Krise von 1961 und die Veränderung der Nuklearstrategie', in M. Salewski (ed.), *Das Zeitalter der Bombe. Die Geschichte der atomaren Bedrohung von Hiroshima bis heute* (Munich, 1995), p. 130.
32. Ibid., pp. 137–40.

close collaboration. Adenauer 'wrapped himself in silence' and made no move to go to Berlin. Indeed, his first reaction was to state that 'calm is the first duty of any citizen'. In response to suggestions from Kennedy and Strauss that the West prepare for war with the Soviet Union, Adenauer replied that he had first to win an absolute majority in the Bundestag elections. War preparations would upset the electorate. When the Soviet Ambassador, Smirnov, saw Adenauer and von Brentano on 16 August the Chancellor thanked him for Khrushchev's greetings and only referred to East Berlin by asking the Russians to ensure law and order there. In the confrontations between Allied troops and the Red Army which occurred in Berlin during the following year, the *Bundeswehr* was nowhere to be seen. Strauss was not at all enthusiastic for the idea that federal German forces should be in the vanguard of any action to protect Berlin. Gerhard Schröder, the Minister of the Interior, who was later to succeed von Brentano as foreign minister, was credited with the notion that West Berlin's population might be moved to settle on the Lüneburg Heath. The fact was that nobody was prepared to 'roll back' the communists – and that applied to the west Germans as well as to their western allies.

Brandt, however, did his best to rally the people of West Berlin, and exemplified their determination to remain free. He it was who welcomed Vice-President Johnson to the city when the Americans did try to restore some of their prestige there. Brandt's demeanour contrasted with that of Adenauer, who blithely carried on with his election campaign in West Germany as if nothing had happened, and made tasteless speeches in which he referred to 'Brandt alias Frahm' – a reference to the fact that Brandt was a *nom de guerre* adopted by the Berlin mayor when working underground in the Third Reich.[33] The Berlin crisis cast doubt on Adenauer's judgement, and some leading figures in his own party began to lose confidence in him. There was renewed speculation about a great coalition with the SPD – under a different chancellor.

An indecisive election

The upshot was that, although the CDU won the elections, it lost its crucial overall majority. The CDU/CSU vote fell by nearly 5 per cent,

33. Hans-Peter Schwarz, *Adenauer Der Staatsmann: 1952–1967* (Stuttgart, 1991), p. 662. For the relative isolation of Berlin in the days after the start of the Wall crisis, cf. Brandt, *My Life in Politics*, pp. 2–3, 48–9, and Willy Brandt, *People and Politics: The Years 1960–1975* (London, 1978), pp. 26–7.

the SPD gained a rather disappointing 4.4 per cent, but the real winners were the FDP, whose share of the poll rose from 7.7 per cent to 12.8 per cent, a result which was to be their best performance in any Bundestag election during the life of the Bonn Republic. This meant that they held the balance in parliament and that Adenauer would have to readmit them to his coalition, the FDP leader, Erich Mende, having already ruled out the possibility of a coalition with the SPD.

Mende wished to inaugurate a Christian–liberal government under Erhard's leadership, the Economics Minister being far more to the liberals' taste than the apparently inflexible Rhineland Chancellor, who was, as Mende unkindly pointed out in public, the same age as Hindenburg had been in 1933. Mende could hope for support from the CSU, whose leader, Strauss, was urging a change of chancellor, and from several leading CDU members, including the president (speaker) of the Bundestag, Eugen Gerstenmaier. Nevertheless, those who thought Adenauer was finished were in for a shock. He secured his position in the CDU party delegation, implied that he might be willing to form a great coalition with the SPD, and finally forced Mende to accept a humiliating coalition settlement in which the FDP swallowed the government's European and security policies as well as allowing the Chancellor to continue in office. However, Adenauer had promised Erhard that he would step down for him before the next election, and he was aware that many other colleagues thought he should do so. Mende, who did not join the new government himself, and the bulk of the FDP were strongly opposed to his continuing as chancellor. Among those on the liberal side intent on ejecting him from office was Rudolf Augstein, the editor of the *Spiegel* magazine.[34]

However, Adenauer's day was by no means done. He was determined to soldier on to prevent the western Allies making concessions to Khrushchev which would seal Germany's division for ever and condemn West Germany to an inferior status in the field of defence, particularly with reference to nuclear weapons. He was very uneasy about the way Kennedy seemed willing to negotiate the German position away during the autumn of 1961, and made great efforts to hold him to a firm course, rejecting concessions to the Soviet Union. Eventually, in May 1962, Kennedy tacitly accepted the West German position, and agreed to stand firm on the status quo with no concessions to the USSR. Although it was not apparent to

---

34. Schwarz, *Adenauer Der Staatsman*, p. 680.

the public, the Berlin crisis was over – so far as the Bonn government was concerned.[35]

Nevertheless, the diplomatic tensions arising from this event had taken their toll. Although in fact the Anglo-Saxon powers had borne the main burden of the confrontation in Berlin, Adenauer was angry at what he saw as the weakness of the Kennedy administration and its readiness to treat with Khrushchev over Germany's future. He thoroughly distrusted Harold Macmillan, the British premier.[36] So he was more inclined to look kindly on the overtures of General de Gaulle who, for his own reasons, wanted to create a Paris/Bonn axis. De Gaulle had pleased Adenauer by urging that no concessions be made to the Soviet Union during the Berlin crisis, though of course he was no more prepared to fight for Berlin than the Anglo-Saxon powers or the West Germans. Adenauer had to be careful to keep de Gaulle enthusiastic for Franco-German co-operation whilst avoiding a clash with NATO, a body of which the French leader was highly critical.

The common ground between the two men was therefore to be found in the area of European integration; both were willing to agree on a vision of a European voice in world politics, and Adenauer was ready to accept de Gaulle's version of a corporatist, tightly knit core group, as against a free trade orientated and looser association which would be favoured by the British if they negotiated entry. This policy was not popular with many of his colleagues, and was especially repellent to Erhard, who much preferred the Anglo-Saxon connection to the French one, since he regarded French economic policy as *dirigiste* and protectionist.

Apart from his suspicions of Macmillan and the Americans, Adenauer was moved by a number of motives in his relationship with de Gaulle. The first was defensive; he wanted to prevent the French leader striking deals with the other powers at west Germany's expense – something which seemed all too likely in the early years of the French Fifth Republic. Secondly, the two men do seem to have got on well personally. Both were authoritarian, conservative Roman Catholics. De Gaulle was well informed about German history

---

35. Cf. the account in ibid., pp. 744–9.

36. His distrust was justified, since Macmillan would have been ready to weaken west Germany's position – by recognizing the GDR and accepting Berlin as a 'free city' – in return for an agreement with the USSR. See V. Mauer, 'Macmillan und die Berlin–Krise, 1958/59', in *Vierteljahrshefte für Zeitgeschichte*, Vol. 44, No. 2 (Munich, April 1996), 229–56.

and culture, and he was nearer to Adenauer in age than Kennedy and his entourage in Washington. Adenauer felt that the French association would prevent Erhard giving in too much to the Anglo-Saxon powers if he became chancellor, and it would encourage de Gaulle to work within the European Economic Community. Even on the economic front Adenauer seems to have feared competition from British coal-mines.

In early July 1962 Adenauer went to Paris and was received with the pomp usually accorded only to heads of state. He was duly flattered, and the Bonn political leadership as a whole was impressed by the rapturous public reception which greeted de Gaulle when he visited the Federal Republic two months later. Early the following year a number of issues were coming to a head. The first British attempt to enter the European Economic Community was meeting French resistance, although much of the press and political leadership in Germany wanted Britain to join, and in London there were hopes that the Germans would assist the British application. At the same time, and in the changed world situation after the American triumph in the Cuban missiles crisis, renewed efforts were being made to obtain a world-wide ban on nuclear testing in the atmosphere. Adenaeur disliked this, both because he wanted West Germany to have the option of developing nuclear weapons in the future and because the GDR would be allowed to sign the test-ban treaty.

It was against this background that, on 22 January 1963, Adenauer, visiting de Gaulle for a Franco-German summit meeting, signed a treaty of co-operation and friendship between Paris and Bonn. Adenauer saw this as a means of binding his successors into a partnership with the French. The reception in Bonn was at least partly one of outrage, not least because a few days earlier de Gaulle had demanded that the British application to join the European Community should be shelved. On 29 January he finally vetoed it. Although the coalition parties could hardly repudiate their chancellor's action, they signalled their displeasure in the Bundestag by tacking a preamble onto the treaty which stressed that it did not affect the FRG's commitment to NATO or the concept of European union. Adenauer accepted this, although de Gaulle regarded it as negating the treaty and spoke bitterly of treaties which were like 'young girls and roses, they only last a morning'. Adenauer assured him in July 1963: 'Roses and young girls naturally have their time, but the rose – which is something about which I really know – is the most resilient plant we have . . . she survives every winter. Yes indeed, this friendship between France and Germany is like a rose, which will blossom perennially and will survive every cold spell wonderfully.'[37]

Adenauer believed that the treaty with de Gaulle was one of the major achievements of his chancellorship, and events were to prove him right. At the time it appeared a mischievous and quirky action, which heralded tensions within the CDU/CSU between 'Atlanticists', such as Erhard and the new Foreign Minister Gerhard Schröder, and so-called 'Gaullists' such as Franz-Josef Strauss. The latter tended to be on the right of their party, playing on a certain brand of nationalist anti-Americanism. This issue was only ephemeral, however, and the lasting benefits of a commitment to collaboration between France and west Germany were much more important. Emotionally the Franco-German link was immensely popular, since it seemed to guarantee that the old days of enmity between the two countries were finally over. Politically France and West Germany could assert their leadership within the EEC. The Adenauer–de Gaulle axis was not extended under Erhard, but later chancellors, such as Brandt, Schmidt and Kohl, worked closely together with their French counterparts. The close Franco-German relationship in Europe became a consistent feature of West German foreign policy to put alongside its commitment to the American security system of NATO. Even though the two policies were not always easy bedfellows, they formed the basis of Bonn's western policy, her *Westpolitik*.

At the end of Adenauer's term of office then, it could be said that the Federal Republic had achieved solid gains in a number of fields. Politically the country was stable and calm. Economically it remained booming; unemployment had ceased to be a problem. Indeed, with the end of the refugee flow from the GDR, labour had to be recruited from other countries. Italians and Yugoslavs came first, to be joined by Spaniards and ultimately by Turks. The currency was stable, and had even been revalued upwards against the dollar in March 1961. The Hallstein doctrine and Adenauer's determined opposition to concessions to the USSR at German expense meant that, even though the division of Germany seemed deeper – and certainly more painful – than ever, the ultimate aim of unification had not been formally jettisoned, and the Federal Republic could maintain its claim to be the only legitimate German state. When the FRG acceded to the test-ban treaty in August 1963, the Kennedy

37. Quoted in Klaus-Jürgen Müller, 'Adenauer and de Gaulle – de Gaulle and Germany: A Special Relationship', *The Konrad Adenauer Memorial Lecture 1992* (Hainault, 1993). For the context of the speech in Bonn see Schwarz, *Adenauer Der Staatsmann*, p. 858.

administration was persuaded to reiterate its recognition of Bonn's claim to speak for all Germans, an important point, since the GDR was also allowed to sign that treaty.[38] Otherwise West Germany was a respected and important member of NATO and the European Economic Community, and her relations with France were better than at any time since the middle of the nineteenth century. It was a pretty good balance sheet.

Yet Adenauer could not last much longer. The signs of his demise had already appeared in the autumn of 1962.

The Spiegel *affair*

The autumn of 1962 was in many ways a fateful one for the Federal Republic. On the one hand it witnessed, from 22 to 29 October, the dramatic crisis over Soviet missiles in Cuba, a crisis which momentarily seemed to bring the entire world to the brink of nuclear disaster, but which quickly culminated in a humiliating climb-down by Nikita Khrushchev. President J.F. Kennedy's calm resolve and his decision to impose a naval blockade against Cuba changed the whole international atmosphere. In the medium term it would end the crisis over Berlin and create a new feeling of security in the Federal Republic.

At the time, however, this was by no means clear. Western leaders expected further pressure from the Soviet side, and there were disagreements about how best to deal with it. Although relations between Bonn and Washington improved markedly as the result of Kennedy's tough stance in the Cuban crisis – Adenauer himself urged the most drastic measures against Cuba, including bombardment and invasion – there were still awkward causes of friction. One of these was defence policy.

The Americans wanted the Germans to build up their conventional forces to counterbalance the huge preponderance enjoyed by the Red Army in central Europe. The Bonn government on the other hand, and in particular Adenauer and Strauss, wanted to obtain access to nuclear weapons. Adenauer was eager to see at least a European nuclear deterrent in which the Federal Republic should participate. In addition to questions of global strategy, Strauss argued that equipping the *Bundeswehr* with more tactical nuclear weapons would enable it to operate with smaller numbers than the Americans

---

38. Schwarz, *Adenauer Der Staatsmann*, pp. 851–2; Schwarz, *Ära Adenauer, 1957–1963*, pp. 303–4.

wanted, thus putting less of a strain on the German economy. One problem about this option, however, was that it might involve the need to engage in a pre-emptive nuclear strike in order to prevent the Red Army overrunning most of Germany in the early stages of a confrontation. Even Adenauer saw the dangers of such a policy, and in the summer of 1992 he toyed with the idea of removing Strauss as defence minister, hoping that he would be content with the premiership of Bavaria instead. Strauss was furious and Adenauer had to back down.[39]

Nor was this all. Strauss made no secret of his contempt for many of his cabinet colleagues. The fact that he had been elected chairman of the Bavarian CSU in spring 1962 had underlined his ambitions, and other ministers in Bonn resented his brash assertiveness. His rise to prominence had been due in no small part to the support he had received from Adenauer, who saw in him a useful Bavarian ally, and an energetic defender of hard-line Cold War policies against backsliders within the government camp. The fact that Strauss was none too finicky in his methods would not have worried Adenauer, so long as he could be sure of Strauss's own personal loyalty. In the summer of 1962, however, Strauss's overweening bombast led him to make openly contemptuous comments about the *Bundeskanzler*, and in particular to imply that he did not understand modern military problems. Adenauer was not amused.

It was against this background that the *Spiegel* crisis blew up.[40] Although it apparently ended without a decisive victory for either side, it was in many ways an important turning point in the history of the Federal Republic. The *Spiegel* was Germany's most successful weekly news magazine, with a circulation of over half a million and a readership estimated at about five million. Although supposedly modelled on the American *Time* magazine, it was far livelier and more controversial. Its proprietor, Rudolf Augstein, stood close to the left wing of the Free Democratic Party, and was critical of right-wing Roman Catholic politicians like Adenauer and Strauss. Strauss was regarded as being unscrupulous and corrupt, and the fact that his power base was in Bavaria did not endear him to journalists operating out of the *Spiegel*'s headquarters in Hamburg.

The *Spiegel* had been targeting Strauss for some time, and this was not unreasonable, since there was a good deal to target. Strauss was

39. Schwarz, *Adenauer Der Staatsmann*, p. 776.

40. Strictly speaking, the title of the magazine is *Der Spiegel*, but in order to avoid clumsy formulations, I shall refer to it hereafter as *Spiegel*.

a clever and dynamic politician, but he was none too scrupulous about his methods or his choice of friends. One of the latter was a Bavarian provincial newspaper publisher called Hans Kapfinger, whose business relationship with Strauss appeared to involve impropriety. The *Spiegel* ran an article implying that there had been underhand dealings involving Strauss and Kapfinger's FIBAG construction company, which benefited from contracts to build barracks for the US 7th Army in Bavaria.[41] Strauss threatened to sue, and the *Spiegel* had to agree not to suggest in future that the minister himself stood to profit by this deal. Nevertheless, indications of impropriety were strong enough for the SPD to insist on a Bundestag enquiry which submitted its report on 20 June 1962. The committee did not find any serious charges proved against Strauss, but asserted that he had been guilty of 'administrative errors'.[42] An unusual combination of SPD and FDP parliamentarians referred the report back, ostensibly to give Strauss more time to clear his name. The final version of the report was due to be debated on 25 October, one day before the *Spiegel* crisis itself burst on the German public.

It was therefore clear that the *Spiegel*'s campaign was damaging Strauss and that he could regard the news magazine as a major obstacle to his ambition. On 8 October there appeared in West German news kiosks the issue of *Spiegel* for 10 October. The main article, complete with cover picture, related to Friedrich Foertsch, the Inspector General of the *Bundeswehr*. It was written by Conrad Ahlers, the *Spiegel*'s deputy editor. He had been a press spokesman for the 'Blank Office', the predecessor of the Federal Defence Ministry, and was therefore well acquainted with defence debates in Bonn. The article described the results of the latest NATO 'Fallex' manoeuvres, and the role of the *Bundeswehr* in western defence. Under the heading 'Only partly capable of defence (*bedingt Abwehrbereit*)' it painted a melancholy picture of the *Bundeswehr*, claiming that NATO had assessed the *Bundeswehr* forces as being in the lowest category of readiness, inferior to those of most of their allies. The NATO 'Fallex' war game had assumed that in the first days of the war West Germany would be attacked and that ten to fifteen million people would be killed in nuclear conflict. The article further claimed that Strauss was trying to have the *Bundeswehr* equipped with nuclear weapons, even if this would mean weakening the German economy or reducing the

---

41. Schwarz, *Ära Adenauer, 1957–1963*, pp. 263–5.
42. Ronald F. Bunn, *German Politics and the Spiegel Affair. A Case Study of the Bonn System* (Baton Rouge, La., 1968), pp. 17–28.

ultimate levels of conventional forces – which were already inadequate. Strauss was also supposed to favour a pre-emptive nuclear strike if war threatened, a policy opposed by the Americans. It was clear that the real target of this article was not Foertsch, but Strauss himself. What the public did not then appreciate was the fact that the nuclear strategy of Strauss, to which the Americans and the *Spiegel* objected, was also largely that of Adenauer.

The article was in many ways a striking example of the frankness and lack of deference to authority displayed by the West German press. On the other hand, the issues it treated were matters of national security and involved classified information. Although the revelations were hardly likely to be news to NATO's enemies, conservative circles in the Federal Republic might conceive them to be a betrayal of the national interest.

When the article appeared, Strauss does not seem to have immediately reacted to it as treasonable. Instead he complained to Adenauer about the 'journalistic terror' being aimed against him which, in his view, was as bad as physical terror.[43] Adenauer was sympathetic, and suggested that they should introduce a law against character assassination.

Soon, however, Strauss took more drastic action. A memorandum was drawn up in the Defence Ministry by a long-serving senior official from pre-war days, Volkmar Hopf, to the effect that the *Spiegel* article was treasonable in that it revealed state secrets and subverted national security. This was not a very serious claim, since West Germany's enemies would learn little from the article they did not already know, apart possibly from the low view of the *Bundeswehr* held in NATO circles. But a legalistic memorandum from a professional member of the higher civil service was enough to convince both the Defence Minister and his Chancellor that they could clamp down on the *Spiegel*.

On 18 October Strauss privately told Adenauer that legal action was planned against the magazine, asking him to preserve secrecy to prevent the miscreants covering their tracks or escaping. Thereafter Strauss kept the Chancellor informed and on 22 October was assured by Adenauer that he could go ahead and pursue those responsible 'without fear or favour'.

One of the most controversial aspects of this matter was that Adenauer and Strauss agreed to deny information about the impending action against the *Spiegel* to the Justice Minister, the Free

43. Schwarz, *Adenauer Der Staatsmann*, p. 777.

Democrat Wolfgang Stammberger. Officially the investigation and prosecution would be in the hands of the state prosecution service which, although formally independent, was nevertheless within the administrative purview of the Ministry of Justice. But instead of telling Stammberger what was going on, Adenauer and Strauss arranged for a confidential channel of communication to be opened between Hopf and Walter Strauss, the senior civil servant in the Justice Ministry, who was in the CDU and who could be counted on to preserve confidentiality even towards his own political chief.

It was helpful to the cause of Strauss and Adenauer that the action against the *Spiegel* coincided with the onset of the Cuban crisis, about which Adenauer was first appraised on the evening of 22 October. Of course, the decision to prosecute the magazine had already been taken well before the Cuban problem appeared, but the crisis distracted public attention from the Bonn government's action, and deepened an atmosphere of Cold War tension useful when justifying charges of treason.

At about 9 p.m. on the evening of 26 October 1962, attorneys from the Federal Prosecution Office, accompanied by security officers of the Federal Criminal Office and uniformed police, entered the *Spiegel* headquarters in Hamburg. They had evidently expected to find only a few members of staff present, and were taken aback to discover about 60 people still at work. When the police tried to clear the building, the staff held a sit-down protest in the corridors and members of the editorial team were able to inform the magazine's legal advisors, despite official occupation of the building's telephone exchange. The authorities had warrants for the arrest of Augstein and Ahlers, neither of whom was actually in the building. Meanwhile the offices were ransacked for incriminating material. Other editors were arrested and their homes searched in the middle of the night. Augstein gave himself up the following day, but Ahlers was on holiday in Spain and was woken up at five in the morning by Spanish police and arrested with his wife. The telephone call which had requested this action came from Strauss's Defence Ministry, and had been preceded by a call from Strauss to Adenauer in which he claimed that Ahlers might run away to Morocco – a claim for which there was not a shred of evidence. The circumstances of Ahlers's arrest were amongst the most controversial of the issues raised during the crisis.[44]

44. Later, Strauss even claimed that Adenauer ordered him to telephone Spain. See Schwarz, *Adenauer Der Staatsmann*, p. 783. For the events on the night of the action, see Bunn, *Spiegel Affair*, p. xviii, 55–8.

The personal involvement of Strauss in this action was perceived to be improper, especially because there was no extradition treaty with Spain covering political offences and because Franco Spain was still a police state of an undemocratic – if not fascist – type.

Adenauer had evidently assumed that the accusations of treason – the term *Landesverrat* has a particularly dishonourable implication in German – would be enough to discredit, if not ruin, the *Spiegel*. He was prepared to ignore or dismiss with contempt those citizens, particularly professors, students and other members of the intelligentsia, who protested against the impropriety of the action. From the Chancellor's viewpoint, Augstein was opposing the foreign policy of the Federal Republic in a scurrilous manner, and using unauthorized contacts with official circles to obtain information. He was therefore quite happy to defend the action against the *Spiegel* with robust – not to say demagogic – enthusiasm.

When the matter was first debated in the Bundestag, Adenauer himself was not in the firing line. The opposition suspected that Strauss was responsible for the impropriety and used question time in the Bundestag to interrogate him. Matters had already been complicated by the threat of the Justice Minister, Stammberger, to resign over the way he had been treated, a threat which Adenauer warded off by suspending the two luckless senior civil servants, Hopf and Walter Strauss. This action itself aroused indignation in the ranks of the CDU. Franz-Josef Strauss, for his part, was disingenuous about his part in the affair, claiming that the matter was one for the police and legal authorities and that he had only acted as a channel of communication to the military attaché in Madrid in the case of Ahlers. For some time this version of events was accepted by the government's supporters, but it soon became evident that Strauss's role in the whole business had been far more central. As for Adenauer, he seemed uninvolved in the matter, which made his intervention in the Bundestag debate on 7 November 1962 all the more sensational. He announced that the country faced 'an abyss of treason'. Despite the fact that nothing had been proved against Augstein in a court of law, Adenauer proceeded to slander him by saying: 'in the person of Augstein we have two complexes . . . on the one side he makes money from treason, and that I find vulgar pure and simple . . . and second, ladies and gentlemen, he makes money from attacks generally on the coalition parties and that pleases you [the SPD], you cannot deny . . .'[45]

45. Bunn, *Spiegel Affair*, p. 133.

It was with this kind of bullying smear tactic that Adenauer sought to bluster his way through the crisis. But it was not to prove successful. In the end he lost his defence minister, and came near to losing office himself.

Very soon after the action became public, it was clear that the prospect of a leading German news magazine being taken over by police and searched at night, and its editor and proprietor being arrested, was going to provoke a strong public reaction. The press itself was overwhelmingly critical of the way the government was handling the matter, and protests from academics and writers followed quickly. On 27 October eight prominent authors, including Günter Grass, Uwe Johnson and Hans Magnus Enzensberger, cabled their solidarity with the *Spiegel*. The following day 49 of the Federal Republic's best-known writers issued a public statement condemning the action and demanding Strauss's resignation. On 30 October 150 students at the University of Frankfurt staged a sit-in and the day afterwards 29 medical and natural science professors in Cologne protested against the threat to press freedom in a letter to Justice Minister Stammberger. These protests and demonstrations rolled on – not, to be sure, with such intimidating power as was to be seen in the rebellious 'happenings' at German universities later in the decade, but with a serious-minded determination which was more impressive. They were reinforced by foreign opinion, which was immediately uneasy at the echoes of the past conjured up by the government's police action. On 30 October the International Press Institute in Zurich protested at the insecurity for the press which would be caused by the government's action.[46] Foreign press comment was overwhelmingly critical.

Nevertheless, despite the unwonted display of dissent by usually cautious middle-class citizens, and the negative judgement of many newspapers usually sympathetic to the government – including the *Frankfurter Allgemeine Zeitung* and *Welt* – the government would probably have shrugged off criticism, relying on public distaste for treason and indifference to the fate of journalists. What prevented the crisis from blowing over was the attitude of Adenauer's coalition partners, the Free Democrats. The fact that without their co-operation he could not govern against the Social Democratic opposition forced Adenauer to trim his sails. It was an example of the way in which the German electoral system, which produces stable but very rarely

46. Ibid., p. 81. For details of protests by writers and academics and the generally negative press reaction, see ibid., pp. 59–77.

one-party governments, is able to enhance the role of parliament and protect the rights of individuals against an over-mighty executive. In Britain, for example, a minister like Strauss would have been able to get away unscathed.

As it was, the FDP was not unnaturally angered by the treatment of Justice Minister Stammberger.[47] Adenauer's sop to their *amour propre* was the suspension of the two civil servants, Walter Strauss and Volkmar Hopf, whom the FDP wanted dismissed. When it became evident that the Defence Minister was inclined to reinstate Hopf, the FDP decided that Franz-Josef Strauss himself, whose involvement in the affair was gradually emerging, would have to go. Adenauer's attack on Augstein in the Bundestag had shocked many members of the FDP parliamentary delegation, and some would have agreed with the *Frankfurter Rundschau* when it said of Adenauer that 'temperamentally he is a fascist'.[48]

On 19 November the FDP decided to withdraw from the coalition. The Christian Democrats' response was to announce the resignation of their own ministers, but since the Federal President was touring in India, and since the Federal Chancellor could not be removed without a positive vote of no-confidence, the government continued on a caretaker basis and Adenauer had time to negotiate his way out of the crisis.

This he did with his usual skill, frightening the Free Democrats by calling on the SPD to form a great coalition. Astonishingly enough, Herbert Wehner and Erich Ollenhauer obligingly agreed to discuss participating in a government led by Adenauer, despite the indignation expressed by their party over his handling of the *Spiegel* affair. The spectacle of the SPD leaders arriving at the Palais Schaumburg for formal negotiations with Adenauer damaged their credibility with their followers and with the public at large.[49] It also weakened the FDP's position, especially since one plank in a Christian/Social Democratic coalition's programme would be an electoral reform designed to squeeze out the Free Democrats. On 4 December 1962

47. The pretext Adenauer and Strauss gave themselves for not warning Stammberger of the action was that the *Spiegel* might have a hold over him because of a court martial case which had occurred during the war. They also suspected him of being too close to Augstein, and this was probably the real reason. See Schwarz, *Adenauer Der Staatsmann*, p. 779.

48. Bunn, *Spiegel Affair*, p. 135.

49. Adenauer's biographer remarks on the fact that: 'Just at the very moment when he [Adenauer] too was being sucked down by the vortex of the *Spiegel* affair, Wehner threw him a life-line': Schwarz, *Adenauer Der Staatsmann*, p. 796. It was, however, noteworthy that Willy Brandt did not participate in these discussions.

Erich Mende, the right-wing leader of the FDP, capitulated and made an agreement with Adenauer to continue the Christian–liberal coalition, something which the Chancellor himself had always wanted.

There were, however, two unpalatable consequences for Adenauer. Firstly, it had become clear that Franz-Josef Strauss would have to be dropped, a sacrifice which naturally angered the Bavarian leader. Secondly, a serious time limit had to be agreed for Adenauer's own term of office. October 1963 was to see the end of *der Alte's* regime.

In December 1962 there would still have been reason to doubt the outcome of the *Spiegel* affair. The cases against the journalists and their accomplices were going on, even if most of them were out of prison by then. On 19 December Adenauer attended a farewell *Bundeswehr* parade for Strauss at the Wahn airforce base and prophesied that he would play a 'great and decisive role' in the political life of the German people.[50] There was no hint of apology or contrition on the part of the Chancellor or his ministers. Thanks to Wehner's misguided *Realpolitik*, the Social Democratic opposition had missed its chance to profit from Adenauer's impropriety and was to remain out of office for over three more years.

The significance of the Spiegel *affair*

Nevertheless, the *Spiegel* crisis was an important turning point for the Federal Republic. The action by Strauss and Adenauer had been typical of the authoritarian tradition inherited from the German *Obrigkeitsstaat*. It was not a nazi operation, even if the nocturnal occupation of press offices aroused uncomfortable memories of the Third Reich. But it was a high-handed suppression of press freedom by official fiat – carried out, to be sure, according to the letter of the law – and would have fitted in well with Bismarck's technique of government, as would Adenauer's demagogic behaviour in parliament. The attitude of the senior officials involved, Walter Strauss and Volkmar Hopf, was also symptomatic. Both were regarded, and doubtless regarded themselves, as respectable civil servants of the old school. Yet they did not find what they were being asked to do extraordinary or reprehensible.

The significance of the *Spiegel* affair was that, for the first time in modern German history, a powerful government was forced to give way over an issue of individual liberty and citizen's rights without

50. He added: 'Bittere Stunden formen den Mann' ('Hard times mould the man'). Schwarz, *Adenauer Der Staatsmann,* p. 810.

insurrection or defeat in war. The affair aroused an unusual amount of public interest; by the end of November polls showed that well over 90 per cent of the public were aware of the issue, and that most people thought Strauss should resign.[51] A combination of passionate but responsible demonstrations by concerned and generally well-educated citizenry, press criticism and parliamentary pressure helped nerve the minority party in the coalition to put its foot down and insist that Strauss pay the penalty for his impropriety. Even the Chancellor knew his days were numbered.

The discomfiture of the government was confirmed by subsequent events. On 13 November a *Spiegel Report* on the affair was drawn up by the government and, after determined prodding by the SPD opposition in the Bundestag, it was published in February 1963. Despite vagueness over many issues, it did reveal that Adenauer had known about the impending action well before it occurred. On 13 May the Third Senate of the Federal Supreme Court dismissed the charges of treason against Augstein and Ahlers. None of those charged was sent to prison. Augstein's reputation was strengthened and the *Spiegel* became a national institution, though still detested by many on the right of the political spectrum. Ahlers was to make a political career under a later administration.

It was symbolic that the *Spiegel* represented the new West Germany – Americanized, materialistic, outspoken, scurrilous perhaps, but absolutely alien to the culture of Wilhelm II, Oswald Spengler, Alfred Hugenberg or Heinrich Brüning. Its victory was a triumph of investigative journalism over bureaucratic intrigue, and of parliamentary power over an autocratic chancellor. For several decades it ensured that politicians and officials could not escape the scrutiny of a well-informed and confident press. It was not until the 1990s that office-holders felt strong enough to begin imposing blocks on 'irresponsible' journalism.[52]

October 1963, therefore, saw the end of the Adenauer era. Despite the old Chancellor's low opinion of Ludwig Erhard, he had to accept the fact that the genial, cigar-smoking Minister of Economics would succeed him. However, Adenauer strung out his departure into the autumn of 1963, making a round of valedictory functions throughout the Federal Republic, as well as visits to Paris and Rome. When, on 15 October, he made his final speech as Chancellor to

51. Bunn, *Spiegel Affair*, pp. 163–78.
52. For an example of tension between some sections of the press and government in 1996, see Gunter Hofmann, 'Nachrichten in Schwarz-weiß' in *Die Zeit*, No. 47, 15 Nov. 1996, p. 3.

the federal parliament, he was able to enjoy an unctuously flattering encomium from the president of the Bundestag, Gerstenmaier, who had been one of those most eager to see him give up office.[53] More fateful for Erhard was the fact that Adenauer hung on to the chairmanship of the CDU, a position from which he was able to do considerable damage to his successor by constant criticism and intrigue.

53. Schwarz, *Adenauer Der Staatsmann*, p. 862.

CHAPTER EIGHT

Growing Pains:
Erhard, Kiesinger and Brandt

When Adenauer stepped down there seemed no reason to suppose that the domination of the CDU in West German politics would decline. The Social Democrats, despite their revised non-Marxist programme, their willingness to accept NATO and European integration and their attractive young chancellor candidate, had failed to break the Christian Democratic hold on power in Bonn. The gradual eclipse of Adenauer had not helped the SPD. On the contrary, the willingness of Wehner and Ollenhauer to treat with the old chancellor after the *Spiegel* crisis had outraged many SPD followers, and seemed to demonstrate a lack of moral fibre in the party's leadership.

Erhard as Chancellor

Erhard's succession to the chancellorship in October 1963 apparently strengthened the government. The founder of Germany's 'economic miracle' was personally well liked in the Federal Republic, and aroused more warmth amongst the population at large than his predecessor had done. He was much closer to the Free Democrats than Adenauer had been. He had no inclination to collaborate with the Social Democrats, whom he regarded as *dirigiste* wolves in newly acquired sheep's clothing.

Furthermore, the success of Erhard's social market economy seemed to be manifesting itself more strongly with every year that went by. Economic growth and prosperity were being taken for granted. This did not only apply to wealthy entrepreneurs or middle-class professionals. Full employment and rising real wages spread a general feeling of security and well-being. The social aspect of CDU policy was also registering impressive achievements. The housing shortage, an apparently insuperable problem in the early 1950s, seemed to have been virtually overcome. In May 1960 the minister of housing construction was able to start gradually dismantling the rent control system, aiming to end it altogether by 31 December 1965. To offset any real tenant hardship, direct rent subsidies, or *Wohngeld*, were provided for poorer families. By the mid-1960s the number of households living as lodgers fell to well under a million. More owner-occupied dwellings began to be built as affluence – especially amongst the middle classes – was reflected in expenditure on homes.[1] Erhard, seen as the father of the 'economic miracle' even if he always denied there was anything miraculous about it, could hope to reap the political reward for this social contentment.

Affluence was also manifesting itself in other ways, and the mid-1960s could be seen as the high point of Americanization in the Federal Republic, a period when mass consumption was fresh enough to arouse enthusiasm, and before a younger generation began to question its ethical foundations. This did not, of course, happen all at once. A symptomatic event had occurred in July 1954, when the finals of the soccer World Cup took place in Switzerland. Despite being unfancied, the West German team won the final in Berne. Travelling back home by train, they encountered wildly enthusiastic crowds, some of them blocking the railway lines so that they could shower gifts and praise on the players. In Bonn the team was greeted by Gerhard Schröder, the Federal Minister of the Interior, who solemnly presented each of them with a leather suitcase. This was in addition to the TV sets and refrigerators they had already received. Finally they came together in the little Bavarian town of Dingolfing, where the local motor firm of Glas gave each man a Goggo moped.[2] This might be seen to symbolize the new way of life in the Federal Republic. The moped and the luggage, in particular, pointed to an almost obsessive interest in travel which was to characterize the west Germans in the decades which followed.

1. See above, Chapter 5. See also Führer, 'Managing Scarcity: The German Housing Shortage and the Controlled Economy, 1914–1990', in *German History. The Journal of the German History Society*, Vol. 13, No. 3 (Oxford, 1995), pp. 348–51.

2. Hermann Bausinger, 'Wie die Deutschen zu Reiseweltmeister werden', in H.W. Hütter, P. Rösgen and S. Diemer (eds), *Endlich Urlaub! Die Deutschen reisen. Begleitbuch zur Ausstellung im Haus der Geschichte der Bundesrepublik Bonn, 6. Juni bis 13. Oktober 1996* (Cologne, 1996), p. 25. This book was produced to accompany an admirable exhibition on German tourism presented in the Museum for the History of the Post-war Period in Bonn. I owe much of the information in the section which follows to the book and to the exhibition.

Tourism and the west Germans

Mass tourism did not, of course, begin in postwar Germany. It had been a western European phenomenon since the second half of the nineteenth century, pioneered by the British entrepreneur, Thomas Cook. German travel firms had existed in the Weimar Republic, but under the Third Reich restrictions on foreign travel had limited tourism, even though the nazis had boasted of their regimented 'Strength through Joy' holidays.

After the end of the war, West Germany hardly appeared able to offer much for tourists. In October 1947 an estimate of the number of holiday beds available claimed that all but about 13 per cent of those existing before the war had been lost to tourism. Bombing, refugees and Allied requisitioning had had a devastating effect. But still, the desire to escape from the grim reality of postwar life encouraged some to take holidays, and there were tour operators eager to reactivate the market. The most famous was Carl Degener, who had already organized holidays in the Bavarian Alps before the war. In December 1947 he rented about 1,000 beds in the little Bavarian town of Ruhpolding and transported winter holidaymakers there in special trains from Hamburg – a journey of nearly 1,000 kilometres which took 23 hours. From 1949 onwards, tourism in the Bavarian Alps blossomed. Ruhpolding itself had 6,000 visitors in 1949; two years later the figure had risen to 23,000 and in 1954 it played host to 34,000 – all attracted by fresh air, Alpine scenery and skiing. Meanwhile, Degener had been developing one of the most important travel firms in West Germany, *Touropa*, which was established with that name in 1951. He bent his efforts to improving the quality of his special trains, which were transformed from dilapidated coaches with wooden seats into plush couchettes boasting modern comforts.

Between 1950 and 1954 almost 400,000 Germans travelled on Degener's organized holiday journeys. *Touropa* also started running holidays abroad, and in this it was not alone. One pre-war firm providing rather adventurous tours had been that of Dr Hubert Tigges and his wife Maria, and they were soon back in business. By 1950 they were organizing pilgrimages to Rome, and two years later they had a foreign travel programme encompassing Portugal, Spain and even Algeria. The year 1953 saw the foundation of *Scharnow Reisen*, the second largest tour operator in the first two decades of the Federal Republic. Another company, Hummel, involved leading Hamburg newspapers like *Die Welt* collaborating with travel agencies.

Nevertheless, in the early 1950s most holiday travel remained within the Federal Republic. Before the war, the northern coasts of Germany and the Baltic coast had been major holiday objectives, but the loss of access to much of the Baltic as the result of the Cold War, and the large refugee population in Schleswig-Holstein, meant that West Germans tended to go south, to Bavaria or the Black Forest. Travel abroad was complicated, owing to the need to obtain visas and permits for foreign currency. Germans were also uneasy about travelling outside the German-speaking area for fear of arousing hostility amongst local populations who might have bitter memories of nazi occupation. Another problem was that, until May 1955, the Federal Republic did not control its own air space, so that flying was not a serious option for the German holidaymaker.

As the 1950s wore on, however, a combination of rising living standards, higher expectations and relaxed travel restrictions meant that holidays abroad became much more popular. Already in 1955, 300,000 West Germans travelled to foreign countries by train. By 1958, most visa requirements within the new European Economic Community had been dropped and West Germans no longer needed to worry about foreign exchange controls; it was not for nothing that Erhard had been called 'Mr Convertibility' by the Americans. The soundness of the German currency meant that foreign holidays were not only exciting but comparatively cheap – a characteristic which became more obvious as the D-Mark steadily appreciated in value throughout most of the Bonn Republic's history.

With the return of German sovereignty in 1955 and developments in civil aviation, the possibilities for air travel improved. In the summer of 1955 Lufthansa, the West German state airline, was established. The same year saw the creation of two air charter companies, LTU and Deutscher Flugdienst. The latter was soon taken over by Lufthansa and retitled Condor. Business flourished and in 1965 the charter companies started flying jet airliners. In 1971 Condor became the first charter airline in the world to fly a 'jumbo jet' Boeing 747. Spain was the prime target for German charter flights, and in 1975 Majorca alone received seven million German visitors.

Flying was not, however, the main means of transport. Railways and bus companies also saw business booming, but above all it was the development of private motor car ownership which transformed the Germans into one of the most enthusiastic travelling peoples in Europe. In 1956 there were four million private cars in West Germany; by 1967 this had risen to fourteen million. Between 1954 and 1960 the percentage of the increasing numbers of West German holidaymakers who travelled in their own cars doubled. Camping became very popular, with the citizens of the Federal Republic heading south in droves, first to Bavaria, Austria and Switzerland, and then to the Mediterranean. Italy became a prestigious holiday destination. At least one small car advertised itself as ideal for camping in Italy.* Italian clothes, popular songs and food became highly fashionable.

The surging tide of German tourism, which was never to ebb in the history of the Bonn Republic, was an interesting example of demand creating supply, and vice versa. The economic 'miracle' of Ludwig Erhard enabled West Germans to afford holidays; the holiday business itself boomed and created jobs. German manufacturers found markets in their own country for all kinds of tourist-related goods, ranging from mass-produced 'Italian' pasta to sun-tan lotions and fashion wear for Mediterranean beaches. German consumers took to tourism with unalloyed enthusiasm. In 1968 there were about as many Germans holidaying abroad as there were choosing to stay in the Federal Republic. Thereafter the percentages tilted in favour of foreign holidays. Destinations became more varied and more exotic as the competition between tour operators intensified and real prices fell. When the Bonn Republic reached its end in October 1990, 70 per cent of its citizens travelled on holiday at least once a year – many more often than that – and most of those holidays were taken abroad.

This emphasis on holidays as the high points of the good life for West German citizens was paralleled, and to a certain extent made possible, by the increase in leisure time afforded to the mass of west Germans after 1949. Entitlement to paid holidays had already been accepted in the western occupation zones as part of workers' rights, and in the early years of the Federal Republic workers could claim twelve working days' holiday per year. In 1963 a federal law was passed which increased the minimum holiday entitlement to eighteen days. In addition, the working week, which was 48 hours in the 1950s, was steadily whittled down, so that by 1990 it was only 38.5 hours.[3] Saturday working became the exception rather than the norm. Already by the end of the 1950s the concept of the 'happy weekend' (*das schöne Wochenende*) was well established, with shops closing at midday on Saturday and families retiring to their balconies and gardens or, increasingly, using their more abundant spare time to go skiing, hiking and camping.

---

* The Zündapp 'Janus', developed by Klaus Dornier in 1955, had back-to-back seats which folded out as beds.

3. G. Langguth, *In Search of Security. A Socio-Psychological Portrait of Today's Germany* (Westport, Conn., 1995), p. 14.

One interesting account of West German tourism has even argued that freedom to travel is a symptom of a change in mentality: 'The upgrading of leisure alters social norms. Spontaneity, mobility, the capacity for enjoyment and an interest in new experiences replaced the old values of order, thrift and self-discipline associated with the work ethic.'[4] A German sociologist who studied West Germans' use of leisure time pointed out that, in the early years of the Federal Republic, survival and recovery caused most people to cling to their work as their main social activity, and that this encouraged a hierarchical way of thinking. In the 1960s, however, the consumer society removed some of the anxieties associated with the work ethic, and generational differences became more important than social hierarchies.[5]

It is not at all clear that Erhard himself would have welcomed this development. In 1963 he rejected trade union claims for even more generous holiday pay as 'social humbug'.[6] But the fact was that West Germany's affluence was partly due to the economic policies associated with his social market economy.

Erhard's election triumph

Erhard's popularity certainly manifested itself at the next Bundestag election, in September 1965, when the CDU/CSU increased its share of the vote to 47.6 per cent, its second highest federal poll percentage since the foundation of the FRG. Although the FDP fell back to just under 10 per cent, and the SPD obtained its best ever result – nearly 40 per cent of the votes cast – the upshot was a clear victory for the government and a personal triumph for Erhard. Brandt, once again the SPD's chancellor candidate, returned to Berlin in despair, believing his career had reached a dead end.

But events were soon to take another turn. Erhard was popular, but he was not a strong chancellor. With the removal of Adenauer's iron hand, many of Erhard's colleagues showed themselves unwilling to exercise even that modicum of discipline they had displayed under the regime of *der Alte*. Erhard allowed Adenauer to continue as chairman of the CDU in Bonn, a post he used to encourage

4. Anegela Stirken, 'Reisezeit–Zeitreise. Ziel, Konzept und Realisierung der Ausstellung', in Hütter, Rösgen and Diemer (eds), *Endlich Urlaub!*, p. 9.

5. Gerhard Schulze, *Die Erlebnisgesellschaft. Kultursoziologie der Gegenwart* (3rd, revised, edn, Frankfurt, 1992), pp. 532–40.

6. Hütter, Rösgen and Diemer (eds), *Endlich Urlaub!*, p. 22.

intrigues against his successor. There were conflicts over foreign policy between 'Atlanticists' – Erhard himself and the Foreign Minister, Gerhard Schröder – and 'Gaullists', like Adenauer and Strauss, who at least pretended they wanted a harder line adopted towards the East based on co-operation with France. This was always an illusory policy, but it served as a stick with which to beat Erhard and his liberal supporters.

Economic problems in the mid-1960s

Erhard could probably have overcome this problem had he not been faced with difficulties in the area that had gained him such prestige – the economy. The West German boom had been surging forward, but the economy was now beginning to overheat. The cost of earlier electoral bribes, such as Adenauer's dynamic pensions, and the loss of a steady flow of cheap but trained labour from the GDR, were beginning to affect the economy. In 1964 the annual growth rate of real GDP reached 6.7 per cent, but signs of inflation were apparent. The following year inflation rose to nearly 4 per cent – certainly not a catastrophic figure – and a budget deficit appeared for the first time since 1951. Being election year, public purse strings were loosened and the deficit grew to 1.4 per cent of GNP.[7]

The Council of Experts Erhard had established to advise the government on economic policy produced a report in November 1965 called *Stabilization without Stagnation*, which drew attention to the stresses in the economy. These seemed likely to produce a typical boom and bust situation unless concerted, gradual and cautious measures were taken to combat inflation. Only in that way could a damaging downturn be avoided.[8] The experts also favoured a revaluation of the D-Mark, which would have made imports cheaper and sharpened the competition for exports. Erhard, however, neglected to follow this wise advice.

Instead, in November 1965, he obtained a Bundestag law to secure the budgetary balance. Interest rates were increased and public spending cut. The intention was to demonstrate the power of the Bundesbank to face down inflationary tendencies. The result was a sharp recession in the years 1966/7: investment went into reverse and in 1967 GDP actually shrank by 0.1 per cent. Unemployment

7. Hans Giersch, Karl-Heinz Paqué and Holger Schmieding, *The Fading Miracle. Four Decades of Market Economy in Germany* (Cambridge, 1992), pp. 142–3.
8. Ibid., p. 143.

rose slightly, though it was still only 3.1 per cent at the trough of the downturn.[9]

By comparison with conditions in western Europe during the 1990s, the situation was almost idyllic, but it aroused great concern in West Germany. Memories of the inter-war economic crisis and its damaging political results still haunted the older generation which had experienced the impact of the 1929 Wall Street crash. The recession, relatively trivial though it was, had dented the aura of constant progress which had characterized Germany's economy since the early 1950s. Public reaction was almost hysterical. A poll taken in the summer of 1966 showed that 20 per cent of those questioned thought a 1929-type slump to be 'certain' and another 42 per cent thought it 'fairly probable'.[10]

Once again, the importance of the federal structure of the West German state was demonstrated when North Rhine-Westphalia, the most populous of all the *Länder* and still one of the most important economically, went to the polls to elect a new *Landtag* on 10 July 1966. The result was a serious shock for the CDU. Erhard's party dropped back by nearly 4 per cent of its vote, but more worrying was the performance of the SPD which, for the first time, outstripped the CDU in North Rhine-Westphalia and obtained nearly 50 per cent of the votes cast.

The result was a crisis in the government because the measures needed to bridge the budget deficit were controversial. The CDU favoured tax increases; the Free Democrats would only contemplate cuts in public expenditure. In the next few months Erhard's government fell apart at the seams, rent by personal rancour and party squabbling. The FDP's more liberal wing had never been happy in the Adenauer coalition and distrusted the 'Gaullists' who were intriguing against Erhard. For his part, Adenauer made no secret of his desire to see his successor replaced with a younger and more authoritative figure.

Erhard's fall

Now that Erhard's power as an 'electoral locomotive' seemed to have deserted him, respect for his economic policy seemed to evaporate

9. Ibid., p. 145.

10. A.J. Nicholls, *Freedom with Responsibility. The Social Market Economy in Germany, 1918–1963* (Oxford, 1994), p. 365. See also Klaus Hildebrand, *Geschichte der Bundesrepublik Deutschland. Vol. IV, Von Erhard zur Großen Koalition, 1963–1969* (Stuttgart, 1984), p. 207.

in Bonn. Those within the CDU who hankered after a great coalition with the SPD were encouraged. They included the federal president, Heinrich Lübke. He used his influence to further an arrangement between the two major parties. On 27 October the FDP ministers in Erhard's government refused to compromise over tax increases and resigned. Erhard's own party then designated as his successor the premier of Baden-Württemberg, Georg Kiesinger, and began to negotiate with the Social Democrats. On 27 November the terms for a CDU/SPD coalition were agreed, and two days later the luckless Erhard resigned.

Doubtless a number of political factors played a part in his downfall. The relentless intriguing of Adenauer, Strauss and others, coupled with a certain lack of ruthlessness on his part, help to explain his extraordinary fall from grace, as do the labyrinthine machinations of the Free Democrats, for whom Erhard ought to have been the ideal chancellor. But some in the FDP reckoned that Erhard himself offered the liberals little chance of broadening their own niche in politics, since his policies were so near to their own. As for the CDU/CSU, many of them were heartily sick of the pretensions of the FDP, associating it with the anti-government campaigns of liberal journalists like Augstein or Ahlers. They saw a great coalition as the opportunity to crush the Free Democrats by reforming the electoral law. Reducing the element of proportional representation would, it was hoped, create a two-party system in which the CDU/CSU would have a built-in advantage.

The NPD

It should not be overlooked, however, that there were more deep-seated signs of malaise in the mid-1960s. The recession punctured economic euphoria; the stagnant situation with regard to East Germany bred resignation over national division. For the first time since the early 1950s, neo-nazi elements began to show their teeth. During the government crisis in November 1966 there had been *Land* elections in Hesse and Bavaria. In each case a new party was returned to the *Land* parliament, the National Democratic Party of Germany (NPD). The NPD was careful to deny any anti-democratic intentions, and unctuously committed itself to upholding the Basic Law of the Federal Republic. It could not, therefore, be prohibited in the same manner as the Socialist Reich Party of Ernst Remer.[11]

11. See above, Chapter 4.

Nevertheless, its associations with the extreme right were all too obvious. It stood for the indivisible unity of Germans and an anti-communist alliance. It accused the 're-educated' citizens of the Federal Republic of having betrayed younger generations by denying their own right to self-determination. It spoke of a national ideal which would develop 'explosive force' against 'foreign domination and imperial forces' – a barely coded message of hatred for Germany's western Allies. It attacked the mass media and the 'so-called pluralistic society', demanding instead a stronger state representing the will of the people. The NPD enthusiastically embraced historical arguments which were surfacing at this time suggesting that Hitler had not been responsible for the outbreak of the Second World War, or at least that Allied policies had been as reprehensible as those of Germany.[12]

It is important to remember that the NPD, which drew support from areas and social groups which had earlier supported the NSDAP in the 1920s, had already emerged before the great coalition of Christian and Social Democrats took office in Germany. It was not that coalition that produced the crisis, but the weaknesses within the two parties that had governed Germany for most of the preceding seventeen years.

West Germany faces up to its past

One of these weaknesses was the failure to face the facts of Germany's nazi past. As we have seen, it was to the advantage of the Adenauer regime that former nazis and collaborators who had valuable professional expertise were able quietly to assimilate themselves within Adenauer's new system, so long as they at least paid lip service to democracy. In the early years of the Federal Republic it could also be argued that most people were too busy with their economic problems to pay much attention to awkward questions of recent history.

There was in actual fact much serious and often brilliant research being conducted into the realities of the Third Reich by scholars such as Karl Dietrich Bracher, a professor of politics at Cologne and Bonn universities, and above all in the Institute of Contemporary History at Munich, two of whose directors, Helmut Krausnick and

---

12. A.J.P. Taylor's *The Origins of the Second World War* (London, 1961) was wilfully misunderstood as an exculpation of Hitler. For a brief description of the NPD and some of its programmatic statements, see A.J. Nicholls, 'Political Parties', in Carl-Christoph Schweitzer *et al.* (eds), *Politics and Government in the Federal Republic of Germany, 1944–1994. Basic Documents* (1st edn, Leamington Spa, 1984), pp. 197, 227.

Martin Broszat, set new standards of scholarship in their investigations of Hitler's nazi system. In 1955 Bracher had produced a monumental study of the collapse of the Weimar Republic, and followed this up five years later with a well-documented account of Hitler's seizure and consolidation of power.[13] Krausnick and his colleagues published a powerful indictment of the nazi system of terror, including the SS and the concentration camps, a study originally produced as background information for a trial of former concentration camp staff.[14] Martin Broszat was to begin a long-standing controversy by pointing out that the Third Reich had not been a monolithic system responding consistently to one man's inflexible will, but rather a confused maelstrom of competing agencies in which ambition and greed for power had played an important role at all levels.[15] Naturally it took time for the results of this research to appear, and even then it was not always communicated very rapidly to the mass of the population. But by the mid-1960s it was becoming more difficult to claim that Hitler was an aberrant figure in German history who had led the less respectable elements in society astray by playing on resentments over problems outside Germany's control.

At the same time some rather laggardly efforts were being made to bring those guilty of serious nazi crimes to justice. In 1958 a Central Office for the Pursuit (*Verfolgung*) of National Socialist Crimes of Violence was set up at Ludwigsburg. Even so, it was not given much in the way of resources, and the results were not initially impressive. In court cases against nazi judges who had sentenced people to death for political 'crimes' under the Third Reich or who had been involved in racial and eugenic persecution, the judges got off better than the widows and orphans of their victims. Judges in the courts of the Federal Republic were willing to accept nazi 'law', despite its arbitrary and even criminal character: 'What was then law cannot count as illegal today.'[16] This was a principle which was to be forgotten after 1990, when the issue of dealing with the former German Democratic Republic came onto the agenda.

13. The second study was a combined effort with Sauer and Schulz. See K.D. Bracher, *Die Auflösung der Weimarer Republik. Eine Studie zum Problem des Machtverfalls in der Demokratie* (Stuttgart and Düsseldorf, 1955); K.D. Bracher, W. Sauer, G. Schulz, *Die nationalsozialistische Machtergreifung. Studien zur Errichtung des totalitären Herrschaftssystems in Deutschland 1933/34* (Cologne and Opladen, 1960).

14. Published in English as H. Krausnick *et al.*, *The Anatomy of the SS State* (London, 1968).

15. Martin Broszat, *Der Staat Hitlers* (Munich, 1969).

16. Kurt Sontheimer, *Die Adenauer Ära: Grundlegung der Bundesrepublik* (Munich, 1991), p. 179.

By the early 1960s, however, a change in the atmosphere could be detected. Contributory causes of this were the trial of Adolf Eichmann in Jerusalem, which went on for the better part of two years and culminated in his execution on 1 June 1962, and the trial of 22 Auschwitz personnel in Frankfurt 1964/5. The former kept the issue of nazi crimes alive in the media; the latter was particularly important for the amount of well-documented information it presented to the public about the mechanism of repression in the Third Reich and the appalling extent of nazi atrocities against the Jews, a subject which many Germans had been reluctant to confront. In the spring of 1965 the statute of limitations affecting nazi crimes of violence so far undetected was due to come into effect. The FDP and the CSU, both of which had many former nazis among their supporters, wanted a line drawn under the issue, claiming that most serious nazi criminals had by now been prosecuted. The cabinet was divided, but agreed to follow the line of the FDP justice minister in favour of applying the deadline. But on 25 March 1965, after an impressive debate, the Bundestag extended the time limit to 31 December 1969. This meant that nazi criminals could not feel safe even if their activities had not so far been the subject of prosecution.[17]

The precedent set by the Bundestag on that occasion was followed throughout the history of the Bonn Republic and finally the statute of limitations was abolished. Whatever criticism may be levelled against the West Germans for their initial indifference towards the issue of complicity in nazi crimes, they never allowed the matter to be swept under the carpet, as was the case in some other European countries. Nor did they content themselves with claiming that they had been 'liberated' from national socialism by their allies and therefore had no responsibility for it, as was the case in Ulbricht's GDR.

The beginnings of student unrest

Paradoxically, the building of the Berlin Wall had made it easier for critical voices to be heard within the Bonn Republic. The steady stream of refugees from the GDR had meant that tension *viv-à-vis* the east was constantly maintained, and the refugees themselves

---

17. Hildebrand, *Von Erhard zur Großen Koalition*, pp. 130–4. Erhard was personally in favour of extending the time limit, and was outvoted in cabinet. His unhappiness about this was known to the Bundestag members when they voted against the government's recommendation. The FDP Justice Minister, Blücher, was forced to give up office by his party for not having enforced the statute of limitations.

influenced West Germans against the concept of Marxist socialism. When the Wall was closed, however, the impact of newly arrived refugees from Ulbricht ceased. This had a particular effect on the Free University of Berlin (FUB), which had been established in west Berlin with American support. The Free University self-consciously stood for democratic rights and academic freedom, in contrast with the communist-dominated Humboldt University in east Berlin. It had more independence than most German universities, which were sub-servient to their *Land* ministries of education. Its constitution estab-lished academic self-government, but it also created an element of student representation and a student assembly, or *Konvent.* In the early days of the Free University, when numbers were small, students were involved in decision-making, including the choice of staff. As time went on, however, professors imported from West Germany refused to consult students on matters of policy or staffing. The students had also refused to allow the traditional German student corporations to establish themselves at the Free University, owing to their anti-democratic and anti-semitic traditions. This too aroused friction with West German authorities.[18]

Another factor which began to be of importance in the 1960s was the opportunity which study in Berlin gave for young west Germans to avoid conscription into the *Bundeswehr*. Under the special arrange-ments agreed for Berlin between the powers, her citizens were not obliged to serve in the West German army.

In addition to this particular problem in Berlin, there was a deeper-rooted discontent in West German universities as the result of increasing student numbers and deteriorating staff–student ratios. In the inter-war period German universities had been relatively small places with an overwhelmingly middle-class clientele. Professors lived sheltered existencies devoting themselves to research, and much of the teaching was carried out by unestablished lecturers – *Privat-dozenten* – who received payment according to the size of their lecture audiences. This system had certainly created a high profes-sional reputation for German scholarship – at least before the arrival of Hitler – but it was not well attuned to the needs of mass education. Students did not have a clear programme of work to follow which would lead them to a qualification within a prescribed period of time. They could register at universities if they had passed their

18. The particular history of the Free University is sometimes neglected when describing the so-called 'student revolution' in west Germany. For a partisan but nonetheless interesting account of this see Uwe Bergmann's chapter in U. Bergmann, R. Dutschke, W. Lefèvre and B. Rabehl, *Rebellion der Studenten oder die neue Opposition* (Rowohlt/Reinbeck bei Hamburg, 1968), pp. 7–32.

secondary school-leaving test, the *Abitur*, and then spend years in self-directed study before presenting themselves for a state examination. The latter was designed to qualify them for some area of the public service: the judiciary, the higher bureaucracy, medicine or teaching – the latter being the only option for most arts students. The main non-vocational qualification was the doctorate, to which only a small minority of students could aspire.

This system worked well enough so long as the student body was self-selecting, with a preponderance of its members being the children of academically trained parents. But as the 1960s wore on, so larger and larger numbers of students began pressing into German universities, lured by hopes of social advancement. This also reflected a trend amongst parents to want to opt for an academic training for their children in schools since that was seen as the passport to genteel, interesting and safe careers. Professors themselves enjoyed high esteem in West Germany; they were well paid and enjoyed the privileges of officials without being directly subservient to state administrations. Pressure grew for higher education to be made accessible to all irrespective of parental wealth, and although there was no comprehensive system of maintenance grants, as in Britain, university fees were very low. Students often had access to low-cost accommodation and enjoyed various financial advantages such as cheap fares, subsidized canteens and reductions on entrance fees to museums, theatres and even cinemas.

The students found themselves in crowded lecture rooms, with little direction for their studies and little hands-on supervision. The purpose of their university life was not made clear to them; on the other hand their parents' new-found affluence meant that most of them could afford to stay on as students for several years. Students were often in their late twenties before they quit university to enter employment. It was a formula for disaster.

The exact nature of the disaster, which was to develop into the greatest trauma of the entire history of the Federal Republic, was not, however, entirely due to the expansion of university student numbers in the postwar period. It was also affected by an obvious gap between the liberal, democratic ideals proclaimed by the political leaders of the country, reinforced by press or radio comments, and the practice in university teaching, which remained hierarchical and authoritarian.[19] To be sure, there had been intellectual currents

19. Rudolf Walter Leonhardt wrote in 1962 that the leadership principle and the personality cult still dominated German universities; see Sontheimer, *Adenauer Ära*, p. 152.

conducive to change. In particular, those academic disciplines relating to politics, social studies or the study of recent history were susceptible to influences from America, and in this the work of German scholars exiled during the Third Reich was often of importance. In sociology Adorno, Horkheimer, König and Plessner became powerful advocates of a critical tendency in theoretical sociology, and Ernst Fraenkel, C.J. Friedrich and Bergstraesser were advocates of pluralistic systems in political science. The fact that many of these scholars were concerned with theory should not obscure the fact that empirical methods of assessment, and in particular sampling techniques in public opinion surveys, were the most obvious gifts of American political science to the West German academic and political culture.

Ambitious younger scholars in the arts and social sciences sought to go to America for at least part of their training and could thus speak and, of course, read fluent English. Yet many other faculties were less affected by 'Americanization', and these included those, like medicine and law (as well as a discipline called 'Allgemeine Staatslehre' – involving a legalistic approach to the subject of government), which remained under the control of men who had been trained in the inter-war period.[20] Many of them had collaborated with the nazis, and some were former party members. They were obviously vulnerable to criticism when they started preaching the values of a western way of life to a generation of students untainted with nazism and for whom the Soviet threat was becoming less of a reality. The building of the Berlin Wall had sealed off West Berlin and West Germany from the refugees from communism who had previously streamed into the country. Khrushchev's defeat in the Cuban missiles crisis seemed to show that the West was strong enough to resist communism, and confrontation was gradually replaced with co-existence. So the younger generation no longer felt threatened by a 'Red Menace'.

The Free University of Berlin

At the Free University of Berlin there was growing discontent over the contrast between the apparently free and democratic constitution

---

20. For a discussion of the nature and significance of *Allgemeine Staatslehre*, E. Vollrath, 'Perspectives of Political Thought in Germany after 1945', in R. Pommerin (ed.), *Culture in the Federal Republic of Germany, 1945–1995* (Oxford, 1996), pp. 37–9. See also Sontheimer, *Adenauer Ära*, p. 155.

of the FUB and the authorities' hostility to political activity on the part of the students. When the student body had been protesting against the totalitarian methods of the communists in the Humboldt University of east Berlin, the professoriat was happy to give it free rein. But when student criticism began to be levelled at the Bonn government or – even more embarrassing – the Americans, tolerance and freedom of speech became less attractive. These difficulties had been manifesting themselves since 1958, when the student *Konvent* had tried to issue a questionnaire to students about the arming of the *Bundeswehr* with atomic weapons and the university authorities (*Rektorat*) had threatened to dissolve the *Konvent*. Attempts by the student executive (*Asta*) to air the issue of ex-nazi judges, prosecutors and doctors active in public service in the FRG were met with moves by the Rector to stop the *Konvent* holding political discussions. In 1965 such a discussion under the title 'Restoration or New Beginning – the Federal Republic twenty years after [the end of the war]' was banned and had to be held in the Technical University, a measure which provoked indignation among many hitherto apathetic FUB students.[21] The FUB had become a pressure cooker which was about to explode.

Extra-Parliamentary Opposition (APO)

The problems afflicting the universities also coincided with domestic political developments to which we have already alluded: the retirement of Adenauer, the eclipse of Erhard and the building of the great coalition between Christian and Social Democrats. The latter was a triumph for party managers like Wehner and opened a window of opportunity for Willy Brandt. It was certainly not unpopular with the mass of the German electorate. But to many of the more idealistic young supporters of the SPD it seemed as if the party had sold out to reaction. The Social Democratic Students' Federation (SDS) had long been a thorn in the flesh of the party's establishment; it had not been enthusiastic about the revisionist implications of the Godesberg Programme and its leaders tended to be embarrassingly outspoken. In 1961 the SDS was expelled from formal association with the SPD, but its members continued to agitate at universities and it not unnaturally continued to move to the left. Once the great coalition was established in 1966, radical

21. Bergmann in *Rebellion der Studenten*, pp. 10–17.

student contempt for what seemed to be a sham democracy in which shifty social democrats collaborated with former nazis became even stronger.

It was unfortunate in view of this that Kiesinger had himself been a member of the NSDAP who had broadcast propaganda on behalf of the Third Reich. Parliamentary opposition to him in the Bundestag consisted only of the very small liberal delegation, the FDP. It was led by Erich Mende, a right-thinking former *Wehrmacht* officer whose photogenic qualities were more striking than his commitment to participatory democracy. So for a radical younger generation of intellectuals, the parliamentary system seemed a fig-leaf for capitalist restoration.

In December 1966 some of the SDS radicals established a movement called the 'extra-parliamentary opposition' (APO – *Ausserparlamentarischer Opposition*) which was designed to express a socialist critique of the way the Federal Republic was developing. Its leader was Rudi Dutschke, who demanded a new system of direct democracy in which the people could vote their representatives in and out of office at will so as to inhibit institutional control.[22] APO was envisaged as an agitational movement to arouse apathetic German citizens to assert their rights. However, the 'extra-parliamentary' aspect of the movement could have sinister implications, and these rapidly manifested themselves.

Economic recovery and political confidence

For the time being, however, the first task of the Kiesinger government seemed to be to restore confidence in the economy. Kiesinger himself was urbane and adept at achieving compromise within his powerful but unwieldy coalition. Despite his former membership of the NSDAP, he was anything but a dogmatic, let alone a fanatical, figure. Like Erhard, he radiated optimism and, being unburdened with his predecessor's political difficulties, he was able to communicate this more cheerful feeling to the public at large.

In some ways the Christian/Social Democratic 'great coalition' marked an important stage in German history. Towards the end of the Weimar Republic the hapless Social Democratic leader, Hermann Müller, had presided over a coalition which had been given that

22. Dennis L. Bark and David R. Gress, *A History of West Germany*, Vol. 2, *Democracy and its Discontents, 1963–1988* (Oxford, 1989), pp. 121–2.

title. It had been a motley collection of parliamentary parties which were willing – albeit grudgingly in some cases – to accept the parliamentary system in the face of extremist movements which wanted to smash it up. There was little consensus or comradeship amongst Müller's colleagues. Kiesinger's coalition was led by an ex-Nazi Party member, its deputy chancellor and foreign minister, Willy Brandt, had been an anti-nazi exile, the minister for all-German affairs, Wehner, was an ex-communist and the finance minister, Franz-Josef Strauss, had been forced to resign his previous cabinet appointment for his part in the arrest of Konrad Ahlers, who now had a post as a junior press spokesman in the new government. Yet, on the whole, the atmosphere in the cabinet was relaxed and co-operative.[23] Parliamentary democracy had become the normal way of conducting German business.

It was the fear of an economic downturn accompanied by inflation that, however unfairly, had discredited Erhard. The new government had two very powerful figures in charge of economic affairs. Professor Karl Schiller, one of the most enthusiastic architects of the modernization of the SPD, became economics minister, and Franz-Josef Strauss finance minister. Of these two, Schiller was the trained economist, Strauss the tougher politician. For the time being they worked well in harness and created a positive atmosphere in business circles. The overheating which had so worried the Bundesbank had already ceased by the time the great coalition took over, and in 1967 GDP actually shrank by 0.1 per cent. By the end of 1966 the Bundesbank was ready to ease interest rates and they fell from 5 per cent in December 1966 to 3 per cent in May 1967. Schiller boosted employment with programmes of public expenditure on infra-structural improvements, such as communications, amounting to DM7.5 billion in 1967. Strauss balanced the budget by cutting expenditure and increasing taxes. By the following year West Germany had returned to her pattern of export-led economic growth. In the first six months of 1968 exports showed a growth rate of 8.4 per cent per annum; in the year 1968 overall, real GDP grew by 5.6 per cent.[24]

Considerable credit for this achievement should go to Karl Schiller for his breezy optimism and his capacity to communicate his faith in Keynesian demand management to a wider German public. He was

23. See the introduction by Karl-Dietrich Bracher to Hildebrand, *Von Erhard zur Großen Koalition*, p. 15.
24. See Michael Balfour, *Germany: The Tides of Power* (London, 1992), pp. 177–80; Giersch *et al.*, *Fading Miracle*, pp. 146–50.

an advocate of macro-economic measures to nudge the economy in suitable directions, provided these did not conflict with market principles. This policy, which included counter-cyclical measures such as public investment or tax cuts to stimulate growth in a recession, was described as 'global steering' and was to be achieved through concerted action between state authorities, trade unions and business leaders. Had the SPD been governing alone or with a left-wing partner, such policies would have been highly controversial. As it was, the CDU/CSU could hardly oppose them, and relied on Strauss to assure fiscal orthodoxy. The result was growth in confidence, since industry could feel that it was being supported by government policy, while the Bundesbank and the financial sector were happy that inflationary pressures were being resisted.

Doubtless the recovery which occurred in 1968 was influenced by many factors other than government action. The western world was still enjoying the long postwar boom, even though the Vietnam War was about to undermine the certainties of the Bretton Woods system of fixed exchange rates based on a powerful US dollar. The German economy, with its huge industrial base and its well-trained work-force, was fundamentally sound. Nevertheless, a weak or wrong-headed government could have damaged German resilience, and the fear that an economic downturn would lead to political crisis was very widespread in West Germany in the mid-1960s. In its most important task, that of restoring a sense of stability, the great coalition had therefore proved itself successful.

Problems of federalism

The more *dirigiste* tendencies of the great coalition put some strains on the federalist aspect of the Federal Republic. Schiller's concept of 'global steering' really implied a centralized approach to the economy, even if the methods to be used were largely indirect forms of financial influence over the economic process. It was in any case inevitable that, as the Federal Republic's commitment to social justice and educational expansion grew, so its power would increase *vis-à-vis* the *Länder*, or federal states. The share of income tax claimed by the federal, as against the *Land*, governments was steadily rising in the 1960s – from 35 per cent in 1962 to 39 per cent in 1968.[25]

25. Kurt Düwell, 'Die Entwicklung des Westdeutschen Föderalismus bis zur Mitte der 1960er Jahre', in J. Huhn and P-C. Witt (eds), *Föderalismus in Deutschland. Traditionen und gegenwärtige Probleme* (Baden-Baden, 1992), pp. 127–44. This issue is discussed on pp. 138–9.

On the other hand, Bonn was handing out subsidies to the *Länder* for all sorts of projects, ranging from building construction and water supplies to sports facilities. The subsidies, which ran into billions of marks even in the 1950s, came with strings attached, so that the *Länder* had to adopt federal policies if they were to receive the money.[26]

There was talk of 'co-operative federalism', following models adumbrated in the USA, where the federal government was also increasing its power *vis-à-vis* the federal states. This development alarmed some of the *Länder* politicians and they urged a proper reform of the financial system to secure their fair share of the finances. From the Bonn government's point of view, a reform would be useful precisely to legalize co-ordinated planning. In June 1967, Article 109 of the Basic Law was altered to ensure that *Land* governments' budgets would take account of the stability of the federal economy and *Länder* would have to accept Bundesbank bonds if this seemed necessary to rectify the business cycle. The government in Bonn was eager to extend its competence still further, and in a way which would expedite planning from Bonn. But the *Länder* proved tough nuts to crack, despite the fact that most of them were relatively new creations.

After much negotiation, a financial reform package was passed in May 1969. This created two new clauses in the Basic Law (91A and B) specifying areas of joint activity in which the federation could, on the basis of federal laws, involve itself in areas which had previously been reserved for the *Länder*, such as the expansion or creation of universities, structural improvements in the regional economy, and the improvement of agriculture or coastal defences. Generally speaking, the federation would bear half the costs of such activities, and the planning was to be shared between Bonn and the *Land* governments. The reform was hailed as 'the most profound and far-reaching reform of the Basic Law' so far carried out, but in practice it did not go nearly as far as some centralizers had hoped. If anything, it might be seen as a defensive victory for the *Länder*, since the new areas of federal competence had been limited in number and circumscribed in execution. Although the major revenues, income tax and corporation taxes, were to be divided between Bonn and the *Länder*, the central government's share of them was not to exceed 50 per cent.[27] The concept of global steering was expressed

26. Hans Boldt, 'Föderalismus im Widerstreit der Interessen. Die Bundesrepublik vor und nach der Finanzreform von 1969', in Huhn and Witt (eds), *Föderalismus in Deutschland*, pp. 145–64, esp. p. 146.

27. Boldt, 'Föderalismus im Widerstreit der Interessen', pp. 150–3.

in the establishment of a Financial Planning Council the same year and a grandiose project for 'concerted action' based on meetings between Bonn and the *Länder*.

In the end these schemes proved largely illusory. By the mid-1970s the gilt was beginning to wear off the gingerbread of economic planning, and in any case CDU victories in the *Länder* made it difficult for the social–liberal coalitions of Brandt and Schmidt to pressurize the federal states, since the Bundesrat majority could block such tendencies. Although Bonn still wielded great financial power *vis-à-vis* the *Länder*, and although it might be claimed that bureaucratic co-operation between federal and *Land* officials was weakening the authority of *Land* parliaments, the federal states retained their identity and continued to exercise an impressive amount of autonomy.

Emergency laws

In another area, however, the activities of the Bonn government helped to stir up the hornet's nest of youthful discontent referred to earlier in this chapter. Ever since West Germany had regained her sovereignty in the mid-1950s there had been discussion of the need for the Federal Republic to have provisions in its constitution to deal with emergencies. This was seen as filling a gap in the Basic Law, which had not provided adequately for measures to be taken by the state to protect itself if there were to be a war or a serious attack on the integrity of the state from within. Such a reform had been mooted since the early 1960s, but even moderate liberal critics were concerned lest West Germany should fall prey to the sort of rule by decree which had played such a fateful role in the collapse of the Weimar Republic, when Article 48 of the constitution had been exploited to the extent that it marginalized parliament. On the other hand, the situation could hardly be left as it was because, in the absence of German arrangements for dealing with emergencies, the Allied powers – or put more bluntly, the former occupiers – reserved the right to act themselves to restore order in West Germany if the need arose. So German politicians, especially on the right, were eager to fill this gap in their sovereignty by emergency regulations of their own.

The conflict over this came to a head in the early years of the great coalition, but it had already been rumbling along under the Erhard administration. In May 1965 a conference was held in the University of Bonn under the title 'Democracy and the State of Emergency', in which the major arguments against a new law were rehearsed. The organizers kept up their critique of government proposals through a body called Emergency of Democracy (*Notstand der Demokratie*). It should be emphasized that by no means all of the protesters were extreme radicals or students; ironically, a number of liberal-minded professors who later became targets of radical abuse were involved in opposing the new emergency laws.

However, in March 1967 the cabinet agreed that the Basic Law should be reformed to include measures necessary in times of emergency, and on 9 November 1967 there was for the first time a public hearing of the issue in the Bundestag. This called forth even more protests, and on 11 May 1968 30,000 demonstrators marched on Bonn. The majority of them were students, because the trade unions stayed aloof and organized their own protests.[28] The law was passed by the Bundestag on 30 May 1968 and established an elected committee of 22 Bundestag members and one representative of each *Land* drawn from the Bundesrat. If two-thirds of this body agreed that parliament was unable to function, it could promulgate a series of decrees which had already been debated and accepted by the Bundestag as part of the emergency package. Once this measure had passed into law in 1968 the issue died down remarkably quickly. The whole matter proved academic, because the emergency provisions were never invoked throughout the history of the Bonn Republic.[29] This was true even during the period of student unrest which had already begun when the Emergency Law was passed, and which intensified in the months that followed.

The 'student revolution', 1967–68

Not all the factors contributing to youth disturbances were domestic. In the student context the atmosphere was worsened by events in the United States. Whereas President Kennedy had been a cult figure for the young, his more effective successor, Lyndon B. Johnson, seemed less attractive and was in any case embroiled in the Vietnam War, a legacy of the Eisenhower and Kennedy administrations. As the war intensified and American involvement became more overt, student radicals at many American universities organized large-scale,

28. Hildebrand, *Von Erhard zur Großen Koalition*, pp. 369–70.
29. Ibid., pp. 369–71; Balfour, *Tides of Power*, p. 183.

and sometimes violent, demonstrations against it. The issue of Vietnam was also conflated with general criticisms of western 'neo-colonialism' in Third World countries. These concerns spread to west German university campuses; they can indeed be seen as an aspect of the Americanization of the Federal Republic.

In West Berlin, where the American protective presence was especially prominent, and where the Free University had been generously underpinned with American financial help, the contrast between the rhetoric of the free world and the behaviour of the American authorities in Vietnam seemed especially crass. German students were also highly critical of their own government, and of the west Berlin Senate, for supporting repressive pro-western dictatorships in Third World countries, such as that of Mobutu in Zaire and of Shah Mohammed Resa Pahlawi in Iran. The Iranian issue had a high profile at some German universities owing to the presence of many articulate and affluent Iranian students who were hostile to the Shah's regime.

Thus it was that, when the Shah made a state visit to the Federal Republic at the end of May 1967, large-scale demonstrations against him occurred in university towns, and above all in west Berlin. On 2 June 1967 the Shah went to the opera in Berlin. The Berlin police – who were augmented by agents of *Savak*, the notoriously brutal Iranian security services – launched an offensive against the demonstrators, and many were savagely beaten. One student participant, Benno Ohnesorg, was shot dead by a policeman, the first such death since the early 1950s. It was fairly clear that the shooting was quite unnecessary, but nobody was punished for it. Tabloid press reports ignored police tactics and concentrated on denouncing the demonstrators. Whatever the rights and wrongs of the incident, it served to inflame student feeling, and to reinforce the views of those who were urging direct action against 'capitalist' tyranny. The APO protests grew stronger.[30]

The student radicals mostly believed themselves to be Marxists, although they rejected the Soviet version of Marxism extant in the GDR. Some of them were even the children of recent immigrants from Soviet East Germany. They disliked Ulbricht's dictatorship but found that western capitalism was almost more distasteful. Dutschke himself was in this category. Ironically, the particular version of

---

30. Stefan Aust, *The Baader Meinhof Group. The Inside Story of a Phenomenon* (trans. A. Bell, London, 1987), pp. 41–2; see also H.K. Rupp, *Politische Geschichte der Bundesrepublik Deutschland* (Stuttgart, 1978), p. 154.

Marxism for which they stood was transmitted to them from North America through the medium of former exiles from the Third Reich. The most influential, if not the most intellectually convincing, of these was the political scientist Herbert Marcuse, whose critique of western capitalist society, *One-dimensional Man*, was published in 1964. This argued that for most people freedom was limited by their lack of economic power, that they were the objects of manipulation by capitalist media and advertising agencies and that they were being atomized into alienated isolation by the division of labour inherent in modern production methods. The capitalist state had no need of overt repression, as had been the case in Stalin's Russia, for instance, because its control over individuals' environment was so great that working people policed themselves. Dutschke and his followers picked up these ideas by inveighing against 'consumer terror' and the 'repressive tolerance' of western society which rendered serious criticism of the system impossible.

Even more seductive was the fact that the APO linked its anti-capitalist message with a demand for sexual liberation. Ideas drawn from post-Freudian socialists, such as Wilhelm Reich – who invented the 'Orgone accumulator' – were mixed up with a wave of self-righteous American pornography, typified by *Playboy*, to produce a heady brew of intellectually pretentious but excitingly erotic permissiveness. January 1967 saw the establishment of 'Commune 1' in west Berlin, a grouping of five men and two women dedicated to breaking down sexual taboos. All this came at a time when contraceptive pills were being made easily available, and when economic opportunities for young people had made independence from parental control easier to achieve than ever before.

The activities of the student radicals soon took on a disturbing character. Professors, and in particular liberal professors of politics or modern history, were heckled in their lectures and sometimes physically prevented from speaking. An ugly atmosphere of mob violence began to pervade the university campuses. Since there were so many students and so few staff, it was difficult to maintain discipline. State authorities and the police were reluctant to interfere in student activities.

In May 1967 extremists produced a number of pamphlets urging German students to follow the example of arsonists in Brussels who had burned a department store, killing 300 people. The thrust of the pamphlets was that, since protests against napalm and civilian bombing in Vietnam had failed, direct action was the only answer: 'For the first time in any big European city, a burning store full of burning people gives that crackling Vietnam feeling.' Not content with praising the action, a later pamphlet clearly urged that it should be imitated: 'Our Belgian friends have at last found the knack of really involving the population in all the fun of Vietnam; they set fire to a department store, three hundred complacent citizens end[ed] their exciting lives and Brussels became Hanoi. None of us need shed any more tears for the poor Vietnamese over our morning paper at breakfast. Now you can just go to the clothing department of Ka-De-We, Hertie, Woolworth, Billea or Neckermann and light a discreet cigarette in the changing room . . .'; 'Brussels has given us the only answer, "burn Warehouse burn".' This last exhortation was rendered in English, with 'Warehouse' being a mistranslation of the German word for department store.

Such stores were particularly offensive to the radical left because they were seen as symbols of capitalist power and 'consumer terror'. It was ironic that the nazis, too, had made department stores a target of their venomous hatred, though in their case it was because many of the stores were Jewish owned. It was to take some time before words were turned into actions, but on the night of 2 April 1968 two of the more extreme radicals, Gudrun Ensslin and Andreas Baader, started fires in two stores in Frankfurt.[31]

University reforms

The radicals did not, of course, represent all students. There were many faculties, such as law and medicine, where they had little impact. It was sad, but predictable, that these were the most reactionary and hierarchical faculties. Medicine also had the largest number of professors tainted by collaboration with nazi atrocities during the Third Reich. In some respects, the result of the student movement was anything but progressive. At a time when the condition of German universities was provoking discussion anyhow, the shrill demands for radical change enunciated by the student leaders led the universities down false paths of reform. Instead of introducing more clearly structured courses, reducing the power of individual professors *vis-à-vis* the rest of the teaching faculty and increasing the number of properly paid lecturers, the reformers were seduced into discussions of 'democratic' restructuring.

31. Aust, *The Baader Meinhof Group*, pp. 33–5, 50. The quotations are in the translated version produced by A. Bell. The fires in Frankfurt did not involve casualties, but caused over half a million D-Marks of damage. See also Hildebrand, *Von Erhard zur Großen Koalition*, pp. 383, 471.

These culminated in the demand for *Drittelparität*, which meant equal representation for students, professors and other staff in the universities' governing bodies. All that did was to create a happy hunting ground for student politicians and a recipe for endless discussions and delays in university administration. Since this form of democratization was bound in the end to be dysfunctional, the really reactionary professors could withdraw comfortably into their shells and await the collapse of the reforms. There were, to be sure, some improvements in the German university system. A number of new universities were opened, although some of them, like Bochum, rapidly became just as impersonal and overcrowded as their more traditional counterparts. Attempts to create smaller and more intimate institutions, such as the University of Constance, were rarely successful. A new category of university teacher, something approaching an American assistant professor or a British lecturer, was established in the form of the 'intermediate academic structure' (*akademischer Mittelbau*), but this was never popular with professors and was allowed to wither as time went by.

Suggestions that the wearisome process of apprenticeship created by the system of *Habilitation*, or second doctorate, should be abolished, were accepted as sensible, but resolutely blocked. Under the *Habilitation* system, a university teacher in his thirties, who had already obtained a doctorate, was forced to remain subservient to a particular professor under whose auspices he would write his second thesis. Without this *Habilitation* he could not obtain a tenured position; once he had achieved it and been elected to a professorial post, he had a job for life and could not be removed. Moderate reformers wanted this system abolished and replaced by one in which all posts would be advertised and appointments would be made on the basis of the candidates' publications and teaching experience. This never happened. In fact, by the time the Bonn Republic ended in October 1990 it was more difficult to attain a university professorship without the *Habilitation* than it had been in the 1950s. The irrelevances of *Drittelparität* had blocked serious reforms which might otherwise have been implemented at a time of affluence.

The impact of the student rebellion

The immediate results of the student rebellion were also damaging for universities. Public buildings were occupied and covered with 'Marxist' graffiti. Maoist and 'Spartakist' minority groups set

206 *The Bonn Republic*

the tone of student discourse in such distinguished universities as Marburg, Heidelberg and Frankfurt. Strikes and demonstrations alienated the general public, who not unnaturally regarded students as a privileged and ungrateful group of young people trying to stir up trouble. Such resentments were exacerbated by a virulent campaign launched against the students in the tabloid press – most prominently Axel Springer's *Bild Zeitung*, which was itself a target of radical denunciation.

When Rudi Dutschke was shot in the head by a young working-class nationalist on 11 April 1968, furious criticism was levelled against the Springer press. Many otherwise moderate students and junior faculty members showed their solidarity with him. Although Dutschke survived the attack, he never really recovered from the shooting, and died in 1979. Nor did the APO campaign lead to any obvious or tangible results. Despite creating disruption in universities and occasional chaos in the streets, the maximalist agenda of the hard left remained a utopian pipe dream.[32] Dutschke accepted that revolution could not be brought about by using the universities as soviet republics, so he urged his followers to adopt the Leninist tactic of the 'long march through the institutions'. In practice that did not amount to much either, though it remained a standard bogey for the German right for the rest of the Republic's history, and was useful in the 1980s to support the repeated – and largely unsubstantiated – claim that the German media were infested with left-wing extremists.

This does not mean, however, that the student revolution was entirely unimportant. On the one hand, it created an atmosphere in which a younger generation could challenge the received wisdom of both the apologists for pre-1945 Germany and the anti-communist westernizers of the postwar era. The fact that many of the ideas adopted by the student radicals were irrational or even dangerous did not entirely undermine the importance of a new confidence among West German youth, and a widespread willingness to be critical of the society in which they found themselves. The political parties, however reluctantly, were forced to adapt to this new atmosphere. Although the SPD rejected the SDS, its leadership, and especially Willy Brandt after he relinquished the chancellorship in 1974, wanted to attract the critical generation without, of course, accepting

32. Rupp, *Politische Geschichte*, p. 154, and Bark and Gress, *Democracy and its Discontents*, pp. 122–6. Over the Easter holidays 1968 it was reported that there had been demonstrations in 27 west German cities, and 827 people had been arrested: Bark and Gress, *Democracy and its Discontents*, p. 125.

the Marxist extremism of a man like Dutschke. A new radicalism began to appear in the SPD – arguably to the detriment of its traditional appeal to working-class voters.

The FDP, faced with the wilderness of opposition in Bonn, also began to shift to the left, and the outspoken attacks on former nazis were also a factor in putting the old guard of Mende's type on the defensive. The left of the party, exemplified by Walter Scheel, Hans-Dietrich Genscher and Hildegard Hamm-Brücher, were supported by a new wave of younger members in pushing the FDP away from nationalism and *laissez-faire* economics towards a policy of socially responsible liberalism, including more stress on individual liberty against the state, on equal opportunities through improved public education, and social peace through new forms of co-determination. It was not until the early 1970s that these tendencies culminated in a new party programme, but they were at work in the late 1960s, and were helped by the general atmosphere of intellectual ferment.

Lastly, the techniques of demonstration, agitation and 'passive' resistance (which frequently degenerated into rioting) learned by the student masses in the late 1960s were to percolate into the political culture of protest in West Germany. This manifested itself during the last two decades of the Bonn Republic over such matters as resistance to nuclear power, campaigns against nuclear weapons, and opposition to building development deemed environmentally unsound or socially unjust. The Green movement, which broke through into the mainstream of German politics after 1980, owed a considerable amount to the activism of radical youth in the 1960s and 1970s. Whether this was an advantage or a drawback still remains to be seen.

However, as a direct assault on the institutions of a 'capitalist' state, the student revolution was, as we have noted, a failure. The great coalition of CDU/CSU and Social Democrats had succeeded in overcoming the economic crisis of the mid-1960s and, more important, the crisis of confidence in the system. It had illustrated that social democrats could function as efficient and responsible ministers, and that they could find considerable common ground with colleagues in the Christian parties. On both sides of the coalition there were those who would have liked it to continue. Chancellor Kiesinger was happy with it, and his CSU colleague Strauss also hoped that the promised electoral reform would eliminate the tiresome liberal Free Democrats, leaving Christian democracy in an unassailable position in Bonn. Within the SPD there were those, like the ex-Communist, Herbert Wehner, and the ambitious leader of the SPD delegation in the Bundestag, Helmut Schmidt, who preferred the fruits of power provided by a great coalition to the risk of an ideologically more defensible alliance with the left wing of the liberal FDP. Brandt, however, had never been particularly enthusiastic about the relationship with the CDU/CSU, and simply accepted it since 'no better solution seemed available'.[33] As mayor of west Berlin he had led a 'social–liberal' coalition with the FDP since 1963–66, and he was more comfortable with the liberals than with Adenauer's former colleagues in the CDU.

Brandt as Foreign Minister

Brandt was Foreign Minister and Deputy Chancellor to Kiesinger, and it was from his Foreign Office that tensions within the coalition often originated. Brandt favoured a much more flexible foreign policy than that traditionally followed by Adenauer and his successors. He thought that the whole concept of continuity between the postwar Federal Republic and the pre-war Reich was very questionable, and subsequently claimed that he would not accept 'any mistaken ideas about continuity, or that faith in miraculous legal formulae whereby Hitler's war was ostensibly consigned to oblivion or its consequences rescinded'.[34] This was at least partly aimed at the Hallstein doctrine, the principle enunciated by Adenauer's government in 1955 and named after Walter Hallstein, the legalistic State Secretary in the German Foreign Office when it was re-established under Adenauer. According to this 'doctrine' the Federal Republic would instantly break off diplomatic relations with countries recognizing the GDR.

Associated with it was the rigidly held position that the Federal Republic was the heir to the German Reich, which legally still existed within the frontiers of 1937 – that is to say, the frontiers established by the Versailles Treaty of 1919. Only a freely negotiated peace treaty could alter that position, which of course implied that Germany had territorial claims, not only on the GDR, but also on Poland and the Soviet Union. The GDR itself could never be referred to as such in public statements, but was always either descibed as the 'so-called' GDR, the 'GDR', the 'Soviet Zone of Occupation' or – most provocatively of all – 'Middle Germany'. The view of hard-line conservatives and their supporters in refugee organizations, which were

33. Willy Brandt, *My Life in Politics* (London, 1992), p. 154.
34. Ibid., p. 157.

well organized and vocal, was that any retreat from these principles would be to betray the cause of German unity and surrender to the Communists. In Kiesinger's own Federal Chancellery, which, as in the Adenauer era, still exercised great influence over foreign policy, there were powerful defenders of the hard-line position, including the Permanent State Secretary, the CDU member Karl Carstens, the long-serving head of the Foreign Affairs Department, Horst Osterheld, and the junior minister in charge, Freiherr Karl Theodor von und zu Guttenberg, a flamboyant Cold Warrior from the CSU. Brandt felt himself hamstrung in the face of such a power structure.[35]

A new policy towards the East – 'Ostpolitik'

The building of the Berlin Wall in 1961 had demonstrated that tough talking alone was not going to change the situation in Germany or Europe. It was also obvious that other western powers, including the USA, were moving towards an accommodation with the USSR in order to reduce the tensions and the expense of the Cold War. Bonn risked isolation if the West German government simply relied on the Hallstein doctrine as the cornerstone of its policy. Adenauer himself had, of course, opened relations with Moscow. After 1961 his foreign minister, Gerhard Schröder, had initiated what was described as a 'policy of movement' aimed at opening some sort of relationship with Soviet satellites in eastern Europe – except the GDR. Schröder pressed on with this also under Erhard but, although the Federal Republic opened trade missions in Poland, Hungary, Romania and Bulgaria, nothing much could be achieved without compromising the Hallstein doctrine.[36]

Meanwhile, in Berlin, Brandt had been developing a much more ambitious concept, born of his despair over the feeble western reaction towards the building of the Berlin Wall. His municipal administration had soon begun to operate its own informal relations with the GDR authorities in order to ameliorate the misery of divided families in the capital. He and his press spokesman, Egon Bahr, adopted a flexible approach to East–West relations, an approach in line with the conciliatory noises being made by President Kennedy in the summer of 1963, when he launched a 'strategy for peace'

---

35. Arnulf Baring, *Machtwechsel. Die Ära Brandt–Scheel* (Munich, 1984), p. 135.
36. Timothy Garton Ash, *In Europe's Name: Germany and the Divided Continent* (London, 1993), pp. 52–3.

based on western security and *détente* with the USSR. On 15 July 1963 Brandt and Bahr addressed a conference at the Protestant Academy in Tutzing, Bavaria, at which Brandt called for 'a policy of transformation'. Bahr went much further and declared that the only way to overcome the status quo was first to accept it, and that 'the preconditions for reunification are only to be created with the Soviet Union. They are not to be had in East Berlin, not against the Soviet Union, not without it'.[37]

Once Brandt became foreign minister in Bonn, he appointed Bahr head of his planning staff. There were numerous contacts with the Soviet bloc at all levels, including communist parties in the West. Needless to say, this aroused suspicions in the Federal Chancellery and Brandt became more and more irritated by the restrictions put upon his freedom of action within the coalition. Kiesinger himself repeatedly indicated his intention of trying to improve relations with the Russians, and denied any intention of destabilizing the eastern bloc countries. But, owing to the limitations of the Hallstein doctrine and the associated claim that Bonn should be accepted as the only representative of the German people, he could not get very far. In January 1967 the Federal Republic opened diplomatic relations with Romania, a nation exhibiting some independence in foreign policy. But this aroused concern in East Berlin and Moscow, so that other Soviet satellites were quickly warned off. Poland and Czechoslovakia signed friendship treaties with the GDR, forming what was decribed as an 'iron triangle' to resist West Germany's diplomatic offensive.[38]

It is sometimes suggested that the main lines of what was to be called *Ostpolitik* – the systematic attempt to improve relations with the USSR and her satellite countries without weakening the Federal Republic's links to the West – had already been adumbrated by Kiesinger during the great coalition, and that Brandt thereafter simply implemented a policy which was almost inevitable given the circumstances. In favour of this argument there is the fact that in mid-September 1969, whilst Kiesinger was still Chancellor, Moscow sent the Bonn government a formal offer of negotiations to reduce tension. Uppermost in the minds of the Soviet leaders seems to have been a desire for economic and technological benefits which might spring from trade with the Federal Republic. The fact that the Soviet suppression of reformist communism in Czechoslovakia in the summer of 1968 had provoked only very muted protests in the west –

37. Cited in ibid., p. 65.
38. Ibid., p. 56.

including West Germany – also encouraged a sense of security in Moscow; the Brezhnev doctrine seemed unchallenged.[39]

In fact, however, the half-heartedness of the CDU, and especially the CSU, and their inclination always to denounce any move towards the East as treason or softness on communism, made it very difficult to envisage rapid progress towards a real rapprochement between Bonn and Moscow. Indeed, the attitude of Adenauer's successors was more concerned with restoring the national status of the Reich to which the Federal Republic was supposedly the heir, than it was to adapting West German policy to the new realities of the international situation.

Such attitudes were displayed over the issue of West German adherence to the Allied nuclear non-proliferation treaty. Adenauer had been strongly opposed to this, and Franz-Josef Strauss described it as 'a new Versailles of cosmic extent'. Since, in the German Treaty of 1955, the Federal Republic had solemnly promised not to build weapons of mass destruction, Strauss's reaction must cast doubt on his good faith as a western ally. When this issue came onto the agenda of the great coalition in 1967, Brandt was willing to accept the treaty, but could not do so whilst harnessed to the Christian Democrats.[40] In this, as in the matter of *Ostpolitik*, Brandt found himself by 1969 much closer to the new leader of the Free Democratic Party, Walter Scheel.

Certainly, the desire for a new flexibility in West German foreign policy was not confined to the SPD. The Free Democrats had always been more willing to take risks for the sake of German unity than had their former coalition partners in the CDU/CSU.

The FDP leader in 1966, Erich Mende, was a cautious, nationalistic figure who clove strongly to a traditional anti-communist line, but other voices began to be heard within his party urging a change of tack. In January 1967 the FDP Central Committee discussed a confidential paper by Wolfgang Schollwer, editor of the party's journal *FD-Korrespondenz*, in which it was proposed to give up the old notion of reunification. Instead, the West Germans should recognize the GDR and the Oder–Neisse frontier in the hope of achieving de-Stalinization in the GDR and peace in central Europe. This point of view was taken up by powerful elements of the left-liberal press, such as Henri Nannen, the proprietor of *Stern*. His example was followed in *Der Spiegel*, *Die Zeit* and the *Frankfurter Rundschau*. Influential

---

39. Cf. ibid., pp. 56–7.
40. Brandt, *My Life in Politics*, pp. 158–62.

churchmen also added their voices to the chorus of criticism demanding a more imaginative policy towards the east. This was especially noteworthy among protestant clergy, who had strong ties to co-religionists in the GDR. Many younger members of the FDP were attracted by the notion of overcoming German disunity by the indirect method of creating a 'lasting all-European peace order'. Mende firmly rejected such ideas, and himself became a target for criticism. Since his party was facing possible extinction on the opposition benches, he was in any case about to lose his position as leader. In February 1968 he was pushed aside and replaced by one of the 'young Turks' from North Rhine-Westphalia, Walter Scheel. His deputy was Hans-Dietrich Genscher, who was destined to become Germany's longest-serving foreign minister and a major practitioner of *Ostpolitik*.[41]

Cracks in the great coalition

If *Ostpolitik* caused friction within the coalition, there were other tensions which in themselves were to prove fatal to it. One appeared at an early stage: the coalition arrangements in West Germany's most populous *Land*, North Rhine-Westphalia. As mentioned above, it had been the CDU defeat in the *Land* election of July 1966 that had heralded the fall of Ludwig Erhard. It had been assumed that this would lead to a great coalition in Düsseldorf, and the SPD's party chiefs in Bonn indicated that they expected this solution. But the rank-and-file supporters of the SPD in the *Land* rebelled and insisted on a coalition with the Free Democrats. It was a collaboration which was to prove very fruitful.

Then there was the issue of electoral reform. The electoral system adopted in the Federal Republic was a careful balance between democratic fairness – ensuring that as many votes as possible counted – and civic responsibility. The former was achieved by the PR element in voting – the second votes cast for party lists – and the latter by having at least half of the parliamentary seats directly elected and by setting up the 5 per cent hurdle to stop too many small parties entering parliament. It is significant that, as many countries have moved from authoritarian to democratic systems since 1980, several of them have taken the West German system as a model, whereas hardly any have chosen the first-past-the-post system favoured in

41. Hildebrand, *Von Erhard zur Großen Koalition*, pp. 340–50.

Britain. It was precisely this latter move that the CDU/CSU now contemplated, arguing that the federal German system made it almost impossible for one party to achieve a majority in parliament, and that this was threatening the stability of the state.

It is conceivable that some in the CDU/CSU, including the Minister of the Interior, Paul Lücke, were seriously concerned to prevent the Bonn Republic going the same way as its Weimar predecessor. It is equally obvious that some – including Franz-Josef Strauss – were mainly concerned to destroy the FDP and give the Union parties an electoral advantage over all others.[42] But that, of course, was hardly likely to please the junior coalition partner, the SPD. In January 1968 a public opinion survey demonstrated that under a first-past-the-post electoral system the SPD would experience a catastrophic defeat at the hands of the Christian parties. This really killed the reform, since SPD votes would be needed to pass it. Kiesinger was too shrewd to press the issue and Lücke resigned. In this, as in foreign policy, the FDP and the Social Democrats clearly shared common interests.

The atmosphere within the coalition became strained. Already in February 1969, when it had been necessary to elect a new president (speaker) of the Bundestag, it had been noted that most Social Democrats did not vote for their CDU colleague, Kai-Uwe von Hassel, who only scraped in with a narrow majority.

The election of President Heinemann

Another, and perhaps even more fateful, issue between the Christian Democrats and their SPD colleagues was that of the election of the Federal President. In 1964 the sitting president, Heinrich Lübke, had been re-elected for a second term of office with the support of the SPD. This had turned out to be unfortunate, since by 1967 he was showing signs of premature ageing. Although he did not in fact retire early, concern about his health focused attention on the problem of finding a successor. Once again, the presidential elections functioned as a political barometer.[43] It was therefore of considerable moment when, in June 1967, Brandt announced that his party would lay claim to the presidency when it fell vacant – after it had been held by a Free Democrat (Heuss) and a Christian Democrat

42. For a defence of Lücke's principled proposals, see ibid., p. 357.
43. See above, Chapter 7. Cf. Baring, *Machtwechsel*, p. 27.

(Lübke). The claim was officially confirmed in letters to Kiesinger and Strauss in August.

This put the CDU/CSU in an awkward position. Since the Chancellor and the President of the Bundestag were both Christian Democrats, there did seem good reason for the SPD to claim one major office. If the CDU/CSU did not support a Social Democratic candidate in the *Bundesversammlung* it might indicate the end of the great coalition. Kiesinger and Wehner hoped to find a candidate who could be acceptable to both parties, but the Chancellor failed to pursue this with sufficient energy. The Christian Democrats were in fact determined to present their own candidate, the defence minister – formerly foreign minister – Gerhard Schröder. So a joint Christian/Social Democratic presidential platform was ruled out. In October 1968 the Düsseldorf coalition partners in North Rhine-Westphalia indicated that they might support Gustav Heinemann, thus opening the possibility of collaboration between the SPD and the Free Democrats over the election of the president. This did not, of course, by itself ensure a Social Democratic victory. In the *Bundesversammlung* there would be 482 Union (CDU/CSU) votes and a further 22 for the NPD which, it could be assumed, would be cast against the SPD. The SPD had only 449 votes, and so to gain election their candidate would have to win 70 out of 83 liberal electors in the *Bundesversammlung*, a very tall order.

However, by the autumn of 1968 it was clear that the SPD would choose the Federal Justice Minister, Gustav Heinemann, as its candidate. Heinemann was personally well suited for the post: he was a man of impeccable moral stature, a member of the protestant confessing church which had obstructed the nazis in the Third Reich, and a champion of humane reforms in the law over such matters as the rights of illegitimate children. But he had begun his career in the CDU as Federal Minister of the Interior under Adenauer and then resigned his post in 1950 as a protest against the policy of rearmament. He had tried to set up his own party in opposition to militarism, and then had reappeared as an SPD Bundestag member, distinguishing himself in 1968 with a bitter attack on Adenauer's German policy. It was obvious that he could not hope for many votes from the Christian camp, but his character and policies might well appeal to the liberals.[44]

As Federal Minister of Justice Heinemann also delivered a remarkable radio speech on 14 April 1968, shortly after the shooting

44. Cf. ibid., pp. 56–63.

of Rudi Dutschke and the turmoil which followed. He had urged the older generation among his listeners to avoid facile condemnation of young people, but to take their criticisms seriously whilst upholding the laws of the land. This response was exactly what the more extreme radicals had not wanted, since they were hoping for violent repression. But it established Heinemann as a minister with sympathy for the younger generation. It did not, of course, imply any softness towards criminal violence; Heinemann was, after all, the minister of justice who had successfully piloted the legislation about a state of emergency through the Bundestag.[45]

Heinemann could certainly appeal to the younger and more reformist members of the FDP, who were looking to Walter Scheel for a rejuvenation of the party. Scheel demonstrated his powers of leadership in the presidential election. He hectored and bullied the FDP members of the *Bundesversammlung* to prevent them breaking into two opposing camps. If the FDP joined with the extreme right NPD in electing the conservative Christian Democrat Schröder as president, they would lose all chance of attracting disillusioned young people into the liberal camp. It was also pointed out that Heinemann's attitudes fitted in well with the flexible *Ostpolitik* favoured by Free Democrats as well as the SPD. Perhaps more important was the thought that the Union parties might yet carry through their intention of altering the electoral system to destroy the Free Democrats. Scheel managed to persuade just enough FDP representatives in the *Bundesversammlung* to vote for Heinemann, and on 5 March 1969 he was elected by simple majority on the third ballot.[46]

Despite the inclination of men like Kiesinger, Wehner and Helmut Schmidt to keep the great coalition going, pressure grew from those in the SPD who wanted to replace a rather stale, conservative nationalism with genuinely liberal reforms in the domestic sphere and a more flexible attitude in foreign affairs. Brandt and the rank and file of his party wanted a genuine change in the German political scene. Overruling the caution of colleagues like Wehner and Schmidt, Brandt made up his mind to go for an SPD-led coalition with the Free Democrats after the Bundestag elections due to be held in September 1969. He accepted that the majority might be very small, and that the new government might not last long because individual members of the Free Democratic Party might be bought off by big

45. See above, p. 201.
46. Baring, *Machtwechsel*, pp. 102–4, 120–1.

business interests. But he calculated that, once he had achieved supreme office, public sympathy would protect him against back-stairs intrigue.[47] His calculations turned out to be prophetic, and his judgement was inspired – a refreshing contrast to the shabby negotiations between Wehner and Adenauer which had so discredited the SPD in 1962.

Karl Schiller: prophet of prosperity

Brandt himself, although he would be the SPD candidate for chancellor and was chairman of the party, did not enjoy great public popularity at this time, nor was he warmly supported by many of his closest colleagues. Kiesinger was far ahead of him in the public opinion polls. But the real star of the SPD in 1969 was the Economics Minister, Karl Schiller, who had now achieved the sort of popularity enjoyed by Erhard in the mid-1950s. A brilliant communicator, Schiller gave the impression that he had personally rescued West Germany from a recession in 1966/7, and the public was duly grateful. The real electoral locomotive of the SPD at this time was not Brandt, but Schiller. It was therefore also not unimportant that Schiller came into conflict with his CDU – and above all CSU – colleagues in the great coalition over the question of revaluing the West German currency.

The Federal Republic at this time had an enormous positive trade balance and a balance of payments surplus. Owing to the Vietnam War, the US dollar was weakening, and the whole Bretton Woods system of fixed exchange rates pegged to the dollar – a system which had fostered an impressive growth in world trade – was under threat. With her low inflation and successful export industry, the Federal Republic seemed the only developed country which could ease the problems of others by raising the exchange rate of the mark. Such an adjustment would be quite compatible with the spirit of the Bretton Woods system, and would in fact make German citizens richer, since their Deutschmarks would be worth more in terms of foreign currency and import prices would fall. The Bundesbank president, Karl Blessing, had been in favour of revaluation for some time, but industrial interests were – as always – against him because revaluation might squeeze their export profit margins.

Kiesinger was too weak to overcome this opposition, more especially because it was vehemently supported by his Finance Minister,

47. Ibid., pp. 133–4.

Strauss, wihout the support of whose Bavarian CSU Kiesinger could not hope to carry on in office. Strauss was not sorry to be able to present himself in opposition to Schiller, who had overshadowed him in the government, and he was able to launch a demagogic campaign suggesting that revaluation would be truckling to foreigners – who were indeed desperately keen that the Federal Republic should revalue. But, as it turned out, the German electorate had more confidence in Schiller than in Strauss. The SPD gained more from this controversy than the CDU/CSU, or for that matter than the FDP, which evaded taking a stand on the issue.[48] It was important for the public perception of the election campaign when Schiller made it clear on 4 September that he would prefer a coalition with the Free Democrats. Although the SPD officially denied that it had made up its mind on the issue, it became obvious that, with Brandt and Schiller against a continuation of the great coalition, its days were probably numbered.

The real problem about this scenario, however, seemed to be the miserable performance of the Free Democrats themselves. Despite their role in Heinemann's election, they had still not come down clearly in favour of change. Opinion polls in the period before the election showed that the public regarded the Social Democrats as the real opposition and would vote for them if they wanted a change. The FDP seemed likely to get less than 5 per cent of the votes cast, and the nightmare scenario presented itself that the crypto-fascist NPD might gain access to the Bundestag just as the liberal Free Democrats were expelled from it. Walter Scheel, like Brandt, was willing to risk his career to stop this happening. Riven by its own internal dissensions, the FDP leadership had agreed not to commit the party to any specific coalition before the elections were over. However disappointing the FDP's ambivalence was to potential voters, Scheel could not risk an open conflict within the party if he committed himself too early. But on 25 September, three days before the elections, Scheel declared in a TV discussion programme – watched by an estimated 30 million people – that, if the election produced a majority for a coalition between FDP and Social Democrats, he would choose that option. The CDU/CSU was worn out after twenty years in office and should be given a period in opposition.[49] This last-minute public commitment to the SPD as coalition partners seems to have been just enough to get the FDP over the 5 per cent hurdle.

48. Ibid., pp. 139–47.
49. Ibid., pp. 148–9.

Kiesinger is defeated

The election of 28 September 1969 was the most exciting in the history of the Bonn Republic. Despite the fact that the CDU/CSU and their chancellor candidate were shown to be holding up well in public opinion polls, there was a widespread perception that west Germany was on the brink of a momentous change. Many writers, actors and intellectuals openly committed themselves to the SPD, and the liberal press was clearly opposed to the CDU/CSU. The slogans adopted by the protagonists were not without significance. The Christian parties stressed the personal stature of Kiesinger ('it all depends on the Chancellor') whereas the SPD presented themselves as a wave of the future ('We are building modern Germany'). In this respect the relative youthfulness of Schiller and Brandt were advantages. Strauss, on the other hand, frightened as many voters in north Germany as he attracted in his home state of Bavaria.

At first, the election seemed to have gone against the Brandt–Scheel option. The Free Democrats gained their worst ever result in a Bundestag election – at 5.8 per cent they were less than one percentage point away from dropping out of the Bonn parliament altogether. Had this occurred, the CDU/CSU would have had an absolute majority of seats in the Bundestag. The right extremist NPD, which had gained nearly 10 per cent of the vote in *Land* elections in Baden-Württemberg the previous year, could only manage 4.2 per cent and was eclipsed thereafter. Of the two major contenders for power, the CDU/CSU only fell back 1.5 per cent and remained the largest party. The SPD, on the other hand, increased its voting share by 3.4 per cent and was within striking distance of its Christian rivals. Between them the Free Democrats and the Social Democrats had won 48.5 per cent of the vote against 46.1 per cent for the Christians. This gave a 'social–liberal' coalition a majority of eighteen seats in the Bundestag. Would it suffice? On the evening of the election, and before the final result, Scheel thought that the CDU/CSU would probably win a majority of Bundestag seats anyhow, and Kiesinger believed he had gained the victory. The Republican president of the USA, Richard Nixon, congratulated him.

But in fact Kiesinger was destined to go down in the history of the Bonn Republic as the only chancellor who lost office as the direct result of a Bundestag election. Although in the SPD Wehner and Schmidt still wanted to continue with the great coalition, and although right-wing Free Democrats remained unconvinced, Scheel and Brandt stuck firmly to their decision to work together. They managed to finesse the doubters in the Free Democratic Party by persuading one of its more conservative Bundestag members, Josef Ertl, to accept the post of agriculture minister in a new coalition. This weakened the case of those like Erich Mende, who were determined to prevent Brandt, the illegitimate working-class socialist who had resisted the Third Reich from Scandinavia, from achieving the post of German chancellor. Despite the attempts of more friendly CDU leaders, like the young premier of the Rhineland-Palatinate, Helmut Kohl, to win the FDP back to an alignment with the Union parties, most of the Free Democrats felt that there was too much animosity towards them on the right – especially from Strauss's CSU. On 3 October Brandt and Scheel informed a sympathetic President Heinemann that they wanted to form a government, and on 21 October Brandt presented himself for election to the Bundestag. He received a narrow majority, although at least three members of his own coalition in the Bundestag apparently did not vote for him.

But he had achieved his goal. The long reign of the Christian Democratic parties was over. In a famous – if famously tactless – reaction, Brandt gave it as his opinion to foreign journalists that now Hitler had finally lost the war.[50] For the first time since 1930 a member of the Social Democratic Party was German chancellor.

50. K.D. Bracher, Wolfgang Jäger and Werner Link, *Geschichte der Bundesrepublik Deutschlands*, Vol. 5/I, *Republik im Wandel, 1969–1974. Die Ära Brandt* (Stuttgart, 1986), p. 24.

CHAPTER NINE

Brandt and the Era of Reform, 1969–1974

October 1969 marked an important stage in the development of the Federal Republic; for the first time a parliamentary election brought with it a new government, and that government was the first which did not include the Christian Union parties. Since the liberal FDP had to be won over with difficulty to the new coalition, it was given a generous ration of posts, including the important ones of Foreign Minister, which went to the party leader, Walter Scheel, and the Ministry of the Interior, held by his deputy, Hans-Dietrich Genscher. In addition, the politically sensitive Ministry of Agriculture went to the Bavarian farmers' leader Josef Ertl, a move which, as we have seen, helped sway some more conservative FDP members in favour of the coalition.[1]

The Brandt–Scheel government began with a fanfare of reformist enthusiasm. Brandt himself spoke of 'daring more democracy', and the impression given by the press – especially those organs which approved of the new regime, such as *Die Zeit*, the *Süddeutscher Zeitung* and *Der Spiegel* – was that West Germany was entering an entirely new era of personal freedom and radical reform. This impression was doubtless exaggerated, and may have helped to create considerable disillusionment in the years which followed. Nevertheless, the Brandt government did carry through important measures to liberalize West German life, and thus create a more open-minded atmosphere in most parts of the Federal Republic. It was a further stage in the westernization of German mores and culture.

1. See above, p. 219. Cf. K.D. Bracher, Wolfgang Jäger and Werner Link, *Geschichte der Bundesrepublik Deutschland*, Vol. 5/I, *Republik im Wandel, 1969–1974. Die Ära Brandt* (Stuttgart, 1986), p. 20.

Social reform

The criminal law was substantially reformed to make it more humane. Censorship of allegedly pornographic books and plays was relaxed and the blanket prohibition of homosexuality was lifted, as was a provision in the law which made landlords liable for prosecution if sex outside marriage took place on their premises (*Kuppelei*). Laws were passed strengthening employees' rights against dismissal and increasing the security of tenants *vis-à-vis* landlords.[2]

The inferior status of women began to be addressed: in 1974 the Bundestag amended the law to enable women to have abortions on demand up to three months into their pregnancies. This was a highly emotive issue in a country where nearly half the population was Roman Catholic, and in which the prohibition of abortion was based on laws going back to the Prussian monarchy. The reform was ruled unconstitutional by the Federal Constitutional Court in February 1975, but the following year saw legal acceptance of abortion which was based on 'due cause' supported by medical advice. The woman's position in marriage was also improved in 1977 by a new marriage law which created more equality between the sexes and replaced the concept of guilt in divorce with that of irreparable breakdown. Contrary to gloomy predictions, this did not result in a huge increase in divorce. West German divorce rates remained reasonably stable. In 1950 1.7 in every thousand marriages ended in divorce. In 1979 the figure was 1.3 per thousand. It was not until the 1980s that a marked upward trend appeared; in 1986 2.9 couples per thousand were divorced.[3] In any case, it should not be thought that this legislation transformed German family life by ushering in an era of matriarchy and permissiveness. The official attitude was that women's consciences should cause them to devote their energies to bringing up children as their first responsibility. The reforms did, however, clear away legal obstacles to female equality in marriage, thus making a feminist agenda for the future at least conceivable, if not very likely. Like many of the measures produced by the

2. From November 1971 landlords could not evict tenants without a warranted interest in so doing, and raising rents was not acceptable as such a warranted interest. Führer, 'Managing Scarcity: The German Housing Shortage and the Controlled Economy, 1914–1990', in *German History. The Journal of the German History Society*, Vol. 13, No. 3 (Oxford, 1995), pp. 349–51.

3. E. Kolinsky, *Women in Contemporary Germany. Life, Work and Politics* (2nd edn, Oxford, 1993), p. 52.

social–liberal coalition in its thirteen-year period of government, emancipation was the objective rather than material gain.

When Brandt introduced the programme of his second ministry to the Bundestag in January 1973, he declared that Germans should cease to be 'bourgeois' and become 'citizens' in the French sense.[4] It was the sort of grandiloquent statement which enraged his conservative critics, but it contained a kernel of truth. The German 'middle class' or *Bürgertum*, to which Brandt himself did not belong, had traditionally regarded itself as exemplifying loyalty to the state. Brandt's ideal was of people who emancipated themselves from subservience to officialdom, whilst being committed to the public good. Shifts in public attitudes during the 1960s and 1970s seemed to demonstrate that his vision was not entirely inappropriate. The CDU, for its part, denied that democracy should be a principle applied to society; it was a political technique used to give a mandate to state governments. In practice there was not too much to choose between the parties, but their different attitudes towards the individual and the state were of considerable importance.

The Brandt–Scheel alliance, which had been cobbled together at the last minute after the election result was known, generated great enthusiasm amongst the rank-and-file membership of both parties, but its programmatic basis was very vague. No clear-cut coalition contract was agreed upon. As a result, the position of the smaller – and electorally much weaker – liberal partner was disproportionately strong, since it could block any measures it disliked without facing the charge that it was going back on commitments made when the government was created.

Hence, when it came to reforms which involved public expenditure, the domestic policies of the social–liberal coalition were actually less adventurous than those of its Christian–social predecessor. This was partly due to its very narrow majority – in the previous Bundestag Kiesinger had enjoyed overwhelming support, and the small FDP opposition could not hope to block government measures. Now the government's majority was tenuous in the extreme. Furthermore, the fact that the CDU/CSU had at last gone into opposition meant that the Bundesrat, the mouthpiece of the *Länder*, could be very much more troublesome than before, because CDU-*Länder* representatives were very powerful within it. This would be a permanent and growing problem for the social–liberal government, because its predictable mid-term drop in popularity was reflected

4. Bracher *et al.*, *Ära Brandt*, p. 94.

in swings to the CDU in the *Länder*. In Bavaria the CSU enjoyed an absolute majority of the votes in *Landtag* elections from November 1970 until the end of the Bonn Republic and beyond. So the CSU always possessed a strident voice in the Bundesrat.

But these difficulties alone did not explain the gap between rhetoric and reality in the domestic reform policies of the social–liberal coalition. The fact was that the FDP was in many respects socially more conservative than its Christian Democratic predecessor. This was particularly the case with respect to co-determination in industry, which the Social Democrats wished to extend, but which the Free Democrats, with their close links to business interests and their commitment to entrepreneurial freedom, wished to block. Higher taxes for the better off were also anathema to the FDP.

The left wing of the FDP did hope for dynamic action on educational reform, but neither Scheel nor Brandt was very enthusiastic about that. However, as we have seen, the issue of reform of the universities was already well on the agenda, and complaints that the school system was inadequate and inegalitarian were also widespread on the left. Ralf Dahrendorf, the rising star of the reformist Free Democrats, spoke of education as a 'civic right'.[5] In practice, arguments about education revolved around student participation in the government of universities and the introduction of comprehensive schools to replace the traditionally divided German secondary schools. It was also argued that school curricula should be more relevant to the needs of contemporary life and contain more natural science. Over this issue the federal system proved an effective barrier to radical change, since the CDU-led *Länder* obstructed the introduction of comprehensive schools and the abolition of traditional subjects like history. In this they were supported by parents, as well as professional bodies like the Conference of University Vice-Chancellors (*Rektorenkonferenz*). The result was that in some states parents could have the choice of using comprehensives or sticking to the old grammar schools, and in others – especially in south Germany – comprehensives made little headway.

So far as the universities were concerned, a Framework Law was passed in 1975 setting out certain model structures for universities. Many universities became 'comprehensive' in that they absorbed teacher training colleges and similar institutions. Faculties were replaced or supplemented by departments. In fact, these changes did

---

5. Bracher *et al.*, *Ära Brandt*, pp. 21, 294. The slogan was the title of a book Dahrendorf published in Hamburg in 1968, *Bildung ist Bürgerrecht. Plädoyer für eine aktive Bildungspolitik.*

not alter the nature of the older universities very much. Model statutes were drawn up involving equal representation for students, professors and other staff, but in practice they did little more than produce tediously long meetings of university senates. The status of professors as the academic leaders of the universities was safeguarded by a decision of the Federal Constitutional Court in 1973, and so the structure of teaching and research was not seriously altered. What did make a difference was the enormous expansion in both the universities themselves and the amount of resources pumped into them. Both old and new universities often found themselves with more than 20,000 students. Yet the size of the teaching staff did not grow in anything like the same proportion.

On the other hand, the social–liberal government did push through the Educational Support Law (BAFöG) in 1971 which provided financial support to help needy families send their children to universities or to the equivalent of sixth-form education if they could not otherwise afford to do so. The previous Bundestag had agreed to fund a programme of new university building on behalf of the various *Länder*, and many new institutions of tertiary education were founded. Between 1965 and 1980 the number of *Gymnasium* students (qualifying for university education) rose from 950,000 to 2.1 million, the number of university students rose from 384,000 to 1.04 million, the cost of education rose from DM264 to DM1,253 per head, and the percentage of education costs in the budget rose from 11.2 per cent to 15.2 per cent.[6]

At the same time the deficit in female education which had existed in the early years of the Federal Republic was being overcome. In 1965 only 40 per cent of *Gymnasium* (grammar school) pupils and only 30 per cent of university graduates were women. By the mid-1980s half the pupils in grammar schools were girls and over 40 per cent of university students were women. Women also made remarkable progress in vocational training, partly thanks to an initiative launched by the government in 1976 under the slogan 'girls in men's jobs'. At that time only 2 per cent of female apprentices were being trained in traditionally 'male' skills; ten years later 80 per cent of them were opting for such possibilities. Young women in the last decades of the Bonn Republic certainly faced the future with far better qualifications than their mothers or grandmothers had done.[7]

In general, West Germany maintained both a high standard of

6. Bracher *et al.*, *Ära Brandt*, p. 135.
7. Kolinsky, *Women in Contemporary Germany*, pp. 100–21.

academic education and broadened its educational base to absorb a mass of ambitious young people whose parents could not themselves have envisaged education beyond the age of fifteen. In this respect the Federal Republic was well placed to meet the economic challenges it would face in the next two decades. However, this achievement cannot be attributed to any one party, nor was it without its negative side, in that too many students were poorly taught and poorly motivated, spending far too long in their search for qualifications. In any case, student radicalism was tending to give the universities a bad name, and the social–liberal coalition could not regard education reform as its main *raison d'être*.

Ostpolitik

The real cement which held the government together, and its major programmatic objective, was the development of a new relationship with the Soviet bloc countries, a policy referred to as *Ostpolitik*.[8] Since discussions about the foreign policy of the Federal Republic from 1969 onwards were dominated by this concept, and since it eventually led to the unification of Germany, it is necessary at this point to review its origins. With hindsight, it is easy to claim that the international constellation was such that a relaxation of tension with the Soviet bloc was in the interests of the western powers as a whole, and that West Germany could not long stay aloof from such a development. However, this is to overlook the obstacles within the Bonn political system to a process of 'normalization'.

As we have seen, Willy Brandt and Walter Scheel had both developed a determination to break out of the rigid Cold War stance which was the legacy of Adenauer so far as Bonn's relations with communist countries were concerned. But Brandt, in particular, was affected by the need to ameliorate the situation of the East Germans in general, and the West Berliners in particular. He had also been negatively impressed by the feebleness of the West's reaction to Ulbricht's coup in August 1961, when East Berlin had been sealed off. As he later put it, the curtain rose on the western Allies' response – to reveal an empty stage. He therefore became impatient with the

---

8. Literally 'Eastern Policy', but referring specifically to the attempt to improve relations with the Soviet Union and its satellites. For a good survey of this issue, see Arnulf Baring, *Machtwechsel. Die Ära Brandt–Scheel* (Munich, 1984), pp. 197–201. Baring writes: 'In its potential for economic and social reform the Great Coalition was markedly to the left of its social–liberal successor' (ibid., p. 200).

pretensions of the Hallstein doctrine and the theoretical claims to Germany's frontiers of 1937. Improvement could only come if the Federal Republic – firmly embedded in the Western Alliance, to be sure – recognized realities and tried to ameliorate relations, initially with the Soviet Union, and then with her satellites, including Poland, Czechoslovakia and the GDR.

The aim of this was threefold: firstly to improve the situation of the Germans living under Soviet control; secondly to ease tensions so that a more peaceable atmosphere could be created in Europe; and last, but certainly not least, to work towards a situation in which the elimination of fear between East and West might lead to the unification – or at least the association – of the two parts of Germany. Egon Bahr, in particular, was regarded with suspicion in the Christian camp because he was feared by some to be a crypto-communist and by others to be a German nationalist. The first accusation was certainly baseless; the second had rather more substance, though the word 'patriot' would have been more appropriate. It was this same patriotism that motivated many of the reformers in the FDP.

Such obvious concern to further reunification by sweeping away Cold War barriers was not always well received among Bonn's allies in London, Paris and Washington. Any sign of rapprochement between west Germany and the Soviet Union was greeted with absurd public speculation about a new 'Rapallo' – a completely unhistorical parallel, but one which illustrated how careful the West Germans would have to be in following any new course. If they did not do enough, they were accused of damaging the prospects for peace by using Cold War tactics. If they took initiatives, the old bogey of a Russo-German alliance was wheeled out to frighten Anglo-Saxon and French newspaper readers.

It should, however, be remembered that within west Germany, too, the reformist path had many enemies. The natural reaction to the building of the Berlin Wall had been one of shock and outrage. West Germans were resentful at their Allies' inaction and guilty over their own. The Springer press, which had built its new headquarters in West Berlin, was particularly strident in its attacks on the 'GDR'. Then there were the refugees, represented before 1969 by their own ministry in the Bonn government, and with strong contacts in the CDU/CSU and in the FDP. The fact that the former FDP leader, Erich Mende, had come from Upper Silesia was not irrelevant to his own position on *Ostpolitik*, although he was considerably more flexible than many others. The general attitude amongst mainstream West German politicians, even in the SPD, was that there ought to be a gradual easing of tension, but that this would have to be handled very cautiously. The Hallstein doctrine would eventually have to go, but the public would only tolerate this after a considerable period of time, and in return for concrete concessions relating to East Germany. Hence, as we have seen, the Kiesinger government appeared half-hearted in its attempts to open up new channels of communication with the eastern bloc.

However, it should not be forgotten that there was also a much more combative, assertive current in West German thinking about the future in the 1960s. This can most easily be identified in the Bavarian CSU, but it was highly vocal elsewhere, and was vigorously supported by the refugee organizations. It was personified by Franz Josef Strauss and the CSU foreign policy expert, Karl Theodor Freiherr von und zu Guttenberg, who demanded a dynamic and even offensive strategy against the East, with the slogan 'the aim is the achievement of freedom'.[9] The formula presented by this sector of the political spectrum, which was supported by populist elements in the press, was that West Germany should work together with France to create a European nuclear power which could function as a European pillar in the Western Alliance, thereby opening the way for a much more forceful attitude towards the Soviet bloc. The fact that General de Gaulle had no intention of sharing the French nuclear deterrent with Bonn was glossed over. This political tendency, which was rather mischievously condoned by Adenauer in his retirement, reflected a certain anti-Americanism and a rebirth of German nationalism, even if it was constrained by the facts of the military situation. It involved strident attacks on any suggestion that the status quo might – even by implication – be recognized.

Yet if *Ostpolitik*, as it came to be known, was to succeed, it would not just have to be a series of slow and grudging compromises dragged out of Bonn by her western neighbours. It would have to be a consistent attempt to improve the atmosphere between Bonn and Moscow. The Soviet government had shown itself ready to work for better relations in its note to the Kiesinger government just before the 1969 Bundestag election. The question was, would the federal government dare to respond in a suitably adventurous manner? Brandt and Scheel were prepared to do so. Many of their colleagues were less confident, and the opposition was eager to torpedo the government by playing the national card.

A new *Ostpolitik* also involved reassuring Bonn's western partners,

9. Karl Theodor zu Guttenberg, *Wenn der Westen Will. Plädoyer für eine mutige Politik* (Stuttgart/Degerloch, 1964), p. 216. See also Baring, *Machtwechsel*, p. 209. Guttenberg and Strauss were not in other respects united, the latter seeing the former as a possible rival.

and especially the Americans. *Ostpolitik* was always a complement to and never a substitute for a clear commitment to NATO and the West. Hence, in his first statement of policy as Chancellor, Brandt announced his intention of accepting the international nuclear non-proliferation agreement, a *bête noire* of the conservatives, and on 28 November 1969 the Federal Republic formally adhered to the treaty. This also pleased the Soviet authorities, since they had no desire to see West Germany become a nuclear power. In his policy statement mentioned above, Brandt had actually gone further than any previous German chancellor when he referred to the existence of two German states, although he went on to claim that they could not be regarded as 'foreign countries' in their relationship to one another. It was noteworthy that Brandt's cabinet did not include a minister for refugee problems, and that the Ministry of 'All-German Questions' was now renamed 'Internal German Relations'.

Brandt and his colleagues were clear that improvements in relations with the other Germany could only be gained through Moscow. The first priority must be to come to terms with the Soviet Union. On 30 October 1969, Walter Scheel, now Deputy Chancellor and Foreign Minister, told the Soviet ambassador that talks about a possible mutual renunciation of force in international affairs – which had run into the sand some time earlier – could be resumed.

By the end of the year Brandt's government obtained agreement from the western Allies to go ahead with negotiations with Moscow on the understanding that the rights of the Allied powers in Germany would not be compromised. The negotiations were to be conducted in Moscow by Egon Bahr, who was now a junior minister in Brandt's Federal Chancellery. In this respect the new government followed the pattern set by Adenauer and Kiesinger: major items of foreign policy, and above all issues which related to East–West relations, were dominated by the Chancellor rather than by the Foreign Ministry. But in his case, unlike that of Kiesinger and Brandt, the Chancellor and his foreign minister saw eye to eye on the objectives of their policy. Indeed, Brandt, Bahr and Scheel were a group of enthusiasts for *Ostpolitik* who had to defend it against doubters within their own respective parties. Thus Brandt found his Defence Minister, Helmut Schmidt, only lukewarm on the issue, and Scheel was forced to part company with his own junior minister in the Foreign Office, Ralf Dahrendorf, who, in May 1970, warned him that *Ostpolitik* was headed for disaster and would ruin the FDP.[10]

10. Baring, *Machtwechsel*, pp. 287–8, 293–7.

This pessimistic conclusion was apparently borne out by the results of *Land* elections in June 1970, in which the FDP fared extremely badly. Scheel was put under pressure from right-wing colleagues to give up his party's chairmanship, but he showed remarkable resilience and carried on. Despite his brave face in public, however, he was contemplating retirement into private life.[11] It was evident that if the government's *Ostpolitik* did not show some rapid results, the FDP might begin to fall apart. In October 1970 three members of the FDP Bundestag delegation, Mende, Starke and Zoglmann, went over to the CDU/CSU, leaving the government with a majority of six. But by that time the crisis had passed its nadir. The new line in foreign policy could demonstrate some real achievements.

This success owed a lot to the tenacity of Egon Bahr. Despite the unyieldingly harsh negotiating tactics of the Soviet foreign minister, Andrei Gromyko, Bahr chipped away at the problem of an acceptable German–Soviet treaty, making repeated visits to Moscow in the early months of 1970. He was rightly concerned that, if the west Germans did not achieve a treaty with Moscow quickly, Ulbricht – who was frightened by *Ostpolitik* – might persuade Moscow that no concessions to West Germany were necessary at all, and that the international recognition of the GDR was just a matter of time – a point that was not lost on Bonn either. Brandt and Scheel were determined to press forward as quickly as possible. They had some cards in their hand, however, and they played them with determination. The Soviet leadership was eager to obtain German help in setting up a European conference on peace and security, an objective in which Bonn was willing to be helpful. More important was the prospect of technical and economic co-operation, financed to a considerable degree by the Federal Republic. Discussions on such matters had preceded Bahr's discussions in Moscow and, just as he began negotiating with Gromyko, an agreement was signed in Essen under which the Federal Republic would provide steel pipes in return for exports of natural gas from the Soviet Union – the whole deal to be funded by German credits.[12]

At the end of May Bahr brought back a memorandum which would serve as a draft treaty. Its basic proposals were that the USSR and the Federal Republic would agree to further the normalization of peaceful relations in Europe on the basis of the actual situation

11. Ibid., p. 303.
12. Timothy Garton Ash, *In Europe's Name. Germany and the Divided Continent* (London, 1993), p. 70. The agreement was signed on 1 February 1970.

which existed there; that both sides would abjure the use of force against the other; that both sides accepted the existing frontiers of Europe as inviolable (*unverletzlich*), including the Oder–Neisse line as the western frontier of Poland and the frontier between the GDR and west Germany. Despite the fact that this paper was leaked and published in the hostile Springer press, Scheel and experts from the relevant ministries decided that it was not incompatible with the west German Basic Law and that the treaty-making could proceed.

Scheel himself then flew to Moscow to conduct more formal negotiations. The only conditions upon which the German foreign office insisted were that the Bonn government should accompany its acceptance with a letter asserting its right to work for unification by peaceful means, and the clear understanding that the agreement would not be ratified in West Germany until a satisfactory settlement had been achieved over the future security of West Berlin. Nothing in the treaty should compromise the rights of the other occupying powers in Germany, nor would it hinder the Federal Republic's commitment to the European Community. Scheel knew that he would have the support of President Pompidou in his efforts in Moscow, and before he went to the Soviet Union he also visited London and Washington to reassure the Allied governments there. Although the new British government under Edward Heath was encouraging, the Americans were uneasy about Bonn's haste and concerned to protect Allied rights in Germany as a guarantee of European security.[13]

The problems which Scheel faced were largely related to the presentation of the agreement with the USSR; they were very important for all that, and they seemed to involve squaring some awkward circles. The West Germans wanted to liberate themselves from the self-imposed restrictions on their freedom of action *vis-à-vis* the countries of the Soviet bloc without giving up the prospect of one day achieving a peace settlement which would bring with it at least the unification of the two Germanys, and possibly some concessions towards those expelled from the territories east of the Oder–Neisse line. The Soviet government, on the other hand, wanted a recognition of the status quo, not just for the time being, but as a permanent settlement which would legitimize the Soviet empire in Europe. So far as the GDR was concerned, the aim of the West Germans was to trade off acceptance of the existence of this east German state for the security of west Berlin and its association with the Federal Republic, and for improvements in the general relationship between the two Germanys

13. Baring, *Machtwechsel*, pp. 320–1.

which might bring with them a liberalization of the regime there. The Russians and the East Germans saw this latter intention very clearly, and were determined to block it. As Brezhnev told Erich Honecker on 28 July 1970, the treaty would strengthen the GDR: 'Brandt also expects advantages. He wants to penetrate you. But he will find that ever harder.' He urged Honecker to ensure that there would not be a process of rapprochement between the FRG and the GDR. He urged the East German to concentrate everything on strengthening the GDR.[14]

This did not augur well for the success of Brandt's grand design, but it is worth noting that Brezhnev's comments to Honecker were understood by both men to be an indication that the latter would soon replace Walter Ulbricht, the epitome of hard-line, anti-western policy, as leader of the GDR. In July 1971 Ulbricht was forced into retirement, a move which could itself be seen as a success for *Ostpolitik.*

Scheel found a frosty reception awaiting him from Gromyko in Moscow, and for several days it seemed as though the essential concessions he needed from the Soviet side would not be forthcoming. On 2 August he visited the Soviet foreign minister in his luxurious dacha on the outskirts of Moscow, and, at the end of what appeared to be a purely social visit, Gromyko produced the draft of a letter which he suggested might be used by the West Germans to explain their position on unification. This was indeed what the Germans had been pressing for, and the text was effectively their own.[15] Although the status of the letter, which reiterated the Bonn government's intention to work towards the peaceful reunification of Germany, was never really clarified, the fact that it was received by the Russians was enough to enable Brandt, Scheel and Bahr to claim that the treaty with the Soviet Union did not alter West Germany's commitment to reunification and was not inconsistent with the preamble to the Basic Law. When the treaty itself was challenged before the Constitutional Court by Franz-Josef Strauss's CSU the interpretation of the government was upheld.

Within days of Scheel's breakthrough, on 12 August 1970, Brandt and Brezhnev signed the German–Soviet treaty in Moscow. Brandt announced that, 25 years after the capitulation of Hitler's Reich and fifteen years after Adenauer had opened diplomatic relations with

---

14. Cited in Garton Ash, *In Europe's Name*, pp. 77–8, based on Honecker's own notes in east German archives: cf. ibid., pp. 478–9.

15. Baring, *Machtwechsel*, pp. 339–40.

the USSR, 'the time has come to found our relationship with the East anew – that is, on unconditional mutual renunciation of force, on the basis of the political situation as it exists in Europe ...'. 'With this treaty', he asserted, 'nothing is lost that has not long since been gambled away.' This latter comment was a side-swipe at those in the FRG who were accusing him of renouncing Germany's national heritage. The criminal gamblers had been the National Socialists and those who supported them.[16]

The Moscow Treaty was the foundation stone of *Ostpolitik*. But while Bahr and then Scheel were struggling to achieve it, action had been carried forward on other fronts also. Negotiations with Poland had opened on 3 February 1970, running parallel with those in Moscow, even though it was not lost on the Poles that their Oder–Neisse frontier had been accepted as inviolable as the result of Russian agreement, rather than concessions made by the Germans to them. In December 1970 Brandt went to Warsaw to sign a treaty which would effectively recognize the Oder–Neisse line, even if legally the Germans could still argue that a final settlement must be legitimized by a peace treaty, which still lay in the future. In fact the Polish agreement was more offensive to hard-liners in Germany than the Moscow Treaty because it not only asserted that the frontiers of Poland were inviolable, but that neither state had any territorial demands on the other. It was therefore difficult to imagine that a future peace treaty negotiated with the wartime Allies would give Germany what she herself had renounced.[17] Although some concessions were made by the Poles about the repatriation of Germans who wanted to leave for the west, the numbers were disappointingly small from Bonn's viewpoint. Perhaps the most significant immediate impact of the treaty was the moment on 7 December 1970 when Brandt graciously knelt down in a gesture of atonement before the memorial to the Jews murdered in the Warsaw ghetto. This image of German repentance, which was instantly published throughout the world, added greatly to Brandt's international stature, even if it was well received by only a minority of his fellow citizens in the Federal Republic.[18]

16. Garton Ash, *In Europe's Name*, p. 73.

17. Werner Link, 'Außen und Deutschlandpolitik in der Ära Brandt 1969–1974', in Bracher *et al.*, *Ära Brandt*, p. 193.

18. Actually, the response in west Germany was surprisingly benign, since 41 per cent of Germans polled thought Brandt's gesture appropriate, as against 48 per cent who thought it exaggerated. Those under 30 years old reacted more positively than their elders. Barbara Marshall, *Willy Brandt* (London, 1990), p. 78.

West Berlin

Two other areas needed immediate attention: the security of west Berlin, and the direct relationship between the Federal Republic and the GDR. West Berlin, despite the relative calm that had descended since the confrontation over Cuba in 1962, was still vulnerable to Soviet and east German pressure over access and supplies. On the other hand, the GDR and Soviet authorities strongly resented federal German institutions, such as the Bundestag and *Bundesversammlung*, meeting in Berlin. The east Germans wanted to separate west Berlin from the Federal Republic altogether, preparatory to its absorption in the GDR. This was totally unacceptable to Brandt and his colleagues; a major objective of *Ostpolitik* was to protect West Berlin and to improve the quality of life for all Berliners. To a great extent they were dependent on their allies, since a treaty about Berlin would have to be negotiated between the Allied occupying powers – in practice by the three western ambassadors in West Germany and the Soviet ambassador in the GDR.

The discussions began in West Berlin on 26 March 1970, but neither the GDR nor the Soviet Union saw any advantage in hastening the negotiations, although Scheel and Brandt had made it clear that, until an agreement was reached on Berlin, the Moscow Treaty would not be ratified. In 1971 the situation eased somewhat because both the Americans and the Russians were seeking agreement over nuclear weapons. President Nixon was due to visit China for the first time, and this stimulated Brezhnev to make progress with his German rapprochement. Ulbricht's removal also helped matters. The Berlin agreement, signed on 3 September 1971, stipulated that the four powers would strive to eliminate tension and avoid the threat of force over Berlin, although it was symptomatic of the difficulties involved that the city itself was not defined, but referred to throughout most of the document as 'the relevant area'. The Soviet government declared that traffic between West Berlin and the Federal Republic would not be impeded. Communications between West Berlin and the GDR would be improved. Residents of West Berlin would be able to visit the GDR (including east Berlin). The western powers agreed that ties between West Berlin and the FRG should be maintained and developed, but that the western sectors would continue not to be a constituent part of the Federal Republic. It was also conceded that state bodies of the FRG would not perform official acts in west Berlin. On the other hand, the FRG could represent the interests of West Berlin internationally and provide its citizens with consular services. The rights of the Allied occupying powers in Berlin were confirmed.[19]

All this was of great benefit to the West Berliners since it formally removed what had been a nagging threat to their security. From this time on West Berlin became more and more of a privileged island, cocooned in a cosy web of western subsidies and special privileges, not the least of which was exemption from military service. Culturally and educationally well served, its citizens had no need to concern themselves about what happened behind the wall which divided their city. Although still a monstrous demonstration of totalitarian repression, the Wall itself was given a cosmetic patina by extensive graffiti, some of considerable artistic merit. Many inhabitants of West Berlin never went through it, and preferred to fly to West Germany rather than travel by train or car across what they still referred to as the 'Zone'.

Relations with the GDR

The last major plank of the first round of *Ostpolitik* was the Basic Treaty (*Grundlagenvertrag*) between the Federal Republic and the GDR on 21 December 1972. The two states agreed to develop good neighbourly relations with each other on the basis of equal rights, and to respect their frontiers as inviolable. They would exchange permanent missions. This clearly implied recognition of the GDR by the Bonn government, but the specific commitment to diplomatic recognition was dodged; the permanent missions, for example, were not described as embassies. The Bonn government also sent a letter to the East German authorities pointing out that the treaty did not conflict with 'the political aim of the Federal Republic of Germany to work for a state of peace in Europe in which the German nation will regain its unity through free self-determination'.[20]

Lastly, the two governments agreed to take steps to apply for membership of the United Nations. This too was acceptable to the victor powers, but only with the proviso that the relevant four-power

---

19. The most important parts of this agreement and its annexes are printed in C.-C. Schweitzer *et al.* (eds), *Politics and Government in the Federal Republic of Germany, 1944–1994. Basic Documents* (2nd edn, Providence, R.I., 1995), pp. 342–6.

20. Ibid., pp. 62–5. Cf. Marshall, *Brandt*, pp. 79–83; Garton Ash, *In Europe's Name*, pp. 75–7; Baring, *Machtwechsel*, pp. 348–55, and Link, 'Außen und Deutschlandpolitik', pp. 214–24.

agreements, decisions and practices would not be affected. So the agreement protected the Allies' postwar rights, but also kept 'the common roof of "Germany" intact in international law'.[21] The two German states were accepted into the UN on 18 September 1973. Although this was perceived to be of more importance for Honecker's East German regime than for the Federal Republic, in practice Bonn had a greater impact on the UN than its communist rival. In its relations with the developing world in general, and with Africa in particular, the UN was a useful forum within which Bonn could exercise influence, not least because of its economic power.[22]

Other agreements either followed or accompanied these major developments, including improvements of communications between the two German states, and a treaty with Czechoslovakia was signed in December 1973. It was no coincidence that in these two years there were also important developments in the relationships between the superpowers. On the same day that a treaty was signed between the two German states easing traffic between them – 26 May 1972 – the USA and the Soviet Union concluded the important agreement on Stragetic Arms Limitation (SALT). In 1972 the USA opened relations with Communist China, an example followed by the Federal Republic in the autumn of the same year. The early months of the following year saw the American acceptance of defeat in Vietnam, the start of preliminary discussions for a Conference on Security and Co-operation in Europe (CSCE) and the opening of Mutual and Balanced Force Reduction talks (MBFR) in Vienna. Had the German government not been willing to take its initiatives in *Ostpolitik* at this time, the Federal Republic would have appeared as a recalcitrant Cold War relic, and its vital interests could have been bartered away by others.

Opposition to Ostpolitik: *the first 'constructive vote of no confidence'*

How serious a possibility that was can be demonstrated by examining the behaviour of the CDU/CSU opposition towards the diplomatic achievements of the social–liberal coalition. The work of Brandt,

21. Bracher *et al.*, *Ära Brandt*, p. 224.

22. For details of the important role which Foreign Minister Genscher played in African affairs, see Wolfgang Jäger and Werner Link, *Geschichte der Bundesrepublik Deutschland*, Vol. 5/II, *Republik im Wandel, 1974–1982: Die Ära Schmidt* (Stuttgart, 1987), pp. 383–97.

Scheel and Bahr was accompanied by a jeremiad chorus in the conservative press and in the Bundestag. It was claimed that Germany's vital interests were being surrendered by irresponsible leftists who were soft on communism. Brandt's record as a wartime resister was played upon to imply that he was not a loyal German, and Bahr was denounced as a dangerous dilettante, easily misled by Soviet blandishments.

The leader of the CDU and its delegation in the Bundestag was Rainer Barzel, a forward-looking and relatively young politician who had himself been minister for all-German affairs under Adenauer. Although he had doubts about the methods used by the new government in its *Ostpolitik*, he sympathized with its general objectives, and thought the opposition should agree to the Moscow and Warsaw Treaties whilst stressing their interpretation that neither German unification nor a future peace conference had been compromised by these new arrangements.

But the CSU leader, Strauss, was much more inclined to exploit nationalist feeling, especially amongst the older generation and the refugee pressure groups, to defeat or discredit the treaties and thus bring down the government. The campaign against 'surrender' to Moscow had been gaining ground, and there had been defections from the FDP and even the Social Democrats in the Bundestag. On 23 April 1972 the loss of yet another FDP Bundestag member meant that the government no longer enjoyed an overall majority in parliament. The opposition decided on a constructive vote of no confidence to replace Brandt by Barzel. It was the first time this provision in the Basic Law had been put to the test. In order to overthrow the government Barzel had to obtain a majority for his own election as chancellor. It appeared that such a majority existed. Feverish lobbying went on behind the scenes in Bonn, but when the vote was taken – by secret ballot – Barzel failed by two votes. Brandt had achieved an important political victory and the opposition was discomfited.

Worse was to follow for Barzel. He and the leaders of the other two Bundestag parties were willing to work out a joint statement which would clarify the Federal Republic's position towards the Eastern Treaties and ensure that they were not seen to be in conflict with the Basic Law. The statement would then open the way to the ratification of the treaties in parliament. It was designed to soothe nationalist sensibilities and was at first accepted by the opposition, including the CSU leader Strauss. After a visit to his die-hard constituents in

Bavaria, however, Strauss reneged on his agreement and insisted that the Bavarian party would vote against the treaties.

Barzel and his supporters in the CDU, including Richard Weizsäcker, who was later to be Federal President, struggled to keep their party behind the agreement, but at a crucial meeting of the CDU parliamentary delegation (*Fraktion*) the venerable Walter Hallstein, author of the inflexible doctrine which bore his name, launched into a legalistic attack on the treaties, and demanded that the CDU should at least abstain when they were voted on. To keep the party together, Barzel weakly agreed to abstention, but even here Strauss insisted that, whereas opponents of the treaties who felt bound by conscience – and this applied particularly to those who came originally from east of the Oder–Neisse – should be allowed to vote 'No', those, like Weizsäcker, who felt equally strongly in favour of the treaties, must be forced to abstain, or the CSU would vote against the treaties *en bloc*. Weizsäcker and his colleagues submitted loyally to party discipline, only to find that there were considerably more 'conscientious' no voters than they had been led to believe.[23]

On 17 May 1972, the Moscow and Warsaw Treaties were ratified by the Bundestag, but in a manner which brought no credit to the opposition. The Moscow Treaty, the cornerstone of *Ostpolitik*, was passed by 248 votes to 10 with 238 abstentions – so only half of those present supported the treaty. In the case of the Polish treaty the result was even less encouraging, since the number of those voting against it rose to seventeen. For the government, the result was all that mattered, but the confusion and malevolence amongst the opposition was fatal for Barzel's authority within his party.

Brandt's election triumph, September 1972

It remained to be seen what impact this fierce political debate would have on the public. The reformers in the CDU had the impression that their party members and voters were far less negatively inclined towards the new course than the Bundestag *Fraktion*. Events were to prove them right. Following his success in the constructive vote of no confidence, Brandt determined to engineer new elections, a perfectly reasonable course, since the government was finding difficulty in conducting parliamentary business. Under the Basic Law, however,

23. Baring, *Machtwechsel*, pp. 440–7.

this was not an easy matter, since elections were supposed to be held at fixed times. By a somewhat dubious manoeuvre, the government engineered a negative vote of confidence in itself on 22 September 1972. Brandt then recommended to the Federal President that new elections should be held and, with the consent of the opposition, President Heinemann duly fixed these for 19 November.

The election campaign, in which Barzel was Brandt's opponent, was virtually a referendum on *Ostpolitik*. The fact that Brandt had been awarded the Nobel peace prize in October 1971 had done his reputation with the electorate no harm. As Brandt, Scheel and Barzel himself had suspected, the new policy of flexibility proved popular with the public, and especially with the young, many of whom were voting for the first time, since the age of voting had recently been lowered to eighteen. The dour rejection of contacts with the GDR and other satellite countries was perceived to be pettifogging obstruction which might endanger peace. Some people may have voted for the government in the hope of easier contacts with relatives in the GDR. Others probably voted to clear away a nagging source of tension and give West Germany a quieter life. Either way, the result was a triumph for Brandt and Scheel.

For the first, and only, time in the Bonn Republic's history the CDU/CSU received fewer votes than the SPD – 44.9 per cent to 45.8 per cent. The Free Democrats' share of the vote rose to 8.4 per cent and the government achieved a comfortable majority. Furthermore, the FDP itself had now swung over to the left, because the rejection of *Ostpolitik* by the opposition ruled out collaboration between the Free Democrats and the CDU/CSU – in particular with Strauss's CSU. For the next ten years the fear of Strauss, with his irresponsible nationalism and his open hatred of the FDP, would be enough to hold the liberals into their coalition with the Social Democrats. The occasion was noteworthy also because it registered the highest turnout in the history of federal elections – an astonishing 91.1 per cent. Of those votes, all but a paltry 0.9 per cent were cast for the three main parties – the extreme nationalist NPD was humiliatingly defeated.

This victory for the Brandt–Scheel coalition was the moment at which the Bonn Republic demonstrated its stability and its commitment to western, democratic and liberal values. Such a result might not have been achieved without determined leaders, willing to risk their careers for important political objectives. In some ways the previous six years had been a period in the Republic's history when there was a real whiff of Weimar in the air. Economic crisis, the appearance of a neo-nazi party, the radical left-wing violence on the streets, which had developed into urban terrorism, might have been enough to unsettle a less stable regime. The narrow, and constantly crumbling, majority of the Brandt–Scheel coalition, and the need to obtain parliamentary sanction for important treaties which were ferociously denounced in some quarters as a national betrayal, could revive memories of Stresemann's struggles in the 1920s over such matters as the Dawes Plan and the Locarno Treaties. But whereas Stresemann – also a Nobel prize winner – had seen his *Westpolitik* only grudgingly accepted by the Reichstag and the electorate, the new course set by Brandt and Scheel received a resounding vote of confidence from the citizens of the Federal Republic. The ghosts of Weimar had been firmly laid.

Terrorism

The pressures on Brandt's government should not, however, be underestimated. Terrorism had become a feature of German life once again, despite the widespread prosperity which most of the FRG's citizens were happy to acknowledge. It was symptomatic of the difficulties faced by an open society that the Olympic Games held in Munich in August and September 1972 were largely ruined by a brutal act of international Arab terrorism, when eleven athletes were callously murdered, nine of them members of the Israeli team who had been held as hostages. The well-intentioned efforts of the Bavarian police to rescue the hostages ended in tragedy, and increased the impression of German powerlessness. The contrast with the 1936 Olympics, which had been a resounding propaganda success for Goebbels and Hitler, could hardly have been greater.[24]

Internally, the radical student movement continued to disrupt both universities and, increasingly, the public peace. Attacks on department stores and violent demonstrations against unpopular politicians began to be supplemented by even more sinister acts. As the extreme leftist groups, a mish-mash of Maoists, Trotskyites and Stalinists, saw little prospect of achieving power through a mass movement, some of them turned to assassination. Whereas Dutschke's APO had at least been a visible, publicity-seeking organization, the

24. The 1936 Olympics had certainly been controversial, but the nazis exploited them to gain respectability. See the German/English publication by R. Rürup (ed.), *1936. Die Olympischen Spiele und der Nationalsozialismus/The Olympic Games and National Socialism* (Berlin, 1996), esp. pp. 79, 84. The book was published in connection with an exhibition in Berlin marking the 60th anniversary of the Games.

new groups were smaller and clandestine. They engaged in robberies to obtain funds and well-planned murder operations.

The most infamous group of terrorists was that named after Andreas Baader and Ulrike Meinhof. Personally, they reflected the mixture of idealism and criminality which characterized their movement. Meinhof was a gifted young intellectual, sincerely committed to the goals of socialism and peace. She had made a good career in left-wing journalism as editor of the radical and satirical journal *Konkret*, but she came to the conclusion that intellectual persuasion alone would not change society. Baader, on the other hand, seems to have been a pathological delinquent, who had little interest in left-wing causes until he saw the chance to become involved in terrorism. At least partly under his influence, Meinhof moved rapidly into the exciting but evil world of political violence. She convinced herself that the Federal Republic's system was fundamentally as evil as national socialism, since it was collaborating with the Americans in their war of aggression in Vietnam.

Baader was actually in custody for an arson attack on a department store, but in May 1970 Meinhof and two other female accomplices rescued him, severely wounding an elderly man in the process. In September that year the group was blamed for three bank robberies in Berlin, and further such crimes followed, often with loss of life amongst the terrorists and police. In February 1972, after a bomb attack by another group on the British yacht club in west Berlin, Brandt himself appealed to both the public and the security services to put a stop to terrorism, and there were some successful arrests, often accompanied by loss of life on both sides. But outrages continued, with attacks on Allied bases and state officials. As time went on, the extent of terrorist violence grew; in May 1972 seventeen people were injured in an explosion at the Springer press headquarters in Hamburg, and three American soldiers perished in Heidelberg when the headquarters of the American Army in Europe was bombed. In June the back of the terrorist organization seemed to have been broken with the arrest of Baader, Meinhof, Gudrun Ensslin and two other leading activists. But the battle against violent extremism had really only just begun.

There were differences of opinion about the tactics to be adopted towards the student 'revolution' and its terrorist offshoots. One view was that the left was now as dangerous as the anti-Republican right had been in the Weimar Republic, and that Brandt's government was weak in dealing with it. The fact that the German Communist Party, albeit under a slightly different name, had re-established itself in 1969 and was not thereafter prosecuted could be seen as an example of such weakness.[25] Certainly the Communists, despite sanitizing their statutes to accept parliamentary democracy, had not changed their spots, and they were undoubtedly supported by Ulbricht's GDR. But they posed no serious threat to the Federal Republic and never looked remotely like gaining access to *Land*, let alone federal, parliaments.

As for the other extreme left groups, to claim that they were as dangerous as their predecessors in Weimar, let alone the NSDAP at that time, was unconvincing. In particular, such arguments overlooked the fact that the defence mechanisms of the state were never really threatened by the left, although at times they were embarrassed by it. Despite Rudi Dutschke's bombastic talk about a Leninist 'long march through the institutions', the APO and its successors had no chance of infiltrating the police, the army or the higher echelons of the civil service. In this respect the whole atmosphere in the Federal Republic differed from that in Germany after the First World War, when what might be called the 'establishment' rejected the new democratic, republican regime.

It was, and still is, commonly claimed that the media in the 1970s were dominated by left-wing critics of the capitalist system. In fact, major parts of the German press – and in particular the Springer concern, which published the mass circulation *Bild*, and popular broadsheets such as *Die Welt* – were hostile to student radicalism. It is true that some presenters and reporters on TV were not sorry to see the German professoriat embarrassed by impertinent students – professional jealousy amongst would-be academics may have played a role there. But the fact was that German universities clearly were in need of reform, and their unhappy role in the Third Reich added a moralistic spice to the criticism which journalists found it hard to resist. It should also not be forgotten that TV and radio stations were under carefully balanced political control, so that the concept of lopsided coverage for the benefit of left-wing anti-capitalists is unconvincing. What did irk the professoriat was that balanced programmes would include the views of APO representatives as well as their own. This helped to create a myth of 'left-wing' television coverage which was to last well into the 1980s and which would encourage the development of privately owned electronic media when the social–liberal coalition was overthrown.

---

25. The old name was the Communist Party of Germany (Kommunistische Partei Deutschlands: KPD); the new one was the German Communist Party (Deutsche Kommunistische Partei: DKP). For other views on this whole issue, see Dennis L. Bark and David R. Gress, *A History of West Germany*, Vol. 2, *Democracy and its Discontents, 1963–1988* (Oxford, 1989), p. 126, and Bracher *et al.*, *Ära Brandt*, p. 83 et seq.

Economic problems: inflation and budget deficits

More damaging to the Brandt government than radicals and terrorists, however, was the state of the economy. When the social–liberal coalition took over in 1969, there was considerable euphoria over the apparent success of Schiller's 'global steering'. Keynesian methods of demand management seemed to have worked in the mini-recession in the mid-1960s. Exports went on booming and the balance of payments was in surplus. In 1970 west Germany exported goods and services to the value of more than DM125 billion and the rate of growth of exports was over 10 per cent. This was not as rapid a rate of growth as in the two previous years, but it was very respectable. At the same time direct investment abroad was rising fast, and by the time the European boom ended in 1973 the Federal Republic had established a respectable network of overseas investments. But this aspect of the economy never achieved the same significance in West Germany as it did in Britain or the USA.[26] German capitalists still invested heavily in their own country.

As the result of retrenchment measures after 1966, wages were held down and profits shot up. This had the effect of generating rapid growth – 7.5 per cent in 1969. The boom was indeed exceptional; in 1970 the degree of capital stock utilization reached the highest level since 1956 and the number of officially registered vacancies climbed to an all-time peak of 800,000. Unemployment was relatively trifling at 150,000 and the number of 'guest workers' was rising steadily. Between 1969 and 1971 well over a million new foreign workers, mostly from Turkey and southern Europe, entered the German labour force.[27] They performed largely unskilled and unattractive jobs which native Germans were reluctant to take up. They also worked for lower wages and under worse conditions than their German colleagues, so that trade unions could satisfy their German members at the expense of foreign labourers, few of whom established any right to permanent residence or long-term employment, let alone German citizenship.

26. For an interesting discussion of this important point, see H.G. Schröter, 'Außenwirtschaft im Boom: Direktinvestitionen bundesdeutscher Unternehmen im Ausland, 1950–1975', in H. Kaelble (ed.), *Der Boom 1948–1973: Gesellschaftliche und Wirtschaftliche Folgen in der Bundesrepublik und in Europa* (Oppladen, 1992), pp. 82–106.

27. For details of the labour market and foreign workers, see Hans Giersch, Karl-Heinz Paqué and Holger Schmieding, *The Fading Miracle. Four Decades of Market Economy in Germany* (Cambridge, 1992), p. 127, and for the boom in the early 1970s, see ibid., pp. 150–8.

The boom lasted until 1973, but its negative aspects were already apparent well before the oil crisis of October 1973 created an entirely different economic environment. Programmes of reform, whether in social welfare or education, were really dependent on the 'magic triangle' of steady growth, low inflation and full employment. Very soon, it became clear that this happy condition was not going to last.

One important cause of this was to be found in Washington. The ill-conceived Vietnam War, which was itself a contributory factor in the growth of student radicalism in western Europe, was beginning to undermine the economic power of the United States, upon which the stability of the free world depended. Above all, the western system of fixed exchange rates, adopted at the Bretton Woods conference in 1944, was under serious strain as the dollar itself lost its value. West Germany was threatened with imported inflation. To prevent this, the government needed to keep revaluing the D-Mark upwards, but such a measure always aroused opposition from industry, which feared for its export prices, and – curiously enough – from nationalist, conservative circles like Strauss's CSU, which saw revaluation as truckling to foreign pressure. When the social–liberal coalition came into office it allowed an immediate revaluation which was beneficial for a period, but the problem kept recurring. Although other measures, such as raising interest rates, demanding special reserve deposits from banks and even introducing foreign exchange controls, were used in the fight to maintain the value of money, they did not work. For the first time in nearly twenty years West Germany began to suffer serious inflation. It averaged from 5 per cent to 7 per cent between 1969 and 1973.[28]

The most effective way of coping with this problem would have been to adopt a floating exchange rate for the D-Mark, letting the currency find its own – higher – level *vis-à-vis* the dollar. Independent economic experts advising the government recommended this. But it was seen as altogether too radical a step, which could at best be used as a temporary measure. In May 1971 the free floating experiment was tried and proved highly successful, but in December of that year another realignment of currencies worked out in Washington created a fixed exchange rate for the D-Mark. By the spring of 1972 Finance Minister Schiller was urging a return to floating, but he was defeated in cabinet and resigned. Yet a year later the flood of hot money into West Germany became insupportable, and on 1 March 1973 the Bundesbank had to buy dollars worth

28. Giersch *et al.*, *Fading Miracle*, p. 151.

DM7.5 billion before closing the country's foreign exchange markets. When they reopened, the D-Mark was left to float.[29]

If this international exchange rate problem was not of West Germany's making, some economic historians have detected weaknesses in the German economy which were self-induced. These were increased labour costs, and the growth of the public sector as an employer. Both developments were consistent with the beliefs of many social democrats and even left liberals. So far as the trade unions were concerned, they had adopted their own pragmatic Düsseldorf programme in 1963, which involved responsible collective bargaining and wage restraint. But by 1969, when profits were soaring ahead of wages, their members were losing patience, and a string of wildcat strikes occurred. From then on the unions determined to push for wage increases ahead of inflation. In 1970 they aimed at an increase of the adjusted wage share in national income by 5.4 per cent in five years, and in this they largely succeeded.[30] The pressure became particularly severe in the public sector, where the unions intended to ensure that their members kept up with those in private industry. This was one reason for increased costs at the municipal and *Land* level, where most such workers were employed. The unions' more aggressive stance did them no harm; in the 1960s they had been stagnating, but between 1969 and 1974 their membership grew by about a million, and unionization of labour rose from 35 to roughly 39 per cent of the workforce.

So far as the growth of the public sector was concerned, this was in line with the general view prevalent in social democratic circles that the quality of life of the masses could only be improved by better and more comprehensive public services. It also reflected a secular trend, in that the older types of manufacturing industry and agriculture were shedding labour and losing market share to the service sector, a considerable part of which was under public ownership or control. The years 1960–73 saw 1.3 million more people employed in the public sector, an increase of over 60 per cent. Nevertheless, this left a proportionately smaller private sector to earn the profits and tax revenues upon which social services could be based. Taxes and social security contributions also rose sharply and by 1973 they accounted for 43.3 per cent of GNP.[31]

Under these circumstances it seems surprising that the West

---

29. On Schiller's resignation, see below, p. 246. For the problems connected with exchange rates, see Giersch *et al.*, *Fading Miracle*, pp. 176–80.
30. Ibid., p. 157.
31. Ibid., p. 160.

German economy fared as well as it did in these years. Certainly the Federal Republic remained a leading exporting country. Two explanations can be advanced for that; the most important is the quality of West German products, especially in the capital goods sector, where the advanced level of West German technology and the expertise available in a skilled labour force meant that foreign customers went on buying German goods even if the prices rose. The second advantage the west Germans possessed was the willingness of their major companies, supported by both *Land* governments and the banks, to invest long-term in modern plant. They weathered economic downturns by re-equipping, and came back strongly when the market recovered.

This happy scene was, however, also dependent on favourable terms of trade which existed in the 1960s and early 1970s. Raw materials were fairly cheap, whereas high value-added manufacturing exports could command high prices. In October 1973 this situation changed almost overnight when the fourth Arab–Israeli war enabled the oil-producers, organized in OPEC, to reduce production in the Middle East and engineer a tripling of the oil price within a few months. Other raw materials also became dearer and the terms of trade changed drastically against west European countries, including West Germany. The deterioration was to continue, with some brief periods of remission, until the middle of the 1980s.[32]

It was against this background that some of the more exaggerated hopes amongst Willy Brandt's followers were revealed to be illusory. The left wing of the party was growing in numbers as more young people joined the SPD – in 1973 the party had a million members, of whom three-quarters were under the age of 40, and two-thirds of the membership had joined the party in the previous ten years. Although they were generally loyal to the leadership, and especially to Brandt, many expected that Social Democracy would create a new form of society based less on a capitalist free-for-all and more on co-ordinated development in which state planning – whether in investment, education, or urban renewal – would play a leading part. Brandt's Federal Chancellery had been put under the control of an ambitious young politician, Horst Ehmke, whose aim was to create a kind of super-ministry to co-ordinate the activities of other departments into a central plan. This proved a costly and largely fruitless exercise, not least because ministers like Schiller, in charge of economic policy, and Helmut Schmidt at defence, had

32. Ibid., p. 159.

no intention of yielding authority to Ehmke. After the Bundestag elections of November 1972, Ehmke was shunted away to become minister for research and technology, and the grandiose planning conceptions were quietly shelved. Nevertheless, rising public expenditure, especially at the municipal and *Land* level, remained an intractable problem.

The result was a permanent budgetary deficit, which the Federal Finance Ministry was unable to close. It was no coincidence that this post saw a rapid turnover of occupants; in May 1971 Alex Möller resigned because he could not stomach excessive public spending by his departmental colleagues, and his place was taken by Karl Schiller, who became a 'super minister', running the departments of economics and finance together. This was not a happy state of affairs, especially since Schiller himself was a committed believer in the market mechanism and sound money. He, like Möller, found himself under fire from ambitious colleagues determined to spend more than the Federal Republic could afford. One of the loudest of Schiller's critics was Helmut Schmidt, the defence minister, who not only promoted his own department with gusto, but was not averse to commenting on the work of other ministries. Much time was spent in recriminations in the cabinet, and Brandt did not have either the tartness of an Adenauer or the emollient gifts of a Kiesinger when it came to dealing with such squabbles.

In May 1971, Schiller insisted that the deficit was going to be so large that there would have to be serious cuts – including DM800 million from Schmidt's defence budget. He was able to obtain agreement to this with great difficulty, but came unstuck over the recurrent problem of the over-valuation of the D-Mark, which he wanted – quite rightly as it turned out – to combat by floating the currency. This was opposed by the president of the Bundesbank, Karl Klasen. The cabinet preferred Klasen's solution of foreign exchange controls which, he promised, would give them a calm period until the next elections. Schiller resigned, going so far as to leave the SPD altogether for a time, and openly supported the CDU in the subsequent Bundestag election campaign. His successor was Schmidt himself, who also took over both ministries as a stop-gap until the Bundestag elections. This whole affair was not helpful for the consistency of West German economic and financial policy. It had as much to do with the ambitions of the two protagonists as with the actual issues involved, although Schiller was probably correct in his judgements. Schmidt was evidently frustrated in his job at the Defence Ministry, especially since Brandt was only five years older than himself, so that he could hardly hope for the Chancellor's position. Schiller was his rival star in the party, and by taking over his posts Schmidt entered the election campaign with a high profile.[33]

The 1973 oil crisis, the guest workers, and Brandt's resignation

For Willy Brandt the October 1972 elections marked the zenith of his career and the beginning of his decline. His party had achieved its best ever result in a history which stretched back into the Bismarckian Empire. His *Ostpolitik* had received public endorsement. But the domestic scene was frustrating, and Brandt himself seemed tired. Immediately after the elections he was in hospital for an operation on his throat and lost his voice for some days. The business of creating the coalition was largely left in the hands of Wehner and Schmidt. Brandt later claimed that too many concessions had been made to the Free Democrats.[34] While Scheel and Genscher remained at their posts, the Free Democrat Friderichs was given the Ministry of Economics, although that department was seriously weakened by losing control of credit and monetary policy to Schmidt's Finance Ministry. This was an area of competence which Ludwig Erhard, for example, had always fought hard to attain, and thereafter the Economics Ministry never enjoyed the prestige and status accorded to it in the first two decades of the Republic. The Free Democrats were given another ministry without portfolio, and, more important, the sensitive job of press spokesman, hitherto exercised by Brandt's admirer Ahlers, went to a Free Democratic nominee, Rüdiger von Wechmar. Generally there was a shift to the right in the cabinet, and Brandt found himself more isolated, with Schmidt and Wehner – whom he largely distrusted – showing less respect for his authority.

It was under these somewhat unhappy circumstances that Brandt's government was faced with the oil crisis of October 1973, an external threat to the country's prosperity over which the government had no control. After some rather panicky reactions, such as the introduction of 'car-free' Sundays, the government recovered its nerve and allowed the free price mechanism to operate, with the ultimate result that oil conservation measures were effective. Speed

---

33. Bracher *et al.*, *Ära Brandt*, pp. 46–54.
34. Willy Brandt, *My Life in Politics* (London, 1992), pp. 280–1; cf. also Bracher *et al.*, *Ära Brandt*, pp. 91–6.

limits on motorways were introduced for the first time; these were in any case highly desirable to reduce the appalling toll of German road accidents, as well as to conserve fuel. But the FDP showed its vulnerability to pressure from vested interests by refusing to allow this measure to become permanent. In any case, no government action could prevent short-term inflation, sharply rising unemployment and very low economic growth.[35]

The most immediate victims of the crisis were the hapless foreign 'guest workers' (*Gastarbeiter*) who had been pouring into west Germany since the mid-1950s. Their contribution to economic growth had been especially important since August 1961, when the building of the Berlin Wall had stopped the flow of East German refugees into the Federal Republic. By 1973 the number of guest workers exceeded two and a half million, many of them from Turkey and Yugoslavia. The beauty of the 'guest worker' system, from the German point of view, was that it did not allow foreigners to stay permanently in West Germany. They were recruited on fixed-term contracts and could therefore be forced to leave the country when these expired. The Federal Republic, as politicians and officials constantly repeated, could not be a target for immigration (*kein Einwanderungsland*).

In 1966, when Erhard's government had experienced a mild recession, the numbers of guest workers had fallen by 400,000, thus alleviating industry's wage burden and safeguarding native German jobs. On 22 November 1973, this tactic was repeated. Recruitment was stopped, and when contracts ran out they were not renewed. The number of guest workers started to fall, and by 1976 it was well under two million. But things did not work out as easily as in Erhard's time. Firstly, the crisis was of a much more fundamental kind, and did not evaporate as had been the case in 1966–67. Secondly, by the mid-1970s many guest workers had actually been allowed to stay for a considerable period, since it suited employers that they should do so. The authorities in some of the *Länder* had implemented the laws regulating guest workers in a more liberal fashion than others, enabling the migrants from Mediterranean countries effectively to become resident in the Federal Republic.[36]

---

35. Growth in 1974 was a mere 0.5 per cent. Of course, it should be remembered that other developed countries faced the same problems and many were worse off than west Germany. Bracher *et al.*, *Ära Brandt*, p. 108.

36. E. Kolinsky, 'Non-German Minorities in Contemporary German Society', in D. Horrocks and E. Kolinsky (eds), *Turkish Culture in German Society Today* (Providence, R.I., 1996), pp. 86–7.

They had established themselves with their families in West Germany. Quite a lot of these workers had obtained skilled or essential jobs, and they were highly unionized. They had also paid social security contributions and could claim benefits for their families. Already many had children born in the Federal Republic, although under federal law this did not entitle them to citizenship, the attainment of which was a lengthy and uncertain business.

In 1973 there were 3.9 million foreigners living in West Germany, and by 1981 this had risen to 4.5 million, of whom 1.5 million were Turks. Their young families tended to be larger than those of the native Germans, who were concerned about their own falling birth rate. Since the foreigners were often concentrated in large cities, such as West Berlin or Hamburg, and since they not unnaturally found themselves only able to afford the poorer type of housing, their presence aroused resentment amongst some less well off West Germans. This would be especially likely where local schools had to cater for a majority of non-German-speaking children. The Turks and Yugoslavs also tended to carry out the least attractive sorts of unskilled work, which meant that they were important for the economy but vulnerable to unemployment.[37] So urban poverty amongst 'guest workers', who were by now more than guests but not accepted as Germans, was a social problem which was never satisfactorily solved during the last decades of the Bonn Republic, and which occasionally caused eruptions of ugly racial friction.

It was thus against a stormy background that two events occurred which were to mark the end of the Brandt–Scheel coalition. The first was the decision by President Heinemann not to run for a second term of office in view of his age. Foreign Minister Scheel, whose own health was not robust, seized the opportunity to announce that only one or other of the coalition party leaders had the right to nomination – and since Brandt did not want to be president, he, Scheel, would take the post. This meant that in May 1974 Scheel would leave the federal cabinet to take up his duties as president. His post as foreign minister would fall to the rather more conservative, but extremely competent, Hans-Dietrich Genscher.

Before this happened, however, Brandt himself had lost the chancellorship. It was discovered that one of the staff in his private office, Günter Guillaume, was an east German agent. This was certainly not

37. For a helpful account of guest workers 1955–81, see H. Esser, 'Gastarbeiter', in W. Benz (ed.), *Die Bundesrepublik Deutschland. Geschichte in drei Bänden: Band 2 Gesellschaft* (Frankfurt, 1983), pp. 127–56.

Brandt's own fault; the responsibility seems to have been shared between Ehmke, who appointed Guillaume, Genscher, who as minister of the interior was responsible for security, and the head of the security service (*Bundesverfassungsschutz*), Günther Nollau.

Nollau does indeed seem to have played an unhappy role in the affair, since he did not report matters directly to Brandt, but to Herbert Wehner, the chairman of the SPD Bundestag delegation, to whom he happened to owe his job. There seems to have been a fear that Guillaume could compromise Brandt by revealing salacious details of his private life, including adulterous affairs with female journalists. Brandt himself later sharply denied this claim. What is clear is that he received very little support from his most important party lieutenants, Wehner and Schmidt, both of whom advised him to leave office. On 6 May 1974 he resigned his post as chancellor, but remained chairman of the SPD, thus ensuring his continuing political importance. The public and the rank and file of his party felt considerable sympathy for him. In general, Brandt had been a people's chancellor rather than a professional politician. The fact that he was socially an outsider was never forgotten in Bonn, and the eagerness with which the bureaucracy and his senior party colleagues seized the chance to be rid of him may have reflected that fact.

His successor was the ambitious, domineering Helmut Schmidt.

CHAPTER TEN

Affluence and Compromise: Schmidt as Chancellor

The new chancellor

Schmidt was in many ways an ideal chancellor for the Federal Republic in the second half of the 1970s. He was at his best when facing disaster, such as floods in Hamburg, the threat of Soviet nuclear missiles or an economic crisis. He had little time for what President Bush once described as 'the vision thing', and was often openly contemptuous of left-wing intellectuals. He began his period of office by berating his Social Democratic parliamentary colleagues for making impossible demands on the state and alienating the electorate with irresponsible promises. So carried away was he with this theme that he arrived half an hour late for his official appointment as chancellor by the Federal President.[1]

Once in charge, Schmidt had a number of advantages over Brandt. As an economist by training, he could inspire confidence at a time of serious economic difficulty. His cabinet was less turbulent than Brandt's, not least because Schmidt himself was no longer a subordinate figure. He had already pushed aside one difficult colleague, Schiller, and was able to drop other possible rivals, like Horst Ehmke and Egon Bahr. Their replacements were mainly safe, middle-of-the-road figures from the trade union wing of the SPD. His other advantage was that the party chairmanship continued to be held by Brandt. A man of lesser calibre might have exploited this position to harass his successor, but Brandt did not follow Adenauer's example vis-à-vis Erhard.[2] Instead, he was able to act as an insulating layer

1. W. Jäger and W. Link, *Geschichte der Bundesrepublik Deutschland*, Vol. 5/II, *Republik im Wandel, 1974–1982: Die Ära Schmidt* (Stuttgart, 1987), p. 12.
2. See above, Chapter 7.

between the new chancellor and his often unhappy left-wing colleagues in the party membership. This did not mean that Brandt and Schmidt saw eye to eye on all issues. By the beginning of the 1980s serious differences were opening up over the strategic objectives to be pursued by the SPD. On balance, however, there was no doubt that Schmidt benefited from Brandt's prestige with the party rank and file.

The main problem faced by the government was the economic crisis: in 1975 unemployment would rise to over one million and in that year also GDP fell by 1.6 per cent, the worst performance since the Great Depression.[3] The left of the Social Democratic Party would have favoured planned government investment and deficit spending as a way of reflating the economy, but the experiences of the early 1970s had created disillusionment with that sort of solution. The public – not to mention the Bundesbank – was worried about inflation. The alternative was to adopt so-called 'supply side' economics, aimed at reducing public expenditure and public debt, and cutting taxes on business to increase profits and encourage investment. This was precisely the type of policy favoured by the Free Democrats' economics minister, Hans Friderichs, whose views also chimed in with those of his new FDP chairman, Hans-Dietrich Genscher.

Schmidt seemed to find the Free Democrats more congenial than his own party at this time, and launched his new regime before the Bundestag declaring 'without investments, no growth; without investments no security of jobs, no higher wages and no social progress'. It was noted that the FDP members applauded this with greater enthusiasm than Schmidt's own party.[4] Business circles also warmed to Schmidt.

The FDP, an uncertain ally

In the FDP itself divisions were apparent which would eventually destroy the coalition. Genscher, now party leader and foreign minister in place of Scheel, had always been less inclined towards the left than his predecessor. He was a friend of Helmut Kohl, the new leader of the CDU after Barzel's election defeat in 1972, and he had always tried to keep a ministerial profile separate from his SPD coalition partners. The move away from social welfare towards more

---

3. Hans Giersch _et al._, _The Fading Miracle_ (Cambridge, 1992), p. 188.
4. Jäger and Link, _Ära Schmidt_, p. 20.

orthodox liberal economic policies pleased him. He wanted above all to complete the work of *Ostpolitik* begun by his predecessor, but he hoped that this could be carried through as well by co-operation with the Christian Democrats.

For his part, Kohl made it clear that he was willing to accept the verdict of the electorate on *détente* with the Soviet bloc. In March 1976 Genscher faced difficulties in the Bundesrat – where there was a Christian majority – over a new agreement with the Polish government which bartered West German credits against more exit permits for ethnic Germans living in Poland. Franz-Josef Strauss was determined to oppose government 'softness' towards the East at every opportunity, but Kohl and Genscher negotiated a form of words which 'clarified' the agreement and assured its ratification. It was no coincidence that at the same time the FDP in Lower Saxony started serious negotiations about joining a coalition with the Christian Democrats, and thenceforth the FDP's loyalty to its Social Democratic comrades in Bonn was always in some doubt. Within the FDP itself Genscher knew that many of the functionaries, as well as the younger rank and file, would regard leaving the social–liberal coalition as a betrayal. But the right wing, which had been severely damaged in 1969, still existed in the shape of politicians like Friderichs and von Lambsdorff. They could afford to wait for a change in the political atmosphere.

Strauss and Kohl

In the mid-1970s the possibility of a rapprochement between the liberals and the Union parties was ruled out by the influence of one man – Franz-Josef Strauss. Strauss hated the Free Democrats, who had twice removed him from office – once after the *Spiegel* affair and then by destroying the grand coalition. He still believed that the social–liberal government could be defeated by beating the nationalist drum against *Ostpolitik*. He also thought that a strong anti-communist line would go down well domestically, and seemed to prove this in October 1974 when his CSU won a smashing victory in its home state of Bavaria. Strauss was encouraged in his hard-line attitude by the prime minister of another large southern *Land*, Hans Filbinger of Baden-Württemberg. Filbinger was typical of a generation of conservative politicians who resented Brandt and his apparent betrayal of German national interests. He also launched a no-holds-barred attack on 'socialism' in the Federal Republic. Using the slogan 'Freedom not Socialism' (*Freiheit statt Sozialismus*) he won a resounding victory at the polls in Stuttgart in April 1976. Strauss and Filbinger denounced the FDP as stirrup-holder for the Social Democrats, and Strauss described the party as a 'solid element in the socialist bloc'. SPD and FDP were described as 'bloc parties' – a reference to communist puppet organizations in the GDR.[5] Under these circumstances association between the FDP and the Union parties was impossible, and Kohl was forced to bide his time.

Nevertheless, in the Bundestag elections of October 1976 the Christian Democrats came very near to winning. The CDU/CSU obtained its second highest ever share of the vote and missed an absolute majority by less than 2 per cent. The social–liberal coalition was left with a majority of two in the Bundestag. Strauss could claim a victory for his tactics because the Christian vote in south Germany was higher than elsewhere. But the fact was that Strauss had frightened off north German voters, who disliked what they saw as his warmongering demagogy. The CDU/CSU would have to wait another six years before it tasted power in Bonn again. Schmidt himself was one of the major causes of the opposition frustration.

Terrorism: a recurrent problem

The Federal Republic was still plagued by terrorism, albeit of a particular kind, since on the whole violence was aimed at specific targets and did not affect the mass of the population. It should be remembered that at the same time terrorism was appearing in various parts of Europe and above all in the Middle East, where Palestinian groups were desperately trying to draw attention to the plight of their expellees from Israel. The extreme left in west Germany regarded Zionism as a tool of capitalist imperialism, and collaborated with some Arab terrorist groups. The 'Red Army Group' (*Rote Armee Fraktion* or RAF) became active once again, targeting leading figures in the state or business, as well as American bases and organizations associated with American 'imperialism'. The campaign of terror seems to have had two aims: the first was to liberate terrorists already in captivity, such as Andreas Baader, Gudrun Ensslin and Jan-Carl Raspe, who were being held in a maximum security prison at Stammheim, near Stuttgart. Ulrike Meinhof had already committed suicide there in May 1976. The second aim was to create anxiety in the Federal

5. Ibid., p. 45.

Republic and provoke reprisals which, in turn, would alienate the masses. Bonn began to look like an armed camp in this period, with heavily armed police and border guards much in evidence and public buildings protected by barbed wire barriers. But the government, despite hectoring criticism from Strauss and some sections of the nationalist tabloid press, refused to overreact.

Terrorism reached a peak in 1977. On 7 April the Federal Attorney General, Siegfried Buback, and two companions were murdered. Buback was responsible for the prosecution of RAF terrorists. In July, Jürgen Ponto, a director of the Dresdener Bank and an admirer of Schmidt, was shot dead at his home near Frankfurt. Then on 5 September, Hanns-Martin Schleyer, who was president of the BDI and the BVDI, the leading associations of west German industrialists and employers respectively, was kidnapped in Cologne, an event which was accompanied by the murder of his chauffeur and three policemen. The kidnappers demanded the release of eleven captured terrorists and a large sum of money.

Schmidt now came into his element. He organized crisis groups in Bonn to report at regular intervals and to co-ordinate both the hunt for the terrorists and public responses to their threats. The opposition parties were associated with the action, as were the governments of *Länder* – mostly under CDU control – where terrorists were imprisoned. This 'solidarity of Democrats' made it difficult for the opposition to make party political capital out of the crisis. Although the aim of government policy was to free Schleyer alive, it was also agreed that the kidnappers had to be captured and that no prisoners should be released. This was a clear toughening of attitude by comparison with an earlier occasion in February 1975, when the CDU leader in Berlin, Peter Lorenz, had been seized and swapped for six members of the Baader–Meinhof group who had been flown to the Yemen.

A news blackout was negotiated with the media, and the terrorists in Stammheim were cut off from their legal advisers, since there was reason to suppose that the RAF action was being orchestrated from the prison. This required a law to be rushed through suspending the prisoners' rights for a temporary period so long as the procedure was accepted by a judge. There were also changes in the law to make house searches easier, but on the whole the Federal Republic did not jeopardize the rule of law – the *Rechtsstaat*, as Germans were proud to call it – in response to terrorist provocation. At first it seemed that the government's tactics might work, since various terrorist deadlines went by without Schleyer being killed. But on 13

October a Lufthansa Boeing 737 flying from Majorca to Frankfurt was hijacked by four Arabs who were evidently in close contact with Schleyer's kidnappers. They threatened that unless the RAF demands were met, together with the release of two Palestinian prisoners in Turkey and a further ransom of US$15 million, all the occupants of the plane and Schleyer himself would be killed. The aircraft was forced to undertake a wearisome flight via Rome, Larnica, Bahrein and Dubai to Aden where, on 16 October, the terrorists murdered the pilot as an earnest of their ill intentions. The plane then left for Mogadishu in Somalia.

For almost the first time, the West German government was determined to fight back. It was also prepared to do so. A specially trained force of West German border guards (GSG 9) was flown to Mogadishu and, just after midnight on 17 October, the hijacked airliner was successfully stormed. All the hostages were rescued, a few with minor injuries. Three of the hijackers were killed. In Bonn the government press spokesman announced this triumph almost immediately and urged the RAF to release Schleyer – a palpably forlorn hope. The first response came from Stammheim where the leading terrorist prisoners, Baader, Ennslin and Raspe, committed suicide, having tried unsuccessfully to make their deaths appear as murder by the authorities. This clearly sealed Schleyer's fate, and his body was found in a car in Mülhausen after his captors had sent a viciously worded message blaming Schmidt for the whole affair.[6]

Despite this tragedy, the outcome of the crisis was a victory for the government, which had shown steadiness and determination throughout. The deaths of the Stammheim group were sensational, but aroused little public sympathy for the RAF, and the circumstances of Schleyer's murder put the kidnappers in an even worse light. Although terrorism did not cease after this, and even increased in the early 1980s, with numerous attacks on American service bases or personnel, it was no longer regarded as a serious threat to the state. In that respect Bonn had again shown that it was very different from Weimar, since in the first German Republic assassinations like those of Erzberger or Rathenau had shaken public confidence in the Republican system itself.

This does not mean that attempts were not made to exploit the outrages for political purposes. In particular, great attention was paid to the so-called 'sympathizers', a penumbra of radical left-wing fellow-travellers who supposedly enabled the terrorists to operate

6. For the details of the affair, see ibid., pp. 74–82.

undetected. In 1971 a survey claimed that 6 per cent of respondents would shelter a member of the Baader–Meinhof gang on the run from the police.[7] After Buback's murder in 1977 an anonymous pamphlet appeared, allegedly written by a student at Göttingen University who claimed that when he heard the news he could not and would not deny feeling a concealed shiver of joy (*klammheimliche Freude*) at the death of a man who had persecuted the left. This phrase became notorious and was picked up by conservative circles to discredit left-wing intellectuals, such as the social democratic novelist Heinrich Böll, who were expressing concern lest the struggle against terrorism should lead to a witch-hunt weakening civil rights.[8] There were, indeed, undertones in the Baader–Meinhof affair that made the struggle against left-wing terrorism in the Federal Republic more complicated than would have been the case elsewhere. The public outrage and mourning after the death of Hanns-Martin Schleyer tended to gloss over the fact that he had been a convinced nazi from an early age – a leading member of the NS student organization at university – and had made a career in the SS during the war.[9] Many of west Germany's business élite had to a greater or lesser extent been compromised by association with the Third Reich, even though they were collaborating happily with parliamentary democracy in the 1970s. This was certainly no excuse for the atrocities committed by the RAF and similar groups, but it helps to explain a certain scepticism towards social élites present in sections of the intelligentsia.

As for the vociferous criticism of left-wing 'sympathizers', it should perhaps be noted that subsequent revelations from the former GDR have proved that radical terrorists were given more material help – and certainly safe havens – by Honecker's *Stasi* east of the Elbe than they received from the chattering classes in West Germany. Nor should it be overlooked that terrorism was not confined to the left. Some viciously lethal outrages were committed by the extreme right, and especially by nationalist groups disillusioned with the failure of the NPD in the 1960s. One sinister paramilitary group

7. The survey was claimed to be a representative sample, but it is difficult to imagine how a scientific observation could be made on this subject. Ibid., p. 86.

8. This concern had originally arisen in December 1971 over a headline in *Bild* which blamed a policeman's murder on the Baader–Meinhof gang before there was any evidence for such a linkage. As a result Böll became a target for Axel Springer's abuse. He responded with the novel *Die Verlorene Ehre der Katherina Blum*. See J. Sandford (ed.), Günter Wallraff, *Der Aufmacher. Der Mann, der bei Bild Hans Esser war* (Manchester, 1990), pp. 17–18.

9. These facts were, however, presented to the readers of Schleyer's not unsympathetic obituary in *The Times*, 21 October 1977.

– 'Defence Sport Hoffmann' – was banned after being suspected of involvement in bomb attacks on foreign workers' hostels.

Strauss and the CSU, who had been quick to tag government supporters with the 'sympathizer' label when the campaign against Baader–Meinhof was under way, minimized these nationalist movements, however murderous they might appear to be. In March 1980 Strauss told a French TV interviewer that it was ridiculous to worry about an eccentric like Hoffmann who thrived on publicity: 'My God, when a man wants to amuse himself by dressing up in a . . . battledress on a Sunday and going out with a rucksack he should be left alone to get on with it.'[10] The matter did not seem quite so amusing when a bomb went off at the Munich Oktoberfest in September killing thirteen people or when, three months later, a Jewish publisher in Erlangen and his common law wife were murdered by killers thought to be from the Hoffmann group.

On both the right and the left there were certainly reservoirs of sympathizers willing to tolerate violent people, but their numbers were not very great. On the nationalist right, the NPD and an organization called the Deutsche Volksunion, headed by a Munich publisher, Gerhard Frey, had between them about 17,000 members in the early 1980s. On the extreme left there was a disparate group of ex-APO Maoists, Trotskyites, alternative lifestyle communists and squatters, who dedicated themselves in one way or another to 'smashing the system'. The former were less well educated and on average older than the latter. Both were malevolent in their intentions. But neither presented a real threat to the Federal Republic so long as its leaders kept their heads.

Schmidt's management of the economy in the 1970s

If Schmidt had gained prestige over the Mogadishu affair, he also received plaudits for his handling of the economic crisis. One reason for this was his international standing. Since he had not been directly involved in the *Ostpolitik* negotiations, and since he was known to be enthusiastic for western solidarity in defence, he was reassuring to the Americans. President Nixon had harboured the ludicrous suspicion that Brandt was trying to undermine the Western Alliance, but even he could hardly believe that of Schmidt. The new chancellor's

10. Jäger and Link, *Ära Schmidt*, p. 88.

perfect command of English and his economics training meant that he could play a leading role in international negotiations to consider the crisis created by OPEC's oil embargo. In the aftermath of the oil crisis international conferences of the world's leading industrial nations became a regular feature of the international scene, starting with a conference at Rambouillet in November 1975.

Schmidt's main aim was to prevent the world sinking back into the kind of small-minded protectionism that had done such damage after the world depression of 1929. In this he was largely successful, though of course the existence of bodies like the IMF and GATT made things much easier for him than they had been for his predecessors in the 1930s. Less useful was the European Economic Community, which had, on 1 January 1973, been enlarged to include Britain, Denmark and Ireland. In the aftermath of the oil crisis the Danes and the Italians introduced import restrictions, despite their incompatibility with the rules of the EEC.[11] Fortunately West Germany, which, with Holland, was the only EEC member to have a positive trade balance in 1974, could put its weight against such infractions. Schmidt was not sentimental about the European Community and, like most economists, had a jaundiced view of its grotesquely protectionist agricultural policy, which was costing the Federal Republic a great deal of money. He made it clear that West Germany was not prepared 'to be a blood donor for others, when the recipients are refusing to take the necessary medicine'.[12]

Schmidt's willingness to accept economic measures unpalatable to his own party, such as VAT increases and cuts in corporation tax, meant that business confidence revived somewhat after 1975, and by 1978 he could once again boast that West Germany was a 'world champion' exporting country. Certainly export industries accounted for a growing share of German jobs. Yet the economic recovery after the oil shock was still faltering, and in 1978 Schmidt accepted pleas from the recently elected American president Carter and other Allied leaders that Germany should take reflationary measures designed to pull the developed world out of recession. This was agreed at a Bonn economic summit in July 1978, at which Schmidt himself not unnaturally played the leading role. West Germany was now evidently a great economic power, even if she was still not in the first division so far as military or diplomatic questions were concerned. Schmidt promised that his country would reflate by an expenditure package

11. Ibid., p. 279.
12. Ibid., p. 279.

equal to 1 per cent of GNP, and in return Carter agreed to combat inflation in the USA and insist that his countrymen should pay more realistic prices for their petrol.[13]

Conventional economists regarded this attempt to use the German economy as a 'locomotive' for world recovery as a mistake, and many economic historians would agree with them.[14] Inflation followed quickly on the Schmidt package, and soon the Bundesbank was having to raise interest rates. But in the short term the initiative seemed to work: in 1979 GDP grew by 4.2 per cent and employment picked up. Unemployment fell to under a million for the first time since 1974 and in 1978 it was down to 876,000, which seemed encouraging, even if it did not compare well with unemployment rates in the 1960s. Schmidt's reputation as an efficient manager of economic affairs was given a boost, and the government's popularity began to rise.

Schmidt as a world leader

Diplomatically, too, Schmidt seemed to be asserting global leadership from Bonn. Despite a lack of personal rapport with the new American president, Carter, Bonn was still seen as Washington's most reliable ally in Europe. On the other hand, Schmidt was able to maintain a reasonably warm relationship with Brezhnev, who himself visited Bonn in 1978. Indeed, that year Bonn was a mecca for high-level visitors, who included Queen Elizabeth II. Although Schmidt had not been intimately connected with Brandt's *Ostpolitik*, and did not have a close relationship with Egon Bahr, he tried to exploit the flexibility for the Federal Republic which Brandt had created.

In 1975 the first major conference on security and co-operation in Europe (CSCE) was held in Helsinki. This was itself a result of the *détente* between East and West, and had been one of the objectives of Soviet policy. If such a conference had taken place before the jettisoning of the Hallstein doctrine and the establishment of formal relations with Soviet satellite countries, the position of the Federal Republic would have been one of embarrassing isolation. As it was, West Germany could play a discreetly important role in the conference, whilst using her membership of the European Economic Community to act as one of a European group. For the time being,

13. Ibid., p. 109.
14. Giersch *et al.*, *Fading Miracle*, pp. 190–1.

Helsinki seemed to do little except present a series of platitudes about peace and co-operation, but the sections of the conference which dealt with human rights, and which established an ongoing institutional concern for these matters, ultimately did work to the advantage of dissidents in the Soviet bloc. This outcome was hardly to be expected in the 1970s. Schmidt was, however, able to use his participation in the conference to make contact with the Polish communist leader, Edward Gierek. Schmidt hoped to achieve a rapprochement with Poland along the lines of the Franco-German reconciliation in the 1960s. Well supported by Foreign Minister Genscher, he was able to achieve agreement on important trade treaties with Poland, which involved substantial credits from west Germany in return for a number of exit permits for Germans east of the Oder–Neisse line. The formal treaty arrangements were supplemented by cultural and youth exchanges, town twinning, and an effort to reform historical textbooks in both countries.[15]

Unhappy relations with the GDR

This improvement of relations with Poland was all the more important because the climate between the two German states remained frosty and even deteriorated. Having achieved international recognition and membership of the UN, Honecker and his East German regime had no intention of pursuing a liberal course which might bring it closer to Bonn. On the contrary, its policy was described as one of *Abgrenzung* or fencing off the East Germans and stressing their separate identity. In October 1974 the GDR constitution was changed to emphasize the independence of the 'workers' and farmers' state' and to eliminate reference to German unification. A crackdown in the cultural sphere saw more restrictions being placed on East German writers and artists. In 1976 the dissident singer, Wolf Biermann, who had voluntarily migrated to the GDR in 1953, was expelled by the government. Despite protests from leading literary figures in East Germany like Christa Wolf and Stefan Heym, Biermann's GDR citizenship was annulled, a measure which brought back memories of similar measures against critics of the Third Reich.

In November 1973 Honecker increased the compulsory daily exchange of western D-Marks into east marks which travellers had to make, a burden on poorer West Germans visiting their relatives.

15. Jäger and Link, *Ära Schmidt*, pp. 307–8.

Journalists from West Germany were harassed and an office opened by the *Spiegel* in East Berlin had to be closed down in January 1978, the same month in which the leader of the opposition in Bonn, Helmut Kohl, was denied permission to make an informal visit to East Berlin. The policy of 'small steps', in which Bahr and Brandt had placed such faith, did not seem to be working. Opponents of *Ostpolitik* were quick to denounce it as a failure.

In actual fact, however, the situation was never to revert to the Cold War confrontation of the Hallstein era. The relationship between Bonn and East Berlin was frigid, but it went on, and contacts between the two parts of Germany developed in the form of intensified visits by West Germans to the East. Furthermore, Bonn could use Honecker's desperate need for hard currency to force him into concessions. The increase in compulsory currency exchange, for instance, was greatly modified – particularly for West German pensioners – as the result of Honecker's need for loans from the Federal Republic. Other agreements were made about improved transport arrangements between the two Germanys in the form of motorway, canal and bridge repairs, although critics could rightly point to the fact that Bonn always paid and East Berlin always took. Nevertheless, a relationship was being created in which the GDR was becoming dependent on the wealth of the Federal Republic. This would have important consequences in the next decade.[16]

Two other aspects of the relationship between the two German states were also noteworthy. The first was that, despite bombastic talk of a new type of workers' and farmers' state, the GDR remained without legitimacy for most of its people. The fact that the Wall in Berlin remained and was constantly strengthened, and that the mined and heavily guarded frontier between the two Germanys was reinforced by orders to the East German border guards to shoot fugitives who tried to escape to the West, was one illustration of the SED's dismal failure to win its people's loyalty.

The Brandt/Bahr settlement with the GDR affected life in Honecker's state in other ways. Although western journalists were harassed in the GDR, they were still allowed to operate there – a result of tough negotiating by Bonn. This meant that western TV – which could be seen in the GDR – carried unvarnished news and features on East Germany. Up to the end of the 1960s Ulbricht's

16. For the development of GDR/FRG relations under Schmidt, see ibid., pp. 353–83. See also Mary Fulbrook, *The Divided Nation: A History of Germany 1918–1990* (Oxford, 1991), pp. 214–18.

regime had tried to suppress access to West German TV and radio; Honecker's government gave up this unequal struggle and in the 1980s even installed a cable for viewers in part of Saxony that could not receive West German TV.[17] A more dubious, but from a humanitarian point of view more urgent, type of relationship was that involving the purchase – one could more properly talk of the ransom – of exit permits for East Germans who had special reasons for leaving the GDR. These included political dissidents and children divided from their families since the building of the Berlin Wall. Such deals had been going on – arranged initially through the churches – since the early 1960s, but after 1973 they were put on a more regular basis, with a 'tariff' for the purchase to freedom of those who had tried to escape from the GDR and were punished for it. Usually such people had to wait two or three years and then they would be transferred to West Berlin at a price of about DM40,000, paid by Bonn. In 1977 this figure rose to DM95,847 – an uneven figure being deliberately chosen to avoid the impression of there being a price per head. The money gained was controlled by Honecker and used for particular political purposes. Over 10,000 persons were bought out of the GDR in this way whilst Schmidt was chancellor.[18] There were also visits by pensioners, with whose presence in the GDR Honecker was cynically willing to dispense. Such contacts kept the notion of inter-German solidarity alive. They also helped to create a sort of mutual dependence between the two states which would ultimately hasten the doom of the GDR.

For the time being, however, it looked quite unlikely that Bahr's programme would do more than bring minor alleviations for the misery of those sixteen million Germans trapped under Soviet rule. In the west there were many who were not unhappy to forget about what went on east of the iron curtain. Public opinion polls showed that, whereas in the 1960s at least 35 per cent of those polled in West Germany thought that the unification of Germany was the most important question with which Germans should be concerned, from the mid-1970s the figure was never more than 1 per cent.[19]

Other issues, including the integration of western Europe, moved much higher up the agenda. For the young especially, East Germany, with its dreary restrictions and its polluted industrial landscape, had

17. Timothy Garton Ash, *In Europe's Name*, p. 136.
18. Ibid., p. 146. On at least one occasion the money was used to import consumer goods for wider distribution: ibid., p. 144.
19. Ibid., p. 134.

few attractions, not least because it presented a dismal picture of what was called 'real existing socialism'. It was far more enjoyable and exciting to talk about socialism with French or Italian communists than to visit Honecker's GDR.

Symptomatic of the German problem was the difficulty caused when the heads of government visited each other. In March 1970, Brandt, at an early stage of his attempt to break the log-jam with the East, had gone to Erfurt in the GDR, where he had talks with the prime minister, Willi Stoph. This had proved highly embarrassing for Ulbricht's regime, because popular enthusiasm for Brandt was spontaneous and unmistakable. Since both premiers had almost the same Christian name, it was easy for demonstrators shouting 'Willy' to pretend to the police that they were not supporting the Chancellor of the Federal Republic, even though it was obvious that they were. On the other hand, when Stoph later visited the Federal Republic, angry anti-communist demonstrators, some of them from the nationalist right, created a tense atmosphere.

After some false starts, Schmidt went to the GDR in December 1981, where he and Honecker jointly visited the city of Gustrow in Mecklenburg. To prevent a repetition of the scenes with Brandt in Erfurt, the streets of Gustrow were sealed off by troops and police so that no contact between Schmidt and the population was possible. The pictures of this event in the press and on TV confirmed just how far the GDR had to go before it earned the respect of its own population.

Ostpolitik *and the threat to* détente

Schmidt's visit came at an important moment in East–West relations, when the whole future of *Ostpolitik* seemed in jeopardy. The Soviet invasion of Afghanistan at the end of December 1979, the election of a fiercely anti-communist president of the USA in the shape of Ronald Reagan the following year – not to mention the earlier election of Mrs Thatcher as prime minister in London – meant that the whole atmosphere of *détente* between the superpowers was deteriorating. Furthermore, in Europe itself there were serious threats to *détente*, particularly in Poland, where a peaceful revolution spearheaded by the trade union 'Solidarity' was causing Moscow great concern. Brezhnev, egged on by Honecker and other hard-line satellite leaders, was contemplating military intervention in Poland similar to that against Czechoslovakia in 1968. Schmidt warned both the Russians and the East Germans against any such move, making clear that it would mean the end of the better relations with the Federal Republic and – by implication – the end of West German economic aid. It is not clear how far this was a factor in protecting the Poles, but it may have weighed somewhat in the Soviet decision against outright intervention. Instead, the Polish army itself intervened, and on 13 December 1981, the last day of Schmidt's visit in the GDR, General Jaruzelski imposed martial law on Poland. Many of Solidarity's leaders were arrested.[20]

To Polish patriots trying to overthrow communism in their country, the attitude of the Bonn government seemed contemptible, since it was apparently ignoring them and dealing happily with Soviet puppet regimes in Warsaw or East Berlin. It must be pointed out, however, that the maintenance of German relations with the eastern bloc governments, and especially with Moscow, helped to prevent a return to the sort of confrontation that had occurred in the 1940s and 1950s, a situation in which any progress towards reform would have been impossible.

Schmidt certainly did not ignore the needs of the Western Alliance or minimize the threat from the Soviet Union. Indeed, he had become very impatient with President Carter's administration for its apparent indifference to western European security, and its willingness to allow the USSR to threaten Europe, especially Germany, with medium-range ballistic missiles. Despite strong protests from an increasingly powerful anti-nuclear element in his own party, Schmidt insisted that the Americans should modernize their medium-range nuclear missiles in western Europe, but that preparations for this should take place simultaneously with negotiations designed to reduce the number of such weapons deployed by both sides. Schmidt was successful in getting this 'twin-track' strategy adopted by the Allied powers at a summit meeting in Guadeloupe in January 1979, and it became NATO policy the following December.

The new weapons would be deployed in 1983, but only if negotiations to reduce the numbers of Soviet missiles had proved a failure. It was symptomatic of the Federal Republic's growing status in the Western Alliance that Schmidt should take the lead in promulgating such a strategy. Hence the furtherance of *détente* was inextricably linked in the minds of both Schmidt and his foreign minister, Genscher, with commitment to an effective Western Alliance. Both knew that the communist leaders with whom they were dealing had no sentimental attachment to the West, and would not hesitate to take advantage of weakness if it revealed itself.[21]

The Franco-German entente

One important aspect of Schmidt's 'western' orientation was his cultivation of links with France. Ever since Adenauer's apparently unconsummated relationship with de Gaulle, the ties between Bonn and Paris had been growing stronger. Brandt had a good rapport with President Pompidou, and his successor, Giscard D'Estaing, knew Schmidt well since they had both been finance ministers in the early 1970s. A personal friendship grew up between the two men, and they collaborated particularly closely over the question of currency stability in Europe following the collapse of the dollar-based system of fixed exchange rates. In September 1978 Giscard and Schmidt held a meeting in Aachen, the birthplace of the Carolingian Empire. Apart from a certain romantic symbolism, the meeting did produce a scheme for a European Monetary System (EMS) within the European Economic Community, with exchange rates based on a European currency unit – the ECU. In fact, the core of the system was the D-Mark, to which other currencies, including the French franc, were linked. The British were only observers, and the Italians had to receive a special dispensation to allow their currency to vary more widely in value than the others. A similar scheme had been tried and failed before, but this one was more solidly based and worked quite well until 1992. It caused some alarm in Anglo-Saxon circles, the British being unwilling to join in, and some Americans regarding the project as an attempt to create a European superpower independent of the USA.[22]

The Franco-German entente was becoming a permanent feature of the European diplomatic scene. It did not mean that Paris and Bonn always saw eye to eye. Giscard made it clear on one occasion to the Russians that he would not wish to see Germany united, a view to which Schmidt could never have subscribed.[23] But generally

---

21. This was demonstrated in a Soviet memorandum about relations with the West which showed that the aim of the communist bloc remained the establishment of a 'proletarian dictatorship', and that parties like the SPD were regarded as enemies. K.D. Bracher, Wolfgang Jäger and Werner Link, *Geschichte der Bundesrepublik Deutschland*, Vol. 5/I, *Republik im Wandel, 1969–1974. Die Ära Brandt* (Stuttgart, 1986), pp. 363–5. For the 'twin-track' decision see Garton Ash, *In Europe's Name*, pp. 93–4.

22. This was the somewhat hysterical view of the *Wall Street Journal*. See Jäger and Link, *Ära Schmidt*, p. 289.

23. Ibid., p. 426.

speaking, by the beginning of the 1980s it could be said that the natural partner to whom Schmidt turned whenever there was an international problem, and especially one involving Europe, was Giscard. In the summer of 1981 Giscard was replaced by a socialist, François Mitterrand. His attempts to reflate and nationalize parts of the French economy did not find favour with Schmidt, but they coincided with conflicts between the European Community and Washington. President Reagan's reckless deficit spending provoked a joint demarche in February 1982, and in the summer of that year even Mrs Thatcher joined in resistance when the Americans attempted to wreck joint natural gas projects with the Soviet Union. So the core Franco-German relationship remained strong. In 1979 Schmidt told the British *Economist*: 'I grew up as an Anglophile, I became up to a point an Americanophile and have, during the last ten years in office, transformed myself into a Francophile.'[24]

Certainly, by the time that Schmidt left office in October 1982, he was no longer the favourite ally in Washington. That role had been taken over by Mrs Thatcher. But, so far as the defence of west Germany's interests was concerned, he had strengthened her position in the Alliance, prevented Soviet domination of western Europe and maintained a reasonably positive relationship with Moscow. It was not a bad record.

West German support for Iberian democracy

There was also another aspect of foreign affairs on which not only the government, but in particular the Social Democratic Party, could congratulate itself. This was the successful establishment of parliamentary democracy in Spain and Portugal. The Iberian peninsula had been the home of authoritarian or – to put it more bluntly – fascist regimes since before the Second World War. In the mid-1970s the situation changed, with the success of the anti-colonial war in the Portuguese colonies leading to a revolution in Lisbon, and Franco's death in 1975 creating a power vacuum in Madrid. In the former case there seemed a strong likelihood that the Communists might come to power in a rather unlikely alliance with radical army officers, whereas in Spain the old fascist ruling élites showed no great enthusiasm for the democratization of their country's political system.

If parliamentary democracy was to succeed in Iberia, it would need some positive support. This was unlikely to be found in either

Washington or London. The British government had always been willing to tolerate right-wing Iberian dictators, and once the Cold War was under way the Americans followed their example. Since the triumph of Castro in Cuba in 1959, the Americans had become increasingly paranoid about any emancipatory movements in Latin America, and changes in the Iberian peninsula might affect the former region. For their part, the French were not particularly enthusiastic about the emergence of a Spanish democracy which might rival their influence in 'latin' Europe.

The German political parties, however, could, and did, intervene in this region by using their powerful political foundations. Funded by public money and private donations, these foundations had the task of political education at home and abroad. The two most important were the Konrad Adenauer Foundation (CDU) and the Friedrich Ebert Foundation (SPD). The Adenauer Foundation did a great deal of good work in Latin America and in Iberia, trying to establish the concept of Christian democracy there. As it happened, however, the social democrats were able to play a stronger role, not least because an SPD-led government was in power in Bonn.

The Portuguese Socialist Party (PSP) was founded in west German exile at Bad Munstereifel in 1973, and its leader, Mario Soares, was assisted financially by the SPD. Through the Ebert Foundation, generous aid was given to the PSP and to the Spanish Socialist Party (PSOE). Willy Brandt himself openly supported the Spanish socialist leader, Felipe Gonzales, and helped to raise his prestige in post-Franco Spain.[25] When creating their constitution the Spaniards looked to Bonn as a model for a democratic, decentralized state. From being an awful example of totalitarian tyranny in the Third Reich, the West Germans had become exemplary democrats. *Modell Deutschland* was an object of admiration for people suffering under authoritarian systems on both sides of the iron curtain. Sometimes, however, it aroused envy and resentment amongst some of its less successful former occupiers.

Difficulties at home: nuclear power and nuclear missiles

Whatever the external achievements of the government, Schmidt's domestic political situation was becoming difficult. This was due to

25. Barbara Marshall, *Willy Brandt* (London, 1990), pp. 114–15.

changes within his own support, the growth of a more effective extra-parliamentary opposition and the machinations of his Free Democratic coalition partners.

As we have seen, Schmidt tended to be impatient with his own Social Democratic Party. One of his SPD colleagues accused him of wanting the party to be like the CDU in the 1950s – an 'electoral association for the Chancellor'.[26] This was certainly not in the tradition of the SPD, which prided itself on its democratic nature, but which was also inclined to develop a self-perpetuating bureaucracy. As the 1970s wore on, the SPD became restless over Schmidt's apparent willingness to jettison social democratic principles on the altar of pragmatism and coalition politics. Some of the younger generation of activists even regarded West Germany as a system dominated by capitalist monopolies which should be replaced by public ownership and planning. According to some of those who held this view, the Christian and Free Democrats were class enemies, whereas the Communists were only 'opponents'.

Willy Brandt, as chairman of the party, was able to fend off such nonsense, and its leading protagonist was expelled from the party, but conflicts between left and right would not die down. More important was the conflict over nuclear power. Like other socialist parties in the 1950s and 1960s, the SPD had welcomed civilian use of nuclear power as a modern and hygenic means of guaranteeing economic growth. But by the 1970s, attitudes were beginning to change. One legacy of the student upheavals during and after 1968 was that the population was no longer so inclined to accept what was decreed for it by experts in government. In October 1973 the federal authorities produced an energy plan to increase electricity production by 90,000 megawatts within twelve years. One hundred new power stations would be built, of which half would be nuclear.[27] The oil crisis of 1973, which broke out a few days later, seemed to reinforce the need for the nuclear option. It was assumed that by 1985 the share of West German power supplies produced by nuclear energy would be 45 per cent, as against 4 per cent in 1973.

Such plans reckoned without the public reaction. Already in 1972 some of the 'citizens' initiatives' (*Bürgerinitiativen*) opposing ecologically unfriendly development schemes had got together to form a 'Federal Association of Citizens' Initiatives for the Protection of the

26. Jäger and Link, *Ära Schmidt*, p. 113.
27. Ibid., pp. 89–90.

Environment' (*Bundesverband Bürgerinitiativen Umweltschutz*, or BBU), and this organization was among several rallying resistance to the power station programme. Two proposed nuclear sites – Wyhl in South Baden and Brokdorf in Schleswig-Holstein – saw scenes reminiscent of a civil war in 1975 and 1976 respectively, as large forces of police fought with thousands of demonstrators protesting against the nuclear projects. The protesters were a mixture of concerned local residents (including farmers), ecologists angry at what they perceived to be irresponsible risk-taking by the authorities, and radical trouble-makers out to exploit a chance to attack 'the system' head on. Whatever the motives, the result was to disillusion *Länder* governments with the nuclear programme, since security was their responsibility.

Although the nuclear issue was an emotional one, since it overlapped with the whole question of possible extinction in global warfare, awkwardly rational arguments began to appear on the antinuclear side. The most important related to the cost of the disposal of nuclear waste, since it began to dawn on politicians that this would be an enormous burden which would not disappear for decades or even centuries to come. This consideration completely altered the economics of nuclear power production. It was no longer a cheap option. Nuclear waste disposal became a bigger issue even than the power stations themselves. A project for a gigantic storage and reprocessing scheme at Gorleben in Lower Saxony was blocked by the CDU *Land* premier, Ernst Albrecht. Large sections of the SPD and FDP were hostile to the nuclear programme, whereas the right wing of the FDP, which seemed to suspend its market theories when it came to nuclear power, and most of the CDU/CSU, supported nuclear expansion – at least in theory. When it came to accepting large new nuclear plants in their own *Länder*, however, the CDU proved less enthusiastic.

On this issue Bonn appeared to be effectively paralysed. In fact, the *Länder* governments' caution turned out to be wise as well as prudent. Disasters at Five Mile Island (1979) and later at Chernobyl in 1986, showed that the potential dangers of nuclear power were greater than had originally been foreseen. Later on, the experience of power privatization in Britain was to demonstrate how uneconomic nuclear power actually was, given the potential costs involved in decommissioning. The checks and balances inherent in the Bonn system had proved their worth.

In the late 1970s such comforting considerations were not available to the Chancellor. He saw his party moving against both nuclear power and nuclear weapons at a time when he was trying to stress the need for the West to modernize its nuclear arsenal against the threat of domination from Moscow. In addition, the economic measures – cuts in taxes for the rich, increased VAT for the poor – which Schmidt was implementing at the behest of the FDP were deeply unpopular with many in Schmidt's own party. The party chairman, Willy Brandt, played an important role in June 1977 in appealing to his fellow Social Democratic Bundestag members not to destroy the social–liberal coalition and thus make the same mistake as the party had done in 1930, when Reich Chancellor Müller had been forced into opposition by his party and the way had been cleared for the enemies of democracy to take over. Of course, the situation was not as bad as that at the end of the Weimar Republic but, as Brandt put it: 'after a few years under the leadership of Strauss and Dregger [a right-wing CDU leader] our electors would not recognise this state . . . .'.[28]

Yet Brandt himself felt that the SPD was moving too far to the right and was in danger of losing its constituency. He realized that the old arguments between Marxists and free marketeers were losing their force in an age when new generations were questioning the whole idea of growth and urging the adoption of ecologically friendly lifestyles. Although many on the right of the SPD, such as the distinguished political scientist, Richard Löwenthal, attacked such notions as unrealistic and irresponsible, the danger existed that younger people might turn away from the party if it did not address these issues at all. There was also the vexed question of equal opportunities for women, an area in which the Federal Republic was not markedly progressive. Brandt showed typical foresight when he warned his party's executive committee that a Green party in Germany could have very damaging consequences for the SPD.[29]

Schmidt was not inclined to heed such warnings from Brandt; nor did he try to use the financial troubles of the government to put taxes on activities which might be regarded as ecologically unfriendly, as his finance minister, Hans Mätthofer, suggested. Instead the Chancellor railed at his own party for its lack of personal support for him, a form of leadership unlikely to arouse unswerving loyalty. Nevertheless, Schmidt's popularity after Mogadishu and his apparent success in coping with the economic crisis in the late 1970s was standing him in good stead with the electorate.

28. Ibid., p. 102.
29. Ibid., p. 106.

The threat from Strauss

He also had another advantage. Franz-Josef Strauss, the leader of the Bavarian CSU, was still determined to impose his leadership on the opposition. Shortly after the elections of 1976 the CSU delegation in the Bundestag agreed to break with the CDU and set up its own party group (*Fraktion*). This was widely seen as a prelude to the creation of a fourth party in the Federal Republic, a nation-wide version of the CSU led by Strauss and playing on authoritarian, anti-socialist and nationalist sentiments. Strauss, however, had reckoned without Helmut Kohl. The chairman of the CDU promptly countered by establishing a separate CDU *Fraktion* in the Bundestag, and announcing that the CDU would extend its activities into Bavaria and campaign there. Public opinion polls in the south German *Land* showed that Kohl was more popular there than Strauss himself and that the CSU might face fatal divisions. Strauss did his reputation no good when he launched a reckless attack on Kohl at a meeting of the CSU Youth Organization in Munich. Having sneered at his colleague as being totally incompetent and lacking the necessary attributes of character, intellect and political know-how to do the job of chancellor, he went on: 'Believe me in one thing, Helmut Kohl will never be Chancellor; when he is ninety years old he will write his memoirs: *I was Chancellor candidate for forty years; lessons and Experiences of a bitter epoch.* Perhaps the last chapter will be written in Siberia or somewhere like that. . . .'[30]

Despite his bombast, it was Strauss who caved in. On 12 December the two parties restored their joint *Fraktion* with Kohl as chairman and a CSU member, Zimmermann, as his deputy. However, the conflicts between left and right in the Christian camp simmered on. Kohl and most of the CDU wanted to keep the party to the middle ground, accept *Ostpolitik* as a *fait accompli* and persuade the FDP to come into a coalition with them. Strauss's CSU and some on the right wing of the CDU, including Dregger and Lothar Späth, the new premier of Baden-Württemberg, wanted to continue attacking *Ostpolitik*, launch a root-and-branch offensive against socialism and work for an absolute majority in the Bundestag which would enable them to destroy the FDP altogether.

Kohl decided it would be unwise to stand again for the chancellorship, and suggested Ernst Albrecht, the photogenic new premier

30. Ibid., p. 72.

of Lower Saxony. However, Strauss announced his own candidacy and Kohl was deserted by one of his own protegés, Kurt Biedenkopf, who began to intrigue with Strauss. Kohl allowed the joint parliamentary CDU/CSU *Fraktion* to vote on the issue and Strauss won. This appeared a defeat for Kohl but in fact it left him in a strong position. Albrecht was knocked out as a rival; Strauss needed Kohl's support in the election and stopped sniping at him. Giving Strauss the chance to stand as chancellor would test out once and for all just how much appeal his strident, rabble-rousing nationalism had amongst the west German electorate.

The election campaign of 1980 was a bitter one, fought on the basis of personalities. Strauss accused the government of being soft on law and order; the SPD presented him as a threat to peace. The issues of abortion and divorce became important when the Roman Catholic Church once again entered the political fray, urging its members to vote for Strauss. Schmidt was furious about this intervention, since he had devoted much time to hearing the views of the church hierarchy. A church-going protestant himself, he had carefully avoided giving any impression of anti-clericalism of the sort that had been so damaging to Schumacher in 1949. As the election campaign started to get under way early in 1980, Genscher appeared to be edging away from his coalition partners and stressing common ground with the CDU. But in May there was an important election in North Rhine-Westphalia at which the SPD scored a success over the opposition while the FDP fell back. It seemed that disloyalty to Schmidt would not benefit Genscher's party, and from then on he stressed his commitment to working with the Chancellor.

The upshot was a considerable victory for Schmidt, whose coalition gained in percentage terms. The CDU/CSU lost 4 per cent, the SPD held its share of the vote and the FDP recorded its best result since 1961, achieving 10.6 per cent. With that victory, the shadow of Strauss was removed from Bonn. It was clear that he had frightened away more voters than he had attracted. The undisputed leader in the Christian camp was Helmut Kohl.

Party squabbles and the break-up of the social–liberal coalition, 1980–82

For the government, the prospects ought to have been optimistic. It had gained votes on its 1976 performance and now had a reasonably safe majority of 45 seats in the Bundestag. But appearances were deceptive. The economic situation was worsening again, partly as the result of a second oil crisis connected with the Iranian revolution. Unemployment and inflation were rising. The policies needed to cope with this problem were deeply controversial. Schmidt seemed inclined to approve of the 'supply side' or monetarist prescriptions of the FDP Economics Minister, Count Otto Lambsdorff, who had taken over from Friderichs in 1977.[31] Lambsdorff was on the right wing of the FDP, and was well thought of by Genscher and Schmidt. For the rank and file of Social Democratic Party members, or even those elected to the Bundestag, policies which seemed to be putting all the burdens of the crisis onto the mass of the population by cutting social benefits, raising health contributions for pensioners and increasing indirect taxes[32] were a betrayal of social democratic principles. Even Schmidt's former allies in the trade union movement turned against him, as union leaders became more determined to protect their members' living standards and job security. They pressed for work creation schemes which were absolutely rejected by the FDP cabinet members.

The SPD was also becoming disillusioned with Schmidt over foreign policy. The advent of Ronald Reagan in Washington dented confidence in the peaceful intentions of the USA, which had never been very strong on the left wing of the SPD. An anti-nuclear peace movement was apparently gaining in popular support, especially amongst the young. The 'twin-track' policy on nuclear missiles, the cornerstone of Schmidt's policy, was attracting much criticism on the left, since it was felt that Reagan did not want to negotiate a settlement with the Soviet Union anyhow. Brandt showed some sympathy with SPD members who supported peace demonstrations, thus adding to the tensions which existed between himself and the Chancellor.

Brandt's fears that the ecological issue could cause a leakage of support from the Social Democrats was proving well founded. During the second half of the 1970s a number of heterogeneous groupings had sprung up in different *Länder* representing a broadly pacifist, environmental and subsequently feminist viewpoint. In some cases, such as Hamburg or Hesse, these had links to the hard left of the APO type, and violence was not uncommon in their demonstrations;

31. It was illustrative of the close links between the FDP and big business that Friderichs resigned his cabinet post to take up the directorship of the Dresdener Bank after the assassination of Ponto in 1977.
32. In February 1982 it was agreed that VAT would be raised from 13 to 14 per cent in July 1983. Jäger and Link, *Ära Schmidt*, p. 214.

others, like that in Baden-Württemberg, were of a more conservative, ecological persuasion. The colour green was associated with these movements to stress their concern for the environment and perhaps also to disassociate them from 'red' Marxist revolutionaries. In March 1979 a party was formed called the 'Other Political Association' (*Sonstige Politische Vereinigung* – SPV) supported by the leaders of the BBU and left intellectuals like Heinrich Böll and Rudi Dutschke. Its most effective leader was a young and articulate German-American woman, Petra Kelly. The SPV fought the European elections in June 1979, gaining 900,000 votes. In October 1979 a 'green' list got into the Bremen *Land* parliament with 5.1 per cent of the vote, and on 13 January 1980 'The Greens', as the new movement was called, founded itself as a federal political party.[33] From then on it was to be a source of concern to both the SPD and the left of the Free Democrats, since it drew support from their natural constituencies of well-educated young urban voters.

The Greens were committed to unilateral disarmament, withdrawal from NATO, the prohibition of civilian and military nuclear power and the abandonment of economic growth in favour of environmental protection. They often combined these views with alternative lifestyles which included child-rearing outside marriage and the open tolerance of homosexuals. This package could hardly have been more incompatible with the aims and policies of Chancellor Schmidt. Yet his SPD party chairman, Willy Brandt, believed that the SPD would have to adapt itself to the idealism represented by the Greens if it was not to see an erosion in its support. As time went on, the Social Democrats in Bonn and in the provinces felt themselves to be spurned by their own chancellor, whilst Schmidt himself fulminated at the ingratitude of a party which owed its role in government to his popularity with the electorate.

The real cause of Schmidt's downfall, however, lay in the machinations within the Free Democratic Party. As we have seen, its leader, Genscher, had always leaned towards a coalition with the CDU, and now that the bogey of Strauss had been banished to Bavaria, where the CSU leader was prime minister, there seemed no further obstacle to the achievement of such an alignment. Kohl's party reiterated its acceptance of the *Ostpolitik*, for which Genscher as foreign minister now felt responsible. Nevertheless, Genscher had to proceed cautiously if he wished to change sides. The majority of his own

33. Carl-Christoph Schweitzer *et al.* (eds), *Politics and Government in the Federal Republic of Germany, 1944–1994. Basic Documents* (2nd edn, Providence, R.I., 1995), p. 249.

party functionaries were committed to the social–liberal coalition, as were many younger members of the party's Bundestag *Fraktion*. The electorate, too, did not appreciate ambivalence in the FDP's loyalty to Schmidt, as was shown in a number of *Land* elections. But two factors pushed the right-wing clique which led the party towards an arrangement with the CDU.

The first was one of the most malodorous scandals of the entire Bonn Republic, the 'party donations affair' which became acute from the autumn of 1981 onwards. This related to the fact that business firms could only make very limited tax-free donations to political parties. Techniques had been developed whereby funds were channelled through apparently genuine charities and used for party political purposes. All of the traditional Bonn parties were involved, but the most deeply compromised were the Free Democrats. In particular Count Lambsdorff, who was party treasurer in North Rhine-Westphalia, was accused of complicity in backstairs funding for the FDP. The plot thickened when it emerged that the Flick business empire – a heavy industrial conglomerate – had been granted capital gains tax relief of DM120 million in August 1981 at a time when the government was desperately trying to plug holes in a gaping budget deficit. The minister responsible for the tax relief decision was Lambsdorff, and Flick had also made generous, though clandestine, donations to the FDP. Rumours circulated in Bonn that Lambsdorff and others might even be arrested.

The affair came at an especially awkward time because the Greens had made a point of differentiating themselves from the existing parties in the Bonn 'system', implying that the latter had become corrupted by the exercise of power. The scandal over party finances seemed to prove their point.

The response of the older parties to this scandal was indeed open to criticism. Those concerned evidently regarded the abuse of charitable donations as a finicky technicality. They proposed to change the law in such a way that such donations would be legal in future and all previous derelictions would be covered by an amnesty. The CDU/CSU and FDP wanted to press on with this 'solution', but to their credit neither the executive committee nor the Bundestag party delegation of the SPD would accept such a questionable arrangement, and the whole affair began to unwind in a series of parliamentary investigations and legal enquiries which would eventually lead to Lambsdorff's resignation in 1984. For the time being, however, he stayed in office. Both he and Genscher blamed the SPD for letting them down over the affair, and Genscher resented the fact that Schmidt, who was not his party's chairman, had held aloof from the whole murky business, whereas Genscher and Kohl were both caught up in it to a certain degree.

The second reason for Genscher might want a change of coalition partner was his party's showing in *Land* elections. The appearance of the Greens meant that it was more difficult for the FDP to attain the 5 per cent they needed for election. In Lower Saxony in March 1982 the FDP had committed itself to a coalition with the CDU in Hanover. Although they did gain representation in the *Landtag*, the Free Democrats fell behind the Greens, whereas the CDU gained an absolute majority and could, if it wished, rule without them. A nightmare possibility opened up that the FDP would become a small fourth party behind the Greens and that the CDU/CSU might not need them at all after the next Bundestag elections.

Lambsdorff, encouraged by Genscher, started to attack the SPD, accusing them of irresponsible economic policies which would weaken the economy and destroy jobs. In the summer of 1982 it was obvious that Genscher and his group were preparing to change sides and torpedo the coalition. A key test would be the *Land* elections in Hesse in September 1982. The FDP made no bones about their opposition to the SPD in that election, and on 31 August Lambsdorff told the conservative tabloid *Bild* that, if the electors decided on a change of coalition partners for the FDP in Hesse, this would be an important signal to the party in Bonn.

Schmidt himself then went over to the offensive. He admonished Lambsdorff in cabinet and ordered him to present a paper on the economy, setting out his ideas for future policy. When this was produced on 9 September it was an extreme version of supply side economics, demanding cuts in public services, bureaucracy and public spending. Lambsdorff's prescriptions were not even officially accepted by his own party, and were roundly denounced by the SPD. Kohl remarked that it was interesting, but contained a mixture of things which were 'sensible, less sensible and positively silly'. As usual, the most trenchant comments came from Franz-Josef Strauss, who asked where Lambsdorff had been for the past thirteen years: 'In a silent camp in Siberia . . . in a diving bell in the South Seas? . . . in the Indian jungle?' It was a fair point to put to a member of a coalition which had been in office since 1969. Strauss compared Lambsdorff to a doctor who, having infected his patient and brought him to a fever bed, then tried to cure him with brutal medicine.[34] The reception of the Lambsdorff paper demonstrated that the social market economy was not about to be jettisoned for *laissez-faire*

34. Jäger and Link, *Ära Schmidt*, p. 249.

economics even if the government did change. But it also showed that a party led by Genscher and Lambsdorff could no longer work with the Social Democrats.

Schmidt's strategy was to provoke new Bundestag elections in which the FDP would fail to enter parliament at all. Genscher's move to the right had provoked anger within his own party, and a damaging split seemed inevitable. On 17 September Schmidt summoned his coalition partner Genscher and showed him the text of a Bundestag speech in which he made the FDP responsible for the end of the coalition. Genscher and his colleagues promptly resigned, leaving Schmidt running a caretaker administration. The Chancellor's version of events, presented with great panache before the Bundestag, was that Genscher had betrayed the social–liberal coalition and the public trust, and that the FDP leader had been working for a break since the previous summer. Schmidt hoped that the CDU/CSU would help him hold new elections, and certainly this was an option that appealed to Strauss, that great hater of the FDP. But Strauss no longer wielded so much influence in Bonn, and even his own Bavarian CSU wanted to get back into office there as soon as possible. Genscher persuaded his parliamentary colleagues to opt for the CDU, although a hard core of eighteen left-wing FDP members of the Bundestag rejected this. On 21 September the CDU/CSU agreed that they should present Kohl as chancellor in a constructive vote of no confidence on 1 October.

Despite this, things seemed to be going Schmidt's way with the sensational results of the Hesse elections on 26 September, in which the SPD, which had been expected to do badly, held most of its ground, the CDU dropped back slightly, and the FDP fell out altogether with a miserable 3.1 per cent of the vote. The only gainers were the Greens with 8 per cent.

But this result was a Pyrrhic victory for Schmidt. It demonstrated to the Free Democrats that they simply could not afford an election at that time and must come to an arrangement with Kohl. It showed the CDU/CSU that an absolute majority for the Christian parties – which Strauss had hoped for – was unlikely; instead they might be forced into a great coalition with Schmidt, which they would not relish, or – in the worst case – they would face a 'Red/Green' majority in parliament. Furthermore, it was clear that in a Christian–liberal coalition the CDU/CSU could call the tune because their parliamentary representation was larger than that of the SPD. In economic discussions, for example, Lambsdorff's 'Thatcherite' programme dropped out of sight.

The real conflict occurred within the FDP. Many on the liberal wing of the party felt that their leadership had betrayed them. The FDP's general secretary, Günter Verheugen, resigned, and later joined the SPD. A number of powerful female Bundestag members, such as Hildegard Hamm-Brücher, Helga Schuchardt and Ingrid Matthäus-Maier, were bitterly opposed to the change, and the two latter also subsequently found their way into the Social Democratic Party.

On 1 October 1982 Helmut Kohl made history in the Bonn Republic by becoming the first federal chancellor elected on a vote of constructive no confidence. He received a majority of seven, which suggests that a substantial minority in the FDP had refused to accept the change of government. It was of no consequence to Kohl. With his election a new era – that of the so-called *Wende* or change – had begun.

CHAPTER ELEVEN

Helmut Kohl and the Unification of Germany, 1982–1990

Just as the social–liberal coalition had been trumpeted as the beginning of a great new democratic era in West German history, so the reappearance of the Christian Democrats and their Bavarian CSU partners in government was hailed as a turning point – or *Wende* – by Helmut Kohl and his supporters. It meant a rejection of socialism and high public spending and a return to the principles of the social market economy. It meant a commitment to the Western Alliance, and an end to the appeasement of Soviet bloc countries to the detriment of West Germany's own security. It meant a return to the common sense policies of Konrad Adenauer rather than the high-flown ideals of radical democrats or unworldly ecologists. If Willy Brandt's election as chancellor had shown that the Federal Republic was capable of carrying through an orderly transition between government and opposition, Kohl's election proved that the great 'people's party' of the right – the CDU – had rooted itself in west Germany and was once again the party of government. Of course, the basis it had enjoyed in many *Land* parliaments, particularly Baden-Württemberg, Lower Saxony, Rhineland-Palatinate and Schleswig-Holstein, had been of crucial importance in maintaining its strength. Strauss's Bavarian CSU was perhaps a mixed blessing, but its success could not be denied.

Helmut Kohl consolidates his power

Kohl was an archetypal Christian Democrat. He consciously saw himself as the heir to Konrad Adenauer, whose policies he greatly admired. But whereas Adenauer had represented the wisdom of age, Kohl personified the dynamism of youth. A Roman Catholic

Rhinelander, he had joined the party in 1946, when he was sixteen. Having obtained a doctorate in modern history, he devoted himself to politics and was elected to the *Landtag* of the Rhineland-Palatinate at the age of 29. He was to become premier there ten years later, the youngest *Land* prime minister. He was now, at the age of 52, the youngest federal chancellor.[1] As a student he had already become a committed European, and had participated in a demonstration removing frontier barriers on the Franco-German border. He stood for all the traditional values of the CDU: federalism as against centralization, the integration of western Europe, resistance against communism, support for the free market tempered by a commitment to social justice. He was, however, also committed to a cause which seemed to be losing its hold on the West German electorate – the reunification of Germany. Whereas for most politicians this issue had become a matter of lip-service, or even a burdensome inheritance to be jettisoned as soon as decently possible, Kohl regarded a commitment to Germans under Soviet control as a matter of personal duty.[2] This did not mean that he expected any rapid progress towards unification, but his assumption that it remained a desirable aim was to prove of great importance by the end of the decade.

For the time being, there seemed no likelihood whatsoever of making progress on that front. Kohl had made it clear that his party would accept the treaties with Moscow and the GDR, and his new FDP coalition colleague, Foreign Minister Genscher, was determined to carry on with the policy of *détente*. In this he faced raucous criticism from Franz-Josef Strauss, whose hatred of the FDP had not diminished, particularly since he had been passed over by Kohl in the new government. However, Kohl and Genscher had been friendly even before the social–liberal coalition, and as chancellor, Kohl had no reason to do Strauss any favours.

The problems seemed to emanate from Moscow, where an ageing Brezhnev – who died in October 1982 – and his successor Andropov

---

1. Werner Maser, *Helmut Kohl, Der deutsche Kanzler* (Ullstein, Frankfurt/M, 1993), pp. 66–7, 203. It is also claimed that Kohl was the youngest member of the Bundestag, but this is not true: he only entered the Bundestag in 1976 at the age of 46. The youngest member until then had been Holger Börner (SPD), who entered the Bundestag in 1957 at the age of 26. Later he was premier of Hessen in the first Red/ Green coalition.
2. For a growing willingness in the FRG to accept the permanence of the GDR, see Timothy Garton Ash, *In Europe's Name. Germany and the Divided Continent* (London, 1993), pp. 210–12. Kohl's commitment to reunification was expressed in public and in private when he visited Oxford to lecture on 2 May 1984: see Helmut Kohl, 'German Foreign Policy Today: the Legacy of Konrad Adenauer', *The Konrad-Adenauer Memorial Lecture* (St Antony's College and the Konrad Adenauer Foundation, 1984).

were continuing the political and military penetration of Africa, the Middle East and Afghanistan; and from Washington, where the right-wing Republican administration under Ronald Reagan was apparently bent on a new arms race. Anti-American feeling in west Germany was not only being fanned by the fear of superpower confrontation leading to a war in Europe. Events in Latin America were not helping good relations between the two countries. The Reagan administration openly supported repressive military regimes, like those of Galtieri in Argentina and Pinochet in Chile. It was also obsessively hostile to a revolutionary government in Nicaragua which had overthrown the corrupt and criminal dictatorship of Somoza. The rebels were regarded as communists and any expression of sympathy with them was denounced as anti-American. Since the German political parties, through their foundations, had been trying to help the development of democracy in Latin America, the Big Brother attitudes emanating from Washington in the early 1980s aroused indignation – loudly voiced by the SPD and the Greens, but also felt by many Christian democrats and liberals.

However, these were matters of foreign policy, and Kohl's first priorities were domestic. The economic situation was gloomy, with rising unemployment, which would exceed two million for the first time in 1983 (see Figure 4). In that year, too, job vacancies were the lowest in the entire history of the Bonn Republic.[3] Rising interest rates caused by Reagan's reckless deficit spending policy were having their effect in west Germany, but it was clear that there were serious structural problems within the domestic economy and there was a general lack of confidence.

The first of these problems could be tackled by stabilizing the political situation, and in March 1983 the government engineered a defeat on a vote of no confidence, enabling the president to dissolve the Bundestag. In the elections that followed, the Social Democrats were led by Hans-Jochen Vogel, formerly justice minister and mayor of Munich and West Berlin. He was a worthy but uncharismatic candidate who was caught in the backlash against Schmidt's 'twin-track' missiles policy. Although of rather conservative disposition himself, he had to oppose the deployment of US missiles to please his party. On the other hand, he flatly rejected any notion of collaboration with the Greens, and so it was unclear how the SPD could be expected to win a majority in the election. As it

3. At 76,000. Hans Giersch, Karl-Heinz Paqué and Holger Schmieding, *The Fading Miracle. Four Decades of Market Economy in Germany* (Cambridge, 1992), p. 127.

FIGURE 4   *Unemployment in the FRG, 1949–90*[a]

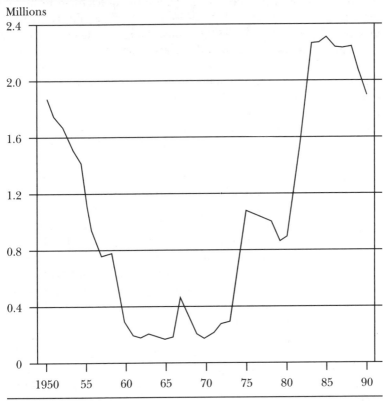

[a] Until 1958, excluding the Saarland.

Source: Statistisches Jahrbuch 1991 für das vereinte Deutschland (Wiesbaden, 1991), p. 119.

turned out, they were soundly defeated, recording their worst result since 1961. Kohl's CDU/CSU romped home with their second best result ever, gaining 48.8 per cent of the vote, and the Free Democrats scraped in with 7 per cent. This meant that they only had 34 seats in the Bundestag, barely ahead of the Greens who obtained 27. The Greens thus became the first new party to enter the federal parliament since 1953. Their appearance was ominous above all for the Social Democrats, since it was from the left of the political spectrum that the Greens drew their support.

The CDU chancellor was thus in a powerful position, since his FDP partners were proportionally far weaker than they had been in the social–liberal coalition, and they needed his protection against the fulminations of the Bavarian CSU. On the other hand Kohl did not have the authority within the coalition of his illustrious role model, Adenauer. By the 1980s the position of a chancellor within a coalition had weakened, in that the practice had become established that each party would select its own ministers. Whereas Adenauer had been able to appoint men of his own choosing, albeit with much difficult negotiation, Kohl really had to accept those his FDP partners presented to him, and even the CSU was really outside his direct control. The situation was exacerbated by the hostility between the Bavarian party – under its obstreperous leader, Franz-Josef Strauss – and the Free Democrats. Kohl did not at first seem very adept at dealing with these difficulties; he did not react very swiftly to problems, but preferred to allow matters to ripen before action. His style was strongly criticized, and by the summer of 1985, when the government was low in the opinion polls, there was talk of a leadership crisis. However, stamina and strong nerves were two of Kohl's most pronounced characteristics. The crisis passed, and he remained.

Meanwhile, the government had launched into a programme of financial retrenchment, but it was far removed from the extremes of Lambsdorff's 'supply side' prescriptions the previous October. Lambsdorff himself remained economics minister, so that the FDP had to share responsibility for the economic situation. His position was weakened, however, by the continuing investigations into the party funding affair. In November 1983 the public prosecutor in North Rhine-Westphalia felt there was enough evidence to bring charges of corruption and tax evasion against both Lambsdorff and Friderichs. Even then, it was not until the following June that Lambsdorff resigned, to be replaced by another FDP economics minister, Martin Bangemann. On 16 February 1987 the two former FDP ministers were found guilty of tax evasion but not of corruption, and both avoided imprisonment. Curiously enough, this did not prevent Lambsdorff becoming the Free Democrats' party chairman in October 1988, and he remained a powerful force within the FDP.

Kohl restores confidence in the economy, 1983–85

Kohl remained true to the principles of the social market economy, although implementing them was not easy. The government made DM5 billion savings in public expenditure, but it was difficult to achieve real cuts in either subsidies or social services. Bonn earmarked DM29 billion for social spending in 1983, two billion more than the Schmidt government had done, and the cost of subsidies to ailing industries – including agriculture and aircraft production – rose by DM21 billion – or 20 per cent – between 1981 and 1985. Tax cuts were announced, but they were spread out in three stages – 1986, 1988 and 1990, and the top rate of tax was only reduced from 56 per cent to 53 per cent.[4] Nevertheless, it was clear that the government was concerned to be more thrifty than its predecessor and more helpful to business. The less practical looking spending proposals of left-wing Social Democrats and Greens were no longer on the agenda. Budget increases over the period 1983–85 were kept down to 3 per cent per annum, whereas they had averaged 10 per cent per annum in the 1970s. Furthermore, the government would support the Bundesbank in its determination to pursue a cautious monetary policy aimed at restricting inflation. Relations between the Bundesbank and the Christian Democratic Finance Minister, Gerhard Stoltenberg, were harmonious. There was thus good reason for confidence to return in business circles, and it seems to have done so.[5]

It should also be pointed out that, although there was much talk of economic downturn in the 1970s and early 1980s, the general strength of the German economy and the standard of living of its people remained enviable by most European standards. For example, in the sphere of housing, there were complaints about high rents in larger cities, but the housing shortage was of an altogether different type from that experienced in the 1950s. The number of single-person households had grown enormously; in 1968 less than 4.5 million one-person households occupied self-contained dwellings, but by 1987 this had risen to well over 8.5 million. The longevity of the elderly had something to do with this, but so did the new affluence of youth.[6] Unemployment might be a nagging problem, but there were still many job opportunities for those with appropriate skills, and the conditions of work – measured in remuneration, the working week and generous holidays – would have seemed utopian

4. Ibid., p. 220; see also M. Balfour, *Germany: The Tides of Power* (London, 1992), p. 221.

5. Article by W. Kannengiesser in *FAZ*, 28 Nov. 1985, reprinted and translated in *The German Tribune: A Weekly Review of the German Press* (Hamburg), No. 1206, 8 Dec. 1985, p. 3.

6. Führer, 'Managing Scarcity: The German Housing Shortage and the Controlled Economy, 1914–1990', in German History. The Journal of the German History Society, Vol. 13, No. 3 (Oxford, 1995), p. 351.

to those who had laboured in the rubble of German cities in the late 1940s.

Nor did the CDU forget its commitment to the family, and thereby to the status of women. In the 1980s there was considerable concern about west Germany's falling birth rate, and a fear that within measurable time there would not be enough young 'native' Germans in the Federal Republic to sustain the burdens of welfare for an ageing population. In 1949 the Federal Republic had 49,200,000 inhabitants. By 1970 migration – largely from East Germany – and a positive birth rate had caused the population to rise by over eleven million. From 1972 onwards, however, deaths exceeded births, so that population levels would have fallen had it not been for the influx of foreign workers – mostly from Turkey and southern Europe – who themselves tended to have larger families than their German hosts.

The average size of a West German family shrank. Whereas in 1950 more than half of West German parents had two or more children, in 1982 58 per cent of families possessed only a single child. The number of couples living together unmarried was rising, as was the number of divorces. Children born in 1980 had three times as much chance of being involved in divorce as those born in 1960. Young people tended to rate marriage less highly in their scale of values than older people. None of this boded well for the future of the German family.[7]

In 1987 it was forecast that the population of the Federal Republic would fall from just over 61 million to less than 60 million by the end of the century. The fact that foreigners were making up an increasingly significant proportion of the people living within the borders of the Bonn Republic also fuelled fears about a possible loss of German national identity. In December 1989, on the eve of unification, there were 4.8 million foreigners living in the FRG – comprising 7.7 per cent of the entire population. As is usually the case, prophesies of doom based on demographic forecasting were soon undermined by events. Unification was to bring another 16 million inhabitants into the Federal Republic, the overwhelming majority of them German; the proportion of foreigners in the whole of Germany in December 1989 was less than 6.5 per cent.[8]

---

7. G. Langguth, *In Search of Security. A Socio-Psychological Portrait of Today's Germany* (Westport, Conn., 1995), p. 12.

8. *Statistisches Jahrbuch 1991 für das vereinte Deutschland* (Wiesbaden, 1991), p. 72. For family structures, see Eva Kolinsky, *Women in Contemporary Germany. Life, Work and Politics* (2nd edn, Oxford, 1993), pp. 81–2. For the general problem, see H. Korte, 'Bevölkerungsstruktur und -Entwicklung', in Wolfgang Benz (ed.), *Die Bundesrepublik Deutschland. Geschichte in drei Bänden*, Vol. 2, *Gesellschaft* (Frankfurt/Main, 1983), pp. 13–34.

However, Kohl's government could not be accused of complacency when facing up to the problems of the German family. One of its earliest measures was the establishment of a publicly funded 'Mother and Child' foundation which should help pregnant women in need. Child allowances were raised. In January 1986 a legislative package was passed which allocated pension rights for mothers who had stayed at home to raise their children. Very generous schemes of maternity leave were established, which included allowances for either parent of an infant to take a 'child-rearing vacation'. European Community rules ensuring equal opportunities in recruitment and equal treatment at work had already been implemented in the Federal Republic in August 1980, and in 1985 an Employment Promotion Act enabled women workers to qualify for retraining if they had been raising children. The aim of all these measures was to encourage working women both to have children and to stay at home to look after them in infancy. In practice, however, it also made it easier for women to move in and out of work, increasing their professional opportunities.[9] Despite the *Wende,* or shift to the right, female emancipation was making impressive progress in the Federal Republic.

Trade and industry

Like all successful politicians, Kohl had a certain amount of luck. In the years after 1974 the terms of trade had been moving against West Germany, with repeated oil shocks rocking an economy which was not fortunate to possess any resources of oil or natural gas. But in the mid-1980s there occurred an oil shock in reverse. Oil prices – which experts had predicted would remain high into the foreseeable future – began to come down. In 1986 surplus production had outstripped demand so far that the price of oil on the Rotterdam spot market fell by nearly half. At that point energy saving by West German industry had become so successful that the oil bill of the Federal Republic was actually lower than it had been in 1973. The West German balance of payments, which had been negative in 1979–81, went back into surplus. The country's export performance thundered on, despite the D-Mark's constant appreciation *vis-à-vis* the dollar (see Figure 5). From 1982 to 1984 there had been an unhealthy boom in the USA, conjured up by reckless deficit spending, radical tax cuts and deregulation. But this quickly ebbed, and the

9. Kolinsky, *Women in Contemporary Germany*, pp. 66–72.

FIGURE 5   *West Germany's trade performance in the 1980s (in millions of DM)*

Year	Imports	Exports	Export surplus
1978	243 707	284 907	41 200
1980	341 380	350 328	8 947
1982	376 464	427 741	51 277
1984	434 257	488 223	53 966
1986	413 744	526 363	112 619
1988	439 609	567 654	128 045
1989	506 465	641 041	134 576

Source: *Statistisches Jahrbuch 1991 für das vereinte Deutschland* (Wiesbaden, 1991), p. 276.

dollar fell steadily against the D-Mark for the rest of the decade. It stood at DM3.50 to the dollar in 1985, but was down to DM1.85 in 1988–89 and DM1.50 in January 1991.[10] Whereas in 1981 west Germany's trade surplus had been only 1.8 per cent of GNP, in 1985 it was 4 per cent of GNP and remained well in excess of 5 per cent for the rest of the life of the Bonn Republic. This was due to the continuing demand for West German industrial exports, which maintained their position owing to high quality and technical excellence. For most of the 1980s West Germany outperformed Japan as an exporting nation.

It is important to note that this was done without undermining the social safety net in the Federal Republic or carrying through the sort of drastic purgative 'cure' (*Rosskur*) so beloved of supply side economists. If we compare the west German performance with that of Great Britain, the European country most committed to the new *laissez-faire* doctrines of the right, we see that the British, despite possessing an extraordinary advantage in the shape of North Sea oil, constantly failed to match the West Germans in almost all indicators of economic success – currency stability, inflation, trade balance, research and development, median living standards and overall competitiveness. Claims that low profit margins were reducing the incentive to invest lose credibility when the actual levels of investment are examined. In the short-lived Reagan boom, US investment rates rose to 19.1 per cent of GNP. In the same period they never fell below 20 per cent of GNP in West Germany.[11] Certainly, the federal

10. Giersch *et al.*, *Fading Miracle*, pp. 246–8. The view of 'Reaganomics' in Giersch's book is far more favourable than mine, but I do not find the case for it convincing.
11. Ibid., p. 246. Giersch and his colleagues claim that US investment was more

structure of West Germany, which meant that the *Länder* controlled a good deal of public spending and could also object to federal budget cuts in the Bundesrat, made it more difficult for the Bonn government to engage in radical deflationary policies. But this was actually a blessing, since such policies did not prove effective elsewhere, and had been notoriously disastrous when put into effect in Germany, 1930–33. In this respect, as in so many others, Bonn was not Weimar.

Prosperity had returned, even if the problem of unemployment, which remained stubbornly over the two million mark, showed no signs of disappearing. However, West German employees were better off than many of their contemporaries in other countries. They mostly enjoyed security of tenure at work, and even though short-term contracts for up to eighteen months were made legal in 1985, it was considerably more difficult to dismiss a German worker than his counterpart in Britain or the USA. Co-determination in larger industrial plants made it easier for entrepreneurs to dismiss staff in factories outside Germany than those at home. Workers who were unemployed received 63 per cent of their last net wage for at least a year and thereafter a means-tested dole of at least 56 per cent indefinitely. They were not obliged to take work offered to them if this would worsen their chances of employment at the level they had enjoyed before. The Kohl government also invested heavily in training schemes, some of which were aimed specifically at the unemployed. In 1983 DM5.4 billion was spent on vocational training; by 1988 this had risen to DM10.7 billion.[12] More German workers were moving from older urban districts to modern suburbs, and there was a shift in labour concentration from the rust-belt area of the Ruhr to the friendlier climes of Bavaria or Baden-Württemberg, where more advanced forms of industry were being developed.

Although young people were finding it harder to obtain jobs than they had in the palmy days of the 1960s, the experience of the average German citizen was one of security and prosperity. The consumer society was well entrenched. Whereas in the early 1960s only 14 per cent of West German households possessed a telephone, just over a quarter could boast a car and 36 per cent a TV set, by 1983 88 per cent of households had telephones, 65 per cent had

dynamic than that of the FRG, but this buoyancy was for a short period only. The rate of return on capital in West Germany rose from 1983 onwards and was above that of the 1970s by the time of unification in 1990. Ibid., p. 210.

12. Ibid., pp. 204–6.

cars and 94 per cent TV sets. Nearly all possessed refrigerators, and the majority had freezers and automatic washing machines.[13]

There was also more time to enjoy such material benefits. The standard working week was already down to 40 hours in the 1970s, and a decade later it was often below that, with the trade unions demanding a 35-hour week. Leisure pursuits were becoming more sophisticated. Whereas in the 1950s tennis, for example, would have been regarded as an élite pastime, well-appointed clubs, many with all-weather courts, mushroomed all over West Germany. In 1985 the young Boris Becker caused a sensation by winning the Wimbledon Lawn Tennis Championships. Thereafter the West Germans were a major force in world-class tennis, as in many other sports, particularly association football. German tourists still flooded abroad with their hard currency. The Federal Republic had not quite fulfilled Ludwig Erhard's dream of 'welfare for all', but it was a nation which enjoyed mass prosperity. Even those who were not successful in the market economy were better off than contemporaries in most other countries, with the possible exception of Scandinavia.

More problems with Strauss

This prosperity was helpful to the government, and Kohl's own genial optimism inspired public confidence. Yet his administration was beset with problems. One was the premier of Bavaria, Franz-Josef Strauss, whose prima donna characteristics had been growing more marked since he had failed to obtain the chancellorship in the 1980 elections. He combined hostility to Genscher's foreign policy with a propensity to meddle in foreign affairs himself. In the summer of 1983, despite his loudly proclaimed anti-communism, he flew to East Germany – piloting his own aircraft – for personal consultations with Honecker. At one stroke, he did more to prop up the SED leader than any other single West German politician by arranging a credit of a billion marks to be raised from private sources through the Bavarian state bank. A further DM950 million followed in 1984. Christian Democrats had accused their SPD predecessors of giving out 'cash against hope' to the repressive SED regime, but nothing quite as spectacular as the Strauss initiative had been seen during the 1970s. Strauss certainly kept Kohl informed, and the loans were guaranteed by the federal government, but Strauss's about-turn was nonetheless astonishing. It upset some of his own anti-communist

13. Kolinsky, *Women in Contemporary Germany*, p. 86.

stalwarts in the Bavarian CSU. Two of them reacted by founding a right-wing nationalist party, the *Republikaner* (Republicans), which was to embarrass the government by making gains in *Land* and European elections, running on a xenophobic ticket which attacked European integration and Turkish guest workers.[14]

Strauss's new-found interest in Honecker did not stop him accusing the government – especially Genscher – of weakness *vis-à-vis* the Soviet bloc, and he remained an obstreperous colleague. In 1987, when the Bundestag election campaign got under way, the FDP decided that it would have to target Strauss in order to persuade moderate voters to strengthen the liberal element in the coalition.

Kohl also had domestic problems of a niggling, if not entirely serious, kind. The party funding affair involved Kohl himself, as chairman of the CDU, in embarrassing revelations, even though he was not held to be personally responsible for any illegal actions. In 1984 his government was able to change the law so that parties could receive donations tax-free, but they had to be publicly declared and accounted for. An attempt to amnesty those who might have evaded tax beforehand had to be withdrawn in the face of popular opposition.

The problem of Germany's past

In foreign affairs Kohl did not at first show sureness of touch. He felt that, as the first German chancellor who had come to maturity after the Second World War, he could assume freedom from complicity in any German outrages committed during it. This was not always well received abroad. In Israel the Chancellor's views on the subject aroused irritation, and the 40th anniversary of Allied victory in Europe – to the celebrations of which the West Germans were pointedly not invited – led to another embarrassment.

Kohl had been particularly pleased when, on 22 September 1984, he had been able to stand together with the president of France, François Mitterrand, at the Douaumont military cemetery to honour the French and German dead in the terrible battle of Verdun during the First World War. He hoped to repeat this symbol of reconciliation with President Reagan when he visited Europe in May 1985. Reagan agreed to join Kohl at the Bitburg cemetery in the Ardennes, where German and American soldiers killed in the last months of the Second World War were buried. Unfortunately it turned out that

14. See below, p. 304.

some of the German dead belonged to the *Waffen-SS*, whose nazi loyalty could not be doubted, even if they were not directly involved in the horrors of the concentration camps. This created a furore and discomfited the Americans, even though Reagan stuck to his promise and took part in the ceremony. Fortunately the poor impression created by this incident was largely offset by the speech delivered to the Bundestag a few days later, on 8 May 1985, by the new president of the Federal Republic, Richard von Weizsäcker. Weizsäcker, a distinguished CDU politician who had been a successful mayor of West Berlin, and who was a leading lay figure in the protestant church, had replaced the somewhat colourless President Carstens in July 1984. Weizsäcker had been an early CDU supporter of *Ostpolitik*.[15] In his speech commemorating the end of Hitler's war he told the Bundestag deputies that for Germans 8 May was not a time for festivities but a time to remember: 'It is not a matter of mastering the past. To do so is impossible. The past cannot be altered or erased retrospectively. But those who shut their eyes to the past will be blind to the future.'[16]

The issues raised by the 40th anniversary of the Allied victory focused attention on West Germany's attitude towards its history. The fact that the Chancellor himself was an historian by training meant that he took historical issues more seriously than some of his colleagues, although Helmut Schmidt had also shown his respect for the historical profession.[17] Two strands of opinion could be detected in the Federal Republic about the Germans' attitude to their past. The first was that reflected in Weiszäcker's speech, which held that the horrors of the Second World War – and especially the mass murder of Jews, gypsies and other 'asocial' categories – should not be forgotten and should be the object of continuing historical investigation. Left-wing intellectuals such as Heinrich Böll and Jürgen Habermas took up a more extreme position which seemed to suggest that national pride was altogether out of place for a people whose history included Auschwitz.

The alternative view was that collective guilt could not be ascribed to all Germans, that there was a lot more to German history than the Third Reich, and that if younger Germans did not have a historical consciousness they could not be expected to defend freedom and democracy against totalitarian subversion.

15. See above, Chapter 9.
16. Cited in Balfour, *Tides of Power*, p. 226.
17. Chancellor Schmidt had delivered the keynote address to the German Historians' Conference (*Historikertag*) in Hamburg in 1978. It is difficult to imagine a British prime minister doing the same for historians in the United Kingdom.

Within the historical profession itself the 1970s had seen a methodological conflict which also had political undertones. There had been a tendency to play down the importance of high politics – and therefore of nationalism – in history, and to concentrate on social movements and class conflict. This tendency – referred to as 'critical' historiography – had gained ground in the 1970s and was particularly associated with a brilliant group of scholars at the University of Bielefeld. With the fall of the social–liberal coalition, however, the opponents of such tendencies took heart. The *Wende* could affect universities too. In fact, the social history lobby had never been very strong in the West German professoriat, especially because most of the *Land* governments, which controlled appointments, were dominated by the CDU. Most chairs of modern history in the 1980s went to more conservative historians, some of whom saw it as their task to rehabilitate the concept of the German nation and create a national consciousness amongst the younger generation. They feared that some young people were seeking inspiration from European rather than German ideals, and others from concepts of social harmony which rejected nationalism altogether. In this latter respect the Greens seemed especially worrying.

Kohl felt that the West Germans should not be denied a healthy feeling of patriotism towards their country, and thought there was much in German history of which they should be proud. He and some of his historical advisers were also worried by the growing opposition to western defence policies that was expressed in the burgeoning peace movement. Young people seemed incapable of distinguishing between totalitarian systems and liberal ones, and history ought to be enlisted to enlighten them. This was especially the case because Honecker's regime was now trying to appropriate for itself historical traditions connected with Martin Luther, Frederick the Great and even Bismarck. Kohl was enthusiastic for the establishment of new museums in Bonn and West Berlin which would present German history from the viewpoint of western scholarship, thereby correcting the picture presented in the Marxist–Leninist museums of the GDR.

Unfortunately, it was difficult to rehabilitate Germany's past without giving comfort to those who had a different agenda – namely the rehabilitation of German nationalism, even if the form it had taken during the Third Reich was agreed to be unacceptable. The writings of the Berlin historian Ernst Nolte, a philosopher by training who had made his reputation with a study of fascism in Germany, France and Italy, conveyed the message that national socialism had been a reaction against the threat of Russian bolshevism, that nazi atrocities had been imitated from bolshevik models, and that measures against the Jews were at least partly explicable – though not justified – by the fact that Zionists openly supported Britain in the war against Hitler.[18] It was also suggested that the nazi atrocities in occupied Europe, however deplorable they were, should not be regarded as unique, because other regimes had tried to kill whole populations. A case which was noted was the massacre of the Armenians by the Turks during the First World War, about which nazi leaders had undoubtedly been quite well informed.

Quite apart from the dubious validity of these claims, they led the whole debate about German identity straight back to issues relating to the nazi past. A furious academic altercation ensued, in which both sides showed a regrettable tendency to lump their opponents together in one pot – as apologists for national socialism on the one side or unpatriotic crypto-Marxists on the other.[19] In fact, most historians held to a perfectly reasonable and moderate line, but the publicity was gained by those on the extreme wings. This so-called 'Historians' row' (Historikerstreit) produced no new insights into the history of national socialism. It did, however, encourage a certain revival of conservative nationalist attitudes amongst sections of the conservative intelligentsia. Its influence on popular opinion, however, was limited. Just as the mass of the German electorate sensibly rejected left-wing calls to abandon NATO, so it showed little enthusiasm for a return to the flag-waving nationalism associated with Bismarck's Germany, let alone Hitler's Third Reich.

Bonn and the European Community: integration moves ahead

Indeed, the most hopeful developments in this period had nothing to do with either national identity or a possible reconciliation with

18. In particular, Nolte implied that a statement by Chem Weizmann published in *The Times* on 5 Sept. 1939 that Jews should regard the war against Hitler as their own – justifiable though it was – could provide a pretext for nazi internment of the Jews. E. Nolte, *Der europäische Bürgerkrieg 1917–1945. Nationalsozialismus und Bolschewismus* (Frankfurt, 1987), pp. 317–18, 509.

19. For an overview of the so-called *Historikerstreit*, see the volume edited by the Piper Verlag, *'Historikerstreit'. Die Dokumentation der Kontroverse um die Einzigartigkeit der nationalsozialistischen Juedenvernichtung* (Munich, 1987). For English language commentaries, see Charles S. Maier, *The Unmasterable Past: History, Holocaust and German National Identity* (Cambridge, Mass., 1988), and R.J. Evans, *In Hitler's Shadow. West German Historians and the Attempt to Escape from the Nazi Past* (London, 1989).

Soviet bloc countries. They related to the western policies of the Federal Republic, and in particular its association with Paris and Brussels. Helmut Kohl was a staunch believer in European integration, and saw himself as carrying the European vision of Konrad Adenauer through to its successful conclusion. In this he was supported by Genscher, who devoted quite as much time to fostering European co-operation as he did to massaging the susceptibilities of the Soviet leaders.

The most important area of development seemed to be that of the European Community. The first enlargement of the Community, on 1 January 1973, had not been entirely successful. It was rapidly followed by the world oil crisis and the first serious postwar industrial recession. Furthermore, the largest new member of the EC, Britain, proved difficult to integrate into the Community. The British had entered for largely negative reasons and few of their political leaders were enthusiastic about the concept of European integration. The major exception, Edward Heath, was ejected from office in 1974. The British were also resentful about what they perceived to be unfairly high British payments into the Community, and a great deal of negotiating time was spent wrangling over this issue. Schmidt and Genscher did their best to be helpful, but reductions in British payments would almost certainly involve even higher contributions by the Federal Republic, and the Germans were already the highest contributors to the EC budget.

Although there remained a strong commitment to European integration in West Germany in the 1970s, the prospects for achieving it seemed very bleak. A cautiously worded report by the Prime Minister of Belgium, Leo Tindemans, published in January 1976, had urged a common defence and foreign policy, a strengthening of the European Commission and its subordination to an effective European parliament. But there was no chance of such a federalist agenda being accepted and the report was shelved, as was a further set of recommendations produced in 1979. Nevertheless, in the second half of the 1970s there was a move towards a third enlargement, as first Greece and then the Iberian countries – Spain and Portugal – applied for admission to the Community. By January 1981 Greece had joined, but negotiations with Spain were proving difficult, largely due to the obstruction of vested interests in France. However, it was clear that the European ideal was important for countries that were emerging from a period of authoritarian – not to say fascist – rule. Morale amongst the pro-Europeans in Bonn and Brussels began to pick up.

In 1981 Genscher, together with the Italian foreign minister, Emilio Colombo, had drawn up a draft European Act which involved the implementation of economic integration, more common policies in the EC, more accountability to the European Parliament, more majority voting in the Council of Ministers, and a greater commitment to the goal of European union.[20] This report also was an apparent failure, but it proved a harbinger of progress to come. The fact that Genscher soon found himself foreign minister in a government with Christian Democrats was not without importance either. The CDU in general, and Kohl in particular, were more genuinely committed to the aim of European union than Schmidt and the Social Democrats had been. In June 1983 a European Council meeting in Stuttgart did not accept the Genscher–Colombo plan, but it did issue a grandiose piece of rhetoric, 'the Solemn Declaration on European Union', which committed participants to further the cause of integration.

Pressure for change within the EC did not all come from Bonn. The European Parliament was also demanding more authority and progress towards a genuine political union. In Paris, Mitterrand wanted to assert France's leadership in Europe at a time when the Americans seemed to have recovered their predominant position in the west and were apparently leading Europe into a new Cold War.

Reagan and SDI

The Strategic Defense Initiative (SDI) announced by Reagan in March 1983 seemed to herald a new stage in the East–West arms race. Known colloquially as 'star wars', the programme – which was highly controversial from both a military and a political point of view – was designed to destroy Soviet missiles in space before they could strike the USA. Theoretically it would enable the Americans to win a nuclear war by bombing the Soviet Union without fear of retaliation. It also involved worrying possibilities for European security, since the Americans might be tempted to retire behind their anti-missile shield and leave western Europe to shift for itself. The French found it particularly repellent because their own *force de frappe* would be rendered completely obsolete and they would have no chance of keeping up with the enormously expensive technology of the SDI

20. Derek W. Urwin, *The Community of Europe. A History of European Integration since 1945* (2nd edn, London, 1995), pp. 221–2.

system. The Germans, on the other hand, remained committed to the American Alliance, and Kohl was willing to consider participation in the SDI project, which might bring many orders for West German firms. Since the French showed no inclination to share their nuclear force with Bonn, the American option remained the safest from the German viewpoint, even though Genscher was uneasy about the effect this would have on *détente* and *Ostpolitik*. The Soviet leadership made threatening noises about the effects on their relations with Bonn if the west Germans participated in SDI.

Other matters caused friction between Bonn and Washington, and made the Greens and SPD even more critical of an unconditional loyalty to Reaganite policies. In the autumn of 1985, even the British were perturbed at the lack of consultation when a Commonwealth country, Grenada, was invaded by American forces seeking to overthrow a left-wing dictatorship there. Nor were the Europeans enthusiastic about American sanctions against Libya to combat its alleged support for terrorism. This dispute culminated in April 1986, when the Americans bombed Libya from bases in Britain, whilst other NATO countries, including West Germany, stood aloof and some even refused air transit rights to the bombers.[21] Then there were economic conflicts. By 1986 West Germany was back on course economically. With virtually no inflation, a booming export industry and the largest share of GNP devoted to research and development in the developed world, the Federal Republic could face the future with confidence. Things were very different in the United States, where deregulation and deficit spending had led to bankruptcies and a serious fall in the value of the dollar. There were also conflicts between the Americans and the European Community over exports of farm products, a highly sensitive issue on both sides of the Atlantic.

Franco-German co-operation in Europe

There was, therefore, good reason for the French and the Germans to try to make progress with the development of the European Community. They, in common with most other continental members of the EC, were concerned that Europe should develop more independence *vis-à-vis* the superpowers, and should be able to withstand competition from rising economic powers like Japan.

21. See article in *FAZ*, 21 April 1986, reprinted in *The German Tribune*, No. 1223, 27 April 1986, p. 1. .

In June 1984 Mitterrand hosted the European Council meeting at Fontainebleau and made a serious effort to clear up outstanding problems, including those of British EC contributions, the long over-due reform of the Common Agricultural Policy (CAP), and the issue of further enlargement. On the matter of political union the meeting agreed to set up yet another enquiry, the Dooge committee, named after its chairman, the former Irish foreign minister, James Dooge. Its recommendations, to the effect that the EC should become a 'true political entity . . . with the power to take decisions in the name of all citizens by a democratic process', were to be discussed at a Council meeting in Milan in 1985. Kohl had meanwhile rhetorically asked the Bundestag in 1984, 'who is prepared to follow us on the way to European Union with the stated objective of a United States of Europe?'[22] The answer was, very few of the larger European powers – but the European bandwagon was certainly rolling again. At the Milan summit the French and the Germans surprised their col-leagues, and angered the British, by bringing forward joint pro-posals for European security co-operation. The German position was not strengthened by the fact that, just before the Milan Council, at a meeting of agriculture ministers in Luxembourg, the German min-ister, Ignaz Kiechle, exercised his veto to prevent a reduction in the price of cereals – the first time the Germans had ever taken such a measure. Both the manner and the cause of this veto cast doubts on the sincerity of German integrationist intentions.

However, although the Milan meeting was not regarded as a great success, it did set an agenda for the EC which turned out to be more radical than was at first imagined. It was agreed to hold an inter-governmental conference which should find ways of creating a genuinely free internal market – an issue over which even the British wanted progress – as well as ways of improving the efficiency of the commission and raising the status of the European Parliament. In all these areas the Germans had a positive interest – none more so than Genscher, whose own position was under threat in the mid-1980s.

Poor *Land* election results led to internal criticism of Genscher within the FDP and he agreed to give up his party chairmanship, which went in 1985 to the ebullient Economics Minister, Martin Bangemann. Furthermore, Genscher was concerned that the Ger-man Foreign Office was being marginalized by Kohl's own Chan-cellery in matters of high policy – especially US/German relations. The CDU/CSU tended to follow a harder, more pro-American line than the FDP. Kohl's foreign affairs adviser, Horst Teltschik, was seen as being highly influential in Bonn's policy-making, and this was not appreciated by Genscher and his colleagues.[23] Progress towards European integration would raise the prestige of the Foreign Office and would not arouse obstruction from Kohl. Furthermore, it might reactivate the concept of a 'European' solution for the German question on the basis of East–West co-operation. Hence Bonn played a generally positive role in the negotiations which led up to the acceptance of the Single European Act at the Luxembourg Council meeting in December 1985, and which set a deadline of 31 December 1992 for the completion of a fully integrated single European market. It also foreshadowed institutional improvements in the EC, including more power for the Parliament and more majority voting in the Council. Meanwhile in June 1985 the Germans, French and Benelux countries had concluded the Schengen agreement designed to establish a 'border-free' zone within the EC. This was envisaged as a model for border controls in the Community as a whole, since a genuinely free market in labour and goods was hardly compatible with internal border checks. The deadline for Schengen was January 1990, but in practice it proved difficult to implement, and had not been properly consummated six years after the Bonn Republic had given way to a united Germany.

From this time forward a clear division within Europe began to emerge, between states like Britain and Denmark, in which there was strong opposition to the implied loss of national sovereignty in the agenda agreed at Luxembourg, and the founding members of the original EEC – reinforced by Spain and Portugal, which became members of the EC in January 1986 – who were enthusiastic for further integration, despite some differences over its implementation. Kohl and Genscher worked with Mitterrand and the dynamic new President of the Brussels Commission, Jacques Delors, to develop the European agenda. The Germans were more interested in strengthening the European Parliament than the French, who tended to regard the democratic deficit in Europe as unimportant. But generally speaking, the Franco-German partnership – which had now assumed the character of a well-established marriage in which quarrels would be expected but not taken as disastrous[24] – was working together for the consolidation and integration of the EC.

23. P. Zelikow and C. Rice, *Germany Unified and Europe Transformed. A Study in Statecraft* (Cambridge, Mass., 1995), p. 78.

24. See the article by H. Schreitter-Schwarzenfeld in *Frankfurter Rundschau*, 9 Nov. 1985 – trans. and reprinted in *The German Tribune*, No. 1204, 17 Nov. 1985, p. 2. At

From confrontation to a new détente: Kohl's Ostpolitik

Otherwise, the international situation looked gloomy in 1985. The west Germans were in danger of being caught between two intransigent superpowers which were still locked in ideological conflict. The colder international climate had impacted on relations with the GDR. Honecker had hoped to visit Kohl in 1984, but in August of that year he was forced to abandon the idea on Soviet insistence.[25] In March 1985 Mikhail Gorbachev took over as leader of the Soviet Union. At first this did not seem to make much difference, although there was some relief that the reign of gerontocracy in Moscow had been replaced by a younger and apparently more dynamic regime. Gorbachev's elevation could be seen as bringing hope for more flexibility in Soviet policy. On the other hand, a more vigorous leader in Moscow could imply a threat to the West, as had been the case with Nikita Khrushchev in the 1950s. Gorbachev received a number of visitors from the Federal Republic, including Willy Brandt and Johannes Rau, the social democratic premier of North Rhine-Westphalia, but he showed no great enthusiasm to meet Kohl. In November 1985 there occurred the first major East–West summit of the Gorbachev era, when the Soviet leader and President Reagan met for three days at Geneva. Although the two men evidently found some personal rapport, Reagan's attitude towards negotiating with what he had described as 'the evil Empire' did not seem to change, and Gorbachev's hostility to SDI was undiminished. As one newspaper commentator put it, citing Raymond Aron in an earlier period: 'peace is impossible; war improbable'.[26] This might bring with it the danger that the German public would turn towards neutralism, a sentiment which was being openly canvassed amongst the Greens and on the left of the SPD.

In January 1986, Kohl sent a letter to Gorbachev welcoming what he described as the progress made at Geneva and claiming credit for German efforts to improve dialogue between East and West. He

the 46th Franco-German consultation that month in Bonn, the French delegation had consisted of 85 people, including the president, prime minister and five ministers. These gatherings were likened by the author to those of medieval times in which emperors and kings travelled around with a huge entourage.

25. Garton Ash, *In Europe's Name*, p. 104.
26. G. Nonnenmacher in *FAZ*, 17 Dec. 1985, trans. and reprinted in *The German Tribune* (Hamburg), No. 1208, 29 Dec. 1985, p. 1.

held out the carrot of economic co-operation if the relations between the two German states could be liberalized. He picked up on a phrase used by the Soviet leader which had referred to a 'common European home' shared by western and Soviet bloc countries, and urged steps to lower tension to make that 'home' habitable. In July 1986, Genscher was able to talk to Gorbachev in Moscow, and it was agreed that a 'new page' should be opened in their relations.

However, it should not be thought that, at this stage, the path to East–West understanding had apparently opened up. On the date of Genscher's visit to Gorbachev the Americans tested a nuclear device, despite the fact that the Soviet leader had implemented a unilateral moratorium on nuclear testing. The problem was that SDI could not go ahead without an extensive nuclear testing programme. It also became evident that the Americans were intending to breach the Anti-Ballistic Missile (ABM) treaty which prevented nuclear tests in space. The fact that Genscher made his distaste for these policies evident to Gorbachev may have helped the Soviet leader's inclination to cultivate West Germany, but the awkward position in which Bonn found itself was obvious.

Kohl's government, as well as the West German public, was divided on the issue. Gorbachev's more liberal policies in Moscow, policies which would soon be associated with the terms 'perestroika' and 'glasnost', were difficult to judge in the West. His talk of a common European home might simply be a ruse to uncouple the western European countries from their alliance with the USA, a traditional Soviet objective. Indeed, the line adopted in Washington was that Gorbachev's skill at public relations was threatening the West by encouraging the growth of neutralism there. This view had support in Bonn from Strauss's CSU and from the right wing of the CDU, exemplified by Alfred Dregger, chairman of the party's Bundestag delegation, and Lothar Späth, prime minister of Baden-Württemberg. Kohl himself seemed inclined to share such opinions. In October 1986, when talking to some American journalists he compared Gorbachev's propaganda methods with those of Josef Goebbels.[27] Not unnaturally, the comparison caused some outrage in Moscow. Gorbachev evidently decided he would await the outcome of the German elections due in January 1987, hoping that a Social Democratic victory might propel the SPD's new chancellor candidate, Johannes Rau, into the chancellorship.

---

27. The interview was with *Newsweek*, 27 Oct. 1986. See Garton Ash, *In Europe's Name*, p. 107.

Kohl's statement came shortly after a superpower confrontation at Reykjavik between Gorbachev and Reagan, which is sometimes – and with hindsight – seen as a turning point in East–West relations. It was not so regarded by contemporaries.[28] Nothing concrete had apparently been achieved in Reykjavik, and the two sides seemed actually to be drifting apart. Furthermore, the American government appeared to be treating its European allies with growing contempt. The abrasive manner adopted by presidential envoys such as Paul Nitze and Richard Perle did not reassure governments in Bonn or Paris, and even seems to have caused some dismay in London. It was evident that Washington was determined to continue nuclear tests and to breach the ABM treaty in pursuit of SDI, despite the anxieties expressed by European allies.

However, in December 1986 domestic events in Washington intruded on world affairs. Reagan became embroiled in a scandal about clandestine payments for arms to Iran and it was clear that his prestige at home was seriously damaged. Since he was now entering the last two years of his final term of office, his political position was in any case weaker than before. The US government moved away from its aggressively anti-communist stance and switched towards a policy of superpower agreement on disarmament. Talk of a 'double-zero' option involving the total abolition of medium-range nuclear missiles, an option initially seen as a propaganda move on both sides, now came to be taken seriously. But, once again, there seemed a danger that German interests might be ignored in a Moscow–Washington dialogue. If the opposition in Bonn won the forthcoming elections, relations with the USA could be expected to deteriorate still further, and concessions might be made to the Soviet Union which could seriously weaken the Western Alliance. Fortunately for Kohl and Genscher, the political climate at home was improving.

Kohl's election victory, 1987

The previous summer, Kohl's chancellorship had, indeed, been looking shaky. But with a constantly improving economic situation, and with signs that the government might be making some progress in foreign affairs, the atmosphere changed in favour of the coalition. The situation was made even better for the government by the

28. The Reykjavik meeting was 11–12 Oct. 1986. See the very pessimistic report on it by L. Wieland in *FAZ*, 14 Oct. 1986, trans. and reprinted in *The German Tribune*, No. 1247, Oct. 1986, p. 1.

problems faced by the SPD. The party had chosen as its chancellor candidate the bluff and ebullient prime minister of North Rhine-Westphalia, Johannes Rau. Rau seemed a good choice, since he could rally the older adherents amongst the SPD's trade union supporters, and was generally middle-of-the-road in his attitudes. But, precisely because of these qualities, he could not appeal to that section of the electorate that was being attracted by the Greens. The party chairman, Willy Brandt, felt Rau was weak in this respect, and barely concealed his disaffection with him. Rau came out firmly against any possibility of a coalition with the Greens – and in truth, the experience of an SPD–Green coalition in Hesse was proving unsatisfactory. But this left the SPD with no coalition partner, since the FDP could not contemplate switching sides again. An overall majority for the Social Democrats was out of the question.

As the election approached it appeared that the SPD would be very badly mauled, and that the Union parties might even get a majority. This possibility was scuppered by Franz-Josef Strauss and his CSU. By launching attacks on Genscher for his softness on the Soviet Union, as well as on the FDP generally for its unwillingness to combat crime or limit asylum-seekers, Strauss frightened moderate voters.[29] He also gave the FDP a splendid chance to present itself as the party which could prevent Strauss from getting influence in Bonn. The elections in January 1987 were a setback for both the larger parties, the CDU/CSU falling back to 44.3 per cent and the SPD losing even more ground, attaining only 37 per cent. The gainers were the FDP, who rose to 9.1 per cent, and the Greens who were only just behind with 8.3 per cent. Political scientists began to talk seriously of the decline of the two great 'people's parties', especially since voter participation in the election had also fallen to the lowest level since 1949.

There certainly were pockets of discontent in West Germany. Despite the stabilization of the economy achieved by Kohl's government, unemployment was proving an intractable problem. For those who were not able to develop marketable skills the outlook was bleak, and the growing prosperity all round them encouraged resentments. Some of these were directed against foreigners, whose numbers had

---

29. In August 1986 Strauss openly called for Genscher to be replaced and implied that a CSU personality should be given his job. Genscher's lukewarm attitude to the USA and his willingness to contemplate sanctions against South Africa were given as reasons for Strauss's denunciation. H.J. Melder, article in *Kölner-Stadt-Anzeiger*, 4 Aug. 1986, trans. and reprinted in *The German Tribune*, No. 1238, 10 Aug. 1986, p. 3.

continued to rise, despite the cessation of guest worker recruitment in 1973. By 1987 there were over four million non-Germans resident in the Federal Republic, considerably more than a third of whom were Turks.[30] It was not difficult for those of extreme right-wing persuasion to argue that the discontents of the unsuccessful were caused by a mixture of liberal permissiveness and truckling to foreigners.

In November 1983 a new political party of the right, the *Republikaner* or *Reps*, had been set up. As we have seen, its founders were two former CSU members of parliament who had been outraged by Strauss's willingness to grant credits to the GDR, and the high-handed manner in which he had rejected criticism of his leadership. The most effective spokesman for the new party was Franz Schönhuber, a charismatic TV presenter who made no apologies for his past experiences in the *Waffen-SS*. The *Reps* were careful to avoid any suggestion that they were threatening the Bonn Republic's democratic structure, nor did they advocate violence. But they did support reforms which would have weakened parliamentary government, such as the direct election of the president and the introduction of plebiscites as a way of achieving popular legislation. One particularly ugly aspect of their propaganda was its hostility to foreign workers and their families, especially the Turks. In January 1989 the *Reps* were to cause something of a sensation by obtaining 7.5 per cent of the votes in *Land* elections in West Berlin, thereby obtaining representation in the city's parliament. They also performed well in the European elections in June the same year. Most of the *Reps* vote seems to have come from disgruntled citizens choosing to upset the major parties, rather than from dedicated nationalists. They were never able to obtain access to the Bundestag in Bonn, suggesting that electors were not prepared to trust them on the national level. Nevertheless, their activities contributed to an unpleasantly tense atmosphere in some parts of West Germany, where intimidation and even violence against migrant communities began to manifest itself.

The *Republikaner* and those like them could dwell on the undoubted fact that more and more outsiders were pressing into West Germany. Ironically, some of these were groups encouraged to settle in the FRG by the policies of successive governments. These were the supposedly German minorities in countries under communist

---

30. In 1987 there were 4,240,500 non-Germans in the FRG, making up 6.9 per cent of the population. Of these, 1,453,700 were Turks. D. Horrocks and E. Kolinsky (eds), *Turkish Culture in German Society Today* (Providence, R.I., 1996), p. 83.

control. According to the terms of the FRG's nationality laws, such people of 'German blood' could claim German citizenship. There had been a consistent policy of trying to achieve such repatriation as the result of *Ostpolitik*, although results had not been very encouraging. In his 1983 government declaration Kohl had stressed his government's wish to welcome 'German' immigrants, but at that time there seemed little likelihood that Soviet bloc states would grant many such people exit permits. Once Gorbachev's reforms got under way, however, the situation changed rapidly and by the end of the decade the West Germans were finding themselves embarrassed by large numbers of immigrants from countries behind the iron curtain, especially Romania, Poland and the Soviet Union. Whereas in 1983 less than 40,000 such 'out-settlers' entered the Federal Republic, in 1988 the number exceeded 200,000, and in 1990 it was nearly 400,000.[31] Far from being welcomed with open arms by their compatriots, these 'German' immigrants, most of whom had never been to Germany and many of whom could not speak their own language very fluently, were regarded as yet another burden on the German social welfare system and a source of competition for already scarce low-skilled employment.

Resentment at such immigration was mixed up with anger over another problem that was growing rapidly in the second half of the 1980s – that of would-be immigrants seeking political asylum. Under Article 16 of the Basic Law, those who suffered political persecution had a right to asylum. This had clearly been intended as a means of giving shelter to political dissidents escaping from totalitarian dictatorships in Europe such as those established by Stalin. But, as time went by, repressive regimes of various sorts sprang up all over the world, especially in Asia and Africa. Furthermore, West Germany was very attractive as a target for migrants from developing countries, famous as it now was for its high standard of living. Hence many would-be migrants were tempted to claim political persecution when their actual motives were economic. Nevertheless, political repression often stimulated a rush of asylum-seekers. In 1980, for example, when there was considerable domestic turmoil in Turkey, nearly 58,000 Turks asked for political asylum. The numbers fell sharply thereafter, but as the 1980s wore on the numbers of asylum-seekers began to rise again, and with more consistency. In 1986 they reached

31. In some cases the Bonn government had to pay large sums of money to regimes such as that of Ceaucescu in Romania for the privilege of receiving German minorities. For a discussion of the 'out-settler' question and statistics, see Garton Ash, *In Europe's Name*, pp. 233–43, 399–400, 660–1.

FIGURE 6   *Asylum-seekers in the FRG during its last decade according to selected nations of origin*

	1980	1985	1987	1988	1989	1990
Europe of which	65 809	18 174	36 629	71 416	73 387	101 631
Romania	777	887	1 964	2 634	3 121	35 345
Turkey	57 913	7 528	11 426	14 873	20 020	22 082
Yugoslavia . . .	–	–	4 713	20 812	19 423	22 114
Africa . . .	8 339	8 093	3 568	6 548	12 479	24 210
Asia	31 996	44 298	15 961	23 006	32 718	60 900
Totals	107 818	73 832	57 379	103 076	121 318	193 063

These figures are for the area covered by the Federal Republic before unification. The number of countries listed is incomplete; that is why the columns do not add up to the totals at the bottom.

Source: *Statistisches Jahrbuch 1991 für das vereinte Deutschland* (Wiesbaden, 1991), p. 73.

100,000, over half of them from Asia. By 1990 the number was approaching 200,000 (see Figure 6).

Over the years procedures of considerable complexity had been developed for processing asylum-seekers, who had to be given food and shelter while their cases were being examined, but who were not allowed to work. Instead, they were spread throughout West Germany and made the responsibility of local authorities, to the considerable anger of native taxpayers. All this was grist to the mill of such parties as the *Republikaner*, and was to prove an even greater source of difficulty once Germany had been unified in October 1990.

Ostpolitik *again*

In practice the 1987 Bundestag election results made little difference to the way west Germany was governed: the Kohl coalition carried on, with the FDP gaining one more ministry – that of education under Möllemann. But the threat to Genscher had been blunted by his obvious popularity *vis-à-vis* Strauss. Public opinion surveys in the *Spiegel* regularly showed the Foreign Minister to be the most popular political figure in West Germany. Meanwhile, Genscher's FDP rival, Bangemann, attracted some bad publicity for his handling of affairs in the Economics Ministry, and was also criticized for being unable to smooth over conflicts within the FDP itself. In 1988 he resigned his position as party chairman and was later seconded to Brussels as a European Commissioner. Count Lambsdorff, who replaced him as chairman, was not in a position to challenge Genscher's pre-eminence in the party.

The public associated Genscher with common sense and peaceful compromise. In that respect the January 1987 Bundestag election was an important lesson for the government, and one which was evidently not lost on Kohl. Even so, it took time for the CDU/CSU to work out a consistent policy towards Moscow. The rather abrupt American decision to drop intermediate-range missiles created concern in German defence circles that the Soviet superiority in short-range nuclear weapons (Scuds) would leave west Germany as a tempting battleground in any future conflict. For a time Kohl seemed willing to obstruct the peace process in order to keep the *Bundeswehr* armed with Pershing missiles. It was not until the autumn that he was willing to brave the contempt of Franz-Josef Strauss and agree to jettison this west German reservation.[32]

Meanwhile, Genscher made strenuous efforts to link disarmament with amelioration in German–Soviet relations. Shortly after the 1987 Bundestag election he addressed a World Economic Forum at Davos and urged its distinguished international audience to 'take Gorbachev seriously; take him at his word!'[33] In July 1987 he accompanied President Weiszäcker to Moscow, where they had a somewhat cool meeting with Gorbachev. When Weiszäcker referred to the continuing awareness of German people that they formed part of one nation, the Soviet censors suppressed this comment in the published record.[34] Nevertheless, the German Foreign Office had been busy encouraging agreements with the USSR over such matters as health and culture, and economic discussions were also proceeding. In the summer of 1987 it became clear that the green light had been given for Honecker to visit the Federal Republic, a sign of a thaw between Moscow and Bonn. Honecker was later able to announce the abolition of the death penalty in the GDR – a punishment that had been used with remarkable frequency in the workers' and farmers' Republic – and the West Germans increased money given to visitors from the GDR from DM30 to DM100.

32. *The German Tribune*, No. 1289, 6 Sept. 1987.
33. Garton Ash, *In Europe's Name*, p. 107.
34. H.-P. Riese, *Deutsche Allgemeines Sonntagsblatt*, Hamburg, 12 July 1987, trans. and reprinted in *The German Tribune*, No. 1282, 19 July 1987, p. 1.

Honecker's reception in Bonn, 9–11 September, was a remarkable event. Outside the Chancellor's office the flags of the Federal Republic and the German Democratic Republic flew side by side, a sight which would have seemed inconceivable fifteen years earlier, when the Eastern Treaties were being bitterly opposed by the Christian Democrats. Now Honecker was fêted in Bonn and in his former birthplace, the Saarland. Commentators feared foreigners might think that the German question and the tiresome *querelles allemandes* could now finally be forgotten.[35] Official statements stressed that West Germany did not accept the Wall in Berlin and the barbed wire dividing Germany as history's last word on the matter, a point which Kohl stressed strongly in his televised speech at the dinner for Honecker in Bonn. 'The awareness of the unity of the nation is as alive as ever', he told his guest.[36] In an interview with the *Frankfurter Allgemeine Zeitung* at the end of November, Kohl stressed that the government had not reconciled itself to the division of Germany, although the issue of reunification 'was not on the agenda of world politics' at that moment.[37]

In view of what happened two years later, it is tempting to see in West German policy at this time a calculated, even Machiavellian, intention to use the changing international situation as a means of achieving German unification. It is very unlikely that this was so. Kohl himself undoubtedly disliked having to socialize with the German communist leader, and he stressed that there could be nothing in common between the two political systems. But the aim of west German policy at this time still seems to have been to reduce tension and ameliorate the living conditions of those Germans unfortunate enough to live under Soviet rule. During his visit to the Saarland, Honecker had declared that the conditions on the frontier between the two Germanys were 'not as they should be' and expressed the hope that the frontier should one day not divide Germans, but unite them in much the same way that the frontier between the GDR and Poland united those countries.[38]

---

35. Article in *Rheinische Post* by J. Sobotta, 5 Sept. 1987. Trans. and reprinted in *The German Tribune*, No. 1290, 13 Sept. 1987, p. 1.

36. Garton Ash, *In Europe's Name*, p. 171.

37. J.C. Reissmüller in *FAZ*, 30 Nov. 1987, translated and reprinted in *The German Tribune*, 13 Dec. 1987.

38. Garton Ash, *In Europe's Name*, p. 198. Garton Ash points out that this reference to the Polish frontier 'could almost be taken for a bad joke' because the GDR frontier with Poland had been almost closed since the emergence of Solidarity. Honecker, however, was not one for jokes; he was assuming that 'socialist' countries enjoyed fraternal frontiers.

Kohl himself, in the interview mentioned above, gave it as his view that 'future generations' might see a reunited Germany, but that 'freedom took precedence over unity, and the nation-state of the nineteenth century had no future'. The real aim of both Kohl and Genscher was evidently to end the inhumane character of the German–German relationship epitomized by the Berlin Wall and the trigger-happy border guards manning the iron curtain. The way to do this was to deepen the co-operation with Moscow and strengthen the European Community so that a new form of European association might eventually supersede the Cold War.

Certainly the international scene was changing fast. In September 1987 Reagan announced that all medium-range missiles were to be scrapped, and at a summit with Gorbachev in December he signed a treaty implementing this decision. Negotiations on conventional disarmament were expected to follow. Franz-Josef Strauss, never a man to let consistency stand in the way of opportunism, promptly flew himself to Moscow to meet Gorbachev, by whom he was duly impressed. Another hard-liner to jump on the bandwagon was Lothar Späth, who visited the USSR in February 1988. Intensive economic negotiations between Germany and the Soviet Union opened in May, and by August Genscher was able to seal those successfully. On 24 October Kohl himself arrived in Moscow for his long-delayed conference with the Soviet leader. They signed agreements on medical and space research, environmental protection and cultural exchanges. This was described as 'the starting signal for normal relations'.[39]

The following summer Gorbachev visited the Federal Republic and received a rapturous reception as a Soviet leader who was bringing new hope of peace and reform. 'Gorbymania' was a phrase coined to describe his popularity, and parallels were drawn on the Soviet side with the Adenauer–de Gaulle rapprochement in the early 1960s.[40] Eleven agreements were signed covering such varied items as investment protection, youth training and the provision of a 'hot line' between Bonn and Moscow. In a grandiosely titled 'Bonn Declaration' the two statesmen asserted their commitment to a new era of peace in which the division of Europe would be overcome. Kohl took the opportunity of privately stressing his commitment to the ultimate goal of German unity, even if he might not live to see

39. Jörg Bischof, *Stuttgarter Zeitung*, 27 Oct. 1988, trans. and reprinted in *The German Tribune*, No. 1346, 6 Nov. 1988.
40. Garton Ash, *In Europe's Name*, p. 113.

it. Gorbachev somewhat enigmatically replied that the USSR had serious economic difficulties, and if he needed help with that one day, would the Chancellor be able to help? Kohl promised to do so.[41] Neither man can have thought that the request would come as soon as it did.

Bonn in Europe: before the Wall came down

Meanwhile, Genscher and Kohl had been making progress on the western European front. For the first six months of 1988 the Germans held the presidency of the European Council of Ministers. Working closely with Mitterrand and Delors, Kohl was able to break a log-jam relating to the Common Agricultural Policy and the EC budget, although this involved West Germany paying more than she had originally wished. At a European Council meeting in Hanover in June 1988 there was discussion of moves towards monetary union and a European central bank and a 'common social structure', which the Germans approved of as a way of preventing the poorer nations in Europe from undermining their living standards. Delors was empowered to investigate the question of monetary union, and in April 1989 presented his report recommending a three-stage process towards the creation of a single European currency, with the first stage beginning in 1990. It was clear that this was seen by its supporters, like Kohl and Mitterrand, as a natural concomitant of the Single Market, and one which was bound to lead to political union.[42]

The vision of the Federal Republic's future in 1989, then, was of a prosperous, export-orientated country with a highly trained and well-educated labour force which would be at the heart of a European community dedicated to promoting peace and improving living standards. It would continue to be protected by alliance with the USA, but would intensify *Ostpolitik* to eliminate tensions and create the most normal possible relationship with Soviet bloc countries, including the GDR. Ultimately the hope might be that, within a European framework, the two Germanys could come together. But this objective seemed a long way off. The West Germans were not at all inclined to try to destabilize East Germany. That would be highly dangerous because it might create turbulence and provoke a backlash. Since the 1950s it had been obvious that the western powers

---

41. Ibid., p. 118.
42. Urwin, *The Community of Europe*, pp. 240–1.

were not prepared to wage war to liberate those Europeans under Soviet rule. The only hope for improvement in the GDR, therefore, was a change of heart in the East German regime.[43]

Yet in 1989 it was not so much the governments as the people themselves who intervened to cause the collapse of European communism. To this proposition there must be added one qualification: the so-called 'velvet revolution' that swept through eastern Europe in the last months of 1989 could not have happened without a major change of policy at the top – in the Kremlin. So far as east Germany was concerned, the regimes of Ulbricht and Honecker lacked any popular mandate, and would have been swept away at any time since 1949 if the shielding hand of the Soviet Union had been removed. The Soviet security forces had created a model pupil in the all-pervasive *Stasi* or East German secret police, the full extent of whose surveillance and terror activities only became apparent after the GDR had collapsed.[44] Above all, there was the presence of the Red Army, with some 400,000 heavily armed men, which gave Honecker and his comrades the feeling of reassurance that their state would not be allowed to disappear. Only if the decision-makers in Moscow came to the conclusion that it was not in their best interests to continue the Brezhnev doctrine, according to which no communist state could ever be allowed to escape from the Soviet orbit, could the GDR be threatened.

The collapse of the GDR: an unexpected revolution

Already in November 1986 Gorbachev had indicated to eastern bloc leaders gathered in Moscow that they might expect more leeway in choosing their own national policies. But this was very far from suggesting that the peoples of their countries might reject communism

43. This is a point discussed by Timothy Garton Ash in *In Europe's Name*. See, for example, pp. 170–5, although he is rather more critical of the West German position than I would be, since the fear of a backlash in Soviet Europe does not seem to me to be entirely misplaced. The massacre on Tienanmen Square in Beijing on 4 June 1989 was the sort of reaction many western observers feared in Soviet satellite countries, and it is well known that some GDR leaders would then have favoured such a course if they could have got away with it.

44. See, for example, M. Fulbrook, *Anatomy of a Dictatorship. Inside the GDR, 1949–1989* (Oxford, 1995), ch. 2; an early revelation of the *Stasi* actions and mentality was a documentary collection brought out in 1990 by A. Mitter and S. Wolle (eds), *'Ich Liebe euch doch alle!' Befehle und Lageberichte des Mfs Jan–Nov 1989* (Berlin, 1990).

altogether. Indeed, right up to the summer of 1989, it could be assumed that Gorbachev's support for reformist leaders in eastern Europe was due to his desire for allies in his own campaign against old-guard conservatives in the Soviet Union who were obstructing *glasnost.*[45]

However, so far as the GDR was concerned, Honecker himself seems to have felt completely secure. In early October 1989 the GDR was to celebrate its 40th anniversary. Honecker could look back on his period of rule with great satisfaction. His regime had been recognized internationally and by the West Germans, albeit in somewhat convoluted language. He had been royally received on a visit to Bonn. The Federal Republic was, in various ways, subsidizing the East German regime to the tune of billions of marks. Yet Honecker was still undisputed ruler of a one-party state. Opposition was actually weaker in the GDR than elsewhere in eastern Europe because would-be dissidents could simply be shipped out to the Federal Republic, an option not open to the rulers of other Soviet satellites. Honecker could also hope that the increased contacts between East and West Germany were all part of a 'normalization' process that would stabilize rather than weaken his government. By allowing more East Germans the chance of short visits to the west, and by relaxing tensions, the communist leadership could hope to generate contentment amongst East Germans who, it was supposed, would appreciate the cosy security (*Geborgenheit*) of the GDR as against the rat-race of the capitalist west – especially as mass unemployment began to be a feature of western economies.

Such illusions were nourished by western commentators on life in the GDR. Few serious investigations of life under communism in East Germany were made in the west. One reason for this was that western scholars needed East German permission to gain access to archival materials in the GDR and did not want to arouse official displeasure. Another was a willingness to accept official East German production figures which seemed to put the GDR quite high amongst the developed countries of the world. The fact that the official exchange rate of the East German mark was at parity with the West German currency made it possible to broadcast misleadingly optimistic statistics about per capita income in Honecker's Republic. There was also an understandable tendency not to want to rock the boat when relations between East and West were at a delicate stage.

---

45. From 1985, relations between Honecker and Gorbachev had deteriorated, but Gorbachev wanted a reformed socialism in the GDR, not a western-style government, let alone German unification. Zelikow and Rice, *Germany Unified*, p. 35.

In 1986 Theo Sommer, a respected editor of the prestigious Hamburg weekly, *Die Zeit*, wrote of a tour in the GDR that life there seemed to be becoming more colourful, and implied that the people were more contented.[46] In fact, the economic situation of Honecker's state was deteriorating. An industrial development plan had proved a failure, and the government was more and more dependent on hard currency injections from the West to keep even its docile command economy going. The expectations aroused within the GDR by increased contacts with the West should not be ignored either. Honecker claimed that in 1987 there had been over five million visits by East Germans to the Federal Republic, of which 1.2 million were by people under pensionable age.[47] Intended to assuage East German resentments, these visits only exacerbated them. The people of the GDR could briefly sample the consumer society and realized that what they saw on western TV was not just a propaganda invention. They also became more conscious of their lack of freedom when they were only allowed brief visits to the West, rather than none at all, as had been the case in the 1970s.

Changes in public opinion in the GDR, especially amongst the youth, were detectable even before the events of autumn 1989. Opinion surveys conducted in May 1989 showed that the proportion of apprentices who claimed to believe in Marxist–Leninism had fallen from 46 per cent in 1975 to 9 per cent. Only 10 per cent of those asked thought that socialism would eventually establish itself throughout the world, whereas in 1975 63 per cent had claimed to believe that. It was reported at the Leipzig church conference in summer 1989 that one in five youths or young men had applied for permission to leave the GDR.[48]

There were, however, other causes of subversion in the GDR, and these should not be overlooked. The activity of the protestant church was particularly important, although subsequently it was to be muddied by controversy. For many years the protestant church had tried to keep itself together as a national faith, bridging the iron curtain that divided Germany. But, especially after the erection

46. Quoted in Konrad Löw, 'Die Bundesdeutsche Politikwissenschaftliche DDR-Forschung und die Revolution in der DDR', in K. Löw (ed.), *Ursachen und Verlauf der deutschen Revolution 1989* (Berlin, 1991), p. 124.

47. These figures were announced by Kohl as given to him by Honecker: see Werner Weidenfled and Hartmut Zimmermann, *Deutschland Handbuch. Eine Doppelte Bilanz 1949–1989* (Munich, 1989), p. 829.

48. Bernward Baule, ' "Wir Sind das Volk!" Politische Bedingungsfelder der Freiheitsrevolution in der DDR', in Löw (ed.), *Ursachen und Verlauf*, pp. 33–4. It is, of course, difficult to judge how reliable the responses were in 1975. The important point is that young people were more willing to express dissent by Spring 1989.

of the Berlin Wall, this had become virtually impossible. Faced with an aggressively atheistic regime which was evidently there to stay, the clergy had to consider how best to protect their faith without arousing direct repression. Their method was to accept the fact of 'socialism' in the GDR and to assert that this need not be incompatible with Christianity – an argument for which there was ample scriptural support. In 1971 the protestant church in the GDR had proclaimed itself a 'church in socialism', and in 1978 Bishop Schönherr had used this ecclesiastical recognition of socialism as a means of obtaining more freedom for the church in such matters as the dissemination of information among its congregations. The churches in many areas became reception centres for complaints and a source of information trusted by the citizenry. This did not mean that the clergy were fomenting revolt. Church leaders sometimes had close links with the *Stasi* or secret police, and were careful to reassure Honecker and his comrades that the church was not interested in destroying the GDR.

After unification it became fashionable to rubbish the church leadership in the GDR as collaborators. Such criticisms came ill from those who had lived comfortably in the west during the 40 years of postwar German history and who had shown no stomach then to fight for the liberty of their East German compatriots. As one East German commentator remarked: 'It will be difficult for somebody brought up in the Federal Republic or in another democratic state to comprehend what it meant to live one's life . . . in the shadow of the Stasi.'[49] In any case, the result of the church's success in maintaining an area outside the total control of the communist state was that in 1989 physical opportunities existed for the organization of dissent.

One area in which this had manifested itself was in the opposition towards nuclear armaments, which had spilt over from the western anti-nuclear movement. The Greens, although themselves not committed to the reunification of Germany, had tried to export their views to the GDR, and had aroused some sympathetic echoes there. Such dissident groups as there were usually looked to an internal reform of the GDR based on the concept of a more humane form

49. Ursula Jaekel, '40 Jahre Staatssicherheit – Ziele, Tätigkeit, Auswirkungen', in Löw (ed.), *Ursachen und Verlauf*, p. 141. Jaekel was born in 1943 and had therefore known no other environment than the Soviet zone and the GDR. For a discussion of the ambivalence of the church's position in the GDR, see Fulbrook, *Anatomy of a Dictatorship*, pp. 115–25. She points to the importance of the 'protective umbrella' of the church to the dissenting movement in the GDR.

of socialism within a disarmed Europe. The slogan 'swords into ploughshares' was taken up by young people, many of whom courted *Stasi* displeasure by wearing peace movement badges in their lapels.

In May 1989 local elections were held. These took the form traditional in communist states: the population was bullied into voting for official lists and where they did not do so the results were simply falsified. Church groups were able to demonstrate that, whereas the official figures showed less than 1.5 per cent of the electors rejecting the official lists, the real figure in many areas was nearer 15 per cent, despite the threats of reprisals which such disobedience might bring with it.

The summer of 1989 saw decisive events outside Germany which would help to undermine Honecker's regime. Already a reformist government in Hungary had replaced that of the hard-line Communist János Kádár, and in June 1989 partly free elections in Poland seemed likely to lead to a government dominated by Solidarity.

Many East Germans had taken holidays in Hungary or Czechoslovakia, where several thousand of them insisted on occupying the West German embassy and demanding the right of migration to the Federal Republic. In previous cases, such matters had been hushed up, and refugees had been returned to the GDR on the understanding that their applications for exit would be processed quickly – on payment of the usual ransom by Bonn to the GDR.[50] But the situation in late summer in the Prague embassy became very difficult owing to the large numbers involved and their determination to go straight to West Germany. Meanwhile in Hungary the 'iron curtain' frontier had been progressively dismantled since the early spring, and on 10 September the Hungarian government announced that it would no longer restrict the movement of East German citizens who wanted to leave for Austria – which meant that they could travel unhindered to West Germany. In the next few weeks 40,000 GDR citizens left by this route.[51] The old East German nightmare of the 1950s was revived. The population was leaking away.

Discontent was now being voiced openly within the GDR. Demonstrations took place in Leipzig, and these became a regular Monday evening event. They formed up around protestant churches and marched peacefully in the centre of the city, demanding liberalization of the government. At first only a few thousand brave souls

50. Zelikow and Rice, *Germany Unified*, p. 37.

51. E. Pond, *Beyond the Wall. Germany's Road to Unification* (Washington D.C., 1993), p. 96.

took part, facing violent intimidation from the *Stasi*. But by the following month tens of thousands were marching, and the police state was facing a serious challenge. October was to see the celebration of the GDR's 40th anniversary, but it took place against a background of impending disaster. In order to smooth over difficulties in Prague, about 5,000 refugees from the embassy were allowed to travel to the West on the understanding that the trains would go through the GDR, but without the refugees having to disembark there. This aroused great interest within the GDR itself. As soon as the embassy was emptied of the first refugees it filled up again, and on 3 October Honecker announced that travel to Czechoslovakia for GDR citizens would be restricted.

When Gorbachev arrived for the anniversary celebrations beginning on 5 October, trains carrying thousands such refugees from Prague were passing through Dresden, and riots broke out as other East Germans vainly attempted to get on board.[52] Gorbachev himself would have had no sympathy for the rioters, but nor was he enthusiastic about Honecker. He made little effort to hide his scepticism when Honecker boasted before the East German Politburo about the achievements of the GDR, and commented that 'life punishes those who come too late' when discussing the need for reform. Gorbachev later denied that this was intended as a direct criticism of Honecker, but it certainly did his career no good.[53] The East German leader could evidently expect little support from Moscow. His days were numbered.

Gorbachev himself was obviously far more popular in east Berlin than the SED. No sooner had he left than more major public demonstrations began to occur. Honecker wanted to use force against the demonstrators, but after Gorbachev's clear signals his colleagues lacked the nerve to do so. On 16 October the Leipzig demonstration attracted an estimated 100,000 people. It was evident that there would either be a blood-bath or the government would have to give way. On 18 October the Politburo dismissed Honecker and replaced him with Egon Krenz. This was hardly a radical change. Krenz was known as a loyal party man who, like Honecker, had made his career

52. Ibid., pp. 101–2.

53. Archie Brown, Gorbachev's biographer, remarks that the comment would have been seen as 'tactful criticism' of Honecker. A. Brown, *The Gorbachev Factor* (Oxford, 1996), pp. 249, 376, fn. See also Garton Ash, *In Europe's Name*, p. 594; Pond, *Beyond the Wall*, p. 106; K.H. Jarausch, *The Rush to German Unity* (Oxford, 1994), pp. 53–4. Zelikow and Rice claim that Gorbachev's remarks were less obviously damning: *Germany Unified*, p. 84, but Honecker's Politburo colleagues must have seen that the Soviet leader would not regret his disappearance.

in the FDJ, the communist youth movement. By now opposition was beginning to become more formalized: in September a 'New Forum' to focus dissent and the demand for reform had been founded, and on 7 October a Social Democratic Party – banned since 1946 – was established in the GDR. Furthermore, some of the subservient 'bloc parties' that had been allowed to continue a formal existence in the GDR – especially the Christian Democrats and Liberal Democrats – started to show signs of autonomy from the SED.

Krenz decided to try to head off the growing discontent by concessions over travel.[54] The urgency of the situation was shown by the fact that on 4 November hundreds of thousands of Germans demonstrated for freedom on the Alexanderplatz in east Berlin. On 9 November it was announced that East Germans would be able to travel abroad freely, and in a televised press conference the SED public spokesman, Günter Schabowski, implied that this freedom would take immediate effect.[55] Versions of his statement were broadcast on western TV and seen by many in east Berlin. That night a huge crowd built up at the Friedrichstrasse checkpoint and the guards at the Berlin Wall were given no clear instructions. Eventually they decided to open the checkpoint and the jubilant demonstrators streamed through the wall into west Berlin, many of them seeing it for the first time in their lives. They were greeted by enthusiastic crowds of west Berliners. Soon the people were climbing on the Wall itself and even starting to hack it down. The division of Berlin – and with it the division of Germany – was at an end.

The popular uprising rapidly swept away the remnants of the SED regime. On 14 November Hans Modrow, a provincial party leader who had suffered in his career through being suspected of reformism, was appointed GDR prime minister. In early December Krenz and the entire Politburo resigned. On 7 December talks between the SED and opposition at a so-called Round Table conference began, but suspicions were aroused when Modrow seemed to be trying to rescue the *Stasi* for the new regime, and the headquarters of the secret police were stormed by indignant crowds.

It became clear that only rapid elections to a genuinely democratic parliament could prevent chaos, and the numbers of East Germans

54. He discussed his 'reforms' with Gorbachev in Moscow on 1 Nov. 1989. His aim was evidently to allow East Germans travel permits but to deny them the right to convert their currency, thus making it difficult for them to travel. Gorbachev evidently agreed to this. Zelikow and Rice, *Germany Unified*, pp. 86–9.

55. Zelikow and Rice sum up this episode by saying: 'the hapless East German government had opened the Berlin Wall by mistake'. Ibid., p. 101.

leaving for the West was causing serious worries in both Bonn and East Berlin. So new elections to the East German *Volkskammer* – the first to be really free and democratic – were fixed for 18 March 1990. The SED dissolved itself, and a new, apparently democratic, successor party, the PDS (Party of Democratic Socialism) was formed, shorn of many of the older communist hierarchy. Meanwhile the West German parties were enthusiastically encouraging their counterparts in the GDR to prepare for the election campaign. Here the former bloc parties – particularly the Liberals and the Christian Democrats – had considerable advantages because they possessed offices, staff and even newspapers which could be used to help disseminate their views. When the elections were held, the 'Alliance for Germany', based on the CDU and supported by Kohl's party in Bonn, won 193 seats, the SPD won 87 and the PDS took third place with 65. The dissident groups that had spearheaded the revolution in the GDR fared badly and lost their political influence. The Alliance (CDU) leader, Lothar de Mazière, became premier.

Helmut Kohl and the unification of Germany

Although before 9 November 1989 the East German demonstrators had been urging reform within their own country, once the Wall was down pressure began to build up for a different future for East Germany – reunification with the West. At first the Bonn government was cautious in its approach to this possibility; but at the Monday demonstrations in Leipzig – which continued despite the opening of the Wall – a new slogan began to be heard. Instead of 'we are the people', demonstrators chanted 'we are one people'. On 28 November Kohl put forward a ten-point programme to overcome the division of Germany, which would have involved a slow progress through 'confederative structures' to an eventual – but rather distant – union.[56]

Here it was important that Kohl himself had always been interested in the East Germans and was predisposed to work for their incorporation in a free, united Germany. He improvised German policy whilst others seemed bewildered by what was happening. The Social Democrats dragged their feet; the Greens and many left-wing intellectuals positively rejected the concept of unification. This distaste for a goal to which NATO was formally committed, but which its members had never imagined they would have to encompass, was

56. Garton Ash, *In Europe's Name*, p. 346.

also apparent amongst some of West Germany's allies. Mrs Thatcher was hostile to the idea of German unification, and President Mitterrand seemed unlikely to support it. On 20 December he arrived in East Berlin for a state visit to the GDR, the first such visit ever paid by a head of state from one of the three western Allies. Opposition to German unification could therefore be expected, not only from the Russians, but also from Germany's western Allies and former enemies, who still had occupation rights in Berlin.

Fortunately for Kohl, the fears in London and Paris were not shared in Washington. George Bush and his Secretary of State, James Baker, showed themselves staunchly loyal to their commitments to the Federal Republic, a state which had for four decades symbolized the American way of life in postwar Europe. Indeed, Bush's support for unification predated the collapse of Honecker's government.[57]

The actual accomplishment of unification presented Kohl and Genscher with their most demanding challenge. Assuming the east Germans wanted to unite with their western compatriots, how was an agreement to be constructed that would satisfy both East and West? Washington and Moscow were the key capitals. Even given Bush's benevolent attitude, the Americans would not agree to a German solution that weakened the NATO alliance. On the other hand, Gorbachev could hardly be expected to accept a united Germany in NATO. And what would happen to the huge Soviet forces in Germany east of the Elbe?

The Americans offered the Germans a way out of the impasse by proposing negotiations between the two Germanys and the four wartime Allied powers. This meant that the German position could be presented – effectively by Kohl – and that the 'victors' would not be drawing up a peace treaty and imposing it on Germany. The Americans also made clear their willingness to offer the Soviet Union agreements on disarmament and weapons control, hence balancing the strategic losses involved by an offer of greater security. Gorbachev could hope for greater co-operation in all fields with the West, a co-operation which would help him achieve the modernization of the USSR.[58]

Meanwhile his own position at home was wracked with economic difficulties. In early January his Foreign Minister, Eduard Shevardnadze, asked for economic help from west Germany, reminding Kohl

---

57. Zelikow and Rice, *Germany Unified*, pp. 80–1, 94–5.
58. Garton Ash, *In Europe's Name*, p. 349.

of his private promise the previous summer. Within hours Kohl was arranging for huge deliveries of German meat to the Soviet Union. In mid-February Kohl and Gorbachev met in Moscow and the former enthused about the prospects of German–Soviet co-operation. In return, the Soviet leader agreed that the Germans could choose their own future. In May Kohl organized a government-guaranteed loan of DM5 billion for the Soviet Union.[59] Hence by a combination of economic aid, personal flattery and optimistic plans for future co-operation, Kohl was able to persuade the Soviet leadership not only to allow the unification of Germany, but to enable the new German state to remain in NATO, albeit with some provisions for the interim period during which the Red Army would still be in occupation of the former GDR. This ticklish problem was resolved by an agreement according to which the Soviet forces would be evacuated from the country by the summer of 1994, in return for large sums of west German money, ostensibly to rehouse the soldiers when they got back to the Soviet Union. The Germans also agreed to reduce the *Bundeswehr* to 350,000 men.

Gorbachev's decision, finally taken at a meeting with Genscher and Kohl in the Caucasus in mid-July 1990, was not only conditioned by his economic needs and his hopes for Soviet–German collaboration in the future. Events in Germany itself were proceeding so fast that to try to put the clock back – or even restrain progress – would have caused a major crisis and possibly a threat of war. The results of the *Volkskammer* elections in March had made clear the east Germans' determination for unity. According to the Basic Law of the Federal Republic (Article 146), reunification should have led to the replacement of the provisional West German constitution by a new one, freely agreed upon by the German people. But the Federal Republic had been so successful that its people had no desire to alter their constitutional arrangements, and the mass of the East German population wanted to achieve the living standards of their West German cousins as quickly as possible. Therefore in April 1990 de Mazière announced that his government favoured joining the Federal Republic under Article 23 of the Basic Law, which simply stipulated that the Law would run in such parts of Germany as decided to enter the existing Federal Republic – the article used when the Saar had rejoined Germany in 1957. This obviously speeded up the whole process of unification, since all that was necessary was for the GDR to establish the *Länder* that could be part of the federal system, and

59. Ibid., p. 351.

to make whatever interim arrangements seemed appropriate to cover the difficult process of assimilation between two completely different social and economic systems.

In this respect the East Germans, unused to the hurly-burly of pluralistic, interest group politics, allowed themselves to be out-manoeuvred. They tended to stress factors such as the right to work – which could hardly be guaranteed in a free market economy – whilst allowing the western negotiators to have their way on the crucial matter of property rights. The East German regime had appropriated property from landowners and entrepreneurs, and this had been used for collective farms, state factories and public housing projects. Many of the former owners had already received some form of compensation under the *Lastenausgleich* system in West Germany. All of them had enjoyed years, if not decades, of prosperity in the West whilst their former neighbours were paying for the Second World War with their liberty and the burden of reparations payments to the Soviet Union. Instead of insisting that property ownership should be accepted as it stood on the day of unification, the east Germans allowed themselves to be saddled with a situation in which former owners could present claims for property that they had not occupied for decades. The result was to put hundreds of thousands of East Germans in a state of uncertainty about the status of their dwellings, and to hamper investment in the former GDR owing to the difficulty of ensuring that land or buildings were unencumbered by property claims. Enthusiastically supportive of this, literally reactionary, property settlement was the West German FDP – which was to be one explanation for its unpopularity in the former GDR in the mid-1990s. Things were not made easier by shady dealings involving former functionaries in the GDR administrative apparatus – including the *Stasi* – who took steps to enrich themselves in the interregnum between the collapse of the SED and the creation of the united Germany.

In other respects, however, the drafting of a treaty of unification between the two Germanys went ahead rapidly. But even before political unification, a decisive step was taken which rendered it almost impossible to unscramble the merging of the two states. On 1 July 1990, monetary union was established. The East German mark was abolished and replaced by the West German D-Mark. Until that point economic developments in the GDR had been hampered by swings in the exchange rate – at one point the East mark was being exchanged at about fifteen to the D-Mark. The Bundesbank was eager that currency union should take place at a realistic rate of exchange to avoid inflationary pressures in the economy, but Kohl overruled it and insisted on a generous treatment of the GDR population. They were therefore able to exchange a substantial part of their savings at one to one, and the rest at two to one. This encouraged a consumer boom in the East, and stimulated West German exports into the GDR. But it was catastrophic for East German enterprises, which found that their debts were insupportable and their price levels uncompetitive.

This is an issue over which economists may argue in the future. Politically, however, Kohl was surely right. The decision to go for a generous exchange rate mollified the east Germans and made them feel that unification really was just around the corner. The temptation to leave for the west – a temptation tens of thousands had already been unable to resist – was reduced.

Helmut Kohl was indeed at his ebullient best in this critical period. Whether he was cheerfully assuring Gorbachev of the benefits a united Germany would bring to the USSR, whether he was assuring the East Germans that their economy would soon be blossoming, or whether he was telling the West Germans that the market economy could cope with unification without the need for major tax increases, his unquenchable optimism and energy carried his country along to the point of unification.

On 23 August the east German *Volkskammer* voted to accede to the Federal Republic. Eight days later the unification treaty between the two Germanys was signed. The twelfth of September saw the representatives of the four Allied powers and the two German states signing the treaty which recognized the Sovereignty of the united Germany. On 3 October 1990 ceremonies were held in Berlin, Bonn and other German cities to mark the 'day of German unity'. It was a relaxed, even downbeat, occasion with fireworks and receptions, but no military pomp and little political bombast. The government remained for the time being in Bonn. The Federal Republic had emerged as a major victor in the Cold War. Communism had not only been defeated; it had effectively disappeared.

But there would be changes in the west too. Bonn had gained the victory, yet the Bonn Republic would no longer exist. The centre of gravity in Germany had already begun to shift. Soon, albeit slowly, Bonn would give way to Berlin.

Suggestions for Further Reading

The books listed below are confined to titles published in English. German sources are referred to in the footnotes to each chapter. I should, however, like to acknowledge my debt to the monumental historical series *Geschichte der Bundesrepublik Deutschland*, published in five volumes and edited by Karl Dietrich Bracher, Theodor Eschenburg, Joachim C. Fest and Eberhard Jäckel. Needless to say, neither my interpretations nor any errors of fact or judgement can be attributed to that work.

Biographies and memoirs

WILLY BRANDT, *My Road to Berlin* (London, 1960)

WILLY BRANDT, *People and Politics: The Years 1960–1975* (London, 1978)

WILLY BRANDT, *My Life in Politics* (London, 1992)

LEWIS J. EDINGER, *Kurt Schumacher: A Study in Personality and Political Behaviour* (Berkeley, LA, 1965)

A.J. HEIDENHEIMER, *Adenauer and the CDU: The Rise of the Leader and the Integration of the Party* (The Hague, 1960)

BARBARA MARSHALL, *Willy Brandt* (London, 1990)

HANS-PETER SCHWARZ, *Konrad Adenauer. A German Politician and Statesman in a Period of War, Revolution and Reconstruction* Vol. 1 *From the German Empire to the Federal Republic, 1876–1952*, trans, Louise Willmot (Providence, R.I., 1995)

General accounts of German politics and society

MICHAEL BALFOUR, *Germany: The Tides of Power* (London, 1992)

DENNIS L. BARK and DAVID R. GRESS, *A History of West Germany*, Vol. 1, *From Shadow to Substance, 1945–1963*, Vol. 2, *Democracy and its Discontents, 1963–1988* (Oxford, 1989)

VOLKER R. BERGHAHN, *Modern Germany: Society, Economy and Politics in the 20th Century* (Cambridge, 1982; 2nd edn, 1987)

MARY FULBROOK, *The Divided Nation: A History of Germany 1918–1990* (Oxford, 1991)

ANTHONY GLEES, *Reinventing Germany. German Political Development since 1945* (Oxford, 1996)

ALFRED GROSSER, *Germany in our Time* (London, 1971)

KONRAD H. JARAUSCH and VOLKER GRANSOW (eds), *Uniting Germany. Documents and Debates, 1944–1993* (Providence, R.I., 1994)

PETER PULZER, *German Politics, 1945–1995* (Oxford, 1995)

GILES RADICE, *The New Germans* (London, 1995)

CARL-CHRISTOPH SCHWEITZER *et al.* (eds), *Politics and Government in the Federal Republic of Germany, 1944–1994. Basic Documents* (2nd edn, Providence, R.I., 1995)

GORDON SMITH *et al.* (eds), *Developments in German Politics* (Basingstoke, 1992)

HENRY ARTHUR TURNER, *Germany from Partition to Reunification* (New Haven, Conn., 1992)

West German economy and society

RALF DAHRENDORF, *Society and Democracy in Germany* (London, 1968)

HERBERT GIERSCH *et al.*, *The Fading Miracle. Four Decades of Market Economy in Germany* (Cambridge, 1992)

EVA KOLINSKY, *Women in Contemporary Germany. Life, Work and Politics* (2nd edn, Oxford, 1993)

ALAN KRAMER, *The West German Economy, 1945–1955* (Oxford, 1985)

A.J. NICHOLLS, *Freedom with Responsibility: The Social Market Economy in Germany, 1918–1963* (Oxford, 1994)

ERIC OWEN SMITH, *The German Economy* (London, 1994)

Monographs

VOLKER R. BERGHAHN, *The Americanisation of West German Industry, 1945–1973* (Leamington Spa, 1986)

ALEC CAIRNCROSS, *The Price of War. British Policy on German Reparations, 1941–1949* (Oxford, 1986)

ANNE DEIGHTON, *The Impossible Peace. Britain, the Division of Germany and the Origins of the Cold War* (Oxford, 1990)

SAKI DOCKRILL, *Britain's Policy for West German Rearmament, 1950–1955* (Cambridge, 1991)

MICHAEL ERMARTH (ed.), *America and the Shaping of German Society, 1945–1955* (Oxford, 1993)

JOHN FARQUHARSON, *The Western Allies and the Politics of Food. Agrarian Management in Postwar Germany* (Leamington Spa, 1985)

TIMOTHY GARTON ASH, *In Europe's Name. Germany and the Divided Continent* (London, 1993)

JOHN GILLINGHAM, *Coal, Steel and the Rebirth of Europe, 1918–1955* (Cambridge, 1991)

JOHN GIMBEL, *The American Occupation of Germany: Politics and the Military, 1945–1949* (Stanford, CA, 1968)

DIETER GROSSER (ed.), *German Unification: The Unexpected Challenge* (Oxford, 1992)

ARTHUR HEARNDON, *Education in the Two Germanies* (Oxford, 1974)

ARTHUR HEARNDON (ed.), *The British in Germany. Educational Reconstruction after 1945* (London, 1978)

GISLEA HENDRIKS, *Germany and European Integration. The Common Agricultural Policy: an Area of Conflict* (Oxford, 1991)

DAVID HORROCKS and EVA KOLINSKY (eds), *Turkish Culture in German Society Today* (Providence, R.I., 1996)

KONRAD H. JARAUSCH, *The Rush to German Unity* (Oxford, 1994)

C. S. MAIER and G. BISCHOF (eds), *The Marshall Plan and West Germany: West German Development Within the Framework of the European Recovery Programme* (New York, 1991)

REINER POMMERIN (ed.), *The American Impact on Postwar Germany* (Providence, R.I., 1995)

REINER POMMERIN (ed.), *Culture in Federal Republic of Germany, 1945–1995* (Oxford, 1996)

ELIZABETH POND, *Beyond the Wall. Germany's Road to Unification* (Washington, D.C., 1993)

NICHOLAS PRONAY and KEITH WILSON (eds), *The Political Re-education of Germany and her Allies after World War II* (London, 1985)

MARK ROSEMAN, *Recasting the Ruhr, 1945–1958. Manpower, Economic Recovery and Labour Relations* (Oxford, 1992)

FREDERIC SPOTTS, *The Churches and Politics in Germany* (Middletown, Conn., 1973)

IAN TURNER (ed.), *Reconstruction in Postwar Germany. British Occupation Policy and the Western Zones, 1945–1955* (Oxford, 1989)

CLEMENS WURM (ed.), *Western Europe and Germany. The Beginnings of European Integration, 1945–1960* (Oxford, 1995)

PHILIP ZELIKOW and CONDOLEEZZA RICE, *Germany Unified and Europe Transformed* (Cambridge, Mass., 1995)

HAROLD ZINK, *The United States in Germany, 1944–1955* (Princeton, NJ, 1957)

Index